THE HISTORICAL REVOLUTION

THE HISTORICAL
REVOLUTION

*English Historical
Writing and Thought
1580-1640*

by

F. SMITH FUSSNER

*New York: Columbia University Press
London: Routledge and Kegan Paul
1962*

Printed in Great Britain
© *F. Smith Fussner 1962*
Library of Congress Catalog Card Number: 62–10147

FOR JANE

CONTENTS

ACKNOWLEDGEMENTS   *page*   ix

A BIBLIOGRAPHICAL PREFACE   xi

INTRODUCTION   xiii

1 THE EUROPEAN BACKGROUND   1
     i *Renaissance Climate of Opinion*   1
     ii *Reformation Politics and Religion*   17

2 THE HISTORICAL CONTEXT   26
     i *Legal influences*   26
     ii *Records and Historical Research*   32
     iii *Libraries and Historical Research*   35
     iv *Censorship and Historical Publication*   37
     v *Genealogy, Heraldry, and History*   42
     vi *Education and History*   44
     vii *History and the Gentry*   49
     viii *History and Middle-class Culture*   53

3 THE INSTITUTIONAL FRAMEWORK   60
     i *Book and Manuscript Collections*   60
     ii *The Public Records and Record Keeping*   69

4 THE ANTIQUARIAN MOVEMENT AND HISTORICAL
     RESEARCH   92
     i *The Elizabethan Society of Antiquaries*   92
     ii *The Impact of the Civil Wars*   106
     iii *The Role of the Church and the Universities*   110
     iv *The Heritage of Antiquarianism*   113

5 POLITICS, PATRONAGE, AND SCHOLARSHIP: THE
     INFLUENCE OF SIR ROBERT COTTON   117
     i *Cotton's Political Career*   119
     ii *The Library and Cotton's Patronage of Learning*   127
         (*a*) *The Court, Officers of State, and Parliament*
             Men   127
         (*b*) *The Legal Profession*   134

CONTENTS

(c) *The Church and the Universities*   *page* 136
(d) *Royal Officials* 139
(e) *The Scholars, Historians, and Others* 142

6 THE VARIETIES OF HISTORY 150
  i *Titles: Problems of Classification* 150
 ii *Content and Purpose* 163
   (a) *Universal History* 165
   (b) *Territorial History* 175
   (c) *Problematic History* 185

7 SIR WALTER RALEGH AND UNIVERSAL HISTORY 191

8 JOHN STOW AND LOCAL HISTORY 211

9 WILLIAM CAMDEN AND TERRITORIAL HISTORY 230

10 SIR FRANCIS BACON AND THE IDEA OF HISTORY 253

11 JOHN SELDEN AND PROBLEMATIC HISTORY 275

12 THE HISTORICAL REVOLUTION: CONCLUSIONS AND
   CONJECTURES 299

  INDEX 323

ACKNOWLEDGEMENTS

TO WRITE HISTORY is to incur intellectual debts—to individuals, to institutions, and to books. These are easier to acknowledge than to repay, and easier to name than to explain. In acknowledging what I owe, I wish to express my thanks to all who have contributed to my understanding of history and its problems.

Professor W. K. Jordan of Harvard has given me encouragement and good advice over a period of years. This book's merits are largely owing to his teaching: to him and to his books I am most deeply indebted.

Professors R. F. Arragon, C. C. Bagg, and F. Peachy of Reed College, and Mr. John Harvey of the University College of North Staffordshire, kindly read sections of the manuscript and made valuable criticisms. Miss Rebecca Pollock, the Librarian at Reed College, has been helpful, both as a librarian and as a critic; and I am indebted to the staff of the Reed Library for providing books on inter-library loan.

The research for this book was carried on at a number of institutions, at all of which I was given every consideration by the librarians and record keepers. Most of the books cited in the text were used in Widener Library or in the Houghton Library and Reading Room at Harvard University. Most of the manuscripts were consulted at the British Museum, and at the Public Record Office in London. Other libraries, both English and American, provided books and manuscripts which proved most useful. My thanks go to all of them.

I am particularly grateful to the American Philosophical Society for a grant which, during the summer of 1954, enabled me to pursue my research in England. During the academic year 1959–60 I was on sabbatical leave from Reed College, under the provisions of the sabbatical programme of the college. Without that leave this book would not have been completed. I wish to thank the President and the Board of Trustees for making the leave possible.

To Mr. C. E. Wright of the British Museum I am indebted for many courtesies and for several valuable references. Mr. Walter F. Oakeshott, Rector of Lincoln College, Oxford, very kindly made available to me the manuscript notebook of Sir Walter Ralegh. Professor Wallace MacCaffrey of Haverford College gave me transcripts from the records of the Court of Aldermen of the City of London, for which I am duly grateful. Many other individuals have helped me in one way or another, and I owe much to the students in my classes at Reed College who have sharpened my awareness of historical issues.

A grant from the F. L. Griffin Fund at Reed College was most helpful in paying for the cost of typing the manuscript. Mrs. Mirth T. Kaplan, who did the typing, deserves much credit for the accuracy and thoroughness of her typing, correcting, and proofreading. To the following editors and publishers I am indebted for permission to quote from copyrighted material:

Allen & Unwin Ltd., for Thomas Fuller, *The Worthies of England*, ed. by John Freeman (1952); Cambridge University Press, for J. G. A. Pocock, *The Ancient Constitution and the Feudal Law* (1957); Chatto & Windus Ltd., for Basil Willey, *The Seventeenth Century Background* (1946); Harper & Bros., for Myron Gilmore, *The World of Humanism* (1952); Harvard University Press, for W. K. Jordan, *The Development of Religious Toleration in England*, Vol. II (1936); Houghton Mifflin Company, for Wallace K. Ferguson, *The Renaissance in Historical Thought* (1948); Secker & Warburg Ltd., for *Aubrey's Brief Lives*, ed. by Oliver Lawson Dick (1950); University of Chicago Press, for A. S. P. Woodhouse, *Puritanism and Liberty* (1951).

A BIBLIOGRAPHICAL PREFACE

THE FOOTNOTES IN THIS BOOK serve two purposes: (1) they identify quotations or paraphrased passages, and (2) they call attention to books and articles which contain further bibliographical information, or which provide important interpretations. There is no formal bibliography—the footnotes to the separate chapters will serve to guide the student to some of the relevant manuscripts, and to useful secondary works. The *Short Title Catalogue*, the *Dictionary of National Biography*, and other standard works of reference, especially the catalogues of the manuscript collections in the British Museum and in the Oxford and Cambridge libraries must be consulted by anyone interested in doing further research. The *Calendars of State Papers, Domestic* and the various calendars published by the Historical Manuscripts Commission are obvious sources of information. No attempt has been made to cite all of the relevant material contained in these, or in other works consulted in writing this book.

In general, I have tried to give the kind of bibliographical comment that would prove useful to interested students. A comprehensive bibliographical essay would have added greatly to the length of this book, and would have duplicated much that can be found readily in such works as the *Cambridge Bibliography of English Literature*, or Douglas Bush's *English Literature in the Earlier 17th Century*. In the notes I have omitted most of the secondary works dealing with well-known writers, or with well-known historical problems. Hence, my bibliographical references must be supplemented—they are meant to provide useful starting points for further research; they are not commentaries on contemporary scholarship. Research specialists will recognize significant omissions (not all of which can be excused as being deliberate), but the works I have cited are, for the most part, important contributions to the subjects discussed in the text. Not all of the books referred to in the text are mentioned in the notes; and no attempt has been made to provide bibliographies of the writings of individual historians. Anyone who wishes to find out more about the ways and means of writing history in the seventeenth century will quickly discover that there are a great many important sources still waiting to be explored.

The abbreviations used in the notes are the following: (1) British Museum manuscript collections are preceded by the initials B.M. Manuscript (MS.) numbers refer to the bound manuscript volume numbers. (2) State Papers at the Public Record Office are designated S.P. All of these are domestic state papers, and may be found by consulting the appropriate Calendars. (3) the *Calendars of State Papers, Domestic*, are abbreviated *C.S.P. Dom.* (4) The *Dictionary of National Biography* is abbreviated *D.N.B.* (5) Books are referred to by short title only, after the initial citation of the full title.

In quoting from manuscripts I have modernized both spelling and punctuation. Quotations from books retain the original spelling, except that certain vagaries of typography have been silently amended; also, in a few cases, I have modernized spelling in the interests of stylistic fluency. Citations from prefaces and from un-numbered pages in books are by Signatures, but this was not thought necessary in short prefaces.

F. S. F.

INTRODUCTION

ALTHOUGH HISTORY HAS BEEN WRITTEN IN many ways and under various titles, the aim of the honest historian has always been to tell a true story of what men have thought and felt, done or left undone in the course of time. The only witnesses of a remote age are the records and remains which the living generation inherits from the dead. Every historian must make use of those records and remains in order to answer the questions he puts to himself. What questions the historian asks, and what arguments and evidence he gives, betray the nature of his interests and the extent of his skill, knowledge, and taste. The skill he shows in questioning his evidence will help to decide his stature as a scholar. But no matter what special techniques he may use to elicit truth, he must ultimately rely on his own knowledge and understanding of men; without this, all interpretation is crippled and limps.

Few historians have loved the past merely for its own sake, or for the sake of its gross remains. It is what living men and women have created or maintained or destroyed that lends to history all its poetry. The past offers little escape or refuge from the present; it is the reality of a once-present life that forms the subject matter of history. The great writers of history have been creators and artificers, not merely recorders and clerks for bygone generations. The best historical writers of the early seventeenth century were men of passion as well as erudition. To them 'a society of the living and the dead' was an unquestioned assumption. Their works may be found catalogued under diverse titles, under headings from Antiquity to Topography, but all have in common a lively interest in the relation of past to present. All contributed, in various ways, to the modern idea of history. The subject of this book is the way in which English historians of the early seventeenth century wrote history, and their ideas about their work.

The word 'history' has sometimes been narrowly defined to mean the events or incidents of the actual past, as distinguished from the records and remains of the past, and from the historian's written account of past events. History, historical evidence, and historiography are a rather pedantic triumvirate, however, and I have preferred to follow the common usage of historians—'history' may mean the evidence, the past, or the historian's account of it; the word's meaning should be clear from the context in which it is used.

The idea of history in any age, like the idea of property, or of progress, is an unstable compound; it is put together as needed, by historians or by philosophers, out of the irreconcilable opinions of men. Every man has opinions about the past, and there is hardly a field of inquiry which does not make some use of 'historical' evidence. In this book I have defined the idea of history in terms of the attitudes and writings of seventeenth-century historians. It is no easy matter, however, to decide which writers were historians. Obviously, not everyone who has written about the past can be called a historian, yet it is equally plain that there have been writers, like John Stow, too modest to call themselves historians, who have, nevertheless, written great historical works. According to the seventeenth-century historical theorists, few men deserved the title of historian. It was easy enough to distinguish invidiously between antiquaries, chroniclers, and historians, but in practice the distinctions made, for example, by Bacon in *The Advancement of Learning*, are too arbitrary to be of much use. In practice, nearly every historian of note in the seventeenth century was interested in antiquarian studies, and profited from them. John Selden, who had no use for the 'sterile part of antiquity' which merely described what had been, knew well how to value the 'precious and useful part of it'. I have therefore disregarded theoretical classifications in favour of a broad common-sense definition: the writer of history was anyone who wrote about the past in order primarily to describe or explain to his contemporaries the actions or traditions of earlier generations.

Writers who were primarily concerned with legal precedents or with theological or political discourse merit consideration only in so far as their research seems to bear directly on the writing of history. A considerable traffic in facts about the past was carried on by lawyers, heralds, genealogists, theologians, and others, but these men were not necessarily interested in the once-actual life of the past. They were more likely to be concerned only with those records and remains of the past which were of immediate use in their work. Historical facts were important to them in terms of a current intellectual coinage; what mattered was the minted value of a fact—its purchasing power, so to speak—not its historical significance. To the herald, for example, armigerous ancestry was a fact to be entered as a credit on some current account. The herald, as such, was not interested in social history and its problems. To what extent writers and investigators in related fields influenced historians is a difficult question which permits of conjecture but not of proof. I have made conjectures, but I have not tried to track the cold trails of particular influences.

The present work is primarily concerned with tracing the origins of certain modern problems of historical inquiry, and with the development of critical historical methods, particularly in the early seventeenth century, when historical research of the highest quality was being accomplished.

The problems and methods of historical research in medieval England have been described by Professor Galbraith, who traces the medieval line of historians to its end in the early sixteenth century.[1] In the century which followed, new techniques, attitudes, and facilities for research were developed, and these revolutionized the study of history. What brought about this 'historical revolution', and what its intellectual effects were, can only be conjectured on the basis of the studies and evidence at present available. The hypotheses of explanation offered in this book are meant only as hypotheses— *caveat lector*. I have examined many different kinds of historical writing with a view to defining the nature and methods of historical inquiry. Had my purpose been to write a history of historiography in the early seventeenth century this would have been a very different book. As it is, certain important writers, such as Spelman, have received only brief notice, while Bacon, Ralegh, Stow, Camden, and Selden have been singled out for discussion in separate chapters. My reason for selecting these writers is simply that I believe they do represent the main currents of historical writing and thought in the period. Other selections could be made and easily justified. Specific works were chosen for detailed study in order to illustrate typical problems in the development of English historiography; the varieties of history are dealt with in a separate chapter.

[1] See V. H. Galbraith, *Historical Research in Medieval England* (London, 1951), 11–12 and 44. This Creighton Lecture of 1949 should be read by all students of English historiography; the present work assumes some familiarity with the problems discussed by Professor Galbraith. My quotations from Selden in this introduction are identified in the notes to the chapter on Selden.

The concrete problems I have investigated cluster around five major features of the historian's work: purpose, method, content, style, and significance. The meaning of these terms will be made clear in what follows.

i PURPOSE

The historian's purpose in writing may or may not be the same as his motive for writing. Boredom with a prison room may have been the motive which first spurred Ralegh to write his *History of the World*, but Ralegh's purpose was to justify the judgments of God upon men. It was this moral purpose even more than the stately roll of his prose that brought Ralegh fame as a historian in his own lifetime. Ralegh's *History* is the archetype of all the moralizing histories of the seventeenth century. Selden's *History* was, in similar fashion, the best expression of history written with a view to its political utility. Selden's purpose in writing the *Historie of Tithes* was to give 'light to the practice and doubts of the present' and the light was meant to expose clerical ignorance and error in a matter of great political concern. In the case of John Stow's *Survey of London* the purpose was not to argue a thesis, nor to teach lessons, but to depict London's greatness. Stow's purpose was antiquarian in the sense that he wished to describe London life and London monuments, past and present. He took it for granted that the study of antiquity was useful and required no apology. As a man of his age, he subscribed to all the Ciceronian platitudes about history's moral utility, but he seldom chose to edify his readers with moral commentary. He was content to let his readers make whatever use they saw fit of his very accurate facts.

Most historical writers of the early seventeeth century thought of the purpose of history in one or another of the ways just described; that is, history served a moral, a political, or an antiquarian purpose. Often all three purposes were combined, or perhaps confused, as the case might be. Elizabethan rhetoric taught that man learns from history 'what is the best course to be taken in all his actions and advices in this world'. Such a statement could mean almost anything. All that can with certainty be said is that most seventeenth-century writers thought of politics, morality, and tradition (*alias* history) as forming a kind of trinity. The modern paradox of historicism was not yet recognized as a paradox. Perhaps only Selden could have appreciated the implications of Troeltsch's epigram—'we get our ethics from our history and judge our history by our ethics'.

ii METHOD

Historical method is the means by which the purpose and end of history are achieved. In the seventeenth century most historians did not argue or write much about their methods. They did not try to define historical method because they were not self-conscious about what they were doing. Method, as Bodin used the word, meant a methodical course of study, not the means by which facts and interpretations could be established. Today historians are far more aware of historical process, and of how their own attitudes and even methods change in a changing world. Because they see themselves as a part of history, not apart from it, they have become more conscious of the problems of method. Fact no longer has a hard sharp outline. On close inspection, fact dissolves into theory. Historical method as a means of establishing truths about the past have been historicized, shown to be relative to time and place.[1] Thus, the evidence available to a historian, the questions he asks, and his theories or hypotheses of explanation are all determined, in part, by his historical circumstance; and all are relevant to the study of his methods. Yet this is not, as is often assumed, a justification for sceptical historical relativism. One reason for studying the methods of seventeenth-century historians is that we may be able to discover why historical methods change and why historians have failed to reach agreement about what constitutes valid method. Instead of assuming that everything is relative, historians must examine their criteria of relevance. The problem of relevance is central, as many modern historians have come to realize.

Historical method presupposes good judgment and common sense,

[1] Starting from different assumptions about the nature of history, R. G. Collingwood in *The Idea of History* (Oxford, 1946), and Raymond Aron in his *Introduction to the Philosophy of History* (Boston, 1961), arrive at this conclusion. It is obvious that different kinds of historical truths have been sought by different generations, and that to some extent historical methods have developed in response to need. The question of how far a historian's fundamental philosophical assumptions about the nature of truth influence written history is also at issue here. See, e.g., *Naturalism and the Human Spirit*, Y. H. Krikorian, ed. (New York, 1944), especially Edward W. Strong's essay, 'The Materials of Historical Knowledge'.

but it has never been the equivalent of those qualities. Every man is free to be his own historian, but only at his own risk; the job requires training and experience. An eye for significant detail, the ability to ask fruitful questions, the intelligence to connect; these can come only with knowledge. In history, as in other arts and sciences, original thought is possible only when a man of intelligence has mastered fundamental facts and skills. The skills required by a medieval historian, for example, should include not only knowledge of languages, but also the very highly specialized knowledge of how and where documents were kept, what significant changes took place in the administration of records, and a host of other complicated topics which modern manuals sometimes refer to rudely as 'ancillary disciplines'. What, in fact, does historical *method* then mean?

For purposes of analysis, historical method will be considered in terms of (1) techniques and special skills, (2) evidence and proof, (3) explanation and relevance. From the Renaissance to our own day there has been progress in the development of special techniques and skills relating to the study of historical documents. It is possible to date a manuscript more precisely, to identify a name or a word more easily, to expose a forgery more confidently now than ever before. In this sense, knowledge in history is cumulative, as it is in science. Historians have borrowed many of their special techniques from other fields of learning. The most important borrowings, at least in the sixteenth and seventeenth centuries, were from philology. John Selden reminded his readers that true philology was 'the only fit wife which could be found for the most learned of the Gods' and every profession 'takes from her to it selfe . . . some necessary part not elsewhere to be sought for'.

Philological studies enabled historians to deal effectively with original documents at a time when quantities of original documents were becoming available for study. Libraries and record offices of all kinds were founded or reorganized, and their administration improved in the late sixteenth and early seventeenth centuries. For the first time in the history of English scholarship it became possible to carry on research with the aid of glossaries, catalogues, calendars, and other technical aids to research. Some seventeenth-century historians acquired a sound, if unsystematic working knowledge of paleography, diplomatics, numismatics, and other special skills. In all matters of technique and special knowledge the seventeenth century was a time of extraordinary discovery and achievement.

Historical method, in its technical aspects, became far more exact, accurate, and professional as a result of the general progress in humanistic scholarship.

If historical method involved nothing more than special technical skills there would be little room for disagreement among scholars. All questions of historical evidence and standards of proof, however, have reference to judgments of *relevance*, or more broadly to ideas of explanation. There can be no question that what especially distinguishes sixteenth- and seventeenth-century historiography from medieval historiography is a new attitude toward historical evidence and proof. The authority of tradition, even the authority of the Bible itself, was slowly undermined by historians who insisted that only by going to 'the fountains', to original documents, could the truth be known. As long as no attempt was made to explain why or how events happened, there could be little question of a conflict between theology and history; what was relevant could be established by an appeal to common sense. Stow's *Survey* provoked no controversy, although it is a classic example of how empirical methods could yield definitive results. The accuracy of the *Survey* is a tribute to Stow's industry in searching for original documents and records; and the relevance of the documentary evidence to the questions which Stow handled has never been questioned. But this was not the case with Selden's *Historie of Tithes*.

Selden wrote to explain how, in practice, tithes had been paid. Even though he did not meddle with divinity, he could not avoid being attacked on the ground that he had made improper use of his evidence. The charge, in effect, was that his *Historie* was subversive of God's Law, and that he had deliberately published evidence which was relevant to a theological, not a historical question. The question of relevance could not be avoided. Consequently, the issue of objectivity was raised by every one of Selden's opponents. The very excellence of Selden's historical methods was an excuse for charging him with bias. The whole controversy about the *Historie of Tithes* turned on the issue of relevance. This might be reason enough to discuss historical method in terms of the problem of relevance, but there are other reasons why I have used the problem of relevance as a touchstone.

It is common knowledge that historians have not reached agreement about the interpretation of certain events: the Reformation, the civil wars in England or America, the Norman Conquest, to name only a few. It is sometimes alleged that these disagreements among historians prove that they are hopelessly biased, but such an argument does not warrant another refutation. It is much more profitable to examine differences of interpretation from the point of view of historical relevance.

Every historian makes use of some theory of explanation or causation, even though he may never state it explicitly, or attempt to defend it. Nevertheless, every historian, at nearly every stage of his inquiry must decide what is relevant to his purposes, and such decisions will reflect in part the psychological and intellectual biography of the historian. For example, Sir Walter Ralegh believed that history could only be explained by reference to God's providence, and that the Bible contained histories which could only be true. For Ralegh, all other evidence had to conform to the authority of the Bible, and all explanations in terms of secondary causes had to be referred to the first cause of all things, which was God. Ralegh could never accept as evidence that which flatly contradicted the authority of the Bible; to Ralegh's mind, the theological doctrine of providence was supremely relevant to the study of history.

The issues which David Hume later argued in his essay on miracles, derive from the issues which historians of the seventeenth century had to face, when they began to apply empirical methods to the study of both sacred and profane history. What facts are relevant, how can they be established, and what constitutes historical proof? What was relevant to Ralegh would not have seemed relevant to Selden, and the differences between the two men could not have been resolved simply by an appeal to documents. The paradox of historical method is that it does not compel agreement. In order to reach agreement about the causes of any event, historians must be able to agree on what is and what is not relevant evidence, and relevant theory. The empirical evidence of documents cannot by itself compel such philosophical agreement. That is why the history of historical method must take into account the beliefs and attitudes of the individual historian with regard to ultimate philosophical and religious assumptions.

iii CONTENT

The content or subject matter of a work of history is evidence for the nature and range of the historian's interests. Although content and purpose are closely related, they must not be confused—the content of a history book may tell more about the author's purpose than anything the author says in his introduction. It was the historical content of the *Historie of Tithes,* not Selden's explicit statements about his purpose in writing it, that alarmed the churchmen. By analysing the contents of works of history it is possible to estimate what kind of information people wanted, how secular their tastes had become, and what problems they thought most important. Scholars like Selden might smile contemptuously at the little digests from which middle-class Englishmen got their history, but such books undoubtedly helped to establish an attitude toward the past which has not yet disappeared. Such books feed traditions.

The content of historical works written in the earlier seventeenth century has been examined in order to show what kinds of inquiry were undertaken by different writers, and what factors of explanation were stressed. No attempt, however, has been made to evaluate the conclusions, or to test the factual accuracy of statements made by these authors.

iv STYLE

In history as in other forms of literature, style can be defined in a number of different ways. In one sense it is simply the ability to say what one wants to say precisely and with economy—without using too many words or too few. By this definition there were a few good prose stylists writing history in the earlier seventeenth century. Ralegh and Bacon were notable stylists, but, for the most part, writers of history were not concerned with the literary value of their works. In analysing the stylistic qualities of the historical writing of this period I have paid attention to style only in the sense of organization or structure. The way in which the historian organized and presented his materials has been the principal object of investigation. The simplest form of organization was a year-by-year account, called a chronicle or annals. The limitations of this particular form were becoming more and more apparent, however, and many historians were attempting to solve the problem of organization in a different way. The development of more rational forms of organization, based on classical models, is one of the features of early seventeenth-century historiography. Of some importance for the later development of the character study by such writers as Clarendon, were the attempts of Camden, Naunton, Bacon, and others to give character sketches of important people. This aspect of style has been noted, but no detailed study of the prose style of seventeenth-century historians has been attempted.

V SIGNIFICANCE

The significance of particular works of history is nearly always measured in more than one dimension. A work of original research, which outlines new hypotheses of explanation or challenges accepted orthodoxies—such a book is measured along the lines of its scholarship. The same standards do not necessarily apply, however, to works of popular history. Historical writing has never been the exclusive property of scholars, and books of popular history (i.e. books written for the market and not based on original research), may be as significant for social and intellectual history as works of consummate scholarship. In discussing the significance of seventeenth-century historiography I have tried to show how certain modern problems in the philosophy of history began to emerge as the result of advances in scholarship. In order to detect significant changes in a broad intellectual landscape, however, one must know what the landscape looks like. I have therefore described in some detail the seventeenth-century historical landscape. That is, I have tried to suggest what the readers of history wanted, what their tastes and attitudes were, in so far as these could be inferred from the popularity of different kinds of published histories or historical works under other titles. Inevitably such a description is somewhat impressionistic, but it will, I hope, be found accurate enough for the purposes it is meant to serve.

There can be no doubt that historical and antiquarian studies of all kinds proliferated and spread throughout the society of seventeenth-century England. The significance of this spreading interest in history has, I believe, received too little attention from students of seventeenth-century thought. In discussing individual works of historical scholarship, I have focused on specific philosophical problems and their significance. In the final section of the book I have outlined some conjectures which may serve as hypotheses for further research. The general thesis of the book is that a 'historiographical revolution' occurred between about 1580 and 1640 in England and that it helped to create those historical attitudes and questionings that we recognize as our own.

Whatever else the seventeenth century was, it was a century of well-marked transition. In that elusively familiar, paradoxical age an intellectual revolution took place which has been commonly described as one in which older scholastic forms of thought were replaced by a new 'scientific' ideal. The results of this change may be seen in philosophy, literature, history, theology, and political thought. Professor Basil Willey has summarized a familiar interpretation as follows:

> It may be said, then, that for the scholastics there was little or no distinction between a 'fact' and a theological or metaphysical 'truth'. For them the important consideration was not how things behave, or what their history might be, but how they were linked with Total Being, and what, in a word, was their metaphysical status. This was satisfying enough to a period in which men's interests were oriented toward a transcendental 'reality' but it was unfavourable to what, since the Renaissance, has been called 'science'.[1]

Whether or not this generalization oversimplifies intellectual history is not the point at issue. That men did shift their interests, both monetary and intellectual, from things sacred to things secular is, I believe, beyond reasonable doubt.[2] Perhaps the English Renaissance and Reformation are as much symptoms as causes of this change. In any case, the slow shift of men's interests, attitudes, and ideas away from their medieval courses can be described in terms of the growth of science, the elaboration of a new rationalism and empiricism, and the rise of the early modern nation state. And there can be no question of ignoring the importance for intellectual history of what we today would call science or at least the scientific temper.

A philosophically rigorous definition of the 'scientific temper' has eluded many eminent scientists. A historically useful definition, however, may be given, and it is all that is here required. In his book, *Science and the Modern World*, Alfred North Whitehead

[1] Basil Willey, *The Seventeenth Century Background* (London, 1941), 14–15.
[2] Anyone wishing to understand the growth of secular attitudes in England will want to read Professor W. K. Jordan's works dealing with English philanthropy. Especially valuable comments are to be found in W. K. Jordan, *Philanthropy in England 1480–1660* (London, 1959), 322 ff. I am indebted to this book for the discussion not only of secularism, but also of class structure and attitudes.

pointed out that it is the 'union of passionate interest in the detailed facts with equal devotion to abstract generalization which forms the novelty in our present society'.[1] That this is a useful definition of the scientific temper is an assumption which I have made; this introduction is not the place to defend it. The issue at stake in the final section of the book is what bearing historical studies had on the development of such a scientific attitude. What did historiography have to do with changes in the climate of opinion? When Whitehead stated that 'The Reformation and the scientific movement were two aspects of the historical revolt which was the dominant intellectual movement of the later Renaissance', he did little to elaborate on what he meant.[2] In the concluding chapter I have tried to suggest the ways in which new ideas of history contributed to, and perhaps eased the acceptance of scientific attitudes and methods. A detailed study of the particular influence of historians on individual writers in other fields would have gone beyond the scope of the present work. For this reason I have preferred to call these interpretations conjectures, and to draw attention to the need for further research.

Finally, concerning the order of the work, I would say with Ralegh, 'I have only taken counsel from the argument.' The organization of the book is apparent from the table of contents. The main themes and definitions are those introduced in the preceding pages. If the reader finds no passages that provide company for an argument, then the book will have failed in its purpose; if the reader is determined by disagreement to examine the evidence for himself, then the writing stands in need of no further apology.

[1] Alfred North Whitehead, *Science and the Modern World* (New York, 1927), 4.

[2] *Ibid.*, 12. Whitehead thought of the historical revolt primarily as a revolt against the rationalism of the later Middle Ages. He did not mean to imply a historiographical revolution, yet he did identify the historical revolt with the study of empirical facts, their antecedents and consequents. (See p. 57.)

1

THE EUROPEAN BACKGROUND

i RENAISSANCE CLIMATE OF OPINION

THE MEANING OF THE RENAISSANCE has been fully, frequently, and fearlessly discussed; it is certainly not a dead dogma of history. Since the nineteenth century, when the word 'Renaissance' first came into widespread use, historians have moved through mountains of evidence in laying out new roads to truth. The Italian Renaissance no longer has the sharp, high contours that Jacob Burckhardt mapped. The great landmarks of European history have changed: more is known of the past, and time has brought new historical perspectives. The northern Renaissance has appeared to some historians to be of greater significance than the Italian. The origins of the Renaissance, relocated in the Middle Ages by many historians, show up as a series of proto-Renaissances (the greatest, still that of the twelfth century), which are links back to classical times. Medievalists in revolt have interpreted the Renaissance as a continuation or decline of the Middle Ages; and economic historians have dwelt on the transition from feudalism to capitalism as the basis of the European Renaissance. Few historians, however, would banish the Renaissance from their vocabulary simply because its definitions are many and various.[1]

---

[1] On this subject generally, see Wallace K. Ferguson, *The Renaissance in Historical Thought* (Boston, 1948), 1–58, and *passim.* Ferguson's bibliography is eminently serviceable.

If the Burckhardtian tradition still persists, after all qualifications have been made, it is because that tradition contains an important truth, namely that the Renaissance was the beginning of our modern world. Similarly, if the medievalists are right, the important truth of their interpretation is continuity: the Renaissance was still part of that agricultural, feudal, and clerical world of Old Europe. The *ancien régime* in this view came to an end in the noise and terror of the French Revolution. Each of these views may be defended, for continuity and change are the two distinct and fundamental premises of historical thought. To balance and reconcile these opposite qualities is the prerogative of great scholarship. For the purposes of investigation it is enough to define the broad context in which events occurred. The Renaissance, the Reformation, and the various native and particular influences on English historical writing and thought form the background and context in which the seventeenth-century historical revolution took place.

Between the fall of Constantinople and the Protestant revolt, the main trends of the European Renaissance were established. The world of humanism as it existed between 1453 and 1517 had many characteristics which it shared with an earlier and a later Europe. During these years, however, significant economic and political indicators showed the direction of coming trends. The transformation of European culture was, of course, slow—even slower than the transformation of the European economy. Self-sustaining economic growth did not occur until late in the history of urban, secularized states. In poor countries today a 'take-off' into self-sustained growth has been shown to depend on many factors, not all of them economic. Indeed, 'economic development' posits a wide variety of changes, having to do with the discovery of additional resources, capital accumulation, population growth, the introduction of new and better techniques of production, as well as changes in the level and distribution of income, in tastes, and in a variety of institutional and organizational arrangements.[1] The analogy between the countries of Renaissance Europe and latter-day poor countries suggests the close connection between economic development and changes in the institutional, intellectual, and psychological environment. By the middle of the sixteenth century the 'policy of provision' was already

[1] The best survey is Gerald M. Meier and Robert E. Baldwin, *Economic Development, Theory, History, Practice* (New York, 1957). See especially pp. 2–3.

being challenged by a 'policy of protection' which recognized long-term economic considerations.[1]

Those changes which were most important for the mobilization of new ideas and attitudes during the Renaissance can be summed up in a few common historical terms. The development of capitalism, including 'economic development' and the rise of an urban middle class; mercantilism, which implied the direction of economic policy in the interest of state-building; nationalism, which took pride in the awareness of belonging to a nation state; secularism, which expressed the slow decay or draining off of medieval religious ideals; and, most importantly, the expansion of Europe overseas: all these movements profoundly affected intellectual life, and helped to create a new sense of time and history. Needless to say, these developments did not proceed apace. Italy failed to become a unified nation, and took little part in the overseas expansion of Europe; the northern countries felt the full tide of the Renaissance only in the sixteenth century. Nevertheless these changes were European in their effects, and cumulatively they produced the Renaissance climate of opinion. A few illustrations will have to serve as symbols of this complex history.

'Written in the annals of mankind in letters of blood and fire' was Marx's savage phrase to describe the historical transition from feudalism to capitalism. The economic and social changes that accompanied the transition to capitalism often were revolutionary. The guildsman, the landlord, the conservative merchant—all might fail, suffer hardship, and look to new Princes or to old Saints for their salvation. Any rational, self-perpetuating system of economic expansion deals hard with those who fail to satisfy its recurrent demands. The successful bankers, businessmen, and officials might watch their world

[1] See Eli F. Heckscher, *Mercantilism*, 2 vols. (London, 1934), I, 19–136, *passim*. A valuable criticism of some of Heckscher's arguments is B. E. Supple, *Commercial Crisis and Change in England 1600–1642* (Cambridge, 1959). Professor Supple's book is indispensable for an understanding of English policy in this period. He denies that there existed a coherent body of principles identifiable as a mercantile *system* (see pp. 225 ff.); he stresses instead the influence of the immediate economic environment on the formulation of policy. In the present chapter and elsewhere in this book, mercantilism should be understood to mean a set of general, often conflicting principles which were used to justify or explain certain policies, especially those having to do with state building. This definition is closer to Heckscher's, which in its main outlines still seems to me to be valid.

through eyes that betrayed that strange, wary satisfaction that Van Eyck noticed in his portrayal of the merchant Arnolfini. But at their backs these men could always hear the anonymous muttering of a bitter discontent.

Early in the history of capitalist institutions, class warfare had broken the urban peace. In Italy, and in the wool centres of the low countries, advances in capitalist methods of organization, and changes in the mode of production, brought violence that seemed to threaten the whole urban social order. Perhaps it is true, as Pirenne has suggested, 'that every class of capitalists is in the beginning animated by a clearly progressive and innovating spirit, but becomes conservative as its activities become regulated'.[1] In any case, some of the early capitalists did not hesitate to enforce their political covenants with the sword; and their conservatism could and often did pave the way for dictatorship.

The example of Italy shows that the weakening of political consciousness in the city states occurred first when the figure of the ruler—the Seigneur—began to emerge as the master and protector of the middle class. The two-fold policy of the Seigneurs was to curry favour with the urban and rural masses on the one hand, and on the other, 'to destroy or at least transform completely, the juridical and political institutions behind which the ruling class of the old Communes were taking refuge'.[2] In this scramble for power, the merely economic elements of capitalism were subordinated to the needs of internal order and a strong foreign policy. Court life and humanistic culture might inculcate into men's minds 'a serene indifference to every form of violent emotion', but nothing could alter the fact that in Italy during the second half of the fifteenth century the city states were exhausting themselves in a series of bloody political and military intrigues. The day of the invasions from the north was soon to come. Meanwhile, 'the "balance of power" policy supervened to demonstrate the impotence to which the Italian States were reduced'.[3]

What had begun as a crisis in the social relations of capitalism

---

[1] Henri Pirenne, *The Stages in the Social History of Capitalism* (Academic Reprints, No. 1, n.d.), 22. Pirenne said this in 1913.

[2] Federico Chabod, *Machiavelli and the Renaissance*, translated by David Moore (Cambridge, Mass., 1958), 55. The importance of keeping in mind both continuity and change is well expressed by Chabod, p. 151.

[3] Chabod, *Machiavelli*, 60.

quickly revealed its intellectual and diplomatic correlatives. Professor Chabod has thus described the new fashion in statecraft:

It was the diplomats who now held the stage—in particular those merchants with hard, secretive profiles who live again in Masaccio's frescoes. These men had long been used to discussing the allocation of financial loans, and they had subsequently been impelled to remedy the shortcomings in communal life. Their calculations no longer had to do with money but with men: they assumed the form of a psychological inquiry, and found concrete expression in subtle specific precepts, which were all the more shrewd in that those who formulated them were so skilled at reading the faces of their adversaries, at deducing their inmost feelings from a mere contraction of their facial muscles. . . . Accordingly, the theoretical maxims of Guicciardini are merely a rationalization of a century of adventures in which the sole criterion was the life of the emotions and of the human intellect.[1]

The idea of *raison d'état* was first clearly formulated by Machiavelli and others in this heavy atmosphere. *Raison d'état* became the dubious hallmark of the new age. It symbolized the rational acceptance of a divorce between individual ethics and the ethics of states, which now knew no law but necessity; and it marked the beginnings of modern historicism.

The sanctions of divine and natural law were, of course, too deeply and extensively rooted to be undermined by any one ruler or writer. Machiavelli began the work of destruction, and Hobbes and Hume and Rousseau carried it on; even so, the ideal of the best state as defined by natural law persisted.[2] From the point of view of *raison d'état*, however, natural law was simply irrelevant. The Prince and his diplomatic officials assumed that the law of *raison d'état* which governed their own actions governed also the actions of other rulers, subject only to the modifications of circumstance and history. 'Thus action in accordance with *raison d'état* developed relatively early into a form of reconnoitring and judgment, which,' as Meinecke observed, 'was already closely related to modern historical judgment.'[3]

Although the genius of Italy was by no means exhausted at the beginning of the sixteenth century, the relative importance of Italy

[1] Chabod, *Machiavelli*, 60.
[2] Cf. R. V. Sampson, *Progress in the Age of Reason* (Cambridge, Mass., 1956), 147–9.
[3] Friedrich Meinecke, *Machiavellism*, translated by Douglas Scott (New Haven, 1957), 19.

for Europe was less in all fields. Bankers and humanists, statesmen and generals commanded greater forces in the North. The commercial revolution of the late fifteenth century had transferred the economic initiative from the Mediterranean to the northern and western countries of Europe. In France, in England, in Germany, in Spain, along the Channel coast, and farther to the North, new patterns of economic development were even more important than the voyages of discovery in setting the pace of change. In varying ways and under differing circumstances, the commercial revolution acted as a stimulant to all kinds of economic activity: new industries were developed, capital was accumulated, new and better techniques of production were introduced; and, inevitably, cracks appeared in the walls of the old social order.

Mercantilism as a policy of state building was now practised almost everywhere, but in France and England, more than in most states, mercantilism became an agent of unification. The adversary of mercantilism was, in the words of Professor Heckscher, 'the medieval combination of universalism and particularism, and its [i.e. Mercantilism's] first object was to make the state's purposes decisive in a uniform economic sphere and to make all economic activity subservient to considerations corresponding to the requirements of the state and to the state's domain regarded as uniform in nature'.[1] The affinity between this doctrine and *raison d'état* is easy to perceive.

The means at the disposal of mercantilist rulers varied as widely as the size of their domains, but an educated urban middle class was everywhere essential to the policies and practices of mercantilism. The middle class not only provided state treasure by foreign trade, it also staffed the state bureaucracy; and it formed the wider audience for the new learning.[2] Its interests were tied to the interests of the state; its sense of time and of opportunity helped to define the secular point of view. Nationalism, mercantilism, and secularism were thus closely related. In spite of the continuing flow of Christian habits of thought and expression, there was a steady draining away of the underground waters of religious feeling. Nothing could be more significant than the change that took place in the direction of

[1] Heckscher, *Mercantilism*, I, 23.
[2] On the definition of the term 'new learning', see Allen G. Chester, ' "The New Learning": A Semantic Note', *Studies in the Renaissance*, II, 1955, 139–47.

charitable bequests in pre-Reformation England. The church received less, the secular schools more.

The middle class understood well the uses of education. Through education middle-class men had found a new way to wealth and a quick way to rise in society. The middle class was especially sympathetic to the programme of Christian humanism which was based on confidence and hope in what education might accomplish for European civilization. At the beginning of the sixteenth century such confidence was possible: there was as yet no history of disenchantment with the human products of a humanistic education. The common bond of the Christian humanists of Erasmus' day was, therefore, 'an acceptance of the new learning and an attempt to apply it to the reform of church and state'.[1]

If an awareness of change was characteristic of much Renaissance thought, the expansion of Europe overseas was one of the most powerful determinants of a new attitude toward past and future. The voyages of discovery made by Portuguese and Spanish explorers, and later continued by Englishmen and others, not only created new markets for goods, but also for ideas and information. The great era of exploration had been prepared for by the earlier growth of commerce; and the printing press, no less than artillery, had given Europe its advantages and its opportunity. As well as opening up the 'Great Frontier', and initiating all the 'idyllic proceedings' which Marx ironically referred to as the chief momenta of the primitive accumulation of capital, the voyages of discovery widened the horizons of European thought. Speculative ventures put a premium on exact information, on maps and charts and histories and descriptions of all kinds. Mercator and Hakluyt and many others like them catered to the new intellectual wants of the sixteenth century. Furthermore, the printing press had by this time changed the habits, and greatly increased the numbers of the European reading public. Practical information was in greater demand and was being supplied in greater quantities than ever before. Popular histories, for example, were written and sold in ever-increasing numbers to the new middle-class public. Many such histories appeared in the sixteenth century with information on roads, weights and measures, and the distances

[1] Myron P. Gilmore, *The World of Humanism 1453–1517* (New York, 1952), 207; also pp. 204–7, *passim*. See also Gilmore's 'The Renaissance Conception of the Lessons of History', *Facets of the Renaissance*. The Arensberg Lectures (University of Southern California Press, 1959).

between towns—for the benefit of those who travelled on business, but who would improve their minds along the way.

Every profession and possibly every social order makes use of symbolic tools: printing, accounting, and the clock are three of the symbolic tools of all modern societies. In the service of the capitalist social order, toward which early modern Europe were advancing, each of these inventions helped to change men's habits and ideas. Accounting brought a new sense of record; the clock a new sense of time; and printing a new sense of communication. Printing affected scholarship in diverse and often surprising ways:

> In 1492, by which time print had become well established, Johann von Trittenheim, abbot of Sponheim, who was naturally a partisan of the old school, awoke to the dangers of this secular innovation and denounced it in an epistolary tract entitled *De Laude Scriptorum*. 'Our writing,' he says, 'if it is on skin may last a thousand years: but how long will a printed paper thing last? It will be doing well if it lasts two hundred years.' With zealous logic, the abbot exhorted scribes to copy over printed books.[1]

Other humanists were quicker to realize the new possibilities of the printed page. The career of an Erasmus would have been impossible in the age of vellum and copied books. Print became the tool of scholarship, and 'the mere fact that a single emendation by a great scholar could now be circulated in thousands of copies without the danger of a copyist's error signified a complete revolution in the conditions of activity of the learned world'.[2]

That the idea of history would be profoundly affected by all the aforementioned changes was only to be expected; modern historiography begins in the Renaissance. The 'rebirth' of classicism had been heralded by the adoring Magi of Italian humanism with something like reverent awe. The Middle Ages of barbarism were happily ending; the revival of Latin and Greek and even Hebrew studies became part of the testimony to the new age. As the study of classical languages led to the recovery of ancient histories, the whole character of historiography was gradually transformed. The style and method of Bruni, and the scholarship and material of Biondo provided Italian humanist historians with native models for a new kind of

[1] See Francis Wormald and C. E. Wright, eds., *The English Library before 1700* (London, 1958), 37. From 'The Bibliography of the Manuscript Book', by G. S. Ivy.

[2] Gilmore, *World of Humanism*, 189; and Chapter VII, *passim*.

history. And both in Italy and in the North, national patriotism was found to be quite compatible with Christian humanism.

The multiformity of humanist thought is perhaps more obvious than the uniformity of humanist activity. Actually, the European humanists formed, in one sense, an international intellectual élite with a common interest in classical and Christian antiquity. Humanism was committed to a holy alliance with Christianity; and most humanist historians were not sceptical about the sources of Christian tradition. Nevertheless, these facts should not be allowed to obscure the differences that separated the humanists from the scholastics. Professor Bush has insisted that humanism opposed 'both the irreligious scientific rationalism—which would separate men from the divine, and the ethical or unethical naturalism—often the eldest child of rationalism—which would link him with the beasts. Common humanistic labels for these two sets of enemies are "Averroists" and "Epicureans".' [1] Humanism fought these enemies, but it is equally true that it fought arid scholasticism in the church and universities. The 'rebirth of good letters' was greeted with hostility by many clerics who felt they had a vested interest in the old educational system. It would be tedious to revive the Reuchlin controversy in order to illustrate the Renaissance quarrel between Christianity and classical culture. It is enough to realize that medieval traditions were tough, and that humanism was challenging many of them.

In the writing of history, this was perhaps even more evident than in philosophy or literature. The classical historians were more interested in ethical and moral problems than they were in examples of divine intervention in human affairs. Augustine's theology of history had dominated the Middle Ages; there had been no Thomistic synthesis in historiography. The humanist historians were thus the first who 'broke with the theological world history of the medieval chroniclers, abandoned the idea of perpetual decline, and established a new periodization on secular grounds, thereby setting up one of the two boundaries of the Middle Ages'.[2] Some comment may appropriately mark the significance of this break.

[1] Douglas Bush, *The Renaissance and English Humanism* (Toronto, 1939), 55. See also Paul Otto Kristeller, *Renaissance Thought, The Classic, Scholastic, and Humanist Strains* (Harper Torchbook, 1961), Chapter 5.

[2] Ferguson, *The Renaissance in Historical Thought*, 17–18. See also R. R. Bolgar, *The Classical Heritage and its Beneficiaries* (Cambridge, 1954), *passim*.

To the waning Middle Ages, the stark alternatives—either salvation or damnation—at times appeared almost as terrifying as they did to later generations of Calvinists. The doctrine of purgatory, with its promise of deferred penance for the worldly sinner (in return for down payments to a wordly clergy) had come into its own in Renaissance Italy. As early as 1439 purgatory was the main topic of discussion at the Council of Florence, and the doctrine naturally became the focal point of Luther's attack on the abuses of the church. The pope, according to Luther, had no power to reduce the penalties of purgatory, because they had been imposed by God. The early humanists were not Lutheran reformers, however, and purgatory was an accepted part of their consciousness. Yet purgatory became intellectually popular precisely because it satisfied an emotional need. The secularism of the Renaissance was fearful, and the men who looked to the *tontine* as a form of insurance in this world looked to purgatory as a form of insurance in the next. A modern scholar has aptly suggested that the doctrine of purgatory was the 'religious counterpart of that capricious and mysterious *Fortuna* popularly believed to govern the unsettled and undisciplined life of Italian society'.[1]

The humanists may have thought themselves above the crasser notions of *fortuna*, but the doctrine of *fortuna* insinuated itself into Italian thought, and Machiavelli was to give it new historical meaning. The transition from providence to *fortuna* was perhaps as symptomatic as the growing popularity of purgatory; the medieval Christian theories of nature and history no longer seemed to satisfy men with secular longings. The humanist historians made the first tentative break from the Augustinian interpretation of the world's history; Machiavelli and Guicciardini made the break irreparable. The Christian interpretation of history did not, of course, cease to rule, but like the universal empire, it no longer commanded the same respect.

The main assumptions of the medieval Christian interpretation of history had been definitively laid down in *The City of God*. First, there was the theory of the two cities, one earthly, and one heavenly, the two 'intermixed until the last judgment effect their separation'. The real concern of Augustine was with 'the pilgrim city of King Christ'.[2] Secular history was meaningful only as an illustration of

[1] Leonardo Olschki, *The Genius of Italy* (New York, 1949), 260.

[2] Saint Augustine, *The City of God*, translated by Marcus Dods (New York, Modern Library, 1950), 38.

divine providence. The history of the world took place in time; God existed in eternity, and was the absolute sovereign of the world of time and history. The sovereignty of God was more than a mere metaphor to Augustine. There could be no cycles in the Augustinian world, for to admit them would be to walk in the circles of the pagans, and 'to measure by [man's] own human, changeable, and narrow intellect the divine mind, which is absolutely unchangeable, infinitely capacious, and, without succession of thought, counting all things without number'.[1]

Freedom and necessity were terms almost as irrelevant to human history as chance or fortune or fate; all belonged to the discredited vocabulary of the pagan historians and philosophers. Cicero was correct in asserting the freedom of the will, but this was only a part of the Truth. Augustine squarely faced the age-old dilemma of historical inevitability, and gave a Christian answer which still attracts adherents. God was prescient of the future, but man's will was free. Christians must embrace both ideas: 'We faithfully and sincerely confess both. The former that we may believe well; the latter that we may live well.' [2] The Augustinian judgment of history (and of its meaning) was above all an act of faith.

The metahistorical judgments of Augustinism could not be empirically verified; nor could the meanings of history be rationally deduced. One had to believe—not only that Christ was the centre of history, but that history's meaning was revealed in every divine-human encounter.[3] Revelation was relevant to history; and miracles warranted the truths of prophecy. The Incarnation became the unique event which was the focal point of universal history. Christian particularism and universalism were thus combined; and Augustine was at least consistent in thinking that secular history could have no ultimate meaning without reference to divine providence. These Augustinian conceptions dominated the historical thought of the Middle Ages.

What humanism, and later Machiavellism did to the Augustinian world-view was not so much to discredit it in argument as to dismiss it as irrelevant. This is an important qualification to the medievalist's

[1] *Ibid.*, 399; cf. 398–402 *passim.*
[2] *Ibid.*, 157.
[3] The illuminating discussion of Augustine's philosophy of history by Robert L. Shinn, in *Christianity and the Problems of History* (New York, 1953), is to be recommended.

11

thesis that 'the Renaissance was essentially a *Stilbegriff*, or, as we may say, a change in the way of putting things, rather than a change in essential ideas about those things'.[1] Naturally, in the writing of history the old traditions did not suddenly go out of style; Ralegh's *History of the World* was certainly in many ways a rich jewel of medievalism. On the other hand, as Professor Ferguson has put it:

> . . . neither the universal view of the medieval churchman nor the narrow particularism of feudal lords and communal burghers could produce the clear perception of the state or the nation as the unit of historical development that resulted from the evolution of the territorial states in Italy and, somewhat later, of the national states in the North. . . . The new political point of view and the patriotic purpose of the humanist historians led them to a new organization and periodization of history. It also reinforced their natural tendency toward a secular interpretation.[2]

The heir of the humanists, whether legitimate or not, was Machiavelli, whose name has become the symbol of modern *raison d'état*, if not of modern historical judgment.

Although many writers have praised or blamed the originality of Machiavelli's thought, a reading of his *Florentine History* or of the *Discourses on Titus Livius* suggests that Machiavelli was an indifferent historian whose ideas were almost all purchased second-hand. The classical historians anticipated much of Machiavelli's thought about history; and many of them, even some who wrote in the rhetorical tradition, had a greater passion for accuracy. What made Machiavelli so important in the history of historiography was not just his pessimistic 'realism', nor his political concentration and patriotism, nor his sense of historical change. Thucydides had known that men often live by greed and the lust for power; Livy, no less than Dionysius of Halicarnassus, was both political and patriotic; and Augustine's sense of the unique—the Incarnation—transcended in importance any classical, or Renaissance theory of cycles.

What gave Machiavelli his right to intellectual eminence, at least as a historical theorist, was just what his critics found most shocking: human history for the first time appeared autonomous. History was divorced from theology—and conventional moral judgments were as irrelevant as hypothetical divine interventions. Religion itself, in

[1] E. F. Jacob, *Essays in the Conciliar Epoch* (Manchester, 1953), 180. See pp. 170–84, *passim*.
[2] Ferguson, *The Renaissance in Historical Thought*, 5.

Machiavelli's thought, was historically conditioned; it could have no absolute validity. To the statesman mindful of history, only the observable effects of religion were important. Not truth but practical utility was the primary consideration.[1]

Machiavelli believed that history was full of lessons for those acute enough to learn them, but such lessons had little or nothing to do with traditional morality or with any Christian philosophy of history. Good and bad were used as relative historical terms, not as metaphysical absolutes by Machiavelli. He believed that all men 'are born and live and die in the same way and therefore resemble each other'.[2] Furthermore, men were by nature vicious, and would 'act right only upon compulsion'.[3] These were obviously not moral judgments; they were simply axioms in Machiavelli's political science. What Machiavelli learned from history was that 'in all our decisions we must consider well what presents the least inconveniences, and then choose the best, for we shall never find any course entirely free of objections'.[4]

Machiavelli's approach to politics was clearly ameliorative—he wanted to bring about changes, especially changes which would make Italy great. His approach to history, by contrast, seemed almost static, lacking in even an awareness of the unique differences between ages. History only provided Machiavelli with examples; he did not have the true historian's passionate awareness of process. Nevertheless, his approach to history was significantly 'relational' in its stress on circumstances, on political purposes, and on the accommodation of means to ends.

Machiavelli carefully related the ruler to the state, and examined his political purposes in relation to what was possible under given historical circumstances; secular means were coherently related to given secular ends. The study of historically necessary relations

---

[1] The commentary on Machiavelli is almost as extensive as that on Augustine. For the present purposes, the bibliography in Chabod, *Machiavelli*, is especially valuable. The essay on Machiavelli in Ferdinand Schevill, *Six Historians* (Chicago, 1956), is short, and penetrating. Cf. also Bolgar, *Classical Heritage*, 297. An important bibliographic article is Eric W. Cochrane's 'Machiavelli: 1940–1960', *Journal of Modern History* (xxxiii, June 1961), 113–16.

[2] Niccolo Machiavelli, *The Prince and the Discourses* (New York, Modern Library, 1940), 149. From *Discourses*, I, xi. Subsequent page references to Machiavelli are to this edition.

[3] Machiavelli, *Discourses*, I, iii, 118.　　　　[4] *Ibid.*, vi, 127.

13

fascinated Machiavelli, who proudly asserted that his methods were both new and capable of refinement.[1] He was far from being a contextual relativist, of course, yet his thought harboured one paradox of relativism. He saw that judgment depended on knowledge of human affairs, affairs which were 'in a state of perpetual movement, always either ascending or descending'.[2] Hence, every judgment of the past would of necessity be relative to the changing viewpoint of the contemporary observer. Machiavelli perceived and stated this problem, but he then blandly ignored it by asserting that his own judgments were manifest, and that, in any case, his instructions were meant to improve the times. However, the implications of his arguments could not be wholly dismissed.

By separating political from individual morality, and by making *raison d'état* the relevant criterion for judging the state and the statesman, Machiavelli cut the traditional moorings of both history and politics. In effect, Machiavelli, as Professor Chabod has argued, 'came to affirm the principle of "politics for politic's sake", or . . . to recognize the "autonomy of politics", regarded as a form of human activity existing *per se* and unconditioned by any assumptions or aims of a theological or moral character'.[3] This was also Machiavelli's greatest contribution to historiography. Moreover, Guicciardini and others helped to set a great tradition of history written in accordance with Machiavellian assumptions.[4]

Whether directly or indirectly, by writing or by reputation, Machiavelli came to England early and stayed late. Richard Morison used some of Machiavelli's arguments in trying to justify English policy during the Reformation, and Cardinal Pole warned, in 1540, that Machiavelli 'had already poisoned England and would poison all Christendom'.[5] The Florentine secretary became, indeed, the European heresiarch of the new secularism. His name was con-

[1] See Machiavelli, *Discourses*, Introduction to Book I, 103–5, and I, xxxix, 216–18.

[2] *Ibid.*, II, 272. Cf. the Introduction to Book II, 271–5, *passim*.

[3] Chabod, *Machiavelli*, 140.

[4] See Myron P. Gilmore, 'Freedom and Determinism in Renaissance Historians', *Studies in the Renaissance*, III, 49–60. Also J. W. Allen, *A History of Political Thought in the Sixteenth Century* (London, 1941), pp. 445–501.

[5] W. Gordon Zeeveld, *Foundations of Tudor Policy* (Cambridge, Mass., 1948), 186. See also p. 189, and Zeeveld's article, 'Richard Morison, Official Apologist for Henry VIII', *Publication of the Modern Language*

demned, but his ideas were considered. In the history of the rise of the inductive method in the social sciences Machiavelli's name has been justly honoured. Modern historical writing and thought would scarcely be intelligible without some knowledge of 'Machiavellism', which, like 'Marxism' subtly permeated the consciousness of later generations.

Before the Reformation there was relatively little to distinguish English from Continental humanism, except, perhaps, the apparent lack of an artistic as opposed to a scholarly tradition. Erasmus, when he came to England, was much impressed by the quality of English Greek and Latin scholarship. The 'Oxford Reformers' were known not only for the newness of their learning, but also for the antique simplicity of their faith. As Colet was wont to advise his theological students, they should keep 'to the Bible and the Apostle's Creed, and let divines, if they like, dispute about the rest'.[1] Yet the Christian humanism of Erasmus, Colet, and More was far from being a fugitive and cloistered faith, isolated from knowledge of the ways of the world. Colet, his life in peril from the sweating sickness, settled the statutes of his school, entrusting it not to clergymen, but to the charge of 'the most honest and faithful fellowship of the *Mercers* of London'.[2] Sir Thomas More was to become fatally engaged with the state, and his life was in some ways symbolic of the dilemma of Christian humanism in an age of secular and religious change.

Both the literary and the biblical humanists of Europe had in common a longing to go backward in time: the mottoes of humanism were '*renovatio, restitutio, restauratio*'.[3] And English humanism conformed to the Italian model in being respectably antiquarian. The first English antiquaries of general importance were John Rous (1411–91), and William of Worcester (1415–82).[4] Both were trusting

Association, LV, no. 2, 1940, 406–25. Cf. Herbert Butterfield, *The State-craft of Machiavelli* (London, 1955). Butterfield's study is especially concerned with historical problems.

[1] Quoted by Frederic Seebohm, *The Oxford Reformers* (London, Everyman, 1914), 227.

[2] Quoted by Seebohm, *Oxford Reformers*, 290.

[3] Johan Huizinga, *Men and Ideas*, Essays translated by James S. Holmes and Hans van Marle (New York, Meridian Books, 1959), 277.

[4] There is an excellent short study of William Worcester by W. B. MacFarlane, 'William Worcester: A Preliminary Study', in *Studies Presented to Sir Hilary Jenkinson* (Oxford, 1951), J. Conway Davies, ed., pp. 196–221.

THE EUROPEAN BACKGROUND

medievalists who suspected no forgery in Geoffrey of Monmouth's account of British antiquity. Buckle's pungent comment on medieval historiography was that the Middle Ages were not satisfied with the absence of truth, but supplied its place by the invention of falsehood. Medieval historians and chroniclers often did begin with the Ark; and Geoffrey of Monmouth was not the only writer to invent a Trojan national ancestry. Nevertheless, the writings of the medievalists, including Rous and William of Worcester, appealed to posterity; and Trojan genealogies were never more popular than in Tudor England.

Sir Thomas Kendrick's fascinating study of British Antiquity makes it clear that the uses of the past, as well as the forgeries of Annius, and the medievalism of antiquaries helped to sustain mistaken theories of remote history in sixteenth- and seventeenth-century England.[1] Leland and Bale, good antiquaries though they were, did not doubt the historicity of Brutus and Arthur. To Bale, Samothes, the grandson of Noah, was the first king of the continental Celts and Britannia; and Albion Mareoticus, the grandson of Isis and Osiris, was one of the two eponymous kings of early Britain. Bale's source was Annius of Viterbo, whose work has been called 'the most mischievous study of the remote past published during the Renaissance', but the fact remains that Bale and many others chose their medievalism deliberately.[2] The rise of historical scepticism during the Renaissance was painfully slow, and in England it did not begin to 'purge history of its errors', as Buckle realized, until late in Elizabeth's reign.[3]

[1] See T. D. Kendrick, *British Antiquity* (London, 1950), *passim*; especially interesting is his comment (p. 77):

The story of the renewed dispute about the age of the two Universities is in itself sufficient to establish our immediate thesis that the struggle to apply to the British History the critical machinery of a new scholarship did not speedily result in an easy triumph of the Renaissance mind, but was one that had to be sustained for over a century against a formidable deadweight of contrary opinion jealously preserved and defended by reactionary scholars of great learning and repute.

[2] *Ibid.*, 71–2.

[3] Buckle's work on the history of civilization in England has been dismissed by all too many students of the seventeenth century. Although Buckle was in many ways the victim of his own sociological ideas, he nevertheless was often acute in his insights. As far as I know he was the first historian to suggest that a major Historical Revolution occurred in the early seventeenth century. See Henry Thomas Buckle, *History of Civilization in England*, 2 vols. (New York, 1910), I, vi, and I, xiii, *passim*.

16

The purpose of the foregoing brief historical survey has been to call attention to some of the significant attributes of the European Renaissance, and, very generally, to indicate presumed connections between events and ideas, between life and literature. Changes in the climate of opinion commonly came after changes in the social and economic institutions of society. Much that happened in Italy or France or Germany happened also, *mutatis mutandis*, in England. What gave the English Renaissance its peculiar and distinctive character, however, was the English Reformation. And in England, no less than on the continent, the Reformation was accompanied by a new series of socio-economic shocks which helped to weaken all the medieval foundations of society.

ii REFORMATION POLITICS AND RELIGION

The Reformation, the Tudor revolution in government, the 'first' great industrialization, the price revolution, the rise of the gentry, and the overseas expansion of English trade—all these far-reaching changes occurred in the sixteenth century; and each had portentous significance for intellectual life. At the same time, the period (at least until about 1580) was one of preparation, not of fulfilment in intellectual history. The connection between English literature and Reformation politics and religion is clearer than that between literature and economic development, yet the latter connection was probably in the long run the more important. The expansion of the market for history cannot be understood without reference to the speculation in monastic lands, the genealogies of the gentry, and the middle-class quest for culture and a measure of legal security along with new political power.

From the very beginning of the English Reformation the new learning of the humanists was put to the test of political and theological debate. Increasingly, after the 1530's, scholars and statesmen turned to history to justify the ways of church and state to Englishmen. On the continent the Reformation and counter-Reformation waged war in print (and on the battlefield) over ostensible issues of theology and church government. History and tradition became the commanding heights which intellectual leaders on each side had to try to capture and hold. For the first time, the study of history became crucial—and crucial it remained, in all the wars of faith, in all countries.

The visible effects of the Reformation on historiography were, first, the intensification of historical research; second, the development of a tradition of historical controversy; and third, particularly in England, the dispersal of historical records. The intensification of research was essential if Protestantism was to substantiate its claim to be a true reformed religion, modelled on early Christianity. Protestants took their stand on the Scriptures and on tradition, as did Roman Catholics; the difference was not so much a matter of what was relevant, as it was of who could speak with authority in matters of faith and tradition. It has been aptly said that, 'If all who denounced abuses and strove for reform in any sense were Protestants, then must we reckon as Protestants Erasmus and Contarini, Ignatius Loyola and Pope Paul IV'.[1] People became Protestants for every conceivable reason, and 'the desire to annex church property made very stout Protestants'.[2] Nevertheless, the 'Protestant Revolt' was a direct challenge to the authority and traditions of the church. Positive consequences were almost bound to follow from Luther's negative declarations of 1520. In that year Luther had utterly rejected the claims of the papacy. If no coercive power belonged properly to the church, if the clergy were as fully subject to secular magistrates as other men, if canon law had no validity, then 'at a blow Christendom was resolved, or dissolved, into a group, if not of "states", at least of independent, secular, territorial magistracies, governing persons and governing bodies. The sacerdotium was abolished and the regnum stood alone'.[3] The implications of all this for political theory have been studied in detail. The implications for historical research were only slightly less, and these require comment.

Although Luther regretted his failure to read widely in history he did make use of some of the critical writings of the humanists (notably Lorenzo Valla's 'Donation of Constantine') in his struggle with the papacy. Melancthon did more—he brought to the German universities at which he taught an enthusiasm for the academic study of history; and he himself provided a Lutheran model of historical interpretation in his pious and learned *Chronicle*. It became a German textbook of universal history which, in spite of Erasmian influence, was unmistakably Lutheran—especially in its treatment of the relations of church and state. The papacy could only be a usurped power to the Lutheran reformer; and temporal rule, divinely hedged, was

[1] J. W. Allen, *Political Thought in the 16th Century*, 3.
[2] *Ibid.*, 4.   [3] *Ibid.*, 5.

necessarily regarded as a dispensation of providence. Doctrine determined interpretation. In turning away from the secular humanist tradition Melancthon, in effect, reverted to an uncritical providential view of history. In this he was typical of Reformation religious historians in general—history became the theatre of God's judgments; and historical criticism was overshadowed by religious piety and polemics. To regard this merely as a retrograde movement is, however, to miss the point.

The Reformation was not a *bloc*. The Lutheran, the Calvinist and the Anglican confessions diverged widely, not only from each other, but also from the Tridentine Catholicism of Rome. Churches had an even greater need than states for the sanction of tradition, and at no time was this more evident than during the Reformation. The churches of the sixteenth century were, furthermore, everywhere allied with territorial states; hence, every question of doctrine also involved a question of church government and church-state relations. The very divergence between confessions was bound to stimulate research in ecclesiastical history, and to result in a widening of the fields of study. The mere amassing of evidence did not, of course, make history, but it helped to make history possible—just as the mere refuting of error did not make truth, although it helped to make truth possible. The Magdeburg 'Centuries' and the folios of Cardinal Baronius illustrated this: they were not true histories, but they helped to make true histories possible.[1]

Theological disputes during the Middle Ages had turned mainly on logical and philosophical (that is, metaphysical) pivots. An appeal to history was seldom made because the church was seldom attacked on the ground that its doctrines were not sanctioned by authoritative tradition. During the Reformation, when papal tradition was challenged, historiography assumed new and strategic importance. The humanists had already begun to question some of the texts and dates of sacred history. Church historians were responsible for extending these investigations and making them count. If the Vulgate was not authoritative, then what was? Erasmus, in editing the Greek manuscripts of the Bible, had perforce posed the question; and the Reformers were often as embarrassed for an answer as the Roman

---

[1] The standard work of reference on the history of historiography is James Westfall Thompson, *A History of Historical Writing*, 2 vols. (New York, 1942). The relevant chapters are XXX and XXXI, both of which contain standard bibliographical references.

churchmen. The great Scaliger remarked that 'our theological disputes all arise from ignorance of grammar'.[1] Not even he realized, however, the extent to which theological disputes helped to extend knowledge of grammar, and of ecclesiastical history.

The dialectic between research and controversy, between religion and learning, was given new direction, power, and impetus by the Reformation. Nothing could be more inaccurate, of course, than to imagine that the clergy of the sixteenth century were primarily concerned with learning, or that they anticipated a scholarly revelation of Christian truth. The Jesuit historical propagandists were quite content to see Catholicism protected from contamination by a papal Index—'the finest secret which has ever been discovered for applying religion to the purpose of making men idiotic', as Fra Paolo Sarpi reminded his readers.[2] Lutherans were, in general, only less efficient policemen of the mind. The Calvinists at Geneva would not pay Casaubon a living wage for teaching there; and Calvin himself had not been backward about burning Servetus. 'Anglicans' were willing to sell English monastic records, and to burn books at Oxford in 1550; and if Tudor Puritans shared with many humanists a detestation of the Catholic Middle Ages, it was because they could not detest popery so much, loved they not learning more. Indeed, even the humanists were men of their age, and not above scholarly suspicion: 'the New Learning created the New Ignorance', according to the epigram of C. S. Lewis.[3] It was the necessity of winning converts, not pure love of truth, that launched historical offensives.

The first general offensive of Protestantism in the field of learning was the great compilation known as the Magdeburg 'Centuries'. Under the direction of Flacius Illyricus, Magdeburg professor and Lutheran controversialist, a group of Lutheran scholars began work on a history of the church since the birth of Christ. The purpose of the 'Centuries' was to demonstrate by means of documentary evidence the increasing corruption of the Roman Church in each century of its existence. The first volume appeared in 1559, and the last, covering the thirteenth century, in 1574. Primarily a work of apologetics, not of historical scholarship, its chief merit was the publication of masses

[1] Quoted by Mark Pattison, *Isaac Casaubon 1559–1614* (London, 1875), 441.

[2] Quoted by Thompson, *Historical Writing*, I, 540.

[3] C. S. Lewis, *English Literature in the Sixteenth Century* (Oxford, 1954), 31.

of source material. Naturally, the sources published were only those which supported the Protestant thesis, but the work put the Catholics on the defensive almost at once.

In the Roman Catholic Church, apart from the Jesuits, the Oratorians were the most important order engaged in the study of church history. The task of defending the church was therefore entrusted to a young Oratorian, Caesar Baronius, who made church history his life's work. The massive answer of Baronius to the Centuriators helped immeasurably to make history the centre of the quarrel between the faiths. Baronius' *Annals* provided the antithesis to the Magdeburg thesis—and now it was the Protestants who were put on the defensive. Baronius compiled with as eager a bias as his Lutheran adversaries, but he enjoyed some advantages that were denied them: at his disposal were the resources of the Vatican press and library, and the wealth of the church. Furthermore, Baronius was singularly gifted for the defence of his faith; his dedication was complete, his industry incomparable, and his mind blissfully incapable of recognizing its own bias. It has been said that, 'while he preserved round the church story that picturesque haze which faith cherished and which historical science would dissipate, he satisfied the requirements of the political churchmen by turning the annals of the church into one long proof of the supremacy of the roman pontiff'.[1] Yet the very success of Baronius' work caused it to be read with critical care, especially by scholarly Protestants.

The foremost Greek scholar of the late sixteenth century was Isaac Casaubon, the Calvinist son-in-law of Estienne, the Genevan printer of classical texts. Casaubon's tribulations at Geneva, Montpellier, and Paris finally caused him to accept an invitation to come to London, where he began work on a refutation of Baronius. On two points Baronious lay entirely at Casaubon's mercy—his lack of any knowledge of Greek or Hebrew, and, in general, of classical learning; and his acceptance of apocryphal literature as though it were matter of fact. Had Casaubon confined his efforts to historical criticism and taken his stand on the principle that church history should be written in conformity with the standards of evidence and proof appropriate to secular history, he might have produced a work of lasting significance. As it was, Casaubon wrote a book that, for all its scholarship, was neither good history nor good theology. He understood the opinions of the church fathers better than his

[1] M. Pattison, *Isaac Casaubon*, 368-9.

less scholarly opponent, but he, too, assumed that when he had ascertained the opinions of the fathers he had obtained truths valid for all time, rather than merely the opinions of a given period of the church. Generally speaking, the fathers and canonical books were exempted by both sides from the application of historical criticism. Conflicting biblical accounts had to be 'reconciled' in order to avoid blasphemy. As yet, it was inconceivable to think of the Bible as a mere historical document; it contained, quite literally, God's words.[1]

The connection between historical studies and Reformation politics and religion could be illustrated by many English examples. In general, the dialectic of development was similar to that which occurred on the continent. Foxe's *Book of Martyrs*, when issued in 1563 as *Acts and Monuments*, was quite consonant in purpose, and in lack of objectivity, to the work of Flacius Illyricus. Hooker's *Laws of Ecclesiastical Polity* summed up and resumed the earlier Admonition controversy, but Hooker went on to provide one of the wisest and most attractive defences of Anglicanism ever written. His views are not without interest to the student of historiography, for he based his defence of the church against Puritan attacks partly on historical arguments, which took cognizance of the differences between ages:

> Our end ought always to be the same; our ways and means thereunto not so. The glory of God and the good of his Church was the thing the Apostles aimed at, and therefore ought to be the mark whereat we also level. But seeing those rites and orders may be at one time more which at another are less available unto that purpose, what reason is there in those things to urge the state of only one age as a pattern to follow?[2]

Hooker was more aware than most religious writers that faith depended ultimately on human testimony: 'For whatsoever we believe concerning salvation by Christ, although the Scripture be therein the ground of our belief; yet the authority of man is, if we mark it, the key which openeth the door of entrance into the knowledge of

[1] On Casaubon's importance in the development of Anglo-Catholic apologetics, see Pattison, *Casaubon*, 373–7.

[2] See Richard Hooker, *Of the Laws of Ecclesiastical Polity*, 2 vols. (London, Everyman, 1907), I, 365.

Scripture.' [1] And the ground of persuasion in matters of history 'can be nothing but man's testimony'.[2]

It is evident that the Elizabethan religious settlement did not and could not appeal to the scriptures alone as earlier Calvinism had done. Hence, historical apologetics in England inevitably was concerned with a wider field of human history. It took some time, however, before historical studies in England reached maturity. One reason for the relative backwardness of English historical research until late in the sixteenth century was simply the dispersal of records that took place after the dissolution of the monasteries. Most of the classical texts had, fortunately, already been edited and printed by the time of the English Reformation, but all manner of religious and legal records of the Middle Ages were dispersed and lost following the dissolution.[3]

There is plenty of contemporary evidence to show that books, records, and manuscripts of all kinds were not only lost, but destroyed, sold, and mutilated during the decades between 1530 and about 1565. John Bale did not exaggerate when he wrote in his 1549 preface to Leland's 'New Year's Gift' that 'a great number of them which purchased those superstitious mansions, reserved of those library books, some to serve their jakes, some to scour their candlesticks, and some to rub their boots. Some they sold to the grocers and soap sellers, and some they sent oversea to the bookbinders, not in small number, but at times whole ships full, to the wondering of the foreign nations.' [4]

Leland and Bale and Matthew Parker were all men who understood the nature and extent of the losses incurred. Matthew Parker, after becoming Archbishop of Canterbury in 1559, was, however, the first scholar who was in a position to do something effective to arrest the process of dispersal. His efforts to bring together scattered manuscripts received official approval in 1568 when the Privy Council directed a letter 'to all and singular' her majesty's subjects who possessed monastic records, to make them available to the deputies of the Archbishop, 'so as both when any need shall require resort

---

[1] *Ibid.*, I, 267.   [2] *Ibid.*, I, 275.

[3] See Wormald and Wright, *English Library*, 149. 'The Dispersal of the Libraries in the 16th Century', by C. E. Wright.

[4] Quoted by C. E. Wright, 'Dispersal of the Monastic Libraries and the Beginnings of Anglo-Saxon Studies', *Transactions of the Cambridge Bibliographical Society*, III, 1951, 208–37. The passage occurs on p. 211; I have modernized the spelling.

may be made for the testimony that may be found in them, and also by conference of them, the antiquity of the state of these countries may be restored to the knowledge of the world'.[1]

The dispersal of monastic records could not, of course, be halted all at once, and historians owed much to those individual scholars and antiquaries—men like William Bowyer, the record keeper, Sir Robert Cotton, the librarian, and many others—who rescued medieval manuscripts for their own reasons. Nevertheless, after Elizabeth came to the throne, the process of dispersal and destruction was arrested:

> The lead was taken by those in authority, who now realized the great importance of much of this material for the purpose of propaganda for the government's policy in church and state alike. Parker early discerned the purposes to which the writings of Aelfric and the early church historians could be put for the more secure establishing of the Ecclesia Anglicana over which he had been appointed by Elizabeth to rule, and Cecil was equally anxious to secure historical material which should feed the rising tide of nationalism and supply the groundwork of the closely-reasoned state papers which were expedient to strengthen Elizabeth's position against hostile controversialists here and abroad.[2]

In short, politics, religion and historical research were linked together during Elizabeth's reign; and the links were not broken thereafter until church and state felt secure in the face of Catholic power.

Even at the popular level, social criticism in the sixteenth century sometimes appeared in the guise of history—especially biblical history—and in the seventeenth century the Puritan reformers nearly all took some interest in sacred and secular history. Prynne and the Presbyterians, Lilburne and the Levellers, Cromwell and the Independents—all held ideas about the relevance of history to their own and England's discontents. In the polemical literature of the seventeenth century, and in the great debates at Putney and Whitehall in 1647 and 1648, the issues discussed in terms of nature and grace nearly always involved some consideration of history, if only by way of questioning the relevance of the 'historical parts of the Gospel'.[3]

[1] B.M. Add. MS. 35831, fols. 279–80; see also J. C. T. Oates, 'The Libraries of Cambridge', in Wormald and Wright, *The English Library*.

[2] Wormald and Wright, *English Library*, 170, by C. E. Wright.

[3] A. S. P. Woodhouse, *Puritanism And Liberty, Being The Army Debates (1647–9) from the Clarke Manuscripts* (Chicago, 1951), 167. The passage occurs in the Whitehall debates, 1648.

Milton saw history in terms of providential progress as did most of the Puritan reformers.

In the sixteenth and seventeenth centuries the Augustinian idea of providence was used to sanction the most diverse interpretations of history. Calvin's theology had given a special urgency to the problem of defining the relationship between divine moral judgments and human history. Providence served to link together the realm of nature, including history, and the realm of grace, but neither Calvin nor anyone else could prove by historical evidence that a particular interpretation of providence was the right one. Intensity of belief was one thing; sound scholarship was another. The Augustinian tradition was not necessarily inimical to science or scholarship— indeed, most of the men of learning in seventeenth-century England believed in a dominating providence. But after the outbreak of the civil wars it became increasingly apparent that a 'principle of segregation' would have to be invoked if the fires of Reformation controversy were to be brought under control.[1] Historical scholarship could profitably be applied only to second causes. By segregating history from divinity it was possible to treat sacred and secular history in the same way. Slowly, yet inevitably, the doctrine of providence receded, and historiography was secularized.[2]

[1] The Puritan idea of history has been discussed by a number of writers. Especially important are the works of William Haller, who edited the standard collection of documents, *Tracts on Liberty*, 3 vols. (New York, 1934). See also Haller, *The Rise of Puritanism* (New York, 1938); and Haller, *Liberty and Reformation in the Puritan Revolution* (New York, 1955). Woodhouse discusses the principle of segregation in his illuminating introduction to *Puritanism and Liberty*. Helen C. White, *Social Criticism in Popular Religious Literature of the Sixteenth Century* (New York, 1944), discusses briefly the argument from history, especially pp. 151 and 217. Herschel Baker, *The Wars of Truth* (Cambridge, Mass., 1952), 84–5, and Chapter II, *passim* deals with historical and eschatological attitudes. Milton and Cromwell, not to mention lesser figures, have been studied in detail, and from nearly every point of view. Further bibliographical reference would be out of place.

[2] The best short discussion of the doctrine of providence in the seventeenth century is that of Herschel Baker in *The Wars of Truth* (Cambridge, Mass., 1952), 12–25. The importance of the doctrine for intellectual history can scarcely be overemphasized. In this paragraph I have necessarily oversimplified a profoundly difficult and complex problem. George L. Mosse, *The Holy Pretence* (Oxford, 1957) discusses the general question of Christianity and Reason of State.

2

THE HISTORICAL CONTEXT

THE RENAISSANCE AND REFORMATION were European movements, with continuing historical effects; in the realms of religion and politics, England was a part of the continent. English institutions and English law, however, were less immediately affected by what happened elsewhere in Europe; and the continuity of English tradition is nowhere more evident than in her laws. Not only was law a matter of custom and record, but also the institutions of local and national government were traditionally record-minded. Among a litigious people even the family muniment room existed less for the sake of prestige than for the sake of protection. No interpretation of English historiography can fail to take account of the pervasive effects of the English legal tradition on English ideas of history.

i LEGAL INFLUENCES

It has been argued that 'the whole effect of the common law upon the Englishman as historian was to keep him isolated, a provincial on the edge of European learning'.[1] The extent to which this was so, at least between about 1550 and 1600, is obviously a matter of considerable importance. It is undeniably true that few revolutionary changes occurred in English historical thought until late in the sixteenth century. Compared with France, England was provincial, yet in the seventeenth century England produced historical scholars

[1] J. G. A. Pocock, *The Ancient Constitution and the Feudal Law* (Cambridge, 1957), 90.

of the first rank. In order to explain this significant difference a short digression must be made to explain the contrast between English and French historical jurisprudence. It will then be seen why the common law tradition inhibited historical understanding, even though it encouraged research.

The French prelude to modern historiography has been admirably discussed by Mr. Pocock, whose observations may be quoted at length:

> It is the peculiar characteristic of a comprehensive system of law like the Roman that it provides a close and extensive description of the principal institutions and many of the ideas of the society for which it was formed; and the historical school—as the humanist lawyers soon became—could not translate the language of Roman law back into its original meanings without reconstructing just such a picture of the society of imperial Rome. They gathered much of their evidence for this picture from the text of the law itself, but much more important was the fact that they sought to interpret the law according to the context of a reconstructed society. Inadequate, piece-meal and *ad hoc* their work may have been, but the essentials of the historical method were there and were known to be there. In this way the legal humanists came to be historians, and the full import of their work on European thought has never yet been measured.[1]

The historical *understanding* of such men as Budé, Alciato, Cujas, Doneau, Hotman, L'Hospital, and Bodin, was far greater than the historical understanding of any of the English legal writers of the sixteenth century. Going beyond mere textual analysis, and developing methods of comparative historical analysis unknown to English lawyers, the French legal humanists laid the foundation for a systematic, indeed, scientific, study of history.[2] Striving for more accurate historical interpretation, these men came close to denying the relevance of the past to the present. Their awareness of the unique characteristics of past societies made them the first modern contextualists. They wrote about and studied Roman law, which was the source of the principles by which their own contemporary society was attempting to govern itself. If they were humanists in the breadth of their learning and in their passion for grammatical exegesis, they

---

[1] *Ibid.*, 9–10. I am indebted to Mr. Pocock's admirable analysis for many of the ideas in this section.

[2] See Linton C. Stevens, 'The Contributions of French Jurists to the Humanism of the Renaissance', *Studies in the Renaissance* (I, 1954), 92–105.

were true historians in their awareness of process. The humanist attempt to restitute, renovate, and restore the past was shown by them to be futile, without first recreating a past society which had few historical continuants into the present. Hence, their investigations raised the most profound and complex problems of relevance.

Questions of relevance necessarily involved religious and political, as well as historical beliefs. It is hardly surprising that these legal humanists differed from one another in their theories of jurisprudence, or that their sceptical ideas of history had little immediate influence on narrative historians. Cujas, when asked to apply his learning to contemporary religious and secular problems is reported to have answered with the question: 'What does it have to do with the Praetor's edict?' A scholar's answer to a layman's request for useful knowledge was likely to provoke charges of apostasy, and this answer did. Cujas, in effect, was saying that the old Roman law was inapplicable to contemporary French society. What was missing was an accepted standard of relevance.

During the 1560's François Baudouin, Jean Bodin, and François Hotman undertook further studies, aimed at bringing law and history back into register with one another. Hotman was perhaps the most influential writer, and his work marked a reaction in favour of customary as opposed to Roman law. The appeal to custom in France was markedly similar to the appeals being made in England and elsewhere to custom or to the 'ancient constitution'. And, by about 1600, 'there was hardly any constitutional movement without its accompanying historical myth'.[1] In France the idealization of custom contributed mightily to an awareness of process in history, yet this awareness was slow to develop in England. In France, legal scholarship showed an awareness of context and process even before it sanctioned the myth of custom. No doubt there are many reasons for this, but the most obvious is simply that in France customary law and Roman law existed side by side; the French king ruled over both *pays de droit écrit* and *pays de coutumes*. This meant that lawyers, political theorists, and historians all had to face the problems of co-existence and competition. In France the dualism of the law promoted comparative historical studies. In England, the uniformity or commonness of the law helped to sanctify the myth of the immemorial antiquity of the law.[2]

[1] Pocock, *Ancient Constitution*, 17.
[2] *Ibid.*, 25–6 and Chapters I–III, *passim*.

In his Rede lecture for 1901, Maitland linked together the legal historian's three R's—Renaissance, Reformation, and Reception. The reception of Roman law in England during the sixteenth century doubtless represented less of a threat to the common law than Maitland supposed, but certainly the common lawyers of the second half of the century rallied to the defence of common law tradition as though the threat were real enough.[1]

Shortly after the turn of the century Sir Edward Coke set his imprimatur on the dogmas of the common law which he himself had done much to define. The common law, by definition, was one which had existed in England since immemorial antiquity—time out of mind. The written records of the law all implied earlier customs which the records only confirmed: 'at however remote a date the series of records had begun, the common-law mind would still have taken their beginning as proof that at that time the laws were already immemorial; since *jus non scriptuus* must by definition be older than the oldest written records'.[2] It is not necessary to pursue all the implications of this argument in order to perceive that it constituted a denial of any idea of changing historical contexts.

If the common law of England was unique—and older than the laws of the Romans, as Fortescue had maintained—then there was little need to study other law, make comparisons, or face the fact that feudal laws might be nothing more than appropriate expressions of a feudal social order. As long as the myth of immemorial antiquity prevailed, the idea of historical process could not mature. Precedent was the antithesis of process. Put very briefly, according to Mr. Pocock, 'What occurred was that belief in the antiquity of the common law encouraged belief in the existence of an ancient constitution, reference to which was constantly made, precedents, maxims, and principles from which were constantly alleged, and which was constantly asserted to be in some way immune from the king's prerogative action; and discussion in these terms formed one of the century's chief modes of political argument.'[3]

---

[1] Maitland's Lecture, 'English Law and the Renaissance', is conveniently reprinted in Helen C. Cam, ed., *Selected Historical Essays of F. W. Maitland* (Cambridge, 1957), 135–51.

[2] Pocock, *Ancient Constitution*, 38.

[3] *Ibid.*, 46. Cf. Margaret Attwood Judson, *The Crisis of the Constitution* (New Brunswick, N.J., 1949), 1–170, *passim*.

In the basic principles of the common law Coke found the 'fundamental law' of this ancient English constitution. The complicated historical relationships between common law, natural law, and fundamental law are of no concern in the present context.[1] The idea of fundamental law was, in Coke's day, significant as an expression of the theory that English law was timeless truth, not the mirror of the times. Legal history for Coke meant contemporary history in the fullest sense. Of Magna Carta Coke wrote, 'this statute is but a confirmation or restitution of the common law', and he added that Magna Carta 'was for the most part declaratory of the principal grounds of the fundamental laws of England'.[2] The fundamental law, defined ultimately in terms of the 'artificial reason' of the common law, was the rock on which Coke founded his church. He has, with some justice been called the first Whig historian because of his habit of reading the present into the past. In doing this, however, he was obliged to ransack the records of the past to find precedents which he thought confirmed existing law. Legal research thus inevitably accompanied the Whig interpretation of legal history.[3]

The theory of confirmations had been part of the legal heritage of the Middle Ages, and the common lawyers who sat in Elizabeth's Parliaments laid claim to new rights and privileges on the basis of precedents which supposedly confirmed existing law—law which was ultimately unwritten custom. During Elizabeth's reign the Commons frequently were guilty of thinking unhistorically, as Sir John Neale has pointed out; and in 1581 an irritated House of Commons saw fit to castigate Arthur Hall for his deviationist views of Parliamentary history.[4] Nevertheless it is clear that historical allusions, parallels, and precedents were the stock in trade of the Parliamentary leaders. In Elizabethan Parliaments common law thought became set in the mould of Custom and the Immemorial. It was unhistorical in what it

[1] Some of these problems are discussed in J. W. Gough, *Fundamental Law in English Constitutional History* (Oxford, 1955), 41 ff.

[2] Quoted by Gough, *Fundamental Law*, 40.

[3] Professor Butterfield was the first to call attention to Coke's Whig view of history. See H. Butterfield, *The Englishman and His History* (Cambridge, 1944), 40.

[4] See J. E. Neale, *Elizabeth I and Her Parliaments 1559–1581* (London, 1953), 420 and 407 ff. On the use of historical arguments in the later Parliaments, see J. E. Neale, *Elizabeth I and Her Parliaments 1584–1601* (London, 1957), 182, 212, and 252 ff.

asserted—that no precedent was an innovation—but it was not necessarily unhistorical in its procedures of documentation.

The toughness of the old common law has been much admired by common lawyers and English historians. Maitland thought that 'taught law' was tough law, and argued that the Inns of Court became the training ground for tough lawyers, because there lawyers learned not from books but from experience.[1] There is no doubt much to be said for this view, yet it is only a part of the truth. The Inns of Court were certainly not isolated from the main currents of humanistic thought, and many students and common lawyers took a lively humanistic interest in the classics and in history. The method of teaching law was by 'conferences and disputations, which they call Mootes, and Pleadings, and putting cases, and Lectures and Readings upon the Lawes and Statutes of England'.[2] Humanism only reinforced the natural tendency of the common law tradition to seek historical knowledge. Sir John Fortescue's historical thought was by no means contemptible, but Fortescue in the fifteenth century, like Coke in the seventeenth century, explained the law in terms of immemorial custom. Moreover, a search for precedents had been going on ever since the days of Bracton. The task of the seventeenth century was to discover a new idea of explanation to replace the doctrine of Custom.

The difference between the English common lawyers and the French legal humanists was primarily, therefore, one of ideas and approach, not of research as such. Lambarde's research in Anglo-Saxon legal history was impressive, but unfortunately the collection of genuine and apocryphal Anglo-Saxon laws, published by Lambarde in his *Archaionomia* (1568), was generally accepted as proof that 'there was no sign in these apparently authoritative texts of any radical breach with the past at the Conquest'.[3] The myth of custom was thus fed by precedents of record. The common law tradition

[1] Cf. Maitland, *Historical Essays* (ed. Helen Cam), 137.

[2] G.[eorge] B.[uck], *The Third Universitie of England: Or A Treatise of the Foundations of All the Colledges, Ancient Schooles of Priviledge, and Of Houses of Learning and Liberall Arts* ... (London, 1631), 1074. On the humanistic interests of the lawyers, see R. J. Schoeck, 'Early Anglo-Saxon Studies and Legal Scholarship in the Renaissance', *Studies in the Renaissance* (V, 1958), 102–10, *passim*.

[3] Pocock, *Ancient Constitution*, 43. The historical thought of Fortescue is discussed in Arthur B. Ferguson, 'Fortescue and the Renaissance: A Study in Transition', *Studies in the Renaissance* (VI, 1959), 175–94.

may have inhibited understanding of the history of the law and of feudalism, but it did contribute to the essential historical task of research in original records.

ii RECORDS AND HISTORICAL RESEARCH

No nation's history can be accurately written without access to its public records and archives. The public records are indispensable to the historian; the recognition of this fact in the seventeenth century by itself constituted a revolution in historical thought. Naturally, the Elizabethan and Stuart medievalists were more confident that the records contained 'the authentic' than are modern historians, who have found that records can lie with as glib a tongue as any literary source. Lawyers like Coke, however, could not be expected to doubt records which were the embodiment of legal memory; unfortunately, historians also were long afflicted with this legalistic assumption. Only gradually did historians learn that the lawyer's predisposition to look for precedents stood in need of historical correctives.

The primary reason for preserving records of all kinds for centuries was a legal reason in England, not a historical one. This may help to account for the strong legal bias in the use of English records by Elizabethan and Stuart historians. The 'courts of record' occupied a special place in English jurisprudence, their records being of the utmost authority at law. All other government records were of secondary importance to lawyers, although not necessarily to historians. Coke exhibited the contemporary attitude toward legal record: 'It [a legal record] hath a sovereigne privilege, that it is proved by no other but by it selfe. *Monumenta* (*quae nos Recorda vocamus*) *sunt vetustatis et veritatis vestigea.* And albeit the cause adjudged be particular, yet when it is entered of Record, it is of great authority in Law, and serves for perpetuall evidence, and therefore ought to be common to all, yea, though it be against the King: as it is declared by act of Parliament in *Anno* 46 E.3 . . .' [1]

King James, by granting that the Commons were 'a court of record and a judge of returns' in Goodwin's case (1604) acknowledged this much of the common law interpretation: Parliament itself

---

[1] Sir Edward Coke, *The Third Part of the Institutes Of The Laws Of England* (London, 1644), 71; the passage occurs in Chapter XIX.

was a high court of record.[1] The relationship between statute law and common law was the subject of considerable dispute even in the seventeenth century, but this controversy belongs properly to constitutional history and must be passed over. The distinction between legal records and other public records, however, should be kept in mind, for it was an article of legal faith, even though 'the public records', then as now, comprised much more than the exclusively legal records of the King's courts of common law and Chancery.

According to a modern definition, ' "The Public Records", then, are the Archives of the Central Government of this Country, Ancient and Modern. . . . Archives are Documents drawn up for the purposes of, or used during, the conduct of Affairs of any kind, of which they themselves formed a part, and [sic] subsequently preserved by the persons responsible for the transactions in question, or their successors, in their own custody for their own reference.' [2] The elements of this definition apply also to the seventeenth century, when matters of custody were of particular interest and concern to historians. In general it must be said that records accumulated naturally in offices for the practical purposes of administration, and that among the ancient records—especially legal records which had been transferred to the Tower—it was seldom an easy task to determine the exact provenance of an archive or to relate it to others in a series. The early seventeenth-century historians thus had to overcome great obstacles before they could reconstruct the history of ancient institutions.

Access to the records of the courts was the legal right of all Englishmen, according to Coke, but he realized that the right was jeopardized by the practice of taking customary fees for search. Still, except for those records having to do with 'mysteries of state', most records could be consulted, and more and more lawyers, historians, and royal officials were consulting them. Books on record searching, published early in the seventeenth century, were meant to satisfy a growing demand. It is clear that bureaucratic disputes of all kinds were being argued out in terms of administrative precedents found in the records. Record repositories existed for the convenience

---

[1] See G. W. Prothero, *Select Statutes and Other Constitutional Documents* (Oxford, 1894), 330.

[2] Public Record Office, *Guide to the Public Records, Part I, Introductory* (London, 1949), 1. This short introduction contains a valuable select bibliography.

of lawyers and officials, not for the benefit of historians, but this fact fortunately did not prove to be too serious a handicap to the serious student of history.

Coincident with the growth of interest in national records on the part of Elizabethan and Stuart historians was a growing concern with local history and local records. The city of Exeter was in many ways typical of the larger provincial towns of England in the period between 1540 and 1640, and it was here that John Hooker, alias Vowel, held office and pursued his antiquarian and historical research. Hooker was a man of ability, whose official duties happily included custody of the city records. These he set in order, and catalogued for his own and posterity's use.[1] Other cities may have been less fortunate in their local officials, but few cities of the seventeenth century were without an antiquary interested in the local records and monuments.

There is no want of evidence for a growth of interest in local history. Carew's *Survey of Cornwall* and Stow's *Survey of London* are only the most prominent examples of a trend in historiography. Moreover, historians were developing a significant interest in family history. This was in part a reflection of the heraldic and genealogical interests of the nobility and gentry, but only in part; historians and antiquaries were often mindful of local and family history because of what it told them of English history at large.[2] Research in a wide variety of records had not been characteristic of medieval historiography, but by the end of Elizabeth's reign, local, family, national, and ecclesiastical archives were all being explored. Antiquaries and historians made transcripts of records and took notes on all kinds of documents which held traces of the past. Some made collections which they hoped would prove useful to them in their work; others no doubt collected information only out of curiosity, or because antiquarianism was a respectable hobby. Indirectly, however, all such activity contributed to the formation of a new attitude toward history as record.

[1] See Wallace T. MacCaffrey, *Exeter 1540–1640* (Cambridge, Mass., 1958), 272–3.

[2] See Michael MacLaglan, 'Genealogy and Heraldry in the Sixteenth and Seventeenth Centuries', in Levi Fox, ed., *English Historical Scholarship in the Sixteenth and Seventeenth Centuries* (Dugdale Society, Oxford Press, 1956), 31–48. A number of manuscript local histories are in the British Museum. For further references to the subject, see my Chapter VI, 'The Varieties of History'.

iii LIBRARIES AND HISTORICAL RESEARCH

Libraries were perhaps even more important for the writing of history than record offices. The study of comparative history would have been impossible without well-stocked libraries. Medieval ecclesiastical documents had very often passed into private hands by the end of the sixteenth century; and the chronicles and literary sources of medieval Europe—the foundation stones of every historical account—were accessible only in libraries. The books, manuscripts, chronicles, annals, and other literary remains of former times were accumulated in Tudor and Stuart libraries, just as public records were accumulated in the Four Treasuries at Westminster and in the Tower.

The growth of private and public libraries in England in the period between the Reformation and the civil wars was not so much the result of state bounty as it was owing to the public concerns of private collectors. The consolidation of the territorial monarchies on the continent had led to the founding of great public libraries under the auspices of the state. In England, libraries were founded mostly by individuals, who might be statesmen like Walsingham and Burghley, bishops like Matthew Parker, or private men of means and position like Bodley and Cotton. Many of the English libraries founded in this period served the interests of the state, as well as the wider interests of the educated public. Libraries were indispensable for the scholarly study of history, and clearly the conditions governing the use of historical materials in libraries directly influenced the development of historiography. Generally speaking, libraries were made accessible to scholars, partly because scholars were serviceable to the state, and partly because statesmen themselves were patrons of learning. In any case, the scope and content of written history was greatly expanded, thanks to the efforts of patrons and collectors who sought to turn history to account.

In seventeenth-century England libraries were more numerous than ever before, and many were expanding both in size and in range of subject matter. Gains were being registered in all the areas of humanistic learning—in classical scholarship, in philology, in literature and languages studies—as well as in the areas of Anglo-Saxon and medieval historical studies. For every book published in these fields one may infer that a sizable number of books and manuscripts had circulated during the course of its preparation. The libraries of England were still small by modern standards, and historians were forced to acquire much of what they needed by purchase. However, by the beginning of the seventeenth century a number of great collections had been made in the different fields of learning; and historians were, for the most part, able to make use of them.

The consolidation of private collections, along with improved institutional arrangements for the care and use of manuscripts and books greatly facilitated the writing of history. By about 1625 the process of consolidation was well advanced. Scholars knew in general where to look for particular materials. Few of England's libraries were as well arranged as Sir Robert Cotton's, but at least the greater libraries were performing their institutional functions. The community of learning was aristocratic and powerful enough to secure privileges for its members, who were able to borrow from, or at least consult, most of the major collections.

The trend toward consolidation meant that various private libraries were being acquired by a few individuals or institutions, either by purchase or through bequests. Camden, for example, had acquired by purchase some of Leland's historical collections which he made use of in his own work. Some of Camden's collections passed to Cotton on Camden's death, and Cotton also acquired by bequest portions of the antiquarian collections of Arthur Agarde, Francis Thynne, Robert Bowyer, Michael Heneage, John Joscelyn, William Lambarde, Laurence Nowell, and Thomas Talbot.[1] By purchase Camden gained some of John Stow's historical manuscripts, and such purchases (on a much larger scale) were often made by Cotton and a few other collectors. The university and college libraries at Oxford and Cambridge were of considerable importance for scholarship in the seventeenth century, although the importance of any one of them was usually owing to the vigor and wealth of an individual donor like Bodley, to the conscientious librarianship of an Abraham Whelock, or sometimes to an accident of fortune, such as the will by which Matthew Parker bequeathed his collections to Corpus Christi College in Cambridge.

Between 1570 and 1700 it has been said that at Cambridge the prime cause of the library's troubles 'was without doubt a general want of respect for the library throughout the university, and hence the want of a continuous tradition of pride in it and affection for it'.[2] The same thing might be said of some Oxford libraries where losses

[1] See Wormald and Wright, *English Library*, 197–8. [2] *Ibid.*, 227.

through carelessness were also sustained, but it would be wrong to infer from this that the universities made only insignificant contributions to librarianship, or to historical studies. Bodley's re-equipment of Duke Humphrey's library became a model for imitation at Oxford and elsewhere; and in the course of the seventeenth century the Oxford University Library became an institution of national, indeed, of international, importance for scholarship.

In general, the universities contributed to historical scholarship in at least three important ways: (1) the collections of certain college libraries were rich in historical books and manuscripts which scholars required; (2) the university library at Oxford was not only growing in size and reputation, but, thanks to Bodley's private agreement with the Stationer's Company for the deposit of new books, it was a place where most such books could be consulted (even though the agreement was not perfectly observed—it was better than none); and (3) English scholars working in fields related to history, did much of their work at one or the other of the two universities. It is true that curricular considerations discouraged the academic study of history in seventeenth-century Oxford and Cambridge, but historical studies were carried on in the name of divinity and other subjects, and the scholarly correspondence of the age testifies to the fact that academic libraries were important institutions of scholarship.[1]

More will be said in the following two chapters about the contents and administration of some of the great private libraries. Here, it is sufficient to observe that the early seventeenth century was a period of growth and consolidation, when the needs of historians were far better provided for than they had been in the past. Libraries were still inadequately catalogued and often uncomfortable to use, but if much still remained to be done, much had been accomplished, especially in the years between the accession of Elizabeth and the outbreak of the civil wars. The number of public and private libraries founded in this period testifies to the great interest on the part of educated Englishmen in all the relations of time past to time present.

iv CENSORSHIP AND HISTORICAL PUBLICATION

Libraries and record offices influenced the study of history;

[1] The most illuminating discussion of this whole subject is that of David C. Douglas, *English Scholars 1660–1730* (London, 1951), an indispensable book for the study of English historiography in the seventeenth century.

licensing authorities, the publication of it. Regulations designed to check the circulation of propaganda against church and state governed the printing of books and pamphlets in England until the Long Parliament began its work. Theoretically, all books had to be licensed, and licensing meant submitting manuscripts to the proper authorities before publication. The censorship as it existed before 1641 was probably not too serious an impediment to pure scholarship, but it must have served as a reminder to historians that they were not free to link the past and the present in any way they saw fit. There was an official policy 'line' on certain subjects, and writers were expected to hew to it. Historians might find themselves in serious difficulties if they published material which, in the opinion of the authorities, was seditious, heretical, or even (to use the modern idiom) subversive.

The actual operation of the licensing system was, like the censorship in eighteenth-century France, ineffective as a means of controlling opinion. The authorities responsible for licensing could not possibly read even a fraction of the manuscripts submitted by printers. They were forced to delegate their authority, and most of the 'correctors' or 'assessors' who were appointed were either clergymen or technical experts, who merely perused a work and took no responsibility beyond giving advice to the responsible official. It was obviously possible for well-placed scholars like Selden to have their works licensed and printed.[1]

According to a regulation of 1599 histories were to be licensed by the privy council; in 1637 it was proposed that one of the two principal secretaries of state be made responsible for licensing works on history and statecraft. Other fields, such as law, heraldry, and religion were each to be made subject to an appropriate authority after 1637, although the King remained the fountainhead of all authority in matters of licensing, as in the days of Henry VIII.[2] It is quite difficult to gauge the effects of this kind of censorship on seventeenth-century historiography, for the historians did not protest,

[1] See W. W. Greg, *Some Aspects and Problems of London Publishing* (Oxford, 1956), 1–20.

[2] Frederick W. Siebert, *Freedom of the Press in England 1476–1776* (Urbana, 1952), is valuable as a summary of problems and procedures. Henry R. Plomer, *A Short History of English Printing* (London, 1915), 150, argues that the 1637 Ordinance was never put into effect. A good deal of documentary evidence may be found scattered through the pages of George William Sanders, ed., *Orders of the High Court of Chancery* (London, 1845), a very rare book in the United States.

and presumably did not feel too restricted in their work. On the other hand, histories were censored, and historians were prosecuted for real or imaginary historical slanders. Of course, to have challenged the censorship would have been to challenge the King's prerogative. In general, historical writers preferred to conform, but the effects of conformity were in all likelihood far from salutary. The persistence of error in popular historical accounts may owe more to the censorship than can ever be proved.

A letter from Richard Bancroft, bishop of London, to Sir Robert Cecil, dated September 27, 1597, affords a good example of the operation of censorship on history:

> I send herewith a history in Latin lately come over. The author of it favours the Gospel and is no papist; he writes more honourably of the Queen and her actions than any foreigner I have yet seen, and continues down to the present journey of the earl of Essex. Still, there are some things in the book which were better omitted; for example on p. 473 are the contents of Sixtus V's bull against the Queen; where, though all the pope's railings and slanderous imputations are omitted, yet the other calumnies against the Queen's government, which Cardinal Allen hath taught the Pope, may hurt those that are popishly inclined. I have therefore ordered the stationers to suspend the sale until I know your pleasure.[1]

The bishop's concern for those 'popishly inclined' may strike the modern reader as disingenuous, but probably it was not. History had too much to say to the present for those in authority to remain neutral and indifferent.

The extremes to which censorship could be carried are illustrated in the case of John Hayward, who was imprisoned from 1599 to 1601 for having published the *First Part of the Life and Reign of Henry IV* in 1599 with a dedication to the Earl of Essex. It is true that Hayward was released, and was even appointed historiographer of Chelsea College in 1610, but his experience with the Star Chamber must have impressed upon him the dangers of analogy in history. He defended himself on the ground that his book was not meant to apply to the present, but Coke had made careful notes pointing out the analogies between Elizabeth and Richard II; and Coke's reasoning as attorney general was not far removed from the common reasoning about history. Justice Popham also submitted a list of questions

[1] Historical Manuscripts Commission, *Salisbury Papers*, I–XVIII (London, 1883–1938), VIII, 406.

to Hayward, one of which asked 'by what means saw you the records of that King which you have set down?'[1] This was an attempt to elicit information about possible accomplices, but it also shows that the authorities were fully aware of the propaganda value of impressive documentation.

Coke was anxious to pursue Popham's line of questioning, and in his examination of Hayward taken at the Tower on the 22nd of January 1600, he noted that Hayward '. . . taketh that to be lawful for any historiographer to insert any history of former time into that history he write about, whether [or not] historians of that . . . time mention the same, and that liberty is allowed by Dionysius Halicarnassus'.[2] Hayward confessed that he had inserted a passage from Foxe's *Acts and Monuments* dealing with Henry II into his own account of Henry IV. Having discovered whole passages from Tacitus in his work, Bacon contemptuously dismissed Hayward on the ground that he deserved prosecution for felony but not for treason. The fact remains, however, that Hayward's scholarship was discredited for reasons of state, not for reasons of scholarship.

Needless to say, there were many excellent reasons for not challenging the censorship, but what is less obvious and perhaps more significant is the fact that censorship was based on premises which most historians fully accepted: history repeats itself, the past is like the present, and the statesman may discover by reading history what is the proper course to be taken in the present. It followed that the purposes of the historian bear watching, that the argument of analogy may be treasonable, and that written history should serve the interests of the state. Fortunately, no such progression was ever explicitly stated, and in practice historians enjoyed a measure of freedom. The first purpose of history was, all agreed, to tell the truth. Censorship probably inhibited the study of recent, especially Tudor, history more than it did study of the remoter past. Yet after all allowances have been made, it remains true that some historians faced a dilemma—how to reconcile their political or moral purposes with the purpose of truth-telling? Moreover, to pry into secrets of

[1] S.P. 12/274 no. 58. (See the list of abbreviations at the beginning of the book for the forms of manuscript citation.)

[2] S.P. 12/278 f. 24–25b. It seems evident from the information in S.P. 12/275 no. 31 that it was possible to evade the censorship. Cf. also S.P. 12/275 nos. 25, 28. Most of these sources have to do with Haywarde's case.

state was not considered proper, nor could historians expect to gain access to state papers unless they agreed not to pry. The dilemma of access has certainly been a recurring one, but it first became a problem in the late Tudor period when historians began to write the history of the modern state, using modern methods of documentation.

An illustration of the dilemma, and of the contemporary attitude, is a letter which Dr. Giles Fletcher wrote to Lord Burghley in November 1590, requesting Burghley's help and patronage in writing a Latin history of Queen Elizabeth's times. He offered to let Burghley choose the relevant documents for him, and correct whatever he might say, adding that he would defend the Queen's parentage by defending Henry VIII and the divorce; he was anxious to tell the truth within these limitations:

> I acquainted your Lordship with my purpose to make trial of myself for writing a Latin story of her Majesty's time. Your Lordship knoweth what is needful, to make it a story not a tale; besides *res gestas* to have *concilia rerum gestarum*. Wherein I shall find defect except your Lordship vouchsafe your help for instructions. I desire not the very *arcana* (which are best when they are secretest), but so much as shall be necessary to explain and justify the actions.[1]

Here, in Fletcher's willingness to justify the Queen and the state, and to accept any conditions Burghley might impose, is the essence of the contemporary doctrine of the political significance and purpose of history. Although historians worshipped at the altar of Truth, they worshipped more than one God.

The censorship of the early Stuarts was at least as restrictive as the censorship of Elizabeth. The rationale of censorship, however, was being gradually undermined as political acts were justified more and more by historical argument. This implied that 'the evidence' was at least as important as the opinions of the censors. Milton's attack on licensing in *Areopagitica* summed up the emerging liberalism of the century; censorship was an evil in any guise, and 'the greatest discouragement and affront that can be offered to learning and to learned men'.[2]

---

[1] B.M. Lansdowne MS. 65, f. 166 no. 5 (cf. Lansdowne MS. 112, f. 134). Throughout, unless otherwise noted, I have modernized spelling and punctuation.

[2] John Milton, *Areopagitica and Other Prose Works* (London, Everyman, 1927), 21.

V GENEALOGY, HERALDRY, AND HISTORY

The renaissance of interest in history was accompanied by a similar renaissance of interest in heraldry and genealogy. A 'hunger for heraldic respectability' was characteristic of the second half of the sixteenth century, when the new gentry and official families sought to acquire older and more dignified arms, impressive by reason of their restrained simplicity.[1] The age of the early Tudors had been the great age of the pedigree makers, whose inventiveness was often expressed in *nouveau riche* quarterings. Under Elizabeth, fashionable families improved their pedigrees in subtler ways, often by the meticulous forgery of suitable documents. The College of Arms, after having received a new charter of incorporation in 1555, was instrumental in setting the higher heraldic standards to which Elizabethan and Stuart forgeries are a tribute.

J. H. Round set himself to expose the frauds and forgeries of the heralds and pedigree makers, 'nailing them up one by one as a gamekeeper nails his vermin'. He shot well and nailed accurately:

> It was under Elizabeth and her successor that the craze reached its height. The Queen herself had set the example with a Tudor pedigree deduced from Adam. The great Burghley was pedigree-mad and sought for the upstart Cecils' ancestors in all directions. Sir Christopher Hatton, that comely person who danced himself into Elizabeth's favour and became her Lord Chancellor, was fitted with a pedigree tracing his family to 'Yvon, a Norman noble, who came in with the Conqueror', which was duly 'seen and registered' by that notorious herald, 'William Dethick, Garter'. To support one of Burghley's ancestries there was forged a document in old French of the days, it was alleged, of the third Edward; to support Hatton's there was duly produced a whole galaxy of charters and seals. . . . For the pedigree maker stuck at nothing; he forged documents not only in Latin, but in Old English and Old French, and these he showed to the heralds, by whom they were greedily swallowed.[2]

It is undeniable that some heralds were guilty of laxity, and that many families were guilty of subornation. Camden, who performed most of his duties as Clarencieux by deputy, was fooled by the

---

[1] MacLaglan, 'Genealogy and Heraldry', in L. Fox, *English Historical Scholarship*, 35.

[2] J. H. Round, *Family Origins and Other Studies* (London, 1930), 69.

Lambert forgeries in the Mildmay case—as were St. George (Norroy), Treswell (Somerset herald), and Segar (Garter). Many examples of fraud and lack of scholarship could be produced. The disagreeable Ralph Brooke attacked Camden's heraldry with some reason; and, with better reason, Augustine Vincent destroyed Brooke's reputation and defended Camden's scholarship in his *Discoverie of Errors . . .* (1622). The important point is not that errors were made, but that the standards of heraldic scholarship were being improved. Heraldry and history progressed together.

A working knowledge of heraldry and genealogy was by no means confined to the armigerous classes in the sixteenth and seventeenth centuries. Many books, from Gerard Legh's popular *Accedens of Armorye* (1568) to Dugdale's learned *Baronage* testify to the widespread interest in descents and blazonry. Lord Burghley copied foreign genealogies in his own hand; Shakespeare could count on some knowledge of heraldry from the man in the pit.[1] Innkeepers and country gentlemen, scholars and lords found pleasure (and often profit) in a knowledge of arms and pedigrees. The long lists of heraldic collections dating from the seventeenth century in the catalogues of the British Museum and elsewhere prove that time and effort and money were expended on the study of heraldry and genealogy. Furthermore, the heralds of the College of Arms performed a multitude of important and necessary functions in a society still ordered in terms of status.

The decline of heraldry in the late seventeenth century coincided with the growth of a more mercantile and contract-minded civilization, in which heraldry had no place. Like astrology, heraldry outlived its usefulness and eventually earned the contempt of many educated men. Meanwhile, however, heraldry was a profession which could attract some of the most eminent scholars and historians; Glover, Camden, and Dugdale were heralds and men of learning, while others less famous, like Francis Thynne and Augustine Vincent

---

[1] Burghley's concern with genealogy is apparent from S.P. 9/206 no. 11. I have drawn on several books, the most recent and best of which is Anthony Richard Wagner, *English Genealogy* (Oxford, 1960). Another useful book by Wagner is *The Records and Collections of the College of Arms* (London, Burke's Peerage, 1952), esp. pp. 15–45. James Dallaway, *Inquiries into the Origins and Progress of the Science of Heraldry in England* (Gloucester, 1743), is still useful. The works of J. H. Round all deserve careful attention, especially since his methods reveal so clearly the historical shortcomings of the Tudor and Stuart heralds.

were scholarly writers who did much to further historical research. The Elizabethan Society of Antiquaries had had many heralds among its members, and was instumental in encouraging sound methods of study.

That the growth of interest in history and antiquity in Elizabethan and Stuart England owed something to the genealogical and heraldic interests of the age cannot be doubted. The dissolution of the monasteries and the subsequent transfer of land through alienation and purchase brought wealth to new families, and wealth encouraged ancestral pride. Perhaps even more important was the fact that litigation put a premium on charters and family records—property created its own pedigrees.

Even the art and architecture of the Tudors, rich in blazonry, recorded the English taste for heraldic splendour. Feudal customs still survived in many houses of the nobility and gentry of Tudor and early Stuart England; and the uniformed retainer, although a dubious asset to the overmighty subject, was still a desirable prop. Order and degree might be untuned from time to time, but custom was obeyed—the new lords and knights soon wore their pedigrees without a difference. The succession from genealogy to history took place easily in a society in which landowners had many good reasons to study the past; and amateur scholars 'passed imperceptibly from their family to their county, and thence to a wider field'.[1]

vi EDUCATION AND HISTORY

Every community of learning is drawn from the wider community of educated men. Successive and overlapping generations pass on not only acquired aptitudes, but also acquired interests and tastes. Education was the means of maintaining traditions, and of instilling social, moral, and intellectual attitudes. Education thus broadly conceived was not confined to schools and universities; it was carried on at home, and throughout society, by all the means available to thought and expression. The painter, the stonemason, the architect and the armourer all helped to educate, along with the poet, the dramatist, the scientist, and the priest. The community of educated men cannot be restricted to graduates of the universities, any more than the community of learning can be confined to those who profess special knowledge by virtue of a higher academic degree. Fetish

[1] See MacLaglan in Fox, *English Historical Scholarship*, 44–5.

worship of the diploma is the appropriate vice of universal education. In an earlier age, it is more profitable simply to distinguish between the educated public, capable of taking an intelligent interest in the arts or sciences, and the men of learning who, whether amateurs or professional scholars, were skilled in special branches of knowledge. This is not to say that formal education was of secondary importance; rather, it is to insist that education, especially education in history, could be acquired in many different ways, and that the sense of the past was compounded from both common and uncommon ingredients.

By and large, English education in the sixteenth and seventeenth centuries made little provision for the formal study of history. The first endowed professorship of history at either university was set up by Camden, while in the secondary schools there was no tradition of formal instruction in history.[1] An education in history had to be sought under different rubrics; and, generally speaking, English history was learned outside of school. In spite of this, there were good reasons for the increase of interest in history. Genealogy and heraldry were helps to the study of history; and the educational system itself made a contribution.

In the secondary schools and at the universities stress was laid on the study of languages, especially Latin, Greek, and Hebrew. Performance in the secondary schools may have been poor, judging by the frequent criticisms that were made by writers ranging from Elyot to Milton, but at least a formal grounding in Latin served both as a preparation for the universities and as a stimulus to thought about the past. The Reformation in England had been a compromise, which meant that England was spared some of the extremes of continental purity in education and religion. Even though educational discipline was sometimes neglected, the humanistic literary ideal

---

[1] See William H. Allison, 'The First Endowed Professorship of History and Its First Incumbent', *American Historical Review* (XXVII, 1922), 733–7. Arthur F. Leach, *English Schools at the Reformation* (Westminster, 1896), 105, and *passim*. Foster Watson, *The English Grammar Schools to 1660* (Cambridge, 1908) and *The Beginnings of the Teaching of Modern Subjects in England* (London, 1909) are valuable. M. L. Clarke, *Classical Education in Britain* (Cambridge, 1959), is a good brief survey. Bolgar, *Classical Heritage*, 360, and *passim*, discusses the nature of the humanist literary tradition in English schools after the Reformation. The appropriate volumes of the *New Cambridge Modern History* should also be consulted.

helped to stimulate an interest in the political and social life of the ancient world.

Throughout the sixteenth century, the middle and upper classes both were sending their children in increasing numbers to the schools and universities, including the Inns of Court. The importance of an education for business and government was becoming obvious to all. The content of the education was probably far less important than the interests which derived from it, and the training in thought and expression which it provided. The study of ancient literature was, for many men, the first formal introduction to the study of history.

History was regarded as a branch of literature by most of the ancients, and by nearly all of the humanists. The rhetorical tradition, which had dominated Greek and Roman historical writing, was exceptionally strong among the humanists. Between 1470 and 1520 humanism had made important scholarly contributions to history in the form of textual criticism, Greek studies, and studies in classical archaeology, mainly Roman. At the same time, however, good style and a high moral tone were accepted virtues in humanist historio-graphy. It was not until the late sixteenth century, when classical studies became highly specialized, that the literary and scholarly traditions of humanism began to diverge.

From the literary and rhetorical traditions of humanism, the 'literary' idea of history derived. In poems and plays and histories authors sought to delight and to instruct their audiences by telling true stories, that is, histories. Whether or not such history was true to the evidence, it had to be true to the literary purposes of the author, that is, true to his moral or patriotic theme, or simply poetically universal in Aristotle's sense—history, like poetry, would then be concerned with 'what a man of a certain sort will say or do, either probably or inevitably'.[1] Something of this attitude appeared in most of the popular histories of the sixteenth and seventeenth centuries.

The difference between the poetic and the scholarly approach to history was, in the early seventeenth century, an accepted one, which permitted the amicable collaboration of Drayton the poet, and Selden the scholar. Selden's learned and witty notes to the *Polyolbion* illustrate admirably the difference between the literary

[1] From Aristotle, 'The Art of Poetry', in Philip Wheelwright's *Aristotle* (New York, 1951). Professor Wheelwright's translation.

and the scholarly traditions. Selden provided illustrations: 'What the Verse oft with allusion as supposing a full-knowing Reader, lets slip; or in winding steps of personating fictions (as sometimes) so enfolds, that sudden conceit cannot abstract a form of the clothed truth; I have, as I might, *illustrated*.' These illustrations served to instruct the reader, but Selden went on to say, 'Being not very prodigal of my Historical faith, after *explanation*, I oft adventured on *examination* and *censure* . . . [and] touching the *Trojan Brute*, I have (but as an advocate of the Muse) argued; disclaiming in it, if alleged for my own opinion.' [1] To argue as an advocate of the muse was one things; to write as a scholarly historian was another. The collaboration between Selden and Drayton was possible because these men could respect each other's puposes. There were historians who wrote history with even less regard for the new scholarship than Drayton showed in his poetry. For these historians Selden had only contempt; he could find no excuse for those who failed to 'seek the fountains, and by that, if means grant it, to judge the *river's* nature'. [2]

In the course of the seventeenth century the rift between the literary and the scholarly traditions widened until, in despair of truth, many writers took part in that Pyrrhonist revolt which became part of the 'crisis of the European conscience'. The European significance of this development has been studied by Paul Hazard; and Mr. Pocock has rightly stressed its importance for the history of historiography in England. [3] New critical techniques, and new ideas of explanation and relevance were being advanced by scholars early in the century, but only very slowly was the new scholarship combined with the writing of history in the form of a literary narrative.

The reasons for the increasing separation between the literary and the scholarly traditions in historiography are no doubt many; obviously important ones are the following: (1) the strength of the literary tradition, fed by poetry and the drama, and encouraged by the methods of study in English schools; (2) the absence of a tradition of teaching history as a separate discipline at the colleges and universities; (3) the relatively slow appearance during the seventeenth century of scholarly monographs, reference works, and reliable

---

[1] *The Complete Works of Michael Drayton*, ed. by Richard Hooper, 3 vols. (London, 1876), I, xxxiii, from Selden's 'To the Reader'.

[2] *Ibid.*, xliv.

[3] Paul Hazard, *The European Mind*, translated by J. Lewis May (London, 1953), Chapter II, *passim*; Pocock, *Ancient Constitution*, 6–8.

narratives written by scholars; (4) the censorship, which discouraged, however capriciously, the expression of original and independent views; and (5) the inevitable time lag, familiar even today, between discovery and application in all branches of learning.

The historical revolution was primarily a revolution in scholarship, but the new historical attitude which became a characteristic of European thought in the seventeenth century was the result of far more general causes—social, economic and intellectual, as well as political and religious. The scholars who wrote history were not isolated from the main currents of thought of the time; they often drew upon work being done in related fields. Moreover, the differences between scholarly and literary historians must not be over-emphasized. From the point of view of the development of a new historical attitude in the seventeenth century, the similarities between the scholarly and the literary traditions are more important than the differences.

The sixteenth and seventeenth centuries witnessed great advances in cartography, philology, geography, and archaeology—fields closely related to history—as well as revolutionary advances in mathematics, astronomy, natural history, and medicine. The relationship between history and science in the seventeenth century will be discussed in a later chapter; here, the important point is simply that the community of learning was still relatively small and relatively unaffected by the growth of specialization. General education went on through a lifetime. The common interests of scholars drew them together, whatever their particular specialties. Physicians like Sir Thomas Browne wrote learnedly on subjects ranging from urn-burials to electrical bodies; Dr. John Dee pursued astrology and antiquity with almost equal devotion; Selden was at home in the Westminster Assembly as well as in law-courts and libraries; Bacon took all knowledge as his province. Under the later Stuarts, the great English scholars were, if anything, even more encyclopedic in their interests and more vigorous in their commitments to the contemporary world.[1] In brief, the community of learning in the seventeenth century was articulated in such a way that respect for historical scholars and scholarship was maintained as a part of the broad humanistic tradition. The whole educational system contributed to this result.

[1] See David Douglas, *English Scholars*, Chapter I, *passim*.

vii HISTORY AND THE GENTRY

Politics and historical research formed a close alliance in the early seventeenth century. It is not surprising that the phrase 'a gentleman and a scholar' had become current by the middle of the century.[1] A higher education was of course expensive, but it opened the way to the high offices of Government and to the fruits of patronage; conversely, powerful and well-educated patrons were indispensable if the community of learning was to fulfil its functions.

Whether or not the English gentry rose or fell, grew richer or poorer, were in sickness for want of office, or in health from sound estates in the years between 1540 and 1640, at least it is clear that as a class the gentry were becoming convinced that their children should have an education at the university, or at one of the Inns of Court.[2]

The gentry was not an economic class, but rather a social and legal class, membership in which was determined by birth and ownership of land and by whether or not a man would bear 'the port, charge and countenance of a gentleman'. In his *Description of England*, Harrison gave a remarkably broad definition of the word gentleman:

> Gentlemen be those whome their race and bloude [or at] least their vertues doo make noble and knowne. . . . [Moreover] as the king dooth dubbe knights, and create the barons and higher

[1] Cambridge University Library, MS. Dd., VIII, 52 f. 2b. A letter from T. B. [Bishop of Lincoln] on the English historians, dated 1656. Thomas Barlow is presumably referred to; he was Bishop of Lincoln, although not at this date.

[2] The 'Storm over the Gentry' shows signs of subsiding. The extensive bibliography on this subject will be familiar to students of the period. The main statements are those of R. H. Tawney, 'The Rise of the Gentry', reprinted in E. M. Carus-Wilson, ed., *Essays in Economic History* (London, 1954), 173–214, and H. R. Trevor-Roper, *The Gentry 1540–1640* (Cambridge, Economic History Society, n.d.). J. H. Hexter, 'Storm over the Gentry', *Encounter* (X, no. 5, 1958), 22–34, sums up, and provides an opportunity for further comment, especially in the following issues. Essential to any student of the period, and its problems is Aylmer's recent book, *The King's Servants, The Civil Service of Charles I 1625–42* (London, 1961). See also the books listed in Chapter V on Sir Robert Cotton. Robert Ashton, *The Crown and the Money Market 1603–1640* (Oxford, 1960), is also useful.

An important contribution to the history of office holding is G. E. Aylmer, 'Office Holding as a Factor in English History, 1625–42', *History* (XLIV, Oct. 1959), 228–40. This article stresses the importance of the general rise in prices, which would affect the prices paid for offices.

degrees, so gentlemen whose ancestors are not known to come in with William Duke of Normandie . . . doo take their beginning in England, after this manner in our times. Who soever studieth the laws of the realme, who so abideth in the universitie [giving his mind to his books] or professeth physicke and the liberal sciences, or beside his service in the roome of a captaine in the warres, [or good counsell given at home, whereby his commonwealth is benefitted,] can live without manuell labour, and thereto is able and will bear the port, charge, and countenance of a gentleman, he shall [for monie have a cote of armes bestowed upon him by heralds (who in the charter of the same doo of custome pretend antiquitie and service, and manie gaie things) and thereunto being made so good cheape] be called master, which is the title that men give to esquiors and gentlemen, and reputed for a gentleman [ever after].[1]

It may be seen from this that 'gentleman' was a title which belonged equally to the aristocracy, the landed gentry, and to those who, by education, service, or wealth could and did live in a certain manner. The yeomen, some of whom rose to become gentry, and the burgesses, many of whom married into gentry families, were technically classes apart. The gentry, considered as a class of landlords and office holders, was, of course, stratified, the great families competing with the peerage, the lesser families not greatly different, at least in income and outlook, from well-to-do yeomen.

The gentry were staunch members of the English governing class, which was made up, roughly speaking, of the nobility, the gentry, the civility in the towns, the higher clergy, and the emerging professional class.[2] The gentry, narrowly defined, consisted of the squirearchy, especially those middling landowners who filled the

[1] The edition used here is that of Frederick J. Furnivall, *Harrison's Description of England* (London, New Shakespeare Society, 1877), 128-9. Furnivall, in collating his texts, made use of the brackets.

[2] The Church was an institution which profoundly affected intellectual life but most of the clergy came from the middle and lower classes of society. A learned ministry did exist, but the economic problems of the Church were such that, before Laud's reforms, relatively few clerical controversialists had been themselves patrons of learning. The Church's influence on scholarship in the early seventeenth century has therefore been subsumed under other headings. See Christopher Hill, *Economic Problems of the Church* (Oxford, 1956), 209 and Chapter IX, *passim*. On the yeomanry, see Mildred Campbell, *The English Yeoman* (London, 1960, reprint of 1942 ed.).

majority of seats in the House of Commons, who served on commissions of the peace, or who were men of some local importance in the country. 'The conception of a squirearchy,' as David Mathew has put it, 'constituted a unifying element in the shifting strata of a class of gentry based technically on the right to coat armour and in practice on a combination of landed property with a certain standard of social custom.' [1] This class was increasingly concerned with education as a means of advancement, and as a token of prestige. Furthermore, it would seem that the much broader class of 'gentlemen' shared this concern, and sought to acquire at least the appearance of learning. Not infrequently the gentleman became in fact a scholar.

That some acquaintance with history was considered an attribute of the gentleman we know from Peacham's manual, *The Compleat Gentleman*, as well as from other contemporary evidence. [2] The 'mere gentry' perhaps found little time for the study of antiquity, but it has been pointed out how genealogical interests could and did spread into wider historical fields. In addition, the fact that many members of the gentry and professional classes took part in politics meant that they were forced to acquire some historical perspective, and probably turn at least to the chroniclers for enlightenment. The men of substance who sat in the Elizabethan and early Stuart Parliaments took their duties seriously and were not, on the whole, either ignorant or ordinary men. Precedents from history served them well.

From the point of view of the higher studies pursued at the universities the century following the Reformation was not, it is true, marked by great achievement. The mercantilist state of the sixteenth century, struggling against the medieval universalism of the church and the particularism of its institutions—monastic orders, canon law, and the universities—succeeded in establishing its own territorial control by about 1560. One result was the virtual destruction of the humanist ideal of a republic of letters, along with the destruction of other forms of universalism; scholars at many universities

[1] David Mathew, *The Social Structure of Caroline England* (Oxford, 1948), 39, and Chapter IV, *passim*.

[2] A great deal of the contemporary evidence has been sorted and discussed by Louis B. Wright in *Middle Class Culture in Elizabethan England* (Chapel Hill, 1935). The book is valuable not only for the comments on middle-class taste, but also for the wealth of bibliography it supplies.

were subjected to more or less severe state control and higher scholarship tended to stagnate. If in the short run this process of 'territorialization of the world of learning' had ill effects, nevertheless it 'made inevitable in the long run the association of science and national prestige and gave governments the right to regard academic institutions as existing primarily for public purposes defined by the statesman'.[1] In England those purposes were to be defined largely in terms of the secular interests of the nobility and gentry.

The social importance of the English universities steadily increased as the upper governing classes made a tradition of sending their children to the university for a time to be educated. Secular control of education by the territorial monarchy probably had less severe effects on scholarship in England than in Germany; and from the point of view of humanistic studies, the state's intervention had at least resulted in increased emphasis on secular humanistic subject matter. A trend toward secularism, remarkable even in the English universities, was thus the quiet counterpart of the blaring religious controversies of the sixteenth and seventeenth centuries.[2]

In the earlier seventeenth century no clear-cut distinction was made between matters of politics and matters of religion; the constitutional conflicts were fused to the religious conflicts, and lines of policy in both church and state were continually justified or attacked in historical terms. However, increasing secular control over education was accompanied at the higher levels by a gradual shift of emphasis away from the older scholastic concerns of the medieval universities; and as the gentry and aristocracy began to acquire a vested interest in higher education, changes in the intellectual atmosphere at the universities began to be noticeable. In the long run, the consumer was to get roughly what he wanted from education. Although it took centuries for medievalism to die in the universities, for history and science to displace the trivium and quadrivium in the colleges, and for historians to be accepted as the peers of theologians, the beginnings of the process of secularization may be traced back at least as far as the sixteenth century.[3]

---

[1] See *The New Cambridge Modern History*, Vol. II, *The Reformation*, p. 435 and Chapter XIII, *passim*.

[2] The best study of the relationship between the English universities and English society is Mark H. Curtis, *Oxford and Cambridge in Transition 1558–1642* (Oxford, 1959).

[3] See M. L. Clarke, *Classical Education*, 21.

The social and economic interests of the gentry and aristocracy—the high governing classes of the secular state—were thus not without significance for the growth of secular learning. Historical studies were immediately relevant to the questions which all governing groups had to face. Moreover, when Oliver Cromwell, in 1646, wrote to deplore excesses committed in the name of religion, he voiced an attitude which was slowly coming to be regarded as fundamental to stable government: 'Sir, this is a quarrelsome age, and the anger seems to me to be the worse where the ground is things of opinion, which to cure, to hurt men in their names, persons, or estates will not be found an apt remedy.' [1] Wherever the ground of things was opinion history was relevant; and the decline of religious 'enthusiasm' in the later seventeenth century was coincident with the rise of empirical (and ultimately rational-historical) attitudes and methods of argument.

viii HISTORY AND MIDDLE-CLASS CULTURE

That recent writers should have reacted against the middle-class formula in historiography is not surprising. Professor Postan, in preparing his attack on another such formula, 'the rise of a money economy', stated the crucial point: 'students will find that the changes in the structure, outlook, and behaviour of the middle classes are much more significant than the mere swelling of their numbers or the inflation of their power through consecutive centuries of English history'.[2] In the sixteenth and seventeenth centuries changes in class structure were rapid; the middle classes were no longer a coherent group, having a determinate social status. The word citizen was still applied to those who lived or worked in the cities and towns, but the 'middle classes' were by no means confined to the urban community. It is well known that rich merchants, lawyers, and professional men often bought country estates and moved into the social orbit of the gentry. Marriages and manors strengthened the bonds between members of the wealthy urban middle class and the class of prosperous country gentry. And during the early part of the seventeenth

[1] Cromwell's letter to Thomas Knyvett, July 1646. See Thomas Carlyle, *Oliver Cromwell's Letters and Speeches*, 3 vols. (London, Everyman, 1907), I, 201.

[2] M. M. Postan, 'The Rise of a Money Economy', reprinted in E. M. Carus-Wilson, ed., *Essays in Economic History*, 1–12; the quotation is on p. 2.

century it was not unusual for substantial gentry families to maintain a town house either in London or in one of the larger provincial towns. The competition for office among gentry families was matched by the competition of business and professional men for a share in the spoils of patronage.

To enter into a detailed examination of the social and economic ties between different groups is unnecessary—the ruling élite of the country was drawn for the most part from the wealthier classes. Wealth eased all processes of social conversion, as contemporaries frequently observed. Harrison, for example, wrote that merchants are 'to be installed, as amongst the citizens [although they often change estate with gentlemen, as gentlemen do with them, by a mutual conversion of the one into the other]'. Yet Harrison was no doubt right in still maintaining the more or less conventional definitions:

> Citizens and burgesses have next place to gentlemen, who be those that are free within the cities, and are of some [likelie] substance to beare office in the same. But these citizens or burgesses are to serve the commonwealth in their cities and boroughs, or in corporat townes where they dwell. And in the common assemblie of the realme wherein our lawes are made, for in the counties they beare but little swaie (which assemblie is called the [high court of] parlement) the ancient cities appoint foure, and the boroughs two burgesses to have voice in it . . .[1]

Harrison does not mention the 'middle classes', but he provides the starting point for a definition. That segment of the urban population which was *of some substance* and at least capable of bearing office formed the unifying element in the shifting strata of a broadly defined middle class. Judged by the sources of their wealth—professional fees, the profits of trade, and fees of office—the well-to-do families of the urban middle classes had much in common with the prosperous or 'rising' gentry. The rise of individual merchants like Lionel Cranfield, who became Lord High Treasurer and Earl of Middlesex, suggests that social mobility was in some sense an established characteristic of English society.

If it was the nobility and gentry who, for the most part, were the patrons of learning and of the arts, it was the middle classes who supplied the numbers which made the printing of all kinds of books and pamphlets profitable. Middle-class culture is too narrow a term

[1] See Harrison, *Description of England*, ed., Furnivall, pp. 130-1.

to apply to the whole Elizabethan Renaissance, but it does describe some of the salient features of the English intellect in the seventeenth century. The middle classes had already begun to assimilate the literature of the past, and to provide new ideas as well as new pedigrees to the aristocracy. In the long run the patterns of middle-class culture would become dominant. The ambiguous nature of this process of assimilation was most evident in its early stages.

In the first place, middle-class culture was not confined to one—specifically bourgeois—segment of the population; in the second, the middle classes were still predominently urban in outlook, although not necessarily so in habitat or behaviour. Clergymen, captains, entrepreneurs, factors, merchants—all might travel far; and some might live, like the poet Herrick, far from London and the varied life of an urban community. Nevertheless, the urban middle classes, intent upon improving themselves and determined to have books and pamphlets to the purpose, now constituted the mass of the book-buying and book-reading public. The literary tastes of a poor journeyman, only one step removed from the class of casual labourers (and only two from the paupers), might differ from the more refined literary tastes of a wealthy merchant or lawyer, but the similarities were deep, and education did not entirely eliminate them. The tastes of a gentleman and a scholar were to be imitated, yet utility remained the grand passion of the middle-class public. Utility in the broadest possible sense was what distinguished the popular literary taste.

The spread of literacy, made possible by cheap printed books, was accompanied in England by a remarkable extension of the book-buying habit. Printers and booksellers helped to provide and sell intellectual wares which, before the sixteenth century, were unknown to the majority of the middle classes. While merchants and other figures in business life showed an extraordinary zeal for culture and education, bestowing gifts on grammar schools, establishing loan funds, and endowing scholarships at the universities, there was an even wider interest being shown in self-education. Moreover, the liveried companies of London contributed much to the support of higher education, even to education which was not immediately practical. Gresham College, founded by an Elizabethan Merchant Adventurer, catered more directly to the practical needs of a busy, urban, port community. And Cranfield's interests in books and the theatre 'suggest that the man of docquets and trade returns was not immune to the civilized tradition of which the achievements of merchants with literary or scientific leanings and historically-minded craftsmen were the fruit'.[1]

The spiritual aristocracy of Puritanism, dedicated to godly discipline and to the religion of trade, showed a more than passing concern with learning and with a learned ministry. Self-help and utilitarianism were doctrines not uncongenial to the ethics of Puritanism, and both satisfied the psychological needs of the commercial population. Above all, the conviction that self-improvement was possible, and within the reach of hard-working, God-fearing men and women of moderate circumstance, made great headway in the England of Elizabeth and her successors. One might find anti-intellectualism among the more extreme Puritan factions, but if learning was sometimes considered a 'great idol', held in higher veneration 'than can strictly be allowed' (in the judgment of Colonel Hutchinson's wife), it was nevertheless true that Puritans in general were convinced of the values of education.[2] And history was one subject which appealed to Puritan saints no less than to unregenerate sinners. In short, both secular and religious influences combined to make the middle classes eager to acquire the practical rudiments, as well as the conversational adornments of education.

Handbooks to improvement were among the most typical expressions of the Elizabethan quest for utilitarian knowledge. Not only were all kinds of practical guides and manuals published, on subjects ranging from needlework to navigation, but there was a significant increase in the number of books devoted to subjects which directly contributed to historical studies. The study of foreign languages was as necessary to the merchant adventurer as to the scholar, and as England entered the first great period of overseas expansion and trade under Elizabeth's rule, those with the gift of tongues found more adequate honour and reward.

The classical interests of the humanists, and the biblical studies of the reformers had already spread knowledge of ancient languages; the demands of travel and trade stimulated the study of modern languages, including slavic, near eastern, and oriental speech. The great Oxford orientalist, Edward Pococke, served as chaplain to the

---

[1] R. H. Tawney, *Business and Politics Under James I, Lionel Cranfield as Merchant and Minister* (Cambridge, 1958), 276.

[2] *Memoirs of the Life of Colonel Hutchinson, written by his Widow Lucy* (London, Everyman, 1908), 41.

Turkey merchants at Aleppo from 1630 to 1636, collecting manuscripts and mastering languages, before he was appointed by Laud as the first Oxford professor of Arabic in 1636. Sir George Buck's *The Third University of England* (1615) described the educational facilities of London, stressing the fact that language teachers were available to teach almost any foreign language. *The Third University* was indeed an appropriate monument to the middle-class interest in utilitarian learning.

In addition to language textbooks, the printers began to supply travel books, maps, and geographical works in increasing numbers in the late sixteenth and early seventeenth centuries. Hakluyt and Purchas were, of course, the most famous compilers of such books; the former was a scholarly enthusiast who once lectured on geography at Oxford; the latter was, like Hakluyt, a preacher, but one intent on finding sermons in geography, if not good in everything. Hakluyt's *Principall Navigations* (1589) and Purchas' *Purchas His Pilgrimage* (1613) appealed not only to lovers of adventure, but also to merchants, to travellers, and to all who were curious about new discoveries, about lands and seas and natural history, and about the strange customs and histories of alien peoples.[1]

The importance of all such geographical studies for history was frequently emphasized. The title of one of Thomas Blundeville's works linked history, geography, and travel: *A Brief Description of Universal Mappes and Cardes, and of their Use: and Also the Vse of Ptholomey his Tables. Necessarie for those that Delight in Reading of Histories: and also for Travailers by Land or Sea* (1589). Other writers of the time made similar connections. Furthermore, new and improved maps of Great Britain and of other European countries were beginning to be produced in the sixteenth century. The work of Saxton and Norden helped to set new standards in English cartography. The surveying of English counties was mainly accomplished by the estate surveyors of the landed gentry; and John Speed, tailor and antiquary, made use of existing maps in producing his great folio, *The Theatre of the Empire of Great Britain* (1611).

All kinds of topographical studies flourished in Elizabethan and Stuart England, as one might gather from the number of works in print bearing the title of *Survey*. Patriotic pride was still a simple unsophisticated pleasure to most Englishmen; and the glorification of England was a theme with infinite variations in Elizabethan

[1] Cf. L. B. Wright, *Middle Class Culture*, 536 ff.

literature. No matter how far from England an English reader might travel, he returned to refresh himself at native springs.

The middle-class interest in utilitarian learning was thus not confined to an interest in impersonal facts and figures, to the learning which, according to Dickens in *Hard Times*, was all that the hard-shelled utilitarians of a later age cared about. No doubt eclecticism has always been a characteristic of popular taste, yet at different times different subjects have won public favour and suffused public opinion. Theology was rising in popularity early in the seventeenth century; by the reign of Queen Anne it was declining. Equally significant is the fact that historical works rose steadily in popular esteem.

The Elizabethan art of translation was making available to the eager but unlearned reading public not only the classics but all kinds of modern works as well. Classical literature provided many of the facts used to illustrate lessons in the Elizabethan handbooks to improvement. Historical works in translation proved to be especially popular, since all writers were in agreement that such history needed no apology. Translations thus greatly enriched the content of English historical literature in the sixteenth and seventeenth centuries; and for those who were to busy, or too lazy to read long books there were brief epitomes of learning which promised ready helps to discourse on a variety of subjects.

'Originating as academic and aristocratic works,' as Dr. Louis B. Wright has observed, 'such compilations gained favour during the latter half of the sixteenth century until, by the end of the century, they were widely popular, not only with cultured readers, but also with busy middle-class folk who prized them because of their concentrated wisdom, their good morality, and their general utility as instruments of instruction.' [1] The fact that history was one of the subjects most frequently epitomized is not surprising. What may cause surprise is the extent to which history had come to be regarded by the middle classes as a subject of surpassing utility.

Saying hosannahs to history was traditional among Renaissance men of letters. The utility of history had, of course, been a constant

---

[1] Cf. L. B. Wright, *Middle Class Culture*, 147–8. I have drawn heavily on Mr. Wright's account. There are a number of studies of Elizabethan translations and translators. Henrietta R. Palmer, *List of English Editions and Translations of Greek and Roman Classics printed before 1641* (1911, n.p.) is a standard reference work.

theme of the ancient Greco-Roman historians and rhetoricians. Biblical history was no less prized by Christians, whether Protestant or Catholic; and the Jews were proud of a history which, as Josephus had contended, was even in his day more ancient and better recorded than that of any other nation. There was no lack of precedents for belief in the value of historical knowledge. Yet not even Ralegh's magnificent apostrophe to history in the preface to his *History of the World* quite sums up the variety of Elizabethan laudations of history.

A catalogue of what history taught would include the following: morals, manners, prudence, patriotism, statecraft, virtue, religion, wisdom, truth; history was equally an antidote to all opposite qualities. History could have tamed the Irish, and history was a salutary remedy for mental sickness. Knowledge of history helped one to rise in the world, and knowledge of God's providence in history solaced those who, like Ralegh, suffered the onslaughts of adversity. The publicity value of history was well understood by projectors and preachers; and history's value as propaganda was firmly grasped by Court, Parliament, and Convocation. The uses of history were almost as various as the understandings of men.

The scope of historical writing was greatly enlarged by popularizers who wrote for the new Elizabethan middle-class audience. Although the 'decline' of standards brought forth scholarly sneers, nevertheless the spread of historical interest and understanding among the populace created a broader and firmer base for enduring scholarship. History was no longer the enclosed property of the upper and privileged orders. In the broadest possible sense, history was being nationalized—and the variety of histories was becoming as wide as the lands known to Englishmen. The classes who would in the long run take control of the state were committed to the view that history was a form of knowledge both useful and exact, and although utility was much commended, utility was not all. The cruelty of time, which shuts up the story of our days at death, was a theme for poets, who, if they had Ralegh's gifts, could discover history's poetic triumphs: '. . . yea, it hath triumphed over time, which, beside it, nothing but eternity hath triumphed over'.

3

THE INSTITUTIONAL FRAMEWORK

i BOOK AND MANUSCRIPT COLLECTIONS

MODERN HISTORIOGRAPHY rests on a framework of institutions. Without libraries, archives, and learned societies, the study of history would become little more than a survey of noble ruins. For every advance in scholarship there has probably been some corresponding advance in the organization of scholarly institutions. Libraries, both public and private; record offices, both national and local; societies of learning, both formal and informal—all have contributed to scholarship, indeed, have made progress possible. Every library catalogue, every calendar of state papers, every personal contact with another scholar adds something to the historian's resources. Not even the brilliance of Thucydides could quite overcome the limitations of his resources—the remote past could not be conjured out of the urn in which it lay buried.

The institutions which were of the greatest importance for historical scholarship in the seventeenth century were not the universities themselves, but the libraries, record offices, and learned societies of England. By informal ties, through friendship and patronage, the antiquaries and historians were associated with librarians and record keepers. The Elizabethan Society of Antiquaries did much to further co-operation between those who kept official historical records, those who collected them, and those who used them. Although this involved no clear-cut division of labour, it is nevertheless obvious that the interests of the record-keeper, the collector, and the antiquary were not identical. Historians and other scholars had to gain access to libraries and record offices as best they could; institutional arrangements affected the study and writing of history at the very outset of research.

The late sixteenth and early seventeenth centuries were a formative period in the history of English libraries. The church, the universities, and the high aristocracy no longer held any kind of monopoly of library facilities. Any survey of libraries would reveal a number of distinct types, ranging from public libraries which were founded for the benefit of the average middle-class reader, to highly specialized collections of manuscripts made by individual scholars in their particular fields of specialty. Many of the great public figures of the day acquired valuable collections of books, manuscripts, and state papers, which might or might not be made available to scholars.[1]

The collections of eminent antiquaries—Leland, Stow, and Camden, for example—rivalled in historical importance the earlier collections of Dukes and Archbishops. The legal collections of Coke and Selden were indicative of the wealth and scholarship to be found among members of the legal profession; and although merchant libraries were seldom used for research they testified to the growing middle-class taste for books and culture. Finally, the great gentry

---

[1] The best general survey is perhaps still Edward Edwards, *Libraries and Founders of Libraries* (London, 1864); the account of English libraries in the *Cambridge History of English Literature* is excellent, though necessarily short. Various topics relating to libraries are discussed in issues of *The Library*. Edward Edwards, *Memoirs of Libraries*, 2 vols. (London, 1859), is still useful. Wormald and Wright, *The English Library*, is, of course, indispensable.

Special topics are dealt with in various books, including John Willis Clark, *The Care of Books*, 2nd ed. (Cambridge, 1902), Chapters V and VIII; Dorothy May Norris, *A History of Cataloguing and Cataloguing Methods* (London, 1939), Chapters VI–VIII, *passim*. Reference books available to scholars are discussed by John Webster Spargo, 'Some Reference Books of the Sixteenth and Seventeenth Centuries', *Papers of the Bibliographical Society of America* (XXXI, 1937). William Dunn Macray, *Annals of the Bodleian Library* (Oxford, 1890), is still a standard work on the subject, but I have not attempted to go into detail on the development of university libraries. Theodore Bestermann, *The Beginnings of Systematic Bibliography* (Oxford, 1935), is a valuable study of an important problem. Sears Jayne, *Library Catalogues of the English Renaissance* (Berkeley, 1956), is also useful. The modern catalogues of the various Oxford, Cambridge, and London libraries naturally contain information on the period, but there is no need to list these here.

collectors brought together historical libraries that were costly, honorific, and gratifying to the learned men who used them.

After the Restoration in 1660 librarians began to have to face the problem of quantity, with all that this entailed in the way of selection, arrangement, and routine. Not since the days of the great Alexandrian libraries had comparable problems emerged, nor had there been comparably large collections.[1] In the century before the Restoration the library resources of scholars had been rapidly augmented; and by 1697, when Richard Bentley published his *Proposal for Building a Royal Library*, the demand for a national library, freely accessible to scholars, had gained strong support. One of the first to recognize the importance of a great public library for scholarship was Sir Robert Cotton. His library was unique in many ways, being the finest and most accessible institution for research in early seventeenth-century England. Other libraries founded or re-formed during Cotton's lifetime were less important but more typical; questioning may properly begin with them.

What kinds of collections were being made? How generally useful were they? Where could they be found? Admittedly, it is hazardous to generalize about the contents and accessibility of different types of libraries, yet this risk must be incurred. The actual resources of libraries, in an age when adequate catalogues were only beginning to appear, could seldom be known by historians except after personal inspection. The Inns of Court libraries, like those of the church, were more specialized than the university libraries. Antiquaries and historians often collected with a view to some particular specialty; and often such collections passed by purchase or bequest from one scholar to another. The libraries of the learned gentry were apt to be rich in historical manuscripts relating to manors, and to genealogical and heraldic matters. The squire's bias in favour of the manor rather than the town or the parish helped to warp the writing of local history for generations.[2]

The transmission of scholarly collections in the sixteenth and seventeenth centuries was of great significance for historical research. Notes, transcripts of records, and written copies of manuscript treatises were as important to scholars seeking knowledge of the past as original manuscripts. Stow's manuscripts and collections (includ-

---

[1] Wormald and Wright, *The English Library*, 10; from the 'General Introduction' by Raymond Irwin.

[2] See W. G. Hoskins, *Local History in England* (London, 1959), 23.

ing his transcript of Leland's *Itinerary*, which Camden used) were known by reputation and were eagerly sought after by scholars. Upon Stow's death, a large part of his collection was purchased by Ralph Starkey, the antiquary whom D'Ewes called 'an ignorant mercenary, indigent man', while allowing that he had 'great plenty of new written collections and divers original letters of great moment'.[1] Starkey died in 1628, whereupon D'Ewes immediately purchased his library. D'Ewes' own library, a very considerable one, was ultimately sold by his grandson to Robert Harley; and as part of the Harleian collection, the D'Ewes' library at last became generally accessible to scholars. Roger Dodsworth, while engaged in research on the *Monasticon* had consulted the Stow papers in Starkey's possession. The transcripts of Leland which Camden had purchased from Stow were apparently not among the manuscripts bequeathed by Camden to Sir Robert Cotton, but they ultimately found their way into the Bodleian in 1736. Some of Stow's other collections were purchased by Cotton in 1613. Before he died Stow himself delivered some of his best collections to Anthony Munday, who used them in subsequent editions of the *Survey of London*.

It may be seen from these examples that the transmission of historical collections was a matter of concern to scholars, and that the larger and more accessible libraries often acquired portions of smaller private libraries. The fact that the Cottonian and the Harleian collections finally were brought together in the British Museum only illustrates the long-term trend toward the consolidation of small holdings, and the ultimate acceptance of the principle of free scholarly access.

The library of the Cecils was in many ways typical of the great libraries founded by high officials of state, and by some members of the aristocracy. The Cecil collection was unusual in that it contained not just a few, but masses of state papers, which had been carted off to Hatfield House (where the bulk of them remained in spite of the efforts of Sir Thomas Wilson to retrieve them for the State Paper Office). Furthermore, Lord Burghley was an unusually avid book collector who had taken great pains to acquire books and manuscripts from the continent. His agents there, of course, enjoyed some

[1] Quoted by Kingsford in his introduction to Stow's *Survey*. I have followed his account in this paragraph. See Charles Lethbridge Kingsford, ed., *A Survey of London by John Stow*, 2 vols. (Oxford, 1908), lxxxvi-xciii.

unique opportunities. Burghley's own work, *The Execution of Justice in England* (1583), shows the historical bent of his mind; and his patronage of Camden enhances his reputation for good judgment. Camden called the Cecil library *bibliotheca instructissima*—with good reason, for he drew heavily on Cecil's collections in writing the history of Elizabeth's reign.

Often the elder Cecil was approached by writers who wished to secure his favour. A Mr. Osborne of the Exchequer, for example, wrote to ask for letters of introduction to continental librarians on behalf of Dr. Hugh Broughton who planned to make a book-buying trip to acquire Greek and Hebrew books of divinity and history.[1] Burghley was well known for his patronage of learning, and for his interest in historical politics. The historian John Clapham owed much of his education to Burghley's benevolence, and although Clapham did not make use of original manuscripts in his popular *Historie of England* (1602), he undoubtedly had become familiar with the Cecils' library while he was in Burghley's service.[2]

The reasons which prompted Burghley to take a semi-official interest in history and scholarship were not lacking in other great officials. It is doubtful that Buckingham was ever seriously interested in his own library, except as a matter of pride, but he did acquire an impressive collection of books and manuscripts. The earl of Arundel was a distinguished collector, and Lord Clarendon acquired a fine library which included a collection of state papers which he used in writing parts of his *History of the Rebellion*.[3] By the end of the century there were a number of fine independent libraries to which historians might hope to gain access. Sir Robert Harley's library came to be an even greater 'seraglio of antiquity' than Cotton's had been; and the tradition of historical politics continued to make historical libraries valuable.

The history of the Bodleian library has been told in greater detail

---

[1] B.M. Lansdowne MS. 64, f. 88.

[2] Burghley's interest in the political aspects of scholarship is evident from his correspondence. See, for example, B.M. Lansdowne MS. 6, f. 170; MS. 65, f. 166; MS. 83, f. 126. Sir Robert Cecil was also interested—see the Parkins correspondence in *Calendar of Salisbury MSS.*, Part IV, pp. 422–3 and 576; Part VI, pp. 122, 262. Information on Clapham may be found in the introduction to *Elizabeth of England . . . by John Clapham*, edited by Evelyn Plummer Read and Conyers Read (Philadelphia, 1951).

[3] See *Calendar of the Clarendon State Papers*, Vol. I, ed. by O. Ogle and W. H. Bliss (Oxford, 1872), 'Preface'.

than that of almost any other English library. A few reminders will suffice to make the point that Bodley's library was an example of what careful planning, personal interest, and foresighted endowment could accomplish. Bodley's original plan had called for the founding of a small, select library of classics, both pagan and Christian— Bodley himself had disdained works in the vernacular. But, thanks to his diligence, and to the efforts of Thomas James, his librarian, the library soon outgrew these modest beginnings. Many eminent men contributed books or money to the library. Bodley probably got fewer books from the royal library than he had been led to expect, but doubtless the King's patronage proved helpful. Bodley bequeathed the bulk of his estate to the library, thereby endowing it. The importance of endowments, and of a tradition of pride in the library had much to do with the success or failure of the library as an institution. Generally speaking, the richer the library collection, the more easily accessible it was to scholars.[1]

The royal library was curiously neglected and meagre until, at the instigation of Prince Henry, Lord Lumley's excellent library was acquired by purchase. Although the royal library was used by scholars during the seventeenth century it was by no means readily accessible. Patrick Young, King James' librarian, did much to enlarge the royal collections and make them more useful to the learned. However, personal influence, not professional courtesy, was still the basis of admission to the royal library, as it was to most other libraries.

The English cathedral libraries, the library at Westminster Abbey, and the Archepiscopal library at Canterbury, all had collections which were of some value to historians, as did the specialized libraries of the Inns of Court. Several English towns, notably Norwich (1608), Bristol (1613), and Leicester (1632), founded public libraries

[1] *C.S.P. Dom.* 1611–18, p. 169. The precise value of the college libraries for historical scholarship cannot be ascertained on the basis of Thomas James' spotty and superficial catalogues of 1601 and 1605. See G. W. Wheeler, ed., *Letters of Sir Thomas Bodley to Thomas James* (Oxford, 1926), 'Introduction'; also John Butt, 'The Facilities for Antiquarian Study in the Seventeenth Century', *Essays and Studies* (XXLV, 1938), 64–79. Edward Edwards, *Memoirs of Libraries*, contains interesting details. See also Falconer Madan, *et al., A Summary Catalogue of Western Manuscripts in the Bodleian Library at Oxford* (Oxford, 1937), II. Part I deals with early seventeenth-century additions. The contrast between sixteenth- and seventeenth-century library practices at Oxford is striking. See N. R. Ker's lectures on the Oxford College libraries in the sixteenth century in *The Bodleian Library Record*, Vol. VI, No. 3, January 1959.

in the period before the civil wars, but these were not important for scholarship and were allowed to decay and disappear before the end of the century. London could boast of several libraries, the most important of which was Sion College Library, founded in 1630, which continued to grow and flourish.[1] Although it is in general true that libraries at this period were either bristling with restrictions, and guarded with a vigilance that kept them from being widely used, or else not properly guarded at all, the plight of the scholar was not thereby rendered desperate. Personal influence and patronage eased the passage from the anteroom to the library; and a tradition of courtesy to scholars was gradually being established. The real tests of a scholar's patience, perseverance, and eyesight were likely to occur after he had secured his *entrée* to the library.

In most libraries books were catalogued by size rather than by author or subject matter. The historian who wished to spend his time working carefully through a poorly catalogued collection might find himself at the mercy of a hurried and possibly ignorant librarian, and (especially at the college libraries) subject to statutory restrictions; not infrequently he had to suit the convenience of a number of indifferent or hostile officers in charge of keys. In winter he might be nearly frozen, and even in summer he might discover that a poorly lighted room was an ill place to examine and transcribe a manuscript. It is no wonder that scholars were unstinting in their praise of Cotton's professionally-run library.

The private libraries of the learned gentry were more widely useful to antiquaries in the seventeenth century than is generally supposed. Sir Christopher Hatton's Book of Seals, begun in 1640, was a transcribed collection of charters and tricked seals which memorialized the heraldic interests of the gentry and nobility. In 1638, an agreement known as *Antiquas Rediviva* was executed by Sir Edward Dering, Sir Christopher Hatton, Sir Thomas Shirley, and Mr. Dugdale. It set out the particular fields of antiquarian research for which each man was responsible, and made provision for the formal exchanges of information; the Book of Seals stemmed from this venture in co-operative research. Dugdale's own historical works, especially his

---

[1] Most of this information is to be found in E. Edwards, *Memoirs of Libraries*, I, 143–61; 415–21; 424–9; 535–43; 577–95; 604–13; 680–5; 714–15; 726–51; Vol. II, Chapter XXII and *passim*. See J. B. Mullinger's article on 'Libraries' in *The Cambridge History of English Literature*, ed. by A. W. Ward and A. R. Waller, 14 vols. (Cambridge, 1932).

History of Warwickshire, owed much to the historical collections of gentry antiquaries, but since the Book of Seals is more narrowly representative of gentry tastes, it is instructive to notice who contributed to it:

> The 529 charters in the Book of Seals were brought together from thirty-two distinct sources which can be grouped under two headings: the collections of individual antiquaries, and the muniment rooms of members of the nobility and gentry of England. A third heading might perhaps be made for two famous seventeenth-century libraries represented in the book, the Arundel Library and the Cottonian Library. Three hundred and thirty-eight charters in the Book of Seals were provided by three collectors who probably welcomed the opportunity of perpetuating the memory of their personal success in accumulating deeds. Sir Henry St. George, John Philipot and Sir William LeNeve, who produced respectively 105, 108, and 125 charters for registration under their names in the Book of Seals, were all Heralds.[1]

The Book of Seals was never completed because the civil wars intervened. Yet even the civil wars, which interrupted the free exchange of information, did not result in the suspension of antiquarian research. In fact, it might be said that the civil wars stimulated the study of political history, and spurred many royalist antiquaries to continue their work. Dugdale, who in 1658 published his *History of St. Paul's Cathedral*, had been encouraged by Sir Christopher Hatton at the beginning of the Long Parliament to preserve the monuments of the church for posterity. And it is clear that the Parliamentary leaders (and later the Cromwellian officials) were determined to preserve the libraries and the record offices of England from the avarice and irrationality of the ignorant.

Long ago Hallam observed that men of learning in the sixteenth century preserved 'an epistolary intercourse' which exceeded even that carried on in the nineteenth century.[2] The habit of correspondence was far more than a matter of literary convention, or of pride in writing elegant Latin—it was a matter of necessity if scholars were to keep abreast of work being done in their fields. In the seventeenth

---

[1] See Lewis C. Loyd and Doris Mary Stenton, eds., *Sir Christopher Hatton's Book of Seals* (Oxford, 1950), xxxiii. This book contains a great deal of valuable information on gentry scholarship.

[2] Henry Hallam, *Introduction to the Literature of Europe*, 4 vols. (Paris, 1839), II, 314.

century this tradition continued, and in England alone the amount of correspondence between scholars, librarians, officials, and others interested in learning was simply prodigious.

The revolutionary changes in historical writing and thought that took place in the seventeenth century must be understood in this context. England was still, by modern standards, a small cohesive society, made up of overlapping communities. Individual members of the community of learning provided one another with scholarly help and information. Correspondence and conversation were often the substitutes for modern printed directives and formal aids to research. To put the matter another way: the individual was more important for contemporary scholarship than the formal institution. The individual librarian or record keeper determined who might use his collections, how they might be used, and, to a large extent, what fees might be charged or abated.

A cropped image of the institutions of scholarship must necessarily exclude details of the general environment. The social milieu of seventeenth-century scholarship was briefly sketched, however, by F. M. Powicke in an address on Sir Henry Spelman and the *Concilia*. Any potential biographer of Spelman or of other scholars like him would, he wrote, have to consider

> . . . the distribution of manuscripts, the state of the public records, the daily intercourse of men discussing and lending books and manuscripts to each other, the correspondence with foreign scholars and the helpful and disturbing influence of foreign learning upon Englishmen's minds; the perplexing interplay of political and ecclesiastical interests with historical inquiry, and the intercourse with the court, counsellors, lawyers, bishops and a crowd of men who, by their curiosity about the historical interpretation of the present, would have been remarkable in any age.[1]

Beyond this, and even more difficult to recapture, would be that seventeenth-century intellectual atmosphere, which was characterized by 'a riot of learning' undisciplined by the modern emphasis on particular specialties. Basic to the whole development of scholarship, however, were studies in the public records. The state of the records

---

[1] F. M. Powicke, 'Sir Henry Spelman and the Concilia', *Proceedings of the British Academy* (VIII, 1930), 13. A useful study is the unpublished doctoral dissertation of Marc Friedlander, 'Growth in the Resources for Studies in Earlier English History', unpublished Ph.D. dissertation, University of Chicago, Chicago, 1938.

conditioned the development of modern historiography and historical politics. Even the tradition of British empiricism owes something to those early modern historians who, by extensive use of the public records, registered the claims of history to be an arbiter of truth.

ii THE PUBLIC RECORDS AND RECORD KEEPING

The public records in the sixteenth and seventeenth centuries were, for practical purposes, divided into two broad groups: first, there were the *arcana imperii*, or documents concerned with 'matters of estate and the crown only'; second, there were various legal and financial records which concerned the rights and interests of the crown and of the subject in such matters as land tenures, titles, bureaucratic precedents, and Acts of Parliament. As Professor Wernham has recently observed, 'only the more formal legal and financial documents in the second group were public records in the sense that the public had reasonably ready and regular access to them upon payment of fees. All the first group, the *arcana imperii*, and many documents in the second group—those that were not matters of record in the strict legal sense—were the private muniments of the King, his courts, and his government.'[1] This helps to explain why the role of the record keepers was crucial in the development of historiography, and why research (especially in diplomatic and administrative history) remained so difficult until the establishment of a public record office in the nineteenth century.

The important historical questions are the following: (1) Where were the public records? (2) Who controlled these records, and how? (3) What was the state of the records? (4) How easy to use were the records? (5) Who used them and for what purposes? The physical obstacles to research in the public records were formidable enough; in addition, there were numerous fees to be paid and formal *entrées* to be sought. Many classes of records were inaccessible except 'by very special grace and favour'.[2] In view of such obstacles the achievements of seventeenth-century antiquaries and historians must appear all the more remarkable, for they did succeed in basing accounts on the study of 'the best approved historiographers and sound records'.[3]

---

[1] See Professor R. B. Wernham, 'The Public Records in the Sixteenth and Seventeenth Centuries', Levi Fox, ed., *English Historical Scholarship*, 11.

[2] *Ibid.*, 14.   [3] Stow, *Survey*, I, lxxxi.

Moreover, these men sometimes found ways to secure immunity from the bureaucratic tribute money levied by officials on those who came to search the records.

According to John Selden, 'out of their own nature it is known to men that are acquainted with Records where they are'.[1] That this was a wry witticism, and not a plain statement of fact becomes obvious when the history of the records is recalled. Although England had acquired a fairly accurate written record of government since the reign of King John, new developments in administration had led to a whole series of administrative expedients in the keeping of records. By the end of the sixteenth century decentralization had already been carried to an extreme.[2]

The Lord Chancellor had a general jurisdiction over records, which he shared, however, with the Master of the Rolls and the Lord Treasurer. Nothing like a clearly defined chain of command existed. The Master of the Rolls was primarily concerned with enrolments in the Court of Chancery; he was responsible also for the recent chancery records which accumulated in the Rolls house, and for those older records that had been pushed into back rooms at the Rolls house and forgotten. The common law courts—King's Bench, Exchequer, and Common Pleas—had accumulated masses of records, some of which rested in the Tower, some in the four Treasuries at Westminster, and some in clerks' offices. The subordinate offices of all the courts, including the Chancery, kept records in their own custody and charged various fees for search.[3]

For example, the Six Clerks Office, the offices of the two Remembrancers, the Clerk of the Pells, and the Clerk of the Pipe's Office all had custody of records, some of which went back more than two centuries. In addition, the archives of the other common law and prerogative courts—Star Chamber, Requests, Admiralty, Augmenta-

---

[1] John Selden, *Titles of Honour*, 2nd ed. (London, 1631), 'Preface'.

[2] The best short survey of medieval administrative policies (with some emphasis on problems of record keeping) is S. B. Chrimes, *An Introduction to the Administrative History of Medieval England* (New York, 1952); the best short discussion of medieval records is V. H. Galbraith, *Studies in the Public Records* (London, 1948).

[3] See George Albert Bonner, *The Office of the King's Remembrancer in England* (London, 1930), 1–48. Also Hubert Hall, *The Antiquities of the Exchequer* (New York, 1891), 47–61, and *passim*; and Hubert Hall, *Studies in Official Historical Documents* (Cambridge, 1908); also the books mentioned elsewhere in the notes to this chapter.

tions, Wards and Liveries—were cared for and disposed of according to different provisions made by the officials of each court. The records of the Court of Augmentations were in the charge of an Exchequer Clerk after 1554; and ancient maritime court records presumably remained under local jurisdiction. State papers containing *arcana imperii* were supposed to be kept in the State Paper Office, but in fact, officials like Burghley, Walsingham and others kept many such papers private for their own use. There was little public or bureaucratic pressure toward centralization, largely because current administration was more important than research, and because the value of records lay 'chiefly in their usefulness for reference in the current business of the office or in the fees that they yielded from searchers'.[1]

In general it may be said that there were four main groups of record repositories at the end of Elizabeth's reign. These were (1) the Rolls House and the Tower of London, (2) the Four Treasuries at Westminster, (3) the State Paper Office at Whitehall, and (4) the various separate offices of the courts and of the departments. The Tower was supposed to contain only ancient records, but owing to disputes over jurisdiction and to other causes, the transfer of ancient records from the Rolls House to the Tower did not always take place. For the same reasons ancient common law court records were not always transferred to the Four Treasuries. After the reign of Edward IV 'there were many conflicts about jurisdiction and about the relative interests in fees and dignities; at one time between the Tower Record Keeper and the Chamberlains of the Exchequer; at other times between the same functionary and the Master of the Rolls'.[2]

Probably around the turn of the century one of the Tower record keepers drew up a list of 'Considerations whether the ancient records of Chancery ought to be laid in the Tower'. The author concluded that they should, that it was 'manifest by record, that about the twentieth year of King Henry VIIIth, there were remaining at the Rolls [House] no records of more ancient time than those of the time of King Henry VIIth—except those few of the years of King Richard the Third'. To the objection that the Tower was not so open or easy of access the author replied 'that the keeping and lawfull

---

[1] Wernham, 'The Public Records', in Fox, *Historical Scholarship*, 15.
[2] E. Edwards, *Libraries and Founders*, 230-1. See also Fox, *Historical Scholarship*, 16–20.

access and use of records within the Tower is no new thing, nor less ancient than the records themselves'. He concluded that the subject would be benefited 'by having the use of more records than he had before for the same fee and all of one place, which otherwise should be forced to double fees in divers places'.[1] This argument in favour of transfers to the Tower was not unrelated to the question of fees, but it is noteworthy that quarrels over jurisdiction stimulated research in the records.

The origin of the aforementioned dispute went back to the quarrels of the 1560's between Edward Stafford, one of the Exchequer Chamberlains, and William Bowyer, Keeper of the Tower Records. In the ensuing war of words and padlocks between the two men a number of interesting facts emerged, which were duly brought to the attention of the Privy Council. The quarrel had begun over the control of keys, that is, over jurisdiction. Bowyer had refused to allow Stafford's lock to be put upon any tower door; Stafford had maintained that the records in the Tower were being improperly and carelessly kept. Some records, Stafford asserted, had been removed to private custody and were only discovered by a 'Mr. Hobbey' while he was searching for a place to store gunpowder. When he found them they were badly eaten by lime from the walls. Furthermore, Stafford charged that Bowyer had demanded excessive fees and removed documents to his own house for copying.[2]

In 1567, the Master of the Rolls, Sir William Cordell, became involved in the quarrel. He had no use for Stafford's claims, but resented Bowyer's successful attempt to secure a warrant from the Queen directing that Chancery records in the Rolls Chapel be delivered to the Tower. Cordell argued that Bowyer was merely his deputy—a claim which Bowyer denied with an impressive show of precedents. The quarrel went on under succeeding officials until it finally was resolved in a case in Star Chamber in the reign of James I. Professor Wernham had summed up the results of the quarrel:

> Eventually, it seems to have been settled in favour of the Master of the Rolls, for it was his nominees Robert Bowyer and Henry Elsyng, not their rival Peter Proby, who were finally confirmed in

[1] B.M. Lansdowne MS. 113, fols. 112–112b.
[2] B.M. Lansdowne MS. 113, fols. 103–4b. See also S.P. Dom. Eliz. 33/f. 2, quoted in part by Wernham, in Fox, *Historical Scholarship*, 17. In the British Museum among the Stowe and Lansdowne MSS. are a number of copies of such letters.

the office by letters patent in December, 1604. Meanwhile, how-ever, the records whose transfer to the Tower Queen Elizabeth had straitly commanded in May, 1567, remained in the Rolls Chapel and Rolls House. They were still there when the Public Record Office took them over in the mid-nineteenth century—an impressive illustration of the power of official inertia.[1]

This instance of bureaucratic imperialism was by no means an isolated one; nor were there wanting other illustrations of the power of official inertia.

According to Thomas Powell's *Direction for Search of Records* (1622) the Tower was supposed to contain records of less value 'by reason of their antiquitie'.[2] Like most other generalizations about the records, this one was somewhat misleading. The Four Treasuries also contained ancient records which, for certain historical purposes, were extremely valuable. The Four Treasuries were located in (1) the Exchequer Court of Receipts, (2) the New Palace at Westminster, (3) the Abbey of Westminster (in the old Chapter House), and (4) in the Cloister of Westminster. Each of these treasuries was kept locked. Each door had three locks, requiring three separate keys which were in the custody of three different officials. The Chapter House contained foreign documents—leagues and treaties between sovereigns and states—while the other treasuries, for the most part, contained domestic legal documents.

A catalogue of the treaties of peace and commerce made between England and other countries was compiled by Arthur Agarde and George Austen in 1611 by order of Sir Robert Cecil. It referred to treaties ranging in date from the twelfth century to 1607, many of which were later damaged or destroyed by dampness, rot and mice. Some idea of the variety of the contents of the Four Treasuries may be gathered from Arthur Agarde's *Compendium* (1610). Copies of Domesday Book, the wills of Henry VII and Henry VIII, secrets of state (which were kept sealed), documents relating to the assay of gold and silver under the Tudors, acknowledgments of the supremacy of Henry VIII, as well as legal records of the courts—all were to be found in one or another of the Four Treasuries.[3]

[1] Wernham, 'Public Records', in Fox, *Historical Scholarship*, 18. On Proby, see *Calendar of Salisbury MSS.*, XVI, 346-51.

[2] Thomas Powell, *Direction for Search of Records* (London, 1622), 16.

[3] On the subject generally, see Hall, *Antiquities of the Exchequer*, 47-61 and Chapter IV, *passim*; also H. C. Maxwell-Leyte, *Historical Notes on the Use of the Great Seal of England* (London, 1926), 400-4. I have also

Before the founding of the State Paper Office at the Palace of Whitehall in the reign of Elizabeth, English state papers had been preserved at the Westminster Treasuries or in the custody of the King's Secretary and chancery clerks. Such state papers comprised 'original treaties or treaty papers, law papers, political reports with royal, departmental, and miscellaneous letters and instruments under the Signet or Sign Manual . . .' as well as less important material.[1] After the reconstruction of the secretariat in 1535 the need for a new repository of papers of state had become urgent. When the State Paper Office was finally instituted medieval documents were left undisturbed in the old repositories at Westminster and the Tower of London. Tudor records and papers were transferred to the State Paper Office, where they were kept for the use of secretaries of state and other government officials.[2]

The Tower, the Rolls House, the Four Treasuries and the State Paper Office were thus the major record repositories, but scattered throughout London were smaller archives in the custody of various clerks eager for fees. Some of these archives contained records which went back as far as the reign of Henry III. Antiquaries and historians had occasion to use these records (as Stow and Selden, for example, did), but it is uncertain whether or not they, like others, paid for the privilege.[3]

The general policy of the government with respect to records could be described as one of orders and lamentations tempered by neglect.

drawn on the following manuscripts: B.M. Stowe, 138 (*passim*); B.M. Cotton Vespasian C. XIV, f. 205 ff.; B.M. Lansdowne 137 (*passim*); and S.P. 14/80/no. 99. A useful article is F. Taylor, 'An Early 17th Century Calendar of Records Preserved in Westminster Palace Treasury', *Bulletin of John Rylands Library* (XXIII, No. 1, 1939). Arthur Agarde, *A Repertorie of Records* (London, 1631), contains an extended version of the *Compendium*. Joseph Ayloffe, ed., *Calendars of the Ancient Charters* (London, 1774), reprints contemporary calendars; and, in more detail, so does Sir Francis Palgrave, *The Antient Kalendars and Inventories of the Treasury of His Majesty's Exchequer*, 3 vols. (London, Commissioners of the Public Records, 1836–7). See also William Prynne, *An Exact Abridgement Of The Records In The Tower Of London . . . Collected by Sir Robert Cotton* (London, 1657). The collection was probably made by Agarde.

[1] See Hubert Hall, *A Repertory of British Archives*, Part I, England, compiled for the Royal Historical Society (London, 1920), xii–xiii. F. S. Thomas, *A History of the State Paper Office* (London, 1849), must be supplemented.

[2] Cf. S.P. 14/20/no. 9, oath of office.

[3] See Bonner, *Office of the King's Remembrancer*, 1–48, *passim*.

This was more true of the two centuries following the civil wars than it was of the preceding century. Under the Commonwealth, and for a long period thereafter, whenever an accumulation of records became inconveniently large, the search for empty cellars and attics began; and the surplus of old records was transferred to a new repository chosen with regard to convenience, but with little or no regard to accessibility or safe keeping. To take but one example, the records of the Court of Wards and Liveries were stored in a dilapidated house belonging to the King's fishmonger who, according to the Parliamentary committee of inquiry in 1709, 'had recourse *to search them*, at pleasure, or to let anybody go in and do as they pleased . . . and it is to be feared many of the Records are embezzled'.[1]

The situation with respect to local records, some ecclesiastical records, as well as Irish and Scottish records, was not much better. The transfer of Scottish records to England during the Commonwealth and their later return resulted in losses. The measures taken by the government of the Commonwealth were aimed at maintenance, not at reform. Hugh Peters proposed that the Tower records be burned on the ground that they contained the evidence and precedents of past tyranny, but fortunately no one paid attention to this *ignis fatuus*. After the restoration, when William Prynne was appointed Tower record keeper, he quickly discovered that a few years of neglect were sufficient to destroy or render useless many records, even in a relatively secure and well-administered 'safe'.[2]

Some of the Elizabethan officials in charge of public records stand out as being among the best who were ever charged with the difficult task of keeping public archives. King James inherited many of Elizabeth's officials, and appointed some able men himself. From the meeting of the Long Parliament until the Restoration, however, little was done to maintain the traditions set by such Elizabethans as Arthur Agarde, William Lambarde, Robert Bowyer, and Thomas Wilson. At the Restoration William Prynne performed Herculean labours in rescuing Tower records from their obscurity in

[1] Quoted by E. Edwards, *Libraries and Founders*, 266.
[2] See William Prynne, *A Brief Register, Kalendar and Survay of Parliamentary Writs*, 4 Parts (London, 1659–64). Part I is hereafter referred to as *Parliamentary Writs*; Prynne's preface 'to the Ingenuous Reader' contains his lament as well as much other valuable information on records. Part III, published as *Brevia Parliamentarium* (1662), contains the story of Prynne's labours in sorting records. On Prynne's career in general, see Ethyn Williams Kirby, *William Prynne* (Cambridge, Mass., 1931).

'Cesar's Chappel in the White Tower of London, like dead men out of mind', and cleansing them of their 'putrefying filth'.[1] Able men succeeded Prynne, but they lacked his apostolic sense of duty.

By the middle of the eighteenth century the problems of storage, access, calendaring, and the like had become insoluble in terms of the unreformed bureaucratic system. The efforts of individuals, even had they been as enthusiastic and as able-bodied as Prynne, could not have overcome the problem of paper, the problem of the daily accumulation of more and more records; and the continuation of the ancient system of fees and perquisites gradually choked off historical research in the records. In the sixteenth and seventeenth centuries, however, the record keepers had achieved real progress in the care and calendaring of records. Furthermore, many of these men took action to make the records in their custody more accessible to scholars. The debt of scholarship to such individuals is enormous.

The foremost Elizabethan and early Stuart record keepers were men of uncommon learning and ability. The quarrel between William Bowyer and Lord Stafford revealed that both men could cite precedents from the records, and that both were aggressive reformers. It is significant that Robert Bowyer, who became keeper of the Tower records in 1604, was a member of the Society of Antiquaries, as were William Lambarde and Arthur Agarde. Lambarde, the historian of Kent and author of *Eirenarcha*, *Archeion*, and other legal works, was appointed deputy keeper of the Tower records in 1600. He prepared and presented to the Queen in 1601 'Pandects of all her Rolls, Bundles, Membranes, and Parcels that be reposited in her majesty's Tower of London'. So large an undertaking could only be partially fulfilled, but Lambarde's work was comparable in importance to Agarde's *Compendium* of the records in the Four Treasuries—both were extremely useful catalogues, drawn up by men who were themselves learned antiquaries. At the State Paper Office Doctor Thomas Wilson, the father of Sir Thomas Wilson (who acquired the office in 1610) was a distinguished scholar, diplomat, and writer.[2] Such men as these were in a position to do a great deal for historical scholarship by

[1] William Prynne, *Brevia Parliamentarium*, Sig. A * 2.
[2] Sir Thomas Wilson worked in the office from 1605 on—he too was an ambassador and writer. Aside from the *D.N.B.* article on Wilson, there is no good short account, either of his career or of his family. Most of the information on Wilson in the text is based on manuscript sources, but Wilson is mentioned in several of the books already cited.

preparing adequate calendars, by preventing losses, by recovering missing records, and by sometimes using their influence on behalf of scholars who required access to certain classes of records.

The State Paper Office, being concerned entirely with 'matters of state', differed from most other record repositories in that no searches were permitted without special warrants. Otherwise, the problems faced by Sir Thomas Wilson at the State Paper Office in the early seventeenth century were very much like those faced by other record keepers.

The oath of office taken by Wilson was necessarily more elaborate than most, for he had to guard state secrets. In part, his oath read, '. . . you shall not willingly suffer any of the same [i.e. records] to be purloined, embezzled, or defaced; you shall carefully, and faithfully keep secret, and conceal from the knowledge of others either by writing or relation all such things therein contained as shall be fit either for reason of state or otherwise for his majesty's service to be revealed and kept secret, except it be to the Lords and others of his majesty's privy council, or such as his majesty shall be content to have them communicated unto . . .' [1] Furthermore, the keeper of the state papers was obliged by oath to try to recover lost records. The oaths taken by other record keepers were less restrictive, but sometimes included a promise not to demand unjust allowances—a promise which was seldom if ever strictly kept.

The problems and duties that Wilson faced he described in a letter to King James, dated about 1615:

> I was appointed to peruse, register, abstract, and put in order, all your majesty's papers for business of state, which I found in extreme confusion, and have reduced them into that due order and form, that your majesty and most of the Lords have seen and approved, wherein I have spent more than 10 painful years. By the pains I have taken therein and in other business (having spent the other former part of my life in schools and universities in the study of civil laws, languages, and other humane learning) your majesty upon trial will haply find me fit to do you other service . . . [2]

Ambitious and hard-working, Wilson was anxious to acquire other offices—partly for reasons of prestige, but also because he was in

[1] Copy in B.M. Harley MS. 39, fols. 766–77. Other oaths are contained in this same volume. See also S.P. 14/20/no. 9, f. 27, Oath of the Clerk of Papers for Matters of State.
[2] S.P. 14/88/no. 48.

need of money. At the State Paper Office it was not feasible to charge privy councillors high fees for searches. The official fees of Wilson's office were only £30 a year plus a £60 allowance for diet; and he had to petition King Charles in 1628 for arrears of pay which amounted to £825. In an earlier petition to the king he had observed that out of his diet allowance he had been forced to keep three clerks, 'two to write and register such things as are called for by the secretaries, privy councillors, ambassadors, and others . . . and one more to bind up those papers that are material into books, whereof I have already made up at least 500 great books of all business of all several kingdoms and states'.[1] The reason for the increase in 'customary' fees in the other record offices is not hard to perceive.[2]

When the State Paper Office had to be enlarged to accommodate the growing bulk of its records Wilson proceeded to make gifts of books and satin suits to sweeten official dispositions. Influence was everywhere the rule of business. A recurrent vexation of office which Wilson had to face was borrowing of records by privy councillors who failed to return them. It was most difficult, he complained, to sue these men's estates; and there was nothing to prevent such borrowed records from eventually becoming private property. Official inertia was, however, the dry rot of every office. Wilson's efforts to overcome it were reasonably successful, but in 1637, when Sir Henry Wotton left valuable papers to the State Paper Office, no one bothered to collect them until the nineteenth century.[3] At other

[1] S.P. 45/20/no. 76.

[2] The problem of fees is discussed by E. Edwards in *Libraries and Founders*, as well as in other books cited. For various reasons fees and gratuities were increasing. Various manuscript sources bear this out—for example, see B.M. Lansdowne MS. 171, f. 390b; B.M. Harley MS. 1576, fols. 157–8; B.M. Lansdowne MS. 25, f. 116 (all these dating from the 1570's). Also Lansdowne MS. 113, f. 112b (probably in the 1580's); and S.P. 12/221, fols. 2–3 and 9–10 (1588); B.M. Lansdowne MS. 76, f. 46 (1594); and Lansdowne MS. 163, f. 331 (1608–10) as well as other manuscripts in this volume. B.M. Stowe MS. 541, fols. 1–45, contains a series of documents relating to the Keeper of the Rolls, done *tempus* Charles II. See also note 2, p. 86.

[3] See B.M. Stowe MS. 548, fols. 2–11, Wilson's own account of the State Paper Office (in an eighteenth-century transcript). See B.M. Harley MS. 94, nos. 58–60—similar complaints by Arthur Agarde. On Wotton's will and the failure of his bequest to take effect, see Logan Pearsall Smith, ed., *The Life and Letters of Sir Henry Wotton*, 2 vols. (Oxford, 1907), I, 217.

record offices political influence, alienation of records, and official inertia presented parallel problems.

Sir Thomas Wilson particularly deplored the influence of Sir Robert Cotton at the Four Treasuries. Yet Arthur Agarde's 'State of the Treasury Records' (the *Compendium* of 1610) owed much to Cotton's knowledge of records. Cotton supplied Agarde with information and with many 'originals of treaties which heretofore have been carelessly lost out of the King's Treasuries'.[1]

In many, perhaps even in most repositories, the office books and calendars were considered private property. Peter Proby, the unsuccessful candidate for the Tower deputy keepership after Lambarde's death, offered to give Lambarde's widow £100 for her calendars.[2] There were no overall regulations governing the care and disposition of records. The individual record keeper's initiative and interests therefore determined many questions of policy. There was thus a degree of latitude in administration, which permitted considerable freedom, especially in the use of records; at the same time this meant that abuses could easily multiply.

The general state of the public records in the early seventeenth century was described by Thomas Powell, the attorney and author who, after 1606, devoted himself to writing legal handbooks and other professional works. Powell published his *Direction for Search of Records* in 1622, and his *Repertorie of Records* in 1631. The former was a practical guide, based on his own experiences in searching the records; the latter was a much larger work, which featured a calendar of those Tower records which were likely to be of special interest to searchers for tenure and title deeds. In both works Powell had in mind the needs of lawyers, but his books would have been almost equally valuable to historians. They are still an excellent starting point for any description of the location and state of the records.[3]

Powell's description of the records was no more systematic than the procedures of storage in the record offices themselves. A searcher might know *in general* from Powell's *Repertorie of Records* what various bags, bundles, chests, tills, etc. contained, but it is clear that

[1] B.M. Lansdowne MS. 137, f. 2 and *passim*. The original of Agarde's *Compendium* is reprinted in part in E. Edwards, *Memoirs of Libraries*; more fully in Palgrave, *Ancient Kalendars*, II, 311–35.

[2] See *Calendar of Salisbury MSS.*, Vol. XI, 350–1.

[3] The best account of Thomas Powell is given in the *D.N.B.*—both his books were published in London. He should not be confused with Robert Powell, a legal antiquary.

nothing like a quick or easy search would have been possible. For example, Powell specified, among other rolls in the chancery '... *Watson's role,* contayning diverse Grants and other things confusedly and promiscuously layd together, which one Watson (sometimes Clarke of the Great Seale, that is to say, betwixt the thirtieth and fortieth years of the late good Queen *Elizabeth*) did for six or seven years together keepe in his Chest, and upon his death they were found and brought into the Chaple of the Rolls'.[1] Powell made it clear that the confused state of the records was not wholly the fault of the record keepers. Administrative changes, as well as administrative carelessness were reflected in the records.

Powell discussed the chancery records under three headings in his *Direction for Search of Records*: Patents, Close Rolls, and Bundles. He attempted to note some of the peculiarities of each series, but he was desperately conscious of the exceptions to all of his generalizations. Chancery records, he observed, were usually deposited in the Rolls Chapel four or five years after they were enrolled. The fees for search among the various chancery records were, generally speaking, as follows: 'For search of anything in the *Index* or *Kalendar*—xii d./ For sight of every Record you call for by the Index or Kalendar— iiii d./ for copying . . . you pay for every sheet viii d./ For hand of the clark to anything you copy ii d.'[2] The fees for search in any chancery records not mentioned in the Kalendar constituted an exception 'out of the foresaid generall rule'. When the search was likely to be 'uncertaine and intricate', then 'your fee must answer the Clarke's extraordinarie paines, &c.'[3] Historians would obviously be more interested in this kind of search than lawyers. Clearly, they would either have to pay out large sums or find influential patrons or friends among the record keepers.

Powell recognized that the Tower was a kind of storage warehouse for ancient records, but he could provide only very general information on exactly what records the Tower contained. As he said, 'there be some records in the *Tower* which, because there is no order taken for reducing them into Kalendars, and their distinct *Classes,*

---

[1] Thomas Powell, *Direction for Search of Records,* 4. The *Direction for Search* is actually more valuable than the *Repertorie* for giving an idea of the conditions of the records.

[2] *Ibid.,* 14. The Kalendar referred to is presumably that of Arthur Agarde.

[3] *Ibid.,* 34.

can neyther be by me, nor any other, here or elsewhere demonstrated'.[1] The fee for search in these Tower records was apparently ten shillings, a sum which entitled the searcher to paw his way through as many documents as he could.

Of the physical state of the records Powell had relatively little to say. In 1599 Lord Keeper Egerton issued orders aimed at preventing abuses in the making up of the chancery rolls, and these show that poor handwriting, careless enrollment, and careless use of forms were common faults. It was the decay and loss of records, however, that caused the greatest anxiety. Dampness rotted parchment and paper alike; rats and mice dieted on the records, and bred and fed generation after generation in vellum labyrinths. As iron was rusted by salt water, so, Agarde complained, was parchment eaten by rat urine. The cats that caught the mice and rats were themselves sometimes coffined in paper—cat carcasses were discovered preserved among the records when they were moved to the Public Record Office in the middle of the nineteenth century. Fire, of course, was an obvious hazard, and one which was likely to result in devastating losses, as the fire in the Six Clerk's Office in 1621 demonstrated.[2]

Perhaps the most urgent problems—from the point of view of the record keepers—were the misplacing of records (less than ten years after the Treaty of Ryswick was signed the original copy could not be found) and the 'plain taking of them away'.[3] The latter cause of losses was extremely difficult to control, since privy councillors,

[1] *Ibid.*, 18–19. Powell gave more detailed information in the *Repertorie*, but, as Prynne observed in the *Brevia Parliamentarium*, most of the records he (Prynne) was publishing were 'unknown to, [and] unperused by any of this or the former generation . . .' See Sig. A *, and ff. Powell, in *Direction for Search* (p. 19), went on to wish that 'some course might be taken in time, for the repayring of Those Records which are worne out with Antiquitie, before it be too late, and past remedie . . .'

[2] See B.M. Harley MS. 39, no. 117, f. 121b. Cf. B.M. Lansdowne MS. 116, fols. 19–19b (complaints of lack of calendars, etc., 1573). Also see B.M. Harley MS. 830, f. 227 ff. The various *Reports* of the Deputy Keepers of the Public Records contain interesting pieces of information, especially the *Thirteenth Report of the Deputy Keeper of the Public Records* (House of Commons Sessional Reports, 1852). A great deal of information on fees, and on the various Chancery offices, including information on the 1621 fire (p. 143), will be found in G. W. Sanders, *Orders of the High Court of Chancery*—consult the excellent index. See also John Selden, *Titles of Honour*, 3rd ed. (London, 1672), Part 2, 587–97.

[3] The lost Treaty of Ryswick is mentioned by Wernham in Fox, *English Historical Scholarship*, 28.

judges, and attorney generals could secure warrants for the release of records into their custody. Moreover, it was noted that 'the lending of books, Rolls, or Records to great officers and others' often resulted in losses.[1] By the same token, however, it is evident that a good deal of lending did take place. The confused state of the records also made it possible for litigants to destroy or embezzle embarrassing legal records—certainly the practice was common enough to draw criticism.[2]

Between 1660 and 1732 little progress was made in improving the state of the records, in spite of Parliamentary committees of inquiry, and in spite of the heroic efforts of William Prynne and a few other dedicated men. The continuing tendency toward administrative decentralization, especially after 1660, virtually ruled out effective piecemeal reform. While it is evident that the state of the public records in the sixteenth and seventeenth centuries was an excellent justification of the decision made in 1838 to concentrate the national archives in a Public Record Office, it must be remembered that these centuries also witnessed real progress. For the first time in English history scholars were able to produce works based primarily on original research in the public records. The worst abuses in the system of fees occurred in the eighteenth century; in the seventeenth century access was easier, fees were lower, and the 'problem of paper' less acute.[3]

A record repository may be important for scholarship even though its contents are imperfectly indexed and poorly calendared. Historians and lawyers no doubt found Powell's guides useful, but long before Powell wrote there were in existence a number of manuscript indexes and calendars of records. The number of manuscript copies of Agarde's *Compendium* suggests that the *Compendium* and other such treatises served as guides to scholarly research. As early as 1592 a series of calendars of the Tower records was available at the Remembrancer's Office at Westminster. Lambarde's *Pandects*, Agarde's

---

[1] B.M. Harley MS. 94, f. 58. Also, B.M. Stowe MS. 162 *passim*—a catalogue of MSS. and State Papers in Walsingham's possession. B.M. Stowe MS. 549, f. 6 contains a copy of a warrant for recovery of papers detained (dated 1611)—see also fols. 7–16. Also B.M. Stowe MS. 1056, *passim*.

[2] See B.M. Lansdowne MS. 116, fols. 19–19b. In Ireland it was a felony also—see *Calendar of Carew MSS.*, 1603–23, p. 156.

[3] See Wernham, in Fox, *English Historical Scholarship*, 30. Kirby, *William Prynne*, 160–71, and B.M. Stowe MS. 543.

Compendium, Le Squyer's catalogue, as well as the catalogues of Wilson and Bowyer, all testify to the fact that the public records were becoming easier to use in the early seventeenth century than they had been for centuries past.

The historians of the nineteenth century were well aware of the debt they owed to the record-minded scholars of the seventeenth century; the 13th Report of the Deputy Keeper of the Public Records, dated 1852, contained a plea for freedom of access, signed by Macaulay and other scholars in which it was pointed out that:

> Many of the most valuable historical works of past ages; such works, for example, as Dugdale's Baronage, the foundation of all our books relating to the peerage; Madox's History of the Exchequer, the basis of much of our legal history; Tanner's Notitia Monastica, the groundwork of our monastic history; and Rymer's Foedera, which first enabled historical writers to put general English history on a firm foundation;—were all compiled from the Records.[1]

It is clear that the advances which enabled these men and others to make good use of the records had already been achieved when they began to write. The Elizabethan and Jacobean record keepers deserve much credit, but they did not work in isolation. They served a precedent-minded generation; and the fact that more and more people were turning to the records helped to make possible the renaissance in good record keeping.

Lawyers and litigants, ambassadors and antiquaries, politicians and bureaucratic officials all had reasons to apply themselves to the study of records. Whether from legal custom grown into habit, or from a sheaf of other historical causes, the argument from records became the characteristic form of English political debate. Abridgments of records, copies and extracts of records, and correspondence about records form no small part of the written remains of seventeenth-century scholarship.[2] The uses of the past were so many and so various that scarcely any collection of records was without relevance to the present.

Abstracts of the rolls of Parliament were especially prized by

---

[1] *Thirteenth Report of Deputy Keeper,* Appendix, p. 530.

[2] It would be quite impossible to give anything like a complete listing of such collections—consult the catalogues of the manuscript collections in the British Museum, and the Oxford and Cambridge catalogues for representative major collections.

politicians and legal antiquaries; Coke owned one such volume which had been given him by the antiquary Francis Tate. The common lawyers' feud with the chancery officials stimulated research in legal history, as the quarrel between 'court and country' stimulated re-rearch in political history. Religion also animated the search for precedents. The reasons that prompted Sir Edward Coke to defend the established religion of England were typical both of the man and of the times. In a letter addressed to Sir Robert Cecil in 1605 Coke explained the purpose and method of his historical research:

> Right Honourable: The papist setteth the supreme jurisdiction ecclesiastical upon the Pope's triple crown; and the sectary upon the Presbytery, thinking the proceedings ecclesiastical to be popish and unlawful, both of them being persuaded as they be taught. It seemed to me very necessary that something were published manifesting (without any inferences or bombasting) the very records of the ancient laws and statutes of England, to the obser-vation whereof the Kings of England have always been sworn; whereby it shall appear what jurisdiction ecclesiastical by the ancient laws of England appertain to the crown, and that the laws made by King Henry 8th or since, are for the most part declara-tive of the old and are not introductive of the new: and thereby both parties, being Englishmen, may the sooner be persuaded to yield their obedience to the ancient English laws, and the Kings proceedings appear to be honourable and just. And I have observed many resolutions of late, and many ancient (book) cases, prece-dents, and acts of Parliament above 400 years old, [and] informed his majesty how necessary it were that somewhat were published plainly and sincerely, touching the matter that the almanac may not serve for the meridian of Westminster Hall alone, but also for all England . . .[1]

The utterance was certainly characteristic of Coke in its stress on custom and the immemorial, but beyond this it was typical of his age, in which record and precedent (with or without bombast) were the touchstones of argument.

The best evidence of the increasing use of records by the seventeenth-century scholars and historical antiquaries is to be found in their works. The scholarly citation of records had become con-ventional by the middle of the century. Some medieval writers had cited evidence from the records, but, generally speaking, few at-tempts were made to write history from original records before the

---

[1] S.P. 14/13/fols. 61–2.

sixteenth century. The subsequent development of historical scholarship was marked by the deliberate inquisition of the public records. Some of the problems and methods of research in the records are revealed by the unpublished notes and collections made by contemporary scholars in the course of their research.

Since a quite considerable number of the Elizabethan record keepers were themselves antiquaries, it is not surprising that their collections and extracts from the records were frequently consulted, or that most of these collections came to rest among the Cottonian, Harleian, and Lansdowne manuscripts in the British Museum. Thomas Talbot, who was one of the clerks of the records in the Tower of London before 1580, was an antiquary who compiled volumes of such manuscript collections. That these early works continued to be used by historians becomes evident from the notations made by Sir Roger Twysden in the late 1650's, in his 'Extracts from the Rolls of Parliament'. Referring to the work done by William Bowyer during Elizabeth's reign he observed that Bowyer had abridged most of the Parliament rolls remaining in the Tower, and that the original leaves of Bowyer's collection subsequently passed into the library of Sir Simonds D'Ewes, where he had consulted them.[1]

In a long letter from D'Ewes to Spelman, dated July 21, 1634, Sir Simonds based his own interpretation of the history and nature of the Sheriff's office in England on evidence drawn from the records:

> ... this was the true reason anciently why the great earls and barons were sheriffs, because the castles in every country [i.e. county] being then the strength of the kingdom were ever in their custodies. I could give you 40 precedents in half an hours view transcribed with my own hand out of the communia rolls. . . . Those rolls of King John and Henry III were never thoroughly overviewed by any before me . . .[2]

In a postcript D'Ewes cautioned Spelman against depending on the manuscript catalogue of Sheriffs—'that catalogue [which began with the reign of Henry II] will nothing but deceive you. Tis false in every leaf, no way worthy your judicious view, much less worthy is it to direct you.'[3] D'Ewes and other scholars worked carefully through masses of original records, and were not content merely to peruse a

[1] B.M. Stowe MS. 347, fols. 3–4. For Talbot's 'Tracts of Records', see B.M. Harley MS. 6723.
[2] B.M. Add. MS. 25384, fols. 27–27b. [3] B.M. Add. MS. 25384, f. 28.

few samples culled from the catalogues. How the historians of the seventeenth century gained access to the public records, and, in particular, how they avoided paying the fees demanded for legal research, must now be considered.

The high cost of searching the records was the direct result of the high prices paid for offices. The value of an office had little to do with the 'official' fees allocated for it by the crown. Office holders were in some respects like feudal lords, possessed of bureaucratic fiefs which could be made to yield a handsome profit. As a result of this 'bureaucratic feudalism' historians and others were frequently obliged to pay large sums for the privilege of seeking evidence from the records. The total income of the Master of the Rolls, for example, was calculated at '£1787-7sh.-7d. in 1608/09, and at £2110-5sh.-10d. in 1609/10'.[1] Some of this income was derived from fees taken in by the clerks under his jurisdiction. Moreover, offices and reversions of offices were bought and sold for large sums. Robert Bowyer was reported to have paid £800 for his post as Deputy Keeper of the Tower records, and to have given over £200 to Mr. Edward Phillips, the succeeding Master of the Rolls, to hold his place. By 1640 the price of the Mastership of the Rolls was pushed up by auction to £15,000. As Professor Trevor-Roper has observed, 'By the time of James I almost every office was bought, either from the Crown, or from the favourites who made a market of the Crown's patronage, or from the previous holder; and the price, in that age of boom and scramble, was continually rising.'[2] Needless to say, this often meant that fees and other charges were multiplied in order to make the office profitable in the shortest length of time. Fees for search in the records increased almost every year. Ordinances aimed at reform seldom achieved their purpose, for the simple reason that they were directed against symptoms not causes.

[1] B.M. Lansdowne MS. 163, f. 324 (dated 1616).
[2] H. R. Trevor-Roper, *The Rise of the Gentry*, 28. The information on Bowyer and Phillips is from B.M. Lansdowne MS. 163, f. 324 (1616). The recent book by G. E. Aylmer, *The King's Servants, The Civil Service of Charles I 1625–42* (London, 1961), adds immeasurably to our knowledge of the royal officials; Chapter IV is especially valuable for information on the sale and value of offices, and forms of payment. Aylmer (p. 222) confirms the price at auction as of 1639. I did not have the benefit of Mr. Aylmer's book when this chapter was written; and although my statements about fees are, I believe, in general correct, they ignore many important qualifications which Mr. Aylmer discusses in detail.

Coke, in *The Second Part of the Institutes of the Lawes of England*, argued vehemently against the taking of excessive fees for the administration of justice, even suggesting that an Act of Parliament justifying fees was a bad act.[1] Lawyers could, of course, pass the cost of fees and other charges on to their clients. Historians could not, and historical scholarship suffered accordingly, especially in the century before the great age of administrative reform beginning in the 1830's. One example will suffice: 'For copying the *Scrope and Grosvenor Roll*, one hundred and eleven pounds were charged in 1828. This was for a simply literary purpose. Indeed, that roll can be applied to no other purpose. The Keeper and the clerks were then in receipt from the Public Purse of £1440 a year.' [2]

A statement made in 1852 by Sir Francis Palgrave, then Deputy Keeper of the Public Records, sums up admirably the operations of the unreformed legal bureaucracy:

> According to the ancient principles adopted in the organization of our Courts of Judicature, they were all intended, in the first instance, not simply to be self-supporting, but something more —fees, and gratuities, and compliments were allowed, exacted, or imposed, partly as a source of Crown revenue, and partly in order to afford to the officers a remuneration rather above than below the ordinary rate of earnings by the employment of time and labour. The benefit of the officers was especially considered; and not infrequently offices were created as a special boon to the parties. . . . Charges were fixed without any definite relation to the labour imposed upon the officers or the interest of the public. . . . In all matters connected with Records, the charges were accumulated to obtain the greatest aggregate profit.[3]

Sir Francis, however, went on to observe that 'under the ancient regulations of the Record Offices, the employment of the Records for historical, topographical, genealogical, or any other literary purposes, was circumscribed; and, with very rare, scanty, and occasional exceptions, they were as sealed Books to all such inquiries'.[4] Now, although, this was perhaps generally true in the

---

[1] Edward Coke, *The Second Part of the Institutes of the Lawes of England* (London, 1642), 198–210.

[2] E. Edwards, *Libraries and Founders*, 288, note. See also B.M. Lansdowne MS. 171, f. 390b; and *Calendar of Salisbury MSS.*, XI, 350–1.

[3] *Thirteenth Report of the Deputy Keeper of the Public Records*, pp. 26–7.

[4] *Ibid.*, 29.

eighteenth century, and in the nineteenth century until the Public Record Office was founded, it is a far from accurate description of seventeenth-century practice.

Scholars in the seventeenth century gained access to the public records in one of four ways: (1) by paying the fees; (2) by consulting records and transcripts of records in private hands; (3) by official warrants; and (4) by influence or patronage. Access by official warrant required unusual influence at court and was relatively rare. Most scholars depended on a combination of the other available methods. Doubtless John Stow was typical of the majority of historians who had occasion to search the records. In his petition to the aldermen of the City of London in 1590 Stow asked for the freedom of the city in order to reduce his expenses: 'And for as much as the search of records in the Arches, and elsewhere, can not but be chargeable to the said John, as heretofore for many years it hath been, altogether of his own charges, besides his other travails and study, he now humbly craveth your honour's and worship's aid . . . to bestow on him the freedom of the city.' [1] Stow was indebted to Robert Bowyer, the Tower record keeper, for scholarly assistance with records, and possibly also to Michael Heneage and Thomas Talbot. It should be remembered that all four men were members of the Society of Antiquaries. Stow himself made searches at the Tower, but it is not clear whether he obtained his abundant extracts from the Patent Rolls and Inquisitions Post Mortem by direct search or by transcribing from collections made by Bowyer, Talbot or Heneage. In any case, Stow clearly did gain access to various public records, as well as to a number of city and city company records.

It was possible to consult many original records and transcripts of records in private libraries, especially in the library of Sir Robert Cotton. On the whole, local records had suffered more from the depredations of antiquaries bent on collecting records than had the national archives in London.[2] The government, however, frequently found it necessary to issue warrants for the recovery of state papers and other records which had passed into private hands.[3] Historical research in the state papers and revenue records of the Tudors was

---

[1] Printed by Kingsford in Stow, *Survey*, I, lxi–lxvii. See also pp. xxxii–xxxiii on the men who assisted Stow.

[2] See Hubert Hall, *Repertory of British Archives*, xxviii.

[3] In addition to B.M. Stowe 549 and 1056, see B.M. Add. MS. 35831, fols. 279–80.

generally discouraged, but access to various transcripts and extracts of records in private libraries could not be controlled.

Undoubtedly the most effective means of gaining access to record repositories without paying the customary fees was by Privy Council warrant. After the Restoration in 1660 such warrants were almost a necessity for scholars who found it necessary to consult many different classes of records. Research at the State Paper Office was at all times restricted, and Sir Thomas Wilson and others naturally refused to permit any unauthorized persons to have sight of state papers except by special warrant. It would seem that heralds sometimes found it expedient to secure special warrants; Randle Holme, who was deputy to the College of Arms for Cheshire, Shropshire, and North Wales, retained in his collections the copy of such a warrant relating to the City of Chester records.[1] Sir Robert Cecil, while Secretary of State, was obliged to have searches made in a variety of archives; he was in a position to secure the necessary warrants, and presumably did so whenever his agents required them. Dr. Parkins wrote to Cecil in 1597 to say that '. . . in conference with the other assigned, we are come so far that we have need to see such treaties as passed between her majesty and Denmark, whereof in such records as are at hand mention is made; for obtaining which your assistance will be necessary by some warrant to the Tower and the Chequer Chamber, where it is thought these treaties are'.[2]

General warrants addressed to all record keepers were very rare, being obtainable only by special grace. Even so, restrictions were usually added. The warrant issued on behalf of Sir Edward Dering in 1627 illustrates the attitude of the government, as well as some of the problems of research in the records. The document was addressed 'To all officers that are Keepers of Records within the Tower of London, the Cities of London and Westminster, or elsewhere within the realm of England'. The full text reads as follows:

> Whereas the Study of Antiquities is by good experience found to be very serviceable and useful to the general good of the State and Commonwealth, and foreasmuch as Sir Edward Dering, Knight and Baronet, is studious in that kind, and that we have good hope and assurance that by his Endeavours therein he may be the more

[1] B.M. Harley MS. 2097, f. 6b.
[2] See *Calendar of Salisbury MSS.*, Part VII, p. 76 and Part XVII, p. 354. Access to State Paper Office: S.P. 14/86/no. 3b, S.P. 14/96/no. 41b. Also B.M. Cotton MS. Vespasian C, XIV, fols. 216–17, and 78.

enabled to promote the public service; We have for his further encouragement herein and by these Presents do will and command all you whom it may concern that forthwith upon the sight hereof you may readily show unto him all or any Records, Rolls, Registers or Books within your several Offices; And that you suffer him to take any notes, or transcribe of them what he shall choose; the which search and transcripts shall by him be made and taken without any fee or fees to be by him paid unto you or any of you; Hereof fail you not as you will answer the contrary at your peril. Given at Whitehall this fourth of April 1627

The warrant was signed by 'A. Cant.[erbury], Tho. Coventry, Marleburgh, E. Worcester, G. Buckingham, Montgomery, Pembrook'. Restrictions were added, providing that '. . . Sir Edward Dering by virtue hereof shall not make search in any Records since the first of King Edward the Sixth which concern the Receipts & Issues of his Majesty's Revenues, within the several offices of Sir Robert Pye or Sir Edward Wardour, nor shall search the records of attainder of treason & felony in the King's Bench without leave granted from the Lord Chief Justice or Mr. Attorney General'.[1]

By far the most common means of gaining access to particular record offices was by personal suit, either to the record keeper or to some powerful patron. Mention has already been made of John Stow's friendships with the record keepers who were members of the Society of Antiquaries. Dr. John Dee wrote to the elder Cecil in 1574 asking for 'your L. hand to a letter, directed to Mr. Harly, keeper of the records of Wigmore Castle, or to whom, in this case, it appertain . . .' Old accounts and other papers formerly belonging to the Abbey of Wigmore were, according to Dee, lying 'spoiled and tossed, in an old decayed chapel, not committed to any man's special charge'.[2] Roger Dodsworth gained access to the records in St. Mary's Tower at York through the agency of Thomas Sandwich, partly because of Dodsworth's father's influence. And Dodsworth, like many other scholars, made extensive use of the collections of other antiquaries.[3] Sir Simonds D'Ewes, although a wealthy man, could scarcely have compiled his parliamentary Journals of the reign of Elizabeth without the co-operation of clerks and record

[1] B.M. Stowe MS. 543, f. 59 (an eighteenth-century copy). Later warrants are contained in B.M. Harley MS. 1760, f. 20, no. 10 and B.M. Stowe MS. 549, *passim.*

[2] B.M. Lansdowne MS. 19, fols. 81–3.

[3] See Joseph Hunter, *Three Catalogues* (London, 1838), 66–8.

keepers. D'Ewes was able, for example, to borrow records from the Treasury of the Exchequer through the courtesy of one John Bradshaw, the elder of two deputy chamberlains of the Tally Office. He cultivated other record keepers and, like most scholars of his generation, was indebted to Sir Robert Cotton for much scholarly assistance.[1]

Instances of favouritism could easily be multiplied, but their importance lies in what they tell about institutional arrangements, and about ways of doing business, not merely in the fact that they illustrate a hardy species of political corruption. The following two chapters will provide more detailed views of the institutional arrangements of scholarship, and grounds for maintaining that patronage and influence profoundly affected the development of historiography in England.

[1] See James Orchard Halliwell, ed., *The Autobiography and Correspondence of Sir Simonds D'Ewes*, 2 vols. (London, 1845), I, 431-2, 438; II, 52-7, 71-83, 239-40, 311-15, and *passim*.

4

THE ANTIQUARIAN MOVEMENT
AND HISTORICAL RESEARCH

---

i THE ELIZABETHAN SOCIETY OF ANTIQUARIES

'THRIFTY OF TIME PAST', and liking death the better because it would gather him to his fathers, the antiquary entered the pages of English literature in the character of an eccentric. Earle's *Micro-cosmography* (1628) recognized the antiquary as a harmless soul, likely to be gulled by any nimble-witted beggar.[1] In John Donne's epigram, the antiquary was deftly exposed to contempt:

> If in his studie he hath so much care
> To hang all old strange things, let his wife beware.

The literary character of the antiquary proved remarkably durable, as some 'mere antiquaries' continued to invite ridicule by exhibiting a pretentious humility toward the past. However, the lawyers, scholars, and 'persons of great Worth' who formed England's first Society of Antiquaries conformed to no stereotype, nor was their interest in antiquity a sterile affectation.[2] If they erred in their views of the past, it was not for lack of rich experience in the present.

Founded about 1586, the organization known as the Elizabethan College of Antiquaries was composed almost exclusively of men of

[1] See [John Earle], *Micro-cosmography, Or A Peece of the World Discovered; In Essays and Characters* (London, 1628). 'The Antiquary' is no. 7. See Sig. Cv. to C3v.

[2] The phrase 'persons of great worth' is from Spelman, one of the original members. Quoted by C. E. Wright in *The English Library*, 180.

substance who, by education and rank in society, belonged to the upper privileged class. With the notable exception of John Stow, all of the forty known members were gentlemen; many were knights, and two were noblemen. The study of law had attracted at one time or another all but eight of the members; about thirty had pursued studies at one or another of the Inns of Court. Twelve of the antiquaries became members of Parliament, while one, Robert Bowyer, became a clerk of Parliament. Four members were heralds, six were active diplomats or statesmen. No fewer than six of the members held office as record keepers. The society was essentially secular—Launcelot Andrewes and Abraham Hartwell were the only representatives of the clergy. Common lawyers were in a majority; and meetings of the society were accordingly scheduled during Term time. Although the earlier antiquarian activities of Archbishop Parker and Laurence Nowell might suggest some continuity of organization, there is no reason to connect the formal and exclusive Society of Antiquaries with any earlier group engaged in co-operative research.[1]

Meetings of the Society were regularly held at Derby House, formerly the seat of the Earls of Derby, and since 1555, the office of the College of Heralds. The heralds were regarded as an especially important group of members, whose opinions were treated with deference. William Camden did not receive his appointment as Clarencieux herald until 1597, but his reputation for both general and heraldic learning was well established by 1586 when he published his *Britannia*. After 1590 the Society met from time to time at the house of Sir Robert Cotton who, although still a young man, was already becoming known as a librarian and antiquary of

---

[1] The fullest and most illuminating study of the Elizabethan Society of Antiquaries is Linda Van Norden, 'The Elizabethan College of Antiquaries', unpublished Ph.D. dissertation, University of California at Los Angeles, 1946. See pp. 38–43, and 200–20. I have followed Miss Van Norden's account in all important respects. The manuscript materials in the British Museum, and nearly all relevant works of modern scholarship have been thoroughly explored in Miss Van Norden's exhaustive study. Joan Evans, *A History of the Society of Antiquaries* (Oxford, 1956), deals primarily with the later society, but Chapters I and II are useful. Thomas Hearne, ed., *A Collection of Curious Discourses Written by Eminent Antiquaries*, 2 vols. (London, 1720), is the standard collection of documents. Later editions of this work are equally valuable. See also the article by C. E. Wright, 'The Elizabethan Society of Antiquaries and the Formation of the Cottonian Library', in Wormald and Wright, *English Library*, esp. pp. 179 and 190.

distinction. Attendance was required at the meetings, which continued to take place until about 1608. It was perhaps the earliest example in English history of a learned society with formal membership, set rules of procedure, and institutionally defined purposes.

At least until about 1590 group research was the accepted practice. Common research problems were assigned to individual members who exchanged 'discourses' on set topics at each meeting. Comments were expected from other members, and judicial or final conclusions were supposed to be set down.[1] In 1598, however, Arthur Agarde complained that by leaving questions undecided 'our assembly might be rather deemed a Courte of Morespeach . . . than a learned conference'.[2] Perhaps the reason for Agarde's criticism was simply that during the 1590's the more voluble experts had taken control of the meetings, ignoring the programme for communal research.[3]

It is entirely likely that the more learned members undertook more ambitious and specialized research projects. On at least two occasions Camden went beyond the ordinary requirements of the meeting by making brief oral reports which he afterwards revised and enlarged for the benefit of his readers.[4] What is most striking, however, is the emphasis put on original research and documentation. For the most part, comment on the spur of the moment and without evidence was discouraged.

Transcripts of records and other materials were regularly brought to the meetings, to be passed around, examined, and finally submitted as evidence in support of particular statements. The legal training of the antiquaries was clearly reflected in their attitudes toward evidence and proof. Moreover, many of the functions of the modern learned society were performed for the first time in England by the Elizabethan Society of Antiquaries.[5]

The disparagement of 'mere antiquarianism' by scholars like Selden was never meant to be a disparagement of all antiquarian research. The best antiquaries were fully aware of contemporary issues, being men whose interest in antiquity most often derived from immediate political or professional concerns. Lawyers, heralds, and diplomats were accustomed to searching for evidence among the

---

[1] See Van Norden, 'College of Antiquaries', 334–6.
[2] Quoted by Joan Evans, *Society of Antiquaries*, 12.
[3] See Van Norden, 'College of Antiquaries', 310–11.
[4] *Ibid.*, 388.
[5] Cf. Joan Evans, *Society of Antiquaries*, 13.

records of the past, and were firmly convinced that the study of antiquity could provide knowledge for use as well as for pleasure. Thomas Smith, the non-juring divine who became librarian of the Cottonian late in the seventeenth century, observed that the purpose of the Elizabethan Society of Antiquaries was the investigation of topics of the greatest moment, those which illustrated the history of ancient times, whereby things of permanent and general use in civil society might be learned.[1] Smith's reasoning was in general correct; he was not predisposed to assume that antiquarian research was necessarily petty or irrelevant.

The purpose of the discourses written by the antiquaries was to investigate the antiquity of the laws, customs, and institutions of England. The antiquity of Parliament and of the Christian religion in England were matters of immediate concern to both the sovereign and the subject. James no less than Elizabeth perceived a fearful symmetry between past and present. The English faith in the moral utility of history was based on recognition of just this symmetry. Historical politics depended equally on a belief in the relevance of remote precedents to immediate constitutional principles—and there was an increasing tendency to hurl precedents in debate. Perhaps this was the reason why, when Spelman and a few other members of the original Society attempted to revive the meetings in 1614 they found that the King took 'a little Mislike of our Society; not being inform'd that we had resolv'd to decline all Matters of State'. It was natural enough for Spelman to exonerate the King; the question is why the antiquaries themselves had, as Spelman said, '... held it sufficient for that time to revive the Meeting and only conceived some Rules of Government and Limitation to be observ'd amongst us; whereof this was one, That for avoiding Offence, we should neither meddle with Matters of State, nor of Religion'.[2] No such formal limitation had been previously thought necessary.

English historiography in the period before the civil wars owed much to the Society of Antiquaries. Far more than either of the Universities, the Society was active in promoting historical research,

---

[1] See Thoma Smitho, *Catalogus Librorum Manuscriptorum Bibliothecae Cottonianae* (Oxford, 1696), viii, Sig. A4v. Quoted in part by Van Norden, 'College of Antiquaries', 311.

[2] See 'The Original of the Four Terms Of the Year' in *The English Works of Sir Henry Spelman*, 2nd ed. (London, 1727), 69–70. See p. 101, n. 2 for details of this edition.

and in bringing together men from different fields and from many parts of England who were united in their belief that to study the past was to further understanding of the present. The group research of the Society had a direct and immediate influence on individual antiquaries, providing them with constructive criticism and examples of good scholarship. The intangible influence of the Society was perhaps even more important.

Access to the public records was undoubtedly facilitated by the fact that record keepers were members of the Society and supported its purposes. The variety of topics chosen for investigation and the variety of evidence cited in the discourses betokened a growing awareness of the importance of original research. The proposed 'Academy for the Study of Antiquity and History founded by Queen Elizabeth', although it was never brought into being, set a precedent for the definition of what a scholarly institution should be, and the purposes it should serve.

The petition for the proposed 'Academy' was signed by Mr. Cotton, Mr. Dodorig [Doderidge], and Mr. James Lee, and was probably presented to the Queen in 1600.[1] From several points of view the petition was an interesting document. It called for the founding of a library which would bring certain public documents into public possession—that is, the principle of freedom of access was asserted, for the benefit of the nation's scholars. Sir Robert Cotton was probably the private gentleman whose library was to become the nucleus of the proposed Academy library. Membership in the Academy would be extended to members of the Society of Antiquaries and to other recognized scholars. Presumably the members of such a national academy would have had exclusive control over the library, and would have used it to further historical scholarship.

The political utility of the Academy was stressed in the petition, which also stated that it would 'not be hurtful to either of the universities, for it shall not meddle with the arts, philosophy, or other final studies there professed, for this Society [i.e. Academy] tendeth to the preservance of history and antiquity, of which the universities, long busied in the arts, take little care or regard'.[2] The

---

[1] See Van Norden, 'College of Antiquaries', 422. The manuscript is B.M. Cotton MS. Faustina E.V., f. 89.

[2] See Thomas Hearne, ed., *A Collection of Curious Discourses*, II, 326; Van Norden, 'College of Antiquaries', 415–17, and 421–9 for discussion. I have modernized the spelling.

failure of the petition had no effect on the conduct of the antiquaries, although it is possible that Sir Robert Cotton may have determined at this time to make his own library into an informal equivalent of the proposed Academy library.

A study of the various papers read at meetings of the Society of Antiquaries leaves no doubt that the members were anxious to get behind the chroniclers and explore the masses of original records of English history. Instead of making a virtue of conjecture, as Ralegh did in his *History*, the antiquaries condemned the use of conjecture as an historical technique. Francis Thynne, the Lancaster herald, wrote, 'But of these conjectural things I will no further intreat, but descend to such matter arising out of our question as record and history will warrant.' [1] Etymological conjectures were considered warrantable, for the antiquaries lacked modern linguistic skills and perforce conjectured about the origin of words—especially the word 'Parliament'. In general, however, the Society members professed to respect only statements founded on specific evidence. Yet William Agarde could refer casually to the founding of Britain by the Trojans, and none of the antiquaries was clear about the early history of representative institutions. In spite of their disapproval of conjectural history these early antiquaries all tended to antedate their sources and to misinterpret early medieval history. To some extent this was because they operated within the legal framework of 'Custom and the Immemorial', but in addition one must reckon with certain methodological limitations which were the distinguishing marks of antiquarian research.

Members of the Society of Antiquaries pursued their researches in a wide variety of sources, in parish records, old chronicles, Parliamentary writs, charters, Rolls, and Exchequer records, as well as in Domesday book, and at times, in collections of ancient coins. The antiquaries gathered to discuss set topics and particular antiquities; as one member supposed, 'our meetings are to afford one another our knowledge of ancient things and not to discourse of things present'. [2] A knowledge of ancient things meant a knowledge of their whereabouts, and of the particular facts contained in ancient documents. The antiquaries investigated the antiquity and dignity of Dukes, or the etymology and antiquity of sterling money, or ancient funeral practices without becoming too deeply involved in 'things present'. When they began to investigate the history of the

---

[1] Hearne, *Curious Discourses*, I, 66.   [2] *Ibid.*, I, 79.

administration of justice, or the 'Antiquity, Power, Order, State, Manner, Persons, and Proceedings of the High Court of Parliament' they inevitably began to tread on uncertain ground.[1] It was not possible to ignore questions of implication and relevance; and it was usually at this point that the limitations of antiquarian methods were most clearly revealed.

It is noteworthy that the members of the Society of Antiquaries showed little or no concern with historical contexts. They wanted to know what and when, not why and how things happened. They set out to discover the antiquity of their country's towns and offices, customs and institutions. They amassed facts, debated the etymology of words, presented all manner of curious details about the past, but never attempted to reconstruct a past age. They failed to examine their methodological assumptions, and hence failed to develop an awareness of the importance of ideas of explanation. Their concepts of evidence or proof were adequate only within very narrow limits. In effect, they assumed a rather simple correspondence theory of historical truth. A statement was warranted or true if it corresponded with some 'fact' found in a document.

The difficulty with this notion was, of course, that it failed to distinguish adequately between true and false 'facts', or between facts at different levels of generality. The problem was that of deciding what evidence was genuine, and also relevant. It was not enough simply to collect information—the authenticity of every statement of fact had to be established and its relevance to the question defined. The antiquaries, generally speaking, failed to solve this methodological problem.

Three reasons help to account for their failure; first, the concept of legal record was misappropriated to antiquarian uses; second, the antiquaries lacked a systematic knowledge of techniques and special skills for studying documents; and third, no long-range programme for research guided their efforts. Papers on inscriptions, mottoes, money, and land dimensions, were mixed in with papers on Parliamentary and legal history, and on heraldic matters. Obviously, something could be said in favour of variety in the choice of topics—for one thing, the discourses showed a recognition of the importance of folk literature rarely expressed by learned writers before the eighteenth century.[2] Nevertheless, the topics were always English, and most of

[1] Hearne, *Curious Discourses*, I, 281–93; cf. II, 277–309.
[2] Van Norden, 'College of Antiquaries', 367.

the documentation was supposed to come from English sources. Although Camden, Spelman, and a few others occasionally broke this rule, no one thought it necessary to undertake comparative historical studies. The French legal antiquaries had been obliged to face the problems of comparative legal history; the English antiquaries at this time remained insular scholiasts.

The English concept of legal record unfortunately lent itself readily to the 'correspondence theory' of historical truth—much to the detriment of antiquarian understanding of the need for *establishing* every fact and placing it in its appropriate context. The antiquaries did not blindly trust authorities, but they seldom showed remarkable critical acumen in interpreting their primary sources. Spelman, it is true, developed a highly sophisticated sense of historical contexts, but he only did so long after the Society of Antiquaries had ceased to meet. The authority of legal record implied a degree of certainty which was out of place in historical work. Moreover, any statement of fact in an early document could easily be transposed to an earlier context by invoking the arguments of Custom and the Immemorial. Lacking the techniques and special skills for the correct dating of documents, the antiquaries tended to antedate their sources whenever they were in doubt.[1]

In short, the antiquaries were learned, they knew the value of records, and they sometimes searched for manuscripts with infatuated patience. In their eagerness to discover new facts about the past, however, these men neglected to make historical comparisons, and they sometimes retailed medieval errors as new-found truths. They were precedent-minded, not yet historical-minded scholars.

Modern historians have put forward three general explanations to account for the remarkable prosperity of antiquarian studies in Tudor and Stuart England. According to the first, the group research of the Society of Antiquaries was 'an expression of the new nationalism that produced *Britannia*, the history plays, and *The Faerie Queene*, and which made peculiarly English both the English Renaissance and the English Reformation'.[2] English antiquarianism in this view was based on 'the conviction that the burning issues which

---

[1] See Herbert Butterfield, *The Englishman and His History* (Cambridge, 1944), 34.

[2] Van Norden, 'College of Antiquaries', 359. Miss Van Norden calls attention to the three following references.

divided contemporary society would best be settled by means of an exhaustive examination of precedent'.[1] The second theory asserts that the antiquarian movement was a by-product of the English Reformation, which flourished through the period of religious controversy and then declined.[2] According to the third theory, the Anglo-Saxon studies of Parker, Lambarde, and later antiquaries developed in relation to 'two configurations of ideas which were to become important—the backward-looking nostalgic admiration for the medieval ... and the modern defence of England's own culture'.[3] In terms of this theory, many of the Society members stood with Bacon and the Moderns, not with the Ancients. The historical and 'Saxon' scholars in particular were associated with modern schools of thought in science and education.

Each of these explanations illuminates a different aspect of the historical significance of the Society of Antiquaries. The strong element of national patriotism in the discourses of the antiquaries disclosed a bias, and at the same time predicated a virtue. The bias of an incipient nationalism distorted, on the one hand, antiquarian perspectives and antiquarian awareness of historical processes; on the other hand, research in the public records was undoubtedly stimulated by patriotic pride in the English nation state.

The interest of the antiquaries in the origins of Christianity and in the history of the English Church owed something to Reformation controversies. The great works of church history written in the seventeenth century—Selden's *Tithes*, Spelman's *Concilia*, and Ussher's *Original of Bishops*, for example—were foreshadowed by the learning of the antiquaries. Finally, it may be said that the Society helped to make the study of history and antiquity a part of modern learning, analogous (in its stress on facts) to natural history and science.[4] The antiquaries were bent on the discovery of truth, and most of them would have agreed with Bacon, that 'Antiquity deserveth that reverence, that men should make a stand thereupon,

[1] David Douglas, 'The Development of English Medieval Scholarship', *Transactions of the Royal Historical Society*, 4th Series (XXI, 1939), 32.

[2] Eleanor N. Adams, *Old English Scholarship in England from 1566 to 1800* (New Haven, 1917), esp. p. 107.

[3] Rosamund Tuve, 'Ancients, Moderns and Saxons', *English Literary History* (VI, 1939), 177.

[4] See Van Norden, 'College of Antiquaries', 360.

and discover what is the best way, but when the discovery is well taken, then to make progression'.[1]

The limitations of the Society, the gradual decay of interest on the part of the members, and the increasing political tension of the time all pointed toward a dissolution. The Society had never enjoyed official recognition, and when it ceased to meet after 1607 no successor was named. Having performed its functions, the Society disappeared; it did not outlive its usefulness. A younger generation of scholars was coming to maturity—Selden's early work dates from about 1607—whose interests were less insular and whose learning was less narrowly antiquarian. A few of the older members of the Society, notably Spelman, led the secession from insular antiquarianism, and slowly established the study of medieval history on new foundations.

The revolutionary importance of Spelman's work on the feudal interpretation of English history was perceived by Maitland long ago, and recent scholarship has thoroughly vindicated Maitland's estimate of Spelman's importance.[2] Spelman's contribution to historiography was his definition of feudalism in terms of the continental *feudum* and his reinterpretation of the history of Parliament and English law in terms of the *feudum*. The essence of his discovery was an idea of explanation, or what he preferred to call a 'theoreme'.[3] Spelman arrived at his new interpretation by an act of creative historical imagination, which provided the fundamental hypothesis in terms of which separate pieces of evidence could be related and arranged. His achievement illustrates perfectly the importance of new ideas of explanation and relevance as opposed to the mere piling up of facts; and his methods were, indeed, analogous

[1] See *The Works of Francis Bacon*, ed. by James Spedding, Robert Leslie Ellis, and Douglas Denon Heath, 15 vols. (Boston, 1864 *et seq.*), VI, 129. All references to Bacon are to this edition, which differs in pagination from the London edition, published 1861–74.

[2] See F. W. Maitland, *The Constitutional History of England* (Cambridge, 1950), 142. Pocock, *Ancient Constitution and the Feudal Law* is, in some ways, a long commentary on the importance of Spelman's ideas of feudal history. A useful study is Jean S. Wilson, 'Sir Henry Spelman and the Royal Commission on Fees 1622–40', in J. Conway Davies, ed., *Essays Presented to Sir Hilary Jenkinson* (London, 1957), 456–70. The *Reliquae Spelmanianae*, to which reference will be made, is the title of the book containing Spelman's posthumous works, edited by Edward Gibson. It is bound as Part II of Spelman's *English Works* in the 1727 edition.

[3] Spelman, *Reliquae*, 61.

to some of the procedures in contemporary natural science.[1] Spelman had to absorb much continental learning, however, before he could assert the relevance of the *feudum* to the whole body of law as it existed in times past.

As an English antiquary Spelman had mastered certain techniques of dealing with documents, and had become aware of the need for further research, especially in linguistic history. As a historian he was able to formulate a theorem which would relate English law to a system of feudal law common to all the nations of the West; furthermore—since he had necessarily become engaged in the comparative study of historical jurisprudence—he was able to perceive the importance of historical contexts.

Spelman was one of the cluster of great early seventeenth-century scholars whose work helped to revolutionize the study of history. Along with Camden, Ussher, Cotton, Selden and others, Spelman was working toward a reappraisal of English historical scholarship in the light of classical and modern continental learning. The writings of the French legal humanists in particular provided Spelman and Selden with fresh viewpoints. The increasing exchange of information between English and continental scholars at this time no doubt also helped to remove the film of familiarity that obscured the defects of the common law interpretation of English history. The full impact of Spelman's historical thought was not felt until late in the seventeenth century; long before this, however, new ideas were beginning to influence the writing of legal history.

The axioms of the common law interpretation continued to be defended with stubborn and sometimes obtuse tenacity, but in the long run, Englishmen were to discover how much less arbitrary their old laws seemed when interpreted as expressions of feudalism. Moreover, the early seventeenth-century revolution in historiography was not confined to the study of legal history; other historical fields benefited from the cumulative advances which were being made in historical method. The immediate question is, how much influence did the antiquarian movement have in setting the pace of change?

Ever since the days of Parker and Nowell, the antiquarian concern with languages had been marked.[2] Anglo-Saxon studies were as necessary for the correct dating and interpretation of pre-Conquest

[1] See Pocock, *Ancient Constitution*, 103.

[2] See Robin Flower, 'Laurence Nowell and the Discovery of England in Tudor Times', *Gollancz Memorial Lecture, British Academy*, 1935. Also,

documents as Greek and Latin studies were for the correct understanding of classical texts. Grammar and etymology, and what was
coming to be known as philology, were important auxiliaries, re-
inforcing historical method. Nearly every antiquary of note was a
student of the history of one or more languages. When Sir Henry
Spelman realized that he could no longer continue his ecclesiastical
and legal studies without providing himself with a glossary of obsolete
medieval words he had reached a turning point in his career as a
scholar. His antiquarian interests led him to undertake a systematic,
comparative study of words: *Archaeologus* was the result. *Archaeologus* was something more than a dictionary compiled on historical
principles; it was a true dictionary of history, which elucidated not
only the medieval legal names of things, but also their historical
significance. By means of a philological inquiry into the names of
various rules, ranks, customs and the like, Spelman arrived at a new
understanding of medieval society.[1] It is hardly surprising that
another learned writer on the law, John Selden, should have observed
that 'the truth is, both it [i.e. the history of tithes] and not a few
other inquiries of subjects too much unknown, fall only under a
far more general study; that is, of true *Philology*, the only fit wife
that could be found for the most learned of the Gods'.[2]

In addition to fostering linguistic studies, the Society of Antiquaries established a tradition of group research and co-operation.
Spelman was indebted to many scholars, foreign as well as native,
and to record keepers for much of his material. The continuing
support of antiquarian and historical research by record keepers was
one of the lasting benefits conferred by the group research of the
Society of Antiquaries.

Camden, along with Spelman, had realized by about 1615 that the
crucial issue was no longer the antiquity of the law, but of Parliament, especially in relation to the Crown.[3] Camden investigated the

on Parker, see E. C. Pearce, 'Matthew Parker', *The Library*, 4th ser.
(VI, 1926), 209–28. Also S. W. Kershaw, 'Archbishop Parker, Collector
and Author', *The Library*, 2nd ser. (1900), 379–83. These are especially
useful articles on the collecting habits of Parker.

[1] An excellent short summary of the significance of *Archaeologus* may
be found in Pocock, *Ancient Constitution*, 94–5.

[2] John Selden, *The Historie of Tithes* (London, 1618), xix.

[3] On Camden, see Frank Smith Fussner, 'William Camden's "Discourse
Concerning the Prerogative of the Crown" ', *Proceedings of the American
Philosophical Society* (Vol. 101, no. 2, 1957), 204–15.

prerogative; Spelman inquired into the history of Parliament. Spelman's opening remarks in the essay 'Of Parliaments' reveal how far he had come in his own realization that contemporary opinion was unhistorical and wrong precisely because it failed to take account of historical process and the historical differences between ages:

> When States are departed from their original Constitution, and that original by tract of time worn out of memory; the succeeding Ages viewing what is past by the present, conceive the former to have been like to that they live in, and framing thereupon erroneous propositions, do likewise make thereon erroneous inferences and Conclusions. I would not pry too boldly into this ark of secrets, but having seen more Parliaments miscarry, yea suffer shipwreck, within these sixteen years past, than in many hundred heretofore, I desire for my understanding's sake to take a view of the beginning and nature of Parliaments; not meddling with them of our time (which may displease both Court and Country), but with those of old; which now are like the siege of *Troy*, matters only of story and discourse.[1]

Here, in short compass, is one of the clearest statements written by an Englishman in the seventeenth century of the principle of contextualism in history, and of the political relevance of antiquarian learning.

The *entente cordiale* between science and antiquarianism in the seventeenth century never developed into an alliance, yet it remained strong enough to discourage intellectual isolation. Many of the antiquaries saw nothing incompatible between their interest in human and natural history. Madox, writing in 1711, could refer to 'the Science of Antiquities' and assert that it 'hath in this last age been cultivated in England with more industry and success than in several ages before'.[2] That there were affinities between antiquarian and scientific learning in the sixteenth and seventeenth centuries can be established by examining the biographies of eminent antiquaries whose greatest reputations were earned in other fields, such as medicine, geography, astronomy, and mathematics.

Dr. John Dee was both an astronomer and an antiquary of con-

---

[1] Spelman, *Reliquae*, 57. The passage is also quoted by Pocock, who casts doubt on the date of composition (1640) as given by Linda Van Norden.

[2] Quoted by David C. Douglas, *English Scholars*, 1660–1730 (London, 1951), 271.

siderable note, whose proposal for founding a national library derived from his own interest in manuscript learning. He owned one of the finest scientific libraries in England—a fact which should refute the common idea that he was merely an astrologer.[1] Thomas Allen, mathematician and antiquary, also amassed a fine library, which he opened to John Selden. Sir Henry Savile, founder of the Savile professorships of geometry and astronomy at Oxford, was himself a distinguished classical scholar and antiquary. Thomas Harriot, Ralegh's friend, was a reputable mathematician, as well as a biblical chronologer. His first-hand account of Virginia appeared in Hakluyt's *Principall Navigations*. Sir Thomas Browne, physician and Baconian scientist, provided an early example of antiquarian archaeological research in his *Hydriotaphia* (1658). 'But we are coldly drawn into discourses of Antiquities,' he wrote, 'who have scarce time to contemplate new things, or make out learned Novelties.' [2]

After the Restoration, Elias Ashmole, Christopher Hatton, and John Aubrey were elected members of the Royal Society, in which Humphrey Wanley was later to become a considerable figure. Archaeology studied in a scientific spirit was perhaps the first antiquarian contribution to the Society's proceedings; in 1667 Sprat observed that the new method of retrieving the lost rarities of antiquity was 'by our labouring anew in the material Subjects whence they first arose [rather] than by our plodding everlastingly on the antiente Writings'.[3] The antiquaries, of course, continued to be record-minded and to work mainly with manuscripts, but the point is that they were not indifferent or hostile to the scientific thought of the age. And it was not surprising that early in the eighteenth century Roger Gale became the first vice-president of the revived Society of Antiquaries, as well as Treasurer of the Royal Society.[4]

Although Gresham College and the Royal College of Physician

---

[1] There is an excellent sympathetic account of John Dee in Francis R. Johnson, *Astronomical Thought in Renaissance England* (Baltimore, 1937), 136 ff.

[2] See *The Works of Sir Thomas Browne*, edited in six volumes by Geoffrey Keynes (London, 1928), IV, 4.

[3] Quoted by Joan Evans, *Society of Antiquaries*, 29.

[4] See D. Douglas, *English Scholars*, 175. Biographies of the founders of the Royal Society may be found in *The Royal Society, Its Origins and Founders*, Sir Harold Hartley, ed. (London, 1960).

and Surgeons contributed more to the tradition from which the Royal Society derived than did the Elizabethan Society of Antiquaries, it is nevertheless remarkable that some of the proposed sequels to the Antiquarian Society were conceived as academies of general learning. Prince Henry's proposed *Academe*, for example, would have investigated everything from heraldry to 'Practical Knowledge of Deeds and Evidences', including the principles and processes of the common law, knowledge of antiquities, husbandry, medicine, mathematics, architecture, fortifications, music, languages, etc.[1] The influence of his proposal was seen in the plans for Chelsea College (1610), and in Edmund Bolton's proposed *Academe* (1617).

The primary purpose of Chelsea College was to confute the errors of Rome. Although King James appointed Camden and Hayward as official historiographers, no money came to the College and hence nothing came of it as an institution. Bolton's elaborate plans for an *Academe Roial* were similarly frustrated, although Bolton continued to try to interest the Crown in his proposals until 1630. Bolton had deliberately attempted to revive the Society of Antiquaries, but with a Roman Catholic bias in the membership, and with the express intent of requiring the *Academe* to provide indexes 'expurgatory and expunctory upon all books of secular learning printed in English . . .' Bolton was not really interested in the disinterested pursuit of truth, but rather in cultivating 'moral learning', 'heroic virtues', and 'the sober desire for glory'.[2] His officious antiquarianism was tied to the rights of monarchy, and to an outworn concept of the courtier as humanist. Other antiquarian societies were founded in England before the Restoration, but except for the *Antiquas Rediviva* scheme of 1638 little is known about them.

ii THE IMPACT OF THE CIVIL WARS

In the history of political theory the English revolution marks a significant, clearly defined turning point; during the revolutionary decades 1640–60, English political thought became the most advanced in Europe. Historical politics received a profound shock when, on the anvils of war-time necessity, writers began to forge

---

[1] By far the best discussion of all these schemes is that by Linda Van Norden in 'College of Antiquaries', 440–87. The quotation is on pp. 479–480.

[2] *Ibid.*, 471, 475–6.

new intellectual weapons designed to win victories for a party. The doctrine of sovereignty, with its implicit appeal to reason rather than to history, was new and symptomatic—'in fact, once the public safety, or reason, or equity, or natural law or any abstract general principle had been accepted as an adequate excuse for what amounted to overriding or ignoring the historic legal powers of the monarchy, there was no limit to the ends for which it might be invoked'.[1]

This very fact, however, led to a renewed, and on the whole success-ful attempt to re-examine past politics with a view to explaining and justifying a variety of present positions. Consistency, in this context, was not to be expected. Both Prynne and Filmer, for example, used historical arguments with skill and effect, yet both men were pressing toward the logical conclusion of sovereignty, which threatened to make any historical argument irrelevant. Historical or antiquarian arguments, however, proved to have at least as strong an appeal as arguments based on logic or abstract general principles. Hence, in the course of the English revolution, royalists and parliamentarians returned again and again to the problems of history; and in the course of debate controversialists broadened the whole concept of historical politics.

One of the clearest statements of the historiographical issue which the civil wars precipitated was that given by Filmer in his *Patriarcha*, the unpublished major work from which most of his pamphlets derived. Custom, according to Filmer, was not a sufficient argument to justify the claims of Parliament. The common law doctrine of Custom and the Immemorial was attacked by Filmer at its weakest point:

> Now concerning customs, this must be considered, that for every custom there was a time when it was no custom, and the first prece-dent we now have had no precedent when it began. When every custom began, there was something else than custom that made it lawful, or else the beginning of all customs were unlawful. Cus-toms at first became lawful only by some superior power which did either command or consent unto their beginning.[2]

Filmer argued that kingly power, patriarchal and sovereign, was the source of those very rights and customs in terms of which the

[1] J. W. Gough, *Fundamental Law in English Constitutional History* (Oxford, 1955), 102.

[2] Sir Robert Filmer, *Patriarcha, and Other Political Works*, ed. by Peter Laslett (Oxford, 1949), 106–7.

Parliament was attempting to justify its assumption of sovereignty. Stated in this way, Filmer's appeal to inheritable rights was no less open to criticism than the doctrines of his opponents. The point, however, was that Filmer had turned the tables on those parliamentary writers who, like Prynne, were attempting to assert the sovereign power of Parliament on the basis of custom and precedent. Filmer denied the relevance of the doctrine of custom, and demanded historical proofs that Parliament had existed before the Norman Conquest. His methodological arguments were effective, especially since he was able to bring evidence and authority (including the authority of Selden) to bear on his contention that the Commons had not been regularly summoned by writ until the reign of Henry III.[1]

The example of Filmer may suggest why the problem of feudalism was to remain one of the central historical and antiquarian problems of the age. It was in terms of feudal tenures and feudal suzerainty that royalist writers were to make their case for political sovereignty; and even Hobbes, whose doctrine of sovereignty few royalists would accept, was able to employ historical arguments to show that the Commons had originated at a late date, and consequently by the King's sovereign will. To argue that every law must have had a particular maker, that the authority of law was not by custom but by command was 'to give every royalist a vested interest in historical research'.[2] Moreover, in Hobbes' case, lack of historical understanding did not prevent a considerable degree of critical insight into the problem of relating facts to rights. Hobbes denied that the monarch received his authority on condition, for, he wrote, 'Covenants being but words and breath, have no force to oblige, constrain, or protect any man but by what it has from the publique sword . . .'[3]

In his own way Hobbes read history backward with as easy a disregard for contexts as Coke, but Hobbes pinpointed some of the difficulties of the Parliamentarians' arguments from antiquity. It was one thing to verify a law or precedent, and another to establish by

---

[1] See 'The Freeholders Grand Inquest', in Laslett, ed., *Patriarcha*, 136–7.

[2] Pocock, *Ancient Constitution*, 163; and Chapters VI and VII. Hobbes' major historical tract was the *Behemoth*, or a history of the civil wars in England. See Francis Maseres, *Select Tracts Relating to the Civil Wars in England*, 2 vols. (London, 1815), II, 529–30, and *passim*. The standard edition of *Behemoth* is that of Tönnies. Hobbes wrote *An Historical Narration Concerning Heresy* (Academic Reprints No. 4, Stanford, 1954), which is also highly revealing.

[3] Hobbes, *Leviathan* (Modern Library ed.), 146–7.

what authority it was made. Hobbes insisted that all laws derived their authority from the command of the sovereign only. The Hobbesian doctrine of sovereignty was unhistorical, but Hobbes forecast many of the arguments which later royalists—including scholars who took advantage of Spelman's feudal learning—were to construct in the years between 1675 and 1688.

It would be no mere paradox to say that the English revolution of the seventeenth century did as much to create feudalism as to destroy it; the historical theory of feudalism was worked out in response to those acts of Parliamentary sovereignty which had destroyed the surviving elements of feudal law and custom in the constitution. To a great extent the new historiography, representing the culmination of the Spelmanist tradition, was discredited in 1688 along with the monarchical powers which it had attempted to defend. Even though Brady and others were able to anticipate many of the modern generalizations about feudalism, and were acutely aware of the importance of historical contexts, they failed to draw the final conclusion that medieval politics were irrelevant to modern politics, because the analogies were irrelevant. Or, as Mr. Pocock has put it:

> We might expect to hear admissions that if the main effect of the Norman Conquest had been to introduce a system based upon feudal tenures, then it could not directly determine the rights and liberties of Englishmen who no longer lived in such a system; and even, that if the authority of the monarch had once been primarily that of a feudal lord over his vassals, then this too was the case in England no longer, and that the prime duty of the historian was to discover by what means the monarchy had survived into the post-feudal age and on what foundations its authority now rested.[1]

Such admissions were not made by the learned Royalist adversaries of the Whig interpretation of history. Yet there can be no doubt that English historical and antiquarian scholarship reached maturity in the years between 1660 and 1730. The promise of the earlier antiquarian movement was abundantly fulfilled. The nature of that fulfilment has been studied in considerable detail and little need here be said about it.[2] A few comments will be in order, however, to point

---

[1] Pocock, *Ancient Constitution*, 210.

[2] Both Pocock, *Ancient Constitution*, and D. Douglas, *English Scholars*, deal with this subject in detail. For the following paragraphs I have relied heavily on the latter book.

up the relation between earlier trends and their fulfilment after the Restoration.

iii THE ROLE OF THE CHURCH AND THE UNIVERSITIES

Civil wars and revolution had stimulated all kinds of historical thought, from the anti-historical anti-Normanism of some of the Levellers, to the Machiavellian meditations of Harrington. When, at the Restoration, England returned to a royalist version of the ancient constitution, the historical and antiquarian debates were continued, but under conditions which were far more favourable to the growth of historical scholarship. The military defeat of the royalists had not been irrelevant, for it served to remind thoughtful men that force was not an argument that could be relied on; and the Restoration itself reanimated historical inquiry aimed at justifying royalist political theory.

In general, it may be said that the antiquarian movement reached fulfilment by proceeding from antiquity to history, that is, by moving from the study of medieval precedents to the re-creation of the historical world of medieval feudalism. Sir William Dugdale, more than any other individual, was the link between the old antiquarianism and the new; his influence was enormous, and his labours served as a starting point for a new generation of great medievalists.

The institutional changes that most notably affected historical scholarship after the Restoration may be summarized in terms of the different roles played by the Universities, the Church, the Inns of Court, and by the Royal Society—the institution that symbolized the new age.

The Universities after the Restoration became centres of historical and linguistic scholarship. Many of the great Anglo-Saxonists held University appointments, and the study of old English antiquities was sustained and enhanced by such academic scholars as Thomas Gale, John Smith, Francis Junius, George Hickes, and Edward Thwaites. The University presses also were publishing all kinds of scholarly editions of medieval chronicles, as well as dictionaries, and other aids to research. Before the Restoration the Universities had played only a minor role in fostering medieval studies. Oxford and Cambridge now became centres of antiquarian research, owing largely to the influence of churchmen.

The Laudian ambition to provide a learned ministry was to a

large extent realized in the decades between 1660 and 1730. Whereas the Church had earlier provided a livelihood for relatively few scholars, the Church after the Restoration set about the official encouragement and patronage of historical and antiquarian learning. Many, if not most of the great books of late seventeenth-century medieval scholarship were written by churchmen; and men in holy orders devoted themselves as never before to the encouragement of secular studies. William Nicolson and Edmund Gibson, both of whom rose to high positions in the Church of England, were passionate students of Anglo-Saxon antiquities who used their influence to promote such studies within the Church. In most fields of learning there were influential churchmen who devoted themselves to furthering research and publication.

It was perhaps fortunate that the Church became, so to speak, a surrogate 'third university', for the Inns of Court were at this time in decline, and they ceased to be teaching institutions before the end of the century. There is perhaps a significant correlation between the decline of the Inns of Court and the re-evaluation of the feudal past by clerical scholars who were in no sense committed to the legal myths of Custom and the Immemorial.

The Royal Society was a symbol of change in more than one sense. On the one hand, it was dedicated to the scientific investigation of nature, and was indifferent to theological questions; on the other hand, scientific investigation represented a challenge to many of the traditional concepts of Christianity. There was bound to be a good deal of questioning and soul-searching about the extent of determinism in the natural order. The scientists of the Royal Society were themselves emphatically Christian; and Robert Boyle even employed the term *The Christian Virtuoso* (i.e. scientist) as the title of one of his books. Nevertheless, in spite of the fact that clergymen were almost as numerous as physicians among the members of the Royal Society, an important minority of Christians saw in the work of the *virtuosi* a threat to their religion. The truths of natural science were arrived at by methods which, if applied to the truths of revelation, would call them all in doubt. In the late seventeenth century Christianity was shaken to its very foundations by the impact of natural science.[1]

The problem of continuity and change is nowhere more evidently

[1] See Richard S. Westfall, *Science and Religion in Seventeenth Century England* (New Haven, 1958), 10, and Chapter I, *passim*.

complex than in the relations between science, religion and the social environment. It is quite true that the scientific movement had behind it a long history before the Restoration, and that the Royal Society was itself more a symptom than a cause of change. Yet as an institution it had no real counterpart in the earlier seventeenth century. In stressing the changes that took place after 1660, no historian would wish to imply that they were unprecedented. Conversely, the continuities which are observable, especially in the institutional arrangements of science and scholarship, did not develop without change.

Earlier trends, interrupted by civil war and revolution, continued after 1660 and reached fulfilment before 1730. To discuss these trends in terms of historical continuity is not to imply a static interpretation of seventeenth-century history and historiography; it is merely to insist that fulfilment depended on the continuing efforts and interests of influential classes and groups of individuals, as well as on the continuing vitality of certain institutions and customs.

The custom of patronage affords an obvious example: historical scholarship after the Restoration was supported by the continuing patronage of the nobility, the gentry, and (to a far greater degree than earlier) the Church.[1] The gentry's interest in local history and antiquities continued without abatement into the eighteenth century. Although heraldic studies tended to decline in the latter part of the seventeenth century, there was no lack of support for, and interest in, record learning; both Madox and Rymer filled the office of Historiographer Royal, and found support for their publications. And the continuity of the antiquarian tradition in the field of politics was not finally broken until after the revolution of 1688.

The tradition of historical politics reached maturity in the years between 1660 and the revolution of 1688. The Brady controversy, which began in 1675, resulted in one of the most significant contributions to the feudal interpretation of medieval history made in the seventeenth century. Brady's royalist convictions animated most of his writing, and politics were the occasion for his decision to devote himself to the study of history. The tithes controversy of the

[1] The literary patronage of the earlier seventeenth century is discussed by Phillip Sheavyn, 'Patrons and Professional Writers Under Elizabeth and James I', *The Library*, 2nd ser. (VII, 1906), 301–36. The best modern survey is Edwin Haviland Miller, *The Professional Writer in Elizabethan England* (Cambridge, Mass., 1959), with chapters on patronage, censorship, etc. D. Douglas, *English Scholars*, discusses the later period and is especially useful on the role of the Church.

early seventeenth century is perhaps the closest parallel, in terms of political interest, and in the quality of the resultant scholarship. It was only after 1688 that historical politics declined, and antiquarian arguments were discredited. Even so, there was no sudden break, for the revolution had made non-jurors of some of the best polemical scholars of the day.

The antiquarian tradition of co-operation in research continued throughout the century.[1] The great *Thesaurus*, or 'Treasury of the Northern Tongues', of George Hickes was but one example of a treatise which manifested the collaboration of many learned men. The spirit of scholarly co-operation, for which the earlier antiquaries of Cotton's and Spelman's generation were noted, triumphed in the long run over political and religious bias. There was perhaps a greater degree of specialization apparent after the Restoration, but more and more English scholars were, in spite of their earnest controversies, prepared to recognize a community of learning beyond politics. The later career of George Hickes, a proscribed non-juror after 1690, was smoothed by the efforts of Whig prelates like White Kennet, Edmund Gibson, and William Nicolson, who looked to Hickes as a leader in scholarship, and as a man to be respected for his intellectual and moral integrity. Nicolson, in his *English Historical Library*, did not hesitate to refer to Hickes as the 'greatest Master of his Subject that hath ever yet appeared in Print'.[2]

iv THE HERITAGE OF ANTIQUARIANISM

To assess properly the contribution of the antiquarian movement to historical scholarship the foregoing changes and continuities must be taken into account. There was no slackening of scholarly effort, and no loss of interest in the problems of antiquity; rather, there was a noticeable increase in both the private and the institutional patronage of learning. Moreover, each of the revolutionary crises of the seventeenth century intensified the dialectic between politics,

[1] Perhaps the most obvious and important example of co-operative scholarship in the seventeenth century was the making of the King James Bible. This was not, of course, strictly speaking, an antiquarian or historical undertaking, yet many eminent scholars collaborated on the work. A recent popular account is Gustavus S. Paine, *The Learned Men* (New York, 1959).

[2] Quoted by Douglas, *English Scholars*, 95.

religion and scholarship. As long as the consequences of the Reformation and the counter-Reformation continued to affect the world of learning, antiquarianism tended to display a polemical purpose. At the same time, historical politics continued to attract the attention of many of the best antiquaries. The difference between the early and the later Stuart antiquaries in this respect was that, after the Restoration, there were fewer antiquaries who, like Cotton, put their knowledge of precedents to use in Parliament, and more who, like Brady, fought from their academic studies.

In the course of the seventeenth century the conventional distinction between the antiquary and the historian tended to disappear, or, rather, to be disregarded by men who thought of themselves primarily as scholars. The problems of feudalism and of the nature of the ancient constitution had been raised at an early date, and these problems continued to occupy scholarly minds throughout the seventeenth century in England. The 'Norman yoke' became a subject for angry dispute not only among scholars, but even among unlettered Levellers.[1] Gradually, and almost unconsciously, antiquaries became historians. Antiquities came to be defined as simply the stuff or raw material of history. When the modern Society of Antiquaries was founded in 1707, the members agreed that the study of antiquities served to introduce and illustrate history:

Friday 12 December 1707

Agreed that the Business of this Society shall be limited to the subject of Antiquities; and more particularly, to such things as may Illustrate and Relate to the History of Great Britain.

Agreed that by the subject of Antiquities and History of Great Britain, we understand only such things as shall preceed the Raign of James the first King of England. Provided, that upon any new Discovery of Antient Coins, books, sepulchres or other Remains of Antient Workmanship, which may be communicated to us, we reserve to ourselves Liberty of Conferring upon them . . .[2]

In short, the antiquaries were to be distinguished by their concern with early English history, its illustrations and remains.

In their discourses the Elizabethan antiquaries had eschewed narrative description and interpretation, concentrating instead on

[1] See Christopher Hill, *Puritanism and Revolution* (London, 1958), 'The Norman Yoke', pp. 50–122.
[2] Quoted by Joan Evans, *Society of Antiquaries*, 36.

precedents and facts. The career of Sir Henry Spelman illustrated the transition from the study of antiquities in isolation to the study and interpretation of the historical context of English feudalism. The conventional distinction between research and interpretation continued to be made, however, largely on the basis of the difference between antiquarian collecting habits, and historical ideas of explanation. Thomas Madox implied this distinction in the title of one of his best-known books: *The History and Antiquities of the Exchequer of the Kings of England* (1711). Individual scholars might equally well be called antiquaries or historians, for the words were used almost interchangeably. It is evident, however, that the antiquarian stylistic habits of the medievalists warped the presentation, and sometimes even the understanding of medieval history.

The stylistic heritage of the antiquarian movement was an extreme emphasis on documentation at the expense of literary style. Few of the great seventeenth-century medievalists were notable stylists; they organized their works largely with a view to presenting evidence, rather than with a view to presenting a narrative with interpretation. Brady's *Complete History of England* (1685) illustrates this point, for the bulk of his stout folio was taken up with conflations of medieval chronicles to which were added transcripts from the Tower records; Brady introduced all of his significant historical arguments in a series of ill-written essays or prefaces. As a method of organization, this left much to be desired; and such antiquarian indifference to stylistic proprieties doubtless had something to do with the decline of medieval studies after about 1730.

The positive contribution of the antiquarian movement to historical writing and thought was most apparent in the area of method. Antiquaries took the lead in developing all those techniques and special skills without which medieval studies could not have progressed. Moreover, the modern idea of historical proof descended directly from the austere 'record' standards of the early antiquaries.[1]

Methodological refinements of all kinds were gradually made in the course of the seventeenth century. Progress was most evident in such matters as the careful collation of manuscripts to establish definitive texts; in the use of diplomatics (Madox applied Mabillon's work to excellent effect in his *Formulare Anglicanum* (1702)—a collection of superbly edited charters); and in comparative historical studies, especially those based on the meticulous collation of medieval

[1] See D. Douglas, *English Scholars*, 125-6, quoting Dr. Brady.

chronicles with medieval public records. In some cases, the standards of textual criticism and analysis attained in the late seventeenth and early eighteenth centuries have only recently been equalled or surpassed.

Finally, it must be said that the feudal reinterpretation of English history, begun by Sir Henry Spelman, constituted by itself a revolution in English historiography. Spelman's 'theorem' or idea of explanation was developed by his successors until it became one of the great categories of interpretation in medieval studies; modern scholarship has modified but never rejected the Spelmanist tradition. The scientific editing of texts, the elaboration of scholarly research methods, and the application of the feudal idea of explanation to English history, are the three most significant legacies of the antiquarian movement. It has been pointed out that these achievements were not owing to the unaided efforts of antiquaries alone, but that they were collaborative achievements which do honour to many scholars in many fields. Historians and linguists, librarians and antiquaries, politicians and patrons, all, in fact, shared in building the towers of learning. The interplay between politics, patronage, and scholarship provides the theme for the following chapter on the influence of Sir Robert Cotton. The details of his career as scholar, librarian, and politician will help to furnish the bare corridors of the foregoing argument.

5

POLITICS, PATRONAGE, AND SCHOLARSHIP: THE INFLUENCE OF SIR ROBERT COTTON

'TO SUBSIST IN LASTING MONUMENTS, to live in their productions, to exist in their names . . .' may, as Sir Thomas Browne observed, 'be nothing in the metaphysics of true belief'.[1] Yet few seventeenth-century writers and men of substance scorned posterity, or failed to erect monuments which tell something of their true beliefs. Sir Robert Cotton's monument was his library, and Cotton's name has been inked by the pens of scholars for over three hundred years. To the lawyers, historians, churchmen, and librarians of the seventeenth century Cotton's manuscripts and his library were even more important than the Cottonian collection in the British Museum is to present-day searchers of the past. Perhaps familiarity has bred neglect, for Sir Robert Cotton remains an enigmatic figure, about whom relatively little is known, even by a posterity which is still greatly in his debt. Yet no man in his time did more to further humanistic scholarship in England than Cotton. The fact that Cotton was an assiduous collector of manuscripts, a purveyor of historical precedents, and an eminent intellectual in politics, might be reason enough to renew his acquaintance; his career will, however, repay study for other reasons as well.

In England's first great age of historical politics it was Cotton's influence and patronage that helped strike a balance between the

---

[1] Sir Thomas Browne, *Hydriotaphia, Works*, IV, 50.

117

study of history as record and the use of history as a weapon. If Cotton's contribution to English politics and historiography had to be summed up in one word, that word would be 'influence'. What gives Cotton a clear title to his fame is not so much what he wrote, but what he did for others who wrote and spoke on both the scholarly and the political issues of the times. Influence was, of course, a means of getting things done in an age when clientage was an approved social and political custom. The relation between patron and client is fundamental for an understanding of early Stuart England, and this relation now depended on influence, not on feudal status. The essence of the relationship in its political aspect, as David Mathew has pointed out, was that both the patron and the client should serve the State.[1] Cotton served the State, but his career is particularly interesting because he combined the Renaissance patronage of letters with the political and bureaucratic patronage and clientage that was to characterize English society until the coming of the great age of reform in the nineteenth century.

Cotton lent books and manuscripts in the way that most men lend money—with the expectation of a return. Cotton's return, or interest, took the form of political privileges. He could expect to be consulted on many important matters, even though he did not hold high office. By administering his library as though it were a source of 'capital' to be invested, Cotton was able to exert political influence on a wide segment of the educated and politically active leaders of the nation. At the same time Cotton stood for sound scholarship, and willingly acted as patron and protector of men of learning.

It has been said that Parliament and the first two Stuart kings engaged in something like a long lawsuit. Into this suit Cotton entered directly, as a servant of the Crown and as a member of Parliament. And (it was characteristic of him) he took part indirectly, as the authority on precedents whose library became the arsenal of the Parliamentary opposition. Cotton himself became many things to

[1] See David Mathew, *The Social Structure of Caroline England* (Oxford, 1948), 4. The system of political patronage has been studied in detail by Sir John Neale. See especially, J. E. Neale, *The Elizabethan House of Commons* (New Haven, 1950), 193–245. There is an excellent study of 'Place and Patronage in Elizabethan Politics', by Wallace MacCaffrey in *Elizabethan Government and Society, Essays Presented to Sir John Neale* (London, 1961), 95–126. The importance of influence is discussed on pp. 112 ff.

many different men: both patron and client, politician and antiquary, a fighter and a forger in the wars of truth. His career embraced both history and politics; it must first be examined in its broad outlines if we are to understand Cotton's unique position and power.

John Selden, writing in 1618, paid handsome tribute to Cotton's contemporary role:

> For, as on the one side, it cannot be doubted but that the too studious Affectation of bare and sterile Antiquity, which is nothing else but to be exceeding busie about nothing, may soon descend to a Dotage; so on the other, the Neglect or only vulgar regard of the fruitfull and precious part of it, which gives necessarie light to the *Present* in matter of *State, Law, History,* and the *Understanding of Good Autors,* is but preferring that kind of Ignorant Infancy, which our short life alone allows us, before the many ages of former Experience and Observation, which may so accumulat years to us as if we had livd even from the beginning of Time. But you [i.e. Cotton] best know this; in whom that usefull part is so fully eminent, that the most learned through *Europe* willing acknowledge it.[1]

Matters of state, law, history, and the understanding of good authors: these were Cotton's main interests.

i COTTON'S POLITICAL CAREER

A great library is an invitation to scholars, and Sir Robert Cotton's library became a central gathering point for educated men. Sir Robert moved in the society of courtiers, scholars, churchmen, lawyers, and government officials. A staunch friend of many English Catholics, he remained a moderate protestant who may even have been something of a sceptic. That he was courteous, charming, and sometimes unscrupulous is clear from his behaviour and his correspondence. With the antiquary's passion for manuscripts, he combined the politician's interest in men, and a lawyer's love of information. He became one of England's greatest librarians and most learned baronets; and also, perhaps, the most distinguished forger of the Stuart century. His influence extended beyond that of a private individual: Cotton was almost as much of a national institution as

---

[1] John Selden, *Historie of Tithes*, 'To the Most Honord Sr Robert Cotton', Sig. A2 and A2v.

his library. And, from the point of view of his later political career, even his genealogy suggests the man fortunate in his inheritance.

Robert Cotton was born in 1571 at Denton, near the family seat of Connington Castle in Huntingdonshire. The Cottons were probably typical of the country gentry who had speculated, profited, and prospered from the land sales following the dissolution of the monasteries. Sir Robert's great grandmother, Mary de Wesenham, was the rich heiress whose estates formed the core of the Cotton family fortune. Through her, Sir Robert could claim descent from the Scottish kings, for she was the grand-daughter of Sir John de Brus whose name supplied Cotton with the justification or pretext for styling himself 'Sir Robert Cotton, Bruceus'.[1] In an age when heraldry often abetted ancestry, and descent might aid ability, Cotton did not find it too difficult to make the most of his claim. When he was knighted by King James in 1603, he was able to call attention to his kinship with the King by including the name of Bruce; and thereafter the King, perhaps in jest, often referred to him as 'cousin'. It was a good beginning for his career as a courtier.

Cotton's early education at Westminster School under the guidance of William Camden, the historian, provided an even better beginning for his career as a scholar. The student shared fully the interests and enthusiasm of the master, and the two men remained close friends until Camden's death. It was probably during the year of the Armada that Cotton began collecting books and manuscripts for a library. He attended Jesus College for a time, and after his marriage he settled in London where he seems to have moved as early as 1586. During the 1590's he was actively engaged in collecting manuscripts and taking part in meetings of the Society of Antiquaries. In fact, meetings of the Society were sometimes held in Cotton's house which, as Mr. C. E. Wright has pointed out, was strategically located next door to the Rolls House.[2] A stairway led down from Cotton's garden to the river, where Cotton could find ready transportation to the record repositories in the Tower. By about 1600, when he

[1] B.M. Harley MS. 807, f. 95. Pedigree of Cotton family. The *D.N.B.* article on Cotton must be supplemented; the best essay is by C. E. Wright (already cited) in *The English Library*.

[2] C. E. Wright, *The English Library*, 195. There are minor points of biographical detail touched on in various issues of *Notes and Queries*; see esp. 3rd ser. vi, 449–451 and 6th ser. vi, 533. *The Calendars of State Papers, Domestic* for the years 1601 to 1631 contain valuable information which I have also used, but without citing every reference.

accompanied Camden on an extensive antiquarian tour to Carlisle, Cotton had met and befriended a large circle of scholars, record keepers, lawyers, and churchmen. His library was becoming famous, and Cotton himself had earned a reputation as an antiquary and patron of learning.

In 1600 he was appointed to serve on a royal commission, and he continued to serve on various special commissions until the end of his life. Even when in disgrace at Court his expert knowledge was respected. He was never, as it has sometimes been asserted, a retiring scholar who was lured away 'from the abstract study of ancient precedents to their application to contemporary affairs, from the peaceful retreat of the scholar to the turbulent publicity of the statesman'.[1] Cotton was a man who went into politics with his eyes wide open. He had his mother's ambitious pride of family, and he was convinced that historical knowledge was for use, that it befitted the port and dignity of a gentleman to further his career by scholarship.

Cotton became an expert in historical precedents, with an expert's enthusiasm, ambition, and self-confidence. In part, his scholarly confidence betrayed him in his career as a courtier. His disgrace at Court was, of course, more directly traceable to the mistakes he made in handling the affairs of his patron, the indiscreet and difficult Earl of Somerset, when that royal favourite fell from grace and was prosecuted for the murder of Sir Thomas Overbury. Cotton's behaviour, during the critical months preceding the trial, can perhaps best be described as the folly of a naïvely confident man. There is no reason to suppose that Cotton deliberately acted as an accessory after the fact in order to further his own political career. All the evidence points to the theory that Cotton forged the dates on Somerset's letters in an effort to protect a patron whom he believed to be innocent. Cotton failed, it is true, to realize what kind of man Somerset was, failed in his efforts to protect him, and failed to realize how dangerous the game was that he played. Nevertheless, an analysis of Cotton's mistakes can be as instructive as the analysis of his successes; and, in the case of Cotton's relations with Somerset, the analysis provides the clue to the nature of Cotton's political role.

---

[1] See Henry Charles Shelley, *The British Museum its History and Treasures* (Boston, 1921), 17. Edward Edwards, *Libraries and Founders*, although out of date in certain respects, is a far more reliable account, containing useful information on Cotton's political career.

Although the evidence does not permit a final judgment, it does suffice to show that Cotton was no mere sycophant. The main facts about Cotton's relations with Somerset are clear enough: Cotton had agreed to act as agent or intermediary for Somerset in the dangerous secret negotiations concerning the Spanish match; he was instrumental in advising Somerset to seek the King's pardon under the Great Seal; and he helped Somerset to destroy, conceal, and forge the dates on some letters which might be regarded as incriminating if Somerset were ever brought to trial for the murder of Overbury. Each of these acts may be regarded as a political mistake, and each may be interpreted as damning evidence of Cotton's naïveté. None of them, however, proves that Cotton betrayed valuable information to Spain, that he changed his religion, or that he planned to seek power for himself by helping to conceal the guilt of a royal favourite.[1]

Cotton was in his early forties when he became involved in the affairs of Somerset; he had had little direct experience with the treacherous currents that swirled about the island court. His respect for precedent, for order and degree, and his own generosity, had ill prepared him to act with the cynical resolution of the Howards, who could so deftly disengage themselves from a falling favourite. He trusted Somerset, and he trusted the King; he was not suspicious by nature. He was, of course, ambitious, and loved the influence he had already acquired among the scholars and government officials of the day. What he was forced to learn from the events of 1615 was that, in politics, influence keeps few friends and provokes many enemies.

The suspense of 1615, culminating in his own arrest on December 29, marked a turning point in his political career. Until then, he had, like many moderates, supported the Crown. He had not criticized the new wine that the King was fermenting in the old constitutional bottles. After 1615, he moved gradually, as Coke and others did, toward opposition. He did not support the Parliamentary opposition in 1625 because he had failed as a courtier in 1615. Rather, he took his stand, as many of his generation did, on the 'ancient constitution' as he understood it. A closer examination of Cotton's actions in 1615

---

[1] This was essentially S. R. Gardiner's view of Cotton, based largely on a reading of Sarmiento's papers. See Samuel R. Gardiner, *History of England from the Accession of James I to the Outbreak of the Civil War* (London, 1883–4), II, 326–7, and *passim*. In general, however, Gardiner's account is factually accurate.

may serve to indicate that his psychological attitudes were at least consistent, and that it was not Cotton so much as the times that changed.

According to S. R. Gardiner, 'Sarmiento was, about the middle of April [1615], surprised by a visit from Sir Robert Cotton, the antiquary'. As Gardiner tells the story, Cotton told the ambassador that he was sent by the King and Somerset, who both wished to see the negotiations for the Spanish match in other hands than those of Digby, the English ambassador at Madrid. Using as his evidence the diplomatic dispatches of Sarmiento (i.e. Gondomar) to Philip III among the Simancas MSS., Gardiner states that Cotton not only acted as agent for James and Somerset (who had urged the pro-Spanish policy), but that Cotton was, as Gondomar wrote, 'mad with delight at having been the channel of such a communication . . .' 'The man who was to be the friend of Eliot and Selden,' Gardiner concludes, 'now assured the Spanish ambassador that he was a catholic at heart, and that he could not understand how a man of sense could be anything else.' [1]

To accept the Spanish ambassador's account of the affair, as Gardiner did, is, of course, to assume that Cotton lied during his examination about his own part in these negotiations. The inference to be drawn from Gardiner's account is that Cotton changed his politics, and probably his religion between 1615 and 1625. This is much too simple a view, even if there were no reason to doubt the accuracy of Gondomar's statements. The Spanish ambassador, however, was a man to whom the wish was often father to the thought.

Whether Cotton was approached by Gondomar, as Cotton himself maintained, or whether the initiative was taken by Somerset, who, according to Gondomar, sent Cotton to the ambassador, is a question which cannot now be definitely settled. The important point is that Cotton acted simply as agent or intermediary. Although he undoubtedly enjoyed this important role and looked forward to suitable rewards, he nevertheless did not aspire to become a policy maker. The control of foreign affairs was still clearly within the King's prerogative. Digby, the ambassador, undertook to carry out a policy of which he disapproved; Cotton, the agent of Somerset and of the King, acted in the same spirit, although he may have been more

[1] Samuel R. Gardiner, *History of England* . . ., II, 326–7. See also S. R. Gardiner, editor and translator, *Narrative of the Spanish Marriage Treaty* (Camden Society, 1869), 295, and *passim*.

sanguine than Digby about the benefits of a Spanish match. Cotton's duty (if he ever thought about it in constitutional terms) was to carry out instructions as smoothly as possible.

Gondomar expressed surprise that Cotton was so sympathetic to Catholicism; he had heard that Cotton was 'accounted a puritan'. Had Gondomar known more about Cotton he would have realized that he was dealing with an urbane and tolerant man who had for years been on good terms with leading Catholic families. Gondomar was even under the impression that Cotton was 'in charge of the King's archives', a pardonable mistake, perhaps, but one which illustrates the danger of accepting Gondomar's statements about Cotton.[1] Flattery and compromise were arts which the antiquary understood as well as the ambassador. The great mistake Cotton made was in thinking that he could serve his patron and his king without danger to himself.

There is no reason to doubt that Cotton thought of himself as a loyal subject who would serve the Crown in whatever capacity he was called upon, be it in Parliament, on Navy commissions, or as secret negotiator. He had no cause to doubt that Somerset was acting with the King's knowledge and support, although a more suspicious man might well have taken warning from the fact that by July 1615 Somerset had become so worried about attacks by his enemies at Court that he had sought Cotton's advice and acted on it by seeking a formal pardon under the Great Seal, which would have saved him from legal prosecution for past offences.[2] The pardon was prepared, but Ellesmere refused to sign it, and so matters stood in September, when the Lieutenant of the Tower, Sir Gervase Helwys, confessed that he had known of attempts to poison Sir Thomas Overbury. This revelation precipitated the final crisis that brought about Somerset's ruin, and almost ended Cotton's career.

The best thing that can be said of Cotton's behaviour at this critical time is that he showed his loyalty most foolishly. He tried to help the almost hysterical earl by altering the dates on some of his letters and helping to destroy others. Cotton's role in all this is

[1] See Gardiner, *History*, II, 346–7.

[2] See D. Harris Willson, *King James VI and I* (London 1956), 352. A good account of the Overbury affair is William McElwee, *The Murder of Sir Thomas Overbury* (London, 1952), which deals with Cotton's role, pp. 171–3, 181–3, 194, 229, 252. See also S. R. Gardiner, 'Account of the Affair of the Earl of Somerset', *Archaeologia*, XLI.

understandable, however, and somewhat less reprehensible than it might seem to a modern lawyer. In the first place, Cotton believed that Somerset was innocent of murder—as he probably was; furthermore, Cotton knew enough history and law to realize that in great state trials it was usually necessary for the defendants to establish innocence, not for the state to prove guilt. Rules of evidence were not yet in customary use, and the temptation to alter evidence or to lie was correspondingly great. What Cotton did was to put his historical training to misuse, in order to protect a man who had already fallen from favour. Somerset, of course, did not merit Cotton's singular steadfastness. Perhaps it might be said that Cotton was more generous than wise; at least he did not display the kind of weakness that made so many 'judicious' decisions easy.

In any case, Cotton's role in the whole affair was primarily that of agent and adviser—the same role he was to play later as a member of the Parliamentary opposition. Cotton was examined by Privy Councillors on the King's orders late in October of 1615. He was fortunate in having once enjoyed the King's favour, and in the fact that no confession could be obtained from Somerset. Having presumably satisfied the Councillors that he had not been implicated in any serious crime, Cotton was finally granted a pardon in July of 1616 and set at liberty.[1] The whole episode, including Somerset's trial, may have taught Cotton to distrust the inconstant favouritism that prevailed at Court. Cotton could not admit that he had been mistaken about Somerset, and he continued to defend his old patron long after Somerset was a forgotten prisoner in the Tower.

It seems probable that Cotton chose to think that both client and patron had faithfully served the state. Yet Cotton must have been shocked by his experiences in 1615. Perhaps he discussed matters with Camden and began to think more seriously about the nature and use of the King's prerogative; perhaps his own embarrassment made him look more than ever to history and precedent as the only trustworthy guides in politics. In any case, he gradually began to draw closer to Selden, Coke, Eliot—the men who were to defend with such stubborn erudition the privileges of Parliament and the subjects' rights. Such men were no more extremists than Cotton was; all believed that they served the true interests of the King and the state.

[1] *C.S.P. Dom.*, 1611–18, Vol. LXXXVII, 373; also Vol. LXXXVIII, 382.

During the critical years of the 1620's, Cotton began to serve the Parliamentary opposition in the capacity of adviser, agent, and adjutant—roles obviously quite similar to those he had played before 1615. Yet Cotton was far better qualified to do research and to write than he was to act as a courtier or secret negotiator. Cotton found his true political vocation in the 1620's. Precedents for Parliamentary speakers came readily from Cotton's library; it was he who drafted the outline of Sir John Eliot's great speech against Buckingham—a speech which, although not delivered by Eliot in the Parliament of 1625, was circulated in manuscript; and Cotton served as adviser, friend, and colleague of the outstanding Parliamentary leaders.[1] At the same time he continued to serve the Crown in various official capacities. He was appointed to the Committee of Inquiry to investigate Chief Justice Coke's affairs in 1621, and was often consulted by Crown officials.

The pattern that emerges from these various activities is significant. Cotton was taking an active part in Parliamentary politics, and at the same time he was behaving almost like a professional civil servant. If he made his learning serve his liberalism in politics, he nevertheless continued to serve the government with expert testimony and impartial advice. He must surely have impressed those who knew him well as a conscientious scholar, who respected evidence and who was not the slave of other men's opinions. To maintain such a reputation would require tact and a high degree of administrative skill in handling his library. The clue to Cotton's character, and ultimately to the nature of his influence, is to be found in the use he made of his library.

Cotton had early become famous for his knowledge of precedents, and for the courtesy he showed to all who sought his help or advice. The unique position he held in early Stuart England depended in part on his ability to influence Tom without alienating Dick or Harry. This does not mean that he lacked political principle, but simply that continued free access to his own library depended on his being fair and impartial in the administration of it. His library was closed on two occasions. First, during the early part of 1616, when he was in disgrace, and again in 1629 owing to the King's anger over Cotton's part in the Parliamentary opposition. The facts suggest that Cotton's library, like some modern corporations or

[1] See Harold Hulme, *The Life of Sir John Eliot* (New York, 1957), 92, 92n., 139n., and *passim*.

foundations, had come to be regarded as a semi-public trust. To abuse the trust would be to invite the anger of the Crown, or, alternatively, the contempt of the learned world. Cotton was able to further the cause of scholarship precisely because he knew how to administer his library professionally; he understood the value of protocol, and enhanced his reputation as a benefactor by purveying historical information to Crown, Parliament, and Community. The network of his influence he kept in good repair, and nearly always put to worthwhile uses.

ii THE LIBRARY AND COTTON'S PATRONAGE OF LEARNING

Cotton seldom let slip an opportunity to extend the number of his acquaintances. Consequently, it is not an easy task to divide his friends, patrons, clients, and acquaintances into a few meaningful categories. As librarian, politician, and man of letters he acquired a reputation among the following social groups: (*a*) the Court, officers of state, and Parliament men, (*b*) the legal profession, (*c*) the Church and the Universities, (*d*) the royal officials, and (*e*) the scholars, historians, and others whom Cotton knew and whose work owed something to Cotton's help. Obviously, there was considerable over-lapping—most of the churchmen Cotton befriended were scholars, for example, and many of the Parliament men were also lawyers or bureaucrats. Yet what is significant is the range of Cotton's acquaintance; he could be said to have sampled accurately the political and intellectual classes of the nation.

More than one hundred names of Cotton's English friends and acquaintances can be readily identified.[1] Of these, most were important enough to find a place in the *Dictionary of National Biography*, or their activities can be traced easily in other works. A full-scale study of Cotton would undoubtedly bring to light further evidence of his influence on scholars, political leaders, government officials and others who ruled and represented Stuart England.

(*a*) The Court, Officers of State, and Parliament Men

Until James came to the throne in 1603, Cotton probably had no direct communication with the sovereign. Possibly it was through

---

[1] A list can easily be compiled on the basis of Cotton's correspondence (especially the letters in B.M. Cotton MS., Julius Caesar III) and on the basis of Cotton's catalogue loan list (B.M. Harley MS. 6018).

Camden, who had enjoyed Lord Burghley's patronage, that Cotton was first brought to the attention of James and the Court circle. In any case, Cotton began early to cultivate the Howards, and their patronage could easily account for his first access to Court favour. In 1603 Cotton drew up a discourse showing the descent of James from the Saxon kings. Clearly, it was an effort at flattery which might easily have pleased the King. By 1608, Cotton was presumably well known at Court, for he was appointed to serve on, and to present the report of the Commission of Inquiry into abuses in the Navy. His service on the Navy Inquiry Commissions was to continue, and his name appears again on a list as late as 1626—long after he had gone over to the opposition. That Cotton was the prime mover behind the scheme to create baronets in 1611 is well known.[1] James no doubt appreciated the additions to the royal treasury which this scheme provided, and if Cotton took the title of baronet more seriously than the King, at least the King took seriously Cotton's reputation as a scholar. Chamberlain, writing to Carleton in Paris in 1612, remarked how the King had refused to grant the baronets precedence over the younger sons of barons, but added that the King had sent Sir Robert Cotton 'out of the way when the case was heard, because he [Cotton] was furnished with records in their favour'.[2]

Knowledge of records was one of the means Cotton used to gain favour at Court and among leading government officials. Robert Acton, the Queen's secretary, wrote to Cotton in March 1614 as follows:

> That I adventure to write to you in this subject it were by her majesty's express commandment, Her majesty having employed this bearer, Mr. Harwell, to make search of all such records and ancient writs as may in any way concern the rights of the Queens of England. And hearing that your industrious and judicious curiosity in all matters of antiquity hath been such as that you may [be] a more present help in this inquiry than any other, hath enjoined me to let you know that if you will do so much at her request as to communicate with Mr. Harwell such things as you have of this nature . . . she [the Queen] will requite it *with such effects of her favour as you shall reasonably desire.*[3] [Italics added.]

[1] The information in this paragraph is all based on the relevant *Calendars of State Papers, Domestic.*

[2] *C.S.P. Dom.*, 1611–18, Vol. LXVIII, 127.

[3] B.M. Harley MS. 7002, f. 371. Spelling, as in all manuscript quotations, has been modernized.

It is perfectly clear from this letter that Cotton could count on returns (in the form of 'favours' or influence) from his scholarly investments. For services rendered Cotton could expect services in return; it is reasonable to suppose that this principle applied even when a correspondent failed to express himself as clearly as the Queen's secretary.[1]

If knowledge of records and history was one pass-key to favour, the lending of books was another. During Cotton's lifetime, printed books were still costly, and large personal libraries were few. Neither Oxford nor Cambridge boasted libraries as great as Cotton's; Coke's library at Holkham was unusually large, with a catalogue which listed only 1200 volumes.[2] It may easily be seen that a first-rate library, well stocked with items of interest to lawyers, churchmen,

[1] As early as 1602 Cotton had provided Lord Henry Howard, Earl Marshal and later Earl of Northampton, with a list of precedents to prove the antiquity of the Earl Marshal's office. Among the high officers of State who sought Cotton's advice, or who were instrumental in having him appointed to royal commissions, were Sir Julius Caesar, who in 1610 requested that Cotton be placed on the commission to investigate the records of Aston, the knight in charge of the King's wardrobe (B.M. Cotton MS., Julius Caesar III, f. 55). George Calvert, Clerk of the Council and later Secretary of State, wrote to Cotton in 1616 requesting information (B.M. Harley MS. 7002, f. 131); and Robert Heath, the Attorney General, wrote to Cotton in 1626 to ask for precedents regarding service in the King's wars (B.M. Cotton MS., Julius Caesar III, f. 193). This was at a time of great unrest, when the government was worried about prosecuting those who refused to fight. Cotton was, of course, at this time closely associated with Sir John Eliot and the opposition. Cotton kept King James' favour, for not only did the King specifically request that Cotton appear before the Council in connection with the Navy reform proposals of 1611, but even in 1621 he approved of Cotton's appointment (along with that of Sir Thomas Wilson, Cotton's old enemy) to search Coke's papers. In 1624 the King requested that Cotton correct Camden's Elizabethan *Annals*. In 1627 Cotton's name appears on a commission to study the law courts, and in 1630, after he was in disgrace and had been denied access to his own library, he was named as a member of the commission on exacted fees (*C.S.P. Dom.*, 1629–31, Vol. CLIX, 179). Salisbury was in touch with Cotton as early as 1607. Sir Francis Bacon sought his help in writing the *History of Henry VII*, and later gave Cotton books. Any man who could be useful to such men was bound to acquire influence. S. R. Gardiner, *History*, VII, 140, argues that Cotton's librarian, Richard James, earned money by 'lending his master's papers to the curious'. This may be so, but I can find no supporting evidence for the statement.

[2] See W. O. Hassal, ed., *A Catalogue of the Library of Sir Edward Coke* (Yale Law Library Publications, 1950), i–xxiv.

politicians, and diplomats would be of the utmost importance for any kind of research. In one sense Cotton enjoyed a monopoly. Not that he owned and administered the only good library in England, but he did control the most convenient, the largest, and the most generally useful library. Hence, the evidence of his lending activities may serve to elucidate not only his own political role, but also the baffling interplay between politics, patronage and scholarship.

Among the members of the nobility to whom Cotton lent books or manuscripts, there were at least eight earls. In addition to North-ampton, Salisbury, and Somerset, Cotton lent materials from his library to Thomas Howard, second earl of Arundel and Surrey, Francis Russell, fourth earl of Bedford, William Cavendish, second earl of Devonshire, John Holles, first earl of Clare (second creation), and David Lindsay, twelfth earl of Crawford. The earl of Arundel, best known for his art collection, was a close friend of Selden, who described the collection in his *Marmora Arundeliana* (1624). It was Arundel, the confirmed enemy of Buckingham, who sponsored Cotton for Parliament in 1625. For his hostility to Buckingham, Arundel was imprisoned from 1626 to 1628. Francis Russell, earl of Bedford, was prosecuted in the Star Chamber in 1629, along with Cotton, Selden, Somerset, and the earl of Clare, for allegedly 'publishing a libel'.

The libel in this case was a tract written in 1614 by Sir Robert Dudley (the illegitimate son of Elizabeth's favourite, Leicester) in which Dudley had proposed, among other things, that the King levy new taxes on his own authority and 'bridle the impertinency of Parliament' by a military occupation of the country.[1] The tract had not alarmed King James, to whom it had been shown in 1614 by Somerset. King Charles, however, was easily persuaded by Went-worth (who had discovered the paper in November 1629) that it was libelous and that those who had circulated it should be prosecuted. As Gardiner goes on to tell the story, 'Cotton, who had quite for-gotten that the original had long been in his own library, fancying that he had before him a revelation of the immediate designs of the Court, sat down to reply to its arguments, no doubt with the inten-tion of publishing a refutation'.[2] This comedy of errors almost had a happy ending, with the King himself ordering the case dismissed upon the news of the birth of his son, Prince Charles. However, an important state paper had been found in Cotton's library, and orders

[1] See S. R. Gardiner, *History*, VII, 138–41. [2] *Ibid.*, VII, 139.

were therefore given to close the library until a catalogue of the manuscripts could be prepared. Cotton was not allowed into his library except in the presence of two clerks of the Council. Charles surely realized that Cotton bore no responsibility for publishing Dudley's tract; and the fact that Cotton had state papers in his library was common knowledge, not something to shock the conscience of the King. The royal revenge was, in fact, political and petty.

What the episode really proved was that Cotton's historical knowledge was feared. Although not a great leader within the walls of Parliament, Cotton was the agent and adviser of some of the most powerful leaders of Parliamentary opinion.[1] Cotton had insisted that his library be free and open to all; equally, he had insisted that the Parliamentary opposition could win its argument on the basis of law, precedent, and evidence. If the kingdom was governed by a 'mixt authority', as his friend Camden had maintained, then there were limits to the King's prerogative, and those limits must be understood by the King and by his subjects.[2] Cotton's role as a true moderate was to testify to the ancient rights and duties of the subject. He had become the agent of a cause which he believed to be historically justified and correct.

The Parliamentary debates of 1628 added little to the nature and scope of the arguments advanced in 1610 and 1614. Yet there was a difference—there was an even greater stress on exact and definite precedents. Royalist judges and councillors increasingly felt obliged to point to established law and precedent favouring the King. Old Lord Ellesmere, as early as 1614, had warned the Lords 'what to expect from the Parliamentary leaders if the Lords went into a joint conference with the Commons on the subject of impositions. He insisted that the Lords had not sufficiently considered the case and the records; whereas the Commons "goe both high and lowe and looke of all things that concern their purpose, and we can say nothinge, having not seen records . . ." ' [3] No doubt it is true that in the course of these debates, both in Parliament and in the law

[1] See Williams M. Mitchell, *The Rise of the Revolutionary Party in the House of Commons 1603–1629* (New York, 1957), 52.

[2] For Camden's views, see F. S. Fussner, 'William Camden's "Discourse Concerning the Prerogative",' *Proceedings of the American Philosophical Society* (Vol. 101, no. 2, 1957), 211.

[3] M. A. Judson, *The Crisis of the Constitution* (New Brunswick, 1949), 239.

courts, neither side answered squarely the arguments of the other. Yet, 'the fact that there were precedents and traditions recognizing the subjects' rights helped to prevent royalist judges and councillors from establishing the complete legal absolutism of the monarch'.[1] Cotton did not create the demand for precedents, but he undoubtedly did much to supply the demand and sustain it during the critical decade of the 1620's.

As early as 1607, Cotton was at work collecting arguments to be used in Parliament, although at this date the arguments were not for use against the Crown.[2] Cotton had by then met Robert Bowyer, member of Parliament, record keeper, and later clerk of the House of Lords. Cotton managed, as usual, to be of service to Bowyer, and to Henry Elsynge when he became clerk of the Parliament. Elsynge provided Cotton with some of the materials he used in his *History of Henry III*, a work which was printed without licence in 1627.[3] Cotton was careful to deny that he had had anything to do with the printing of it, merely acknowledging that he had written it 'some 15 years ago', and allowing it to be assumed that neither he nor Elsynge bore any further responsibility. Both Elsynge and Bowyer were clearly on good terms with Cotton, and in all probability Cotton's Parliamentary career owed something to the expert advice these men could give.

During the last decade of his life, Cotton sat in three Parliaments. He was elected M.P. for Old Sarum in 1624, Thetford in 1625, and

---

[1] Judson, *Crisis*, 156.

[2] *C.S.P. Dom.*, 1603–10, Vol. XXVII, 360.

[3] On Bowyer, see D. H. Willson, *The Parliamentary Diary of Robert Bowyer* (Minnesota, 1931), x–xi; Cotton's relations with Bowyer, and Cotton's activities in the House are discussed 52n., 115n., 314n., 332–3, and *passim*. See also B.M. Harley MS. 6018, f. 154b. Henry Elsynge, senior, is briefly mentioned in Orlo Cyprian Williams, *The Clerical Organization of the House of Commons* (Oxford, 1954), a useful book. The best study is Catherine Strathman Sims, ed., *Expedicio Billarum Antiquitus . . . by Henry Elsynge* (Louvain, 1954), xvii–li. On the publication of the *History of Henry III*, see S.P. 16/54, nos. 4 and 5, 'A brief of the several examinations taken before the Lord Bishop of London this week touching the Book entitled A view of the Long Life and Reign of Henry the Third . . .' Most of Cotton's political and historical tracts are reprinted in *Cottoni Posthuma*, ed. by Edmund Goldsmid, 4 vols. (Edinburgh, 1884). The large number of manuscript copies of Cotton's works in the British Museum and at the Public Record Office and elsewhere suggest that they were widely circulated in the seventeenth century.

served in 1628–9 as M.P. for Castle Rising. Since he took little part in debate, the question is, how could he keep the patronage of important men, and continue to be elected? The answer may be found in the scattered references to Cotton's services to Parliament, and in particular to the opposition members. As early as May 20, 1614, there is a reference to a letter sent from Sir Robert Cotton, 'wherein is conteyned his servisable dutye to the house, and that he beinge sick at Cambridge had sent the keye of his studye to Sir Edward Mountague and his brother to searche for such recordes as should be fore the benefit of the Common wealthe . . .' [1] What use, if any, Montague made of these records is not known. The point is that Cotton was acting almost as an information bureau, or research agent for the House. Montague was appointed Lord Chief Justice in 1616, and thereafter became a strong supporter of the Crown. During the Parliament of 1621, Cotton addressed his treatise dealing with Floyd's case ('A Brief Discourse shewing that the House of Commons hath Equal Power with the Peers in Point of Judicature') to Sir Edward Montague, who is reported to have replied, 'I have ben to search presidents and we have cause rather to lett them alone that see and reade them.' [2]

Early in the course of the Parliament of 1621, a question had arisen whether or not Sir Dudley Digges should be admitted to the House, since he had been chosen to represent Tewkesbury while he was beyond the seas. In reporting to the House, 'Mr. Hackwell' [i.e. Hakewill] reported as follows: '*Absens Reipublicae causa videtur presens.* By dirreccion of the Howse he had spoken with Sir Robert Cotton. There was no President in the case soe that nowe we are left to reason.' [3] It is clear that Cotton was being consulted as an authority on precedents. During the course of the debates in December, many of the precedents cited were taken from Cotton's 'The Antiquity and Dignity of Parliaments, A Relation to prove that the Kings of England have been pleased to consult with their

---

[1] See Wallace Notestein, Francis Helen Relf, and Hartley Simpson, eds., *Commons Debates, 1621,* 7 vols.(New Haven, 1935), VII, App. C, pp. 642–3. A good deal of scattered comment on Cotton's political career may be found also in *The Letters of John Chamberlain,* ed. by Norman Egbert McClure, 2 vols., American Philosophical Society Memoir XII (Philadelphia, 1939), I, 325, 332, 345, 541, 607; II, 10, 418, 524, 557.

[2] Notestein, Relf, Simpson, *Commons Debates,* III, 229; on Montague, see W. Mitchell, *Rise of the Revolutionary Party,* 53, n. 112.

[3] Notestein, Relf, Simpson, *Commons Debates,* IV, 54.

Peers in the Great Councell and Commons in Parliament'. It is therefore not surprising that Cotton was sought after by members of the opposition group in this and in later Parliaments. Cotton had probably met Sir John Eliot by 1620, and in 1621 Eliot, Wentworth, Pym, Selden, and Coke were meeting together at Cotton's house during the sessions of Parliament. No doubt Cotton was able to be of even greater service when he was himself a member of the House.

In January 1628, Cotton is known to have sent word to a man named Scudmore for a book 'against the parliament'.[1] In other words, Cotton was getting ready for the session by collecting evidence for whatever arguments he or others expected to use when Parliament convened. Perhaps the impeachment of Mountague was already being considered, for on the 29th of May 1628, Nathaniel Hall in Ireland sat down to answer a letter from Cotton in which Cotton had asked for Irish precedents on impeachment.[2] Taken altogether, the evidence suggests that Cotton acted as the agent not only of the Parliamentary opposition, but also, in some matters, as a general agent of the House of Commons. How important his influence was on the men who stood and spoke against Buckingham, and who supported the Petition of Right, must remain uncertain. Still, it should be obvious that Cotton was in a position to help make key decisions, that his political influence stemmed from his knowledge of the books and records in his library, and that his role in Parliament would certainly enhance his influence with government officials as well as with members of the legal profession.

(b) The Legal Profession

The close connection between the Parliamentary opposition and the common lawyers was obvious even to contemporaries. The massive figure of Sir Edward Coke stands out as the symbol of the common law opposition to the exercise of arbitrary power by the Crown. Coke's authority, his knowledge of matters of record and history, and his ponderous scholarly arguments, made him both feared and famous. He was the foremost common lawyer to oppose the Crown—'Reason of State lames Magna Carta' was his phrase,

[1] B.M. Cotton MS., Julius Caesar III, f. 337. Meetings were held at Cotton's house as early as 1621, but there is some doubt about the later meetings. See Catherine Drinker Bowen, *The Lion and the Throne* (Boston, 1956), 422; cf. Hulme, *Life of Sir John Eliot*, 184n.

[2] B.M. Harley MS. 7000, f. 219. Richard Mountague is surmised.

and it tells much about the man. Yet, since Coke could not command, he had to persuade; and he was persuading many of his contemporaries both in and out of Parliament that 'no man ought to be wiser than the law'. The law was not a matter of authority or faith; it was a matter of evidence and record. The stated purpose of Coke's *Institutes* was to 'open some windowes of the law, and to let in more light to the student, or to move him to doubt'.[1] In other words, the law must be learned by scholarly processes. The legal scholar, or the politician, for that matter, must discover the truth by going to the records, by acquiring knowledge of law and history. Coke's Whiggish appeals to history are well known, and there is an aptness about Coke's offer in Parliament of £300 for three manuscripts, one being Lambarde's 'Abreviate of Tower Records'.[2] The reason why Coke spoke with such authority to his generation was that he had thoroughly mastered its learning, and could cite evidence that all men respected.

Sir Edward Coke was of course not the only lawyer to take his stand in favour of liberty and property, nor was he the only lawyer or judge to turn to Cotton for precedents. John Selden was greatly in Cotton's debt and dedicated his best-known and most controversial book, *The Historie of Tithes*, to Cotton. Although Selden accumulated one of the best libraries in England he still found Cotton's storehouse indispensable. That Selden returned Cotton's generosity there can be no doubt. Cotton could, furthermore, open doors which were closed even to Selden. Perhaps because of the notoriety of the *Historie of Tithes*, Selden had to ask Cotton for help in 1624, in order to borrow materials from the Westminster Library of the Lord Bishop of Lincoln.

Among the more moderate lawyers who borrowed from Cotton was Thomas Coventry, first Baron Coventry, who was appointed Solicitor General in 1617, and Attorney General in 1621; in 1629 he attempted to mediate between Crown and Parliament in the course of the debates on the Petition of Right. Among the extremists who borrowed from Cotton's library was Sir Roger Owen, treasurer of Lincoln's Inn in 1613, who was later dismissed from the post for anti-royalist speeches. The list of names of lawyers and judges who made use of the library could easily be extended. Although it is seldom clear just what kinds of materials these men wanted to

[1] Quoted by Bowen, *The Lion and the Throne*, 510.
[2] See Bowen, *The Lion and the Throne*, 491.

borrow, there is some evidence that lawyers wrote to Cotton for information about purely legal precedents.[1] In any case, the legal profession was exceptionally well represented in the lists of Cotton's borrowers. Sir John Hobart, Attorney General; Sir James Ley, attorney for the Court of Wards; Sir John Doderidge, Justice of the King's Bench, and author of *The English Lawyer*; and James White-locke, Justice of the King's Bench: these were only some of the more prominent examples. James Whitelocke was to turn to Cotton for help in 1613 when he was sent to the Fleet for opposing the Commission on Naval Reform. Although Cotton himself was a member of the Commission, Whitelocke wrote to him to ask for precedents *ab antiquo* to support his own defence.[2] This curious behaviour suggests again that Cotton's library was, in fact, if not in name, a public library, and that Cotton presided over an institution of recognized national importance.

(c) The Church and the Universities

The Church and the Universities were also much indebted to Cotton for assistance in scholarly matters. Bishop Mountague, who, next to Spelman, was Selden's ablest opponent, called Cotton's library 'the magazine of history'; the phrase is apt, for Cotton rendered services to nearly everyone in the English community of learning.[3] A church 'flourishing with learned and extraordinary men' was supplied with 'oil to feed those lamps' partly by Cotton's generosity.[4] He was a close friend of Archbishop Ussher, and he dealt cordially with many of the prominent churchmen of his day. James Ussher, whose well-known chronology became the standard adopted in editions of the English Bible, frequently wrote to Cotton to borrow or exchange manuscripts and historical information, especially on topics relating to ecclesiastical history. It was Ussher who wrote to warn Cotton that the Jesuits were negotiating in

[1] B.M. Cotton MS., Julius Caesar III, f. 79. The loan list (B.M. Harley MS. 6018) is the source of all statements about borrowers from Cotton's library.

[2] B.M. Cotton MS., Julius Caesar III, f. 400.

[3] See the *D.N.B. sub* Cotton. The extent of Cotton's correspondence alone would suffice to prove this. Many of the letters addressed to him are in B.M. Cotton MS., Julius Caesar III.

[4] The phrases are Clarendon's. See Edward, Earl of Clarendon, *The History of the Rebellion and Civil Wars in England*, ed. by W. Dunn Macray, 6 vols. (Oxford, 1888), I, 95.

Antwerp to purchase the only 'Oriental Press' (i.e. the only supply of print in Oriental languages) in Europe.[1] Archbishop Ussher's long friendship with Cotton seems never to have been marred by the kind of discourtesy that Laud displayed when he abruptly insisted that Cotton return borrowed books to Oxford. Laud's sense of academic responsibility may have been admirable, but Laud was not above scoring off an opponent of the Crown; and he certainly knew and ignored the fact that Cotton had been one of the first to make generous gifts to Bodley's library at Oxford.

At least three translators of the English Bible appear among Cotton's correspondents or on the lists of borrowers from Cotton's library. The international reputation of Cotton as a benefactor of learning, if not of the Church of England, is evident from a letter he received from the Benedictine monk, Augustine Baker, in 1629, appealing to him to send printed or manuscript books to be used in the English nunnery at Cambrai.[2] In all matters of religion, Cotton was an Erastian, who put his trust in rational principles, and not in persecution. His written treatise on the subject of English Catholicism contained suggestions which were 'moderate, sane, and, as it happened, remarkably tolerant'. As Professor W. K. Jordan goes on to observe, 'Most illuminating was his considered opinion that English public sentiment would no longer support a policy of outright persecution. Cotton may have strained fact slightly to his theory, but there can be no doubt that in England a powerful body of opinion was crystallizing which was earnestly opposed to further spiritual coercion . . .' [3]

From members of both Universities Cotton also received appeals for help and information, as well as favours and gifts. Richard James, the man who was later to become Cotton's librarian, was

---

[1] B.M. Cotton MS., Julius Caesar III, f. 383. See also the correspondence of Ussher in *The Whole Works of the Most Reverend James Ussher D.D.*, 17 vols., ed. by C. R. Elrington and J. H. Todd (Dublin, 1847–64), Vols. XV and XVI, *passim*. This correspondence sheds much light on all aspects of scholarship and is valuable for what it tells about libraries other than Cotton's. A few of the more important letters are Vol. XV, 2, 13, 31, 33–5, 48–50, 56, 64–5, 68–9, 74, 77, 81, 83, 85–6, 89, 92–6, 98, 103, 110–15, 135, 137, 143–4, 146, 155, 159; Vol. XVI, 215, 218, 233, 262, 343, 357, 373, 375, 379, 388, 401, 417, 423.

[2] B.M. Cotton MS., Julius Caesar III, fols. 12, 12b.

[3] W. K. Jordan, *The Development of Religious Toleration in England*, 4 vols. (Cambridge, Mass., 1932–40), II, 479.

pleased to do Cotton favours while still a fellow of Corpus Christi College in Oxford. In an undated letter to Cotton, James wrote, 'Your council of Constance is with an honest dilatorie man yet when you please it shall be speedily and thankfully returned with a promise from the party to make some addition unto your most excellent Seraglio of Antiquity.' [1] In another letter, James requested that Cotton pay some bills for him, and added that he had gained from a Mr. King 'the use of two Ensham Leger Books, which I doubt not in time shall come to your freer keeping . . .' [2] Judging by the tone of his remarks, James knew where Cotton's political sympathies lay; he observed that in one of the manuscripts he had found 'an excellent instance for the prerogative of the Parliament interpreting the sense of our great charters if any doubt their drift . . .' Almost as an afterthought he advised Cotton to send to Mr. Allen (the mathematician and antiquary) a gift of some green ginger, for 'peradventure, besides comforting the good old man, it will also open some odd corner of antiquity'.

That Richard James found life at Oxford during the early 1620's extremely uncongenial may be gathered from a letter he wrote to Cotton pointing up the ageless analogy between state and college politics:

> We are here governed also by a prerogative and one of the most ugly favourites that ever imaginary prince made choice of. Doctor Holt may have amongst us love, honour and profit, if he would not as it were fatally rather embrace his own scorn and our injury. Wherefore my brief litany still continues that God would raise me some kind friend to deliver a poor captive from the contagion of this brangling collegiate life. [3]

It was probably not long after writing this letter that he was delivered; and in the service, first of Sir Robert, and then of his son, Richard James found felicity.

When Sir John Bennet, judge of the Prerogative Court of Canterbury and M.P. for Oxford, was accused of corruption by the House of Commons in 1621, he did not hesitate to write to Cotton to ask 'what doth appear in any parliamentary rolls to have been done in the parliament house, against any ordinary or ecclesiastical officers, or what particular offences any of them have been charged withal in those parliaments wherein several statutes have been made against

---

[1] B.M. Harley MS. 7002, f. 118. [2] B.M. Harley MS. 7002, f. 120.
[3] B.M. Harley MS. 7002, f. 125.

their oppressive extortions and exactions . . .' [1] If Cotton could not tell him the answer he requested that Cotton tell him how to go about searching the records in the Tower. This letter, written on the 24th of July 1621, just three months after the charges had been made in Parliament, is further proof that Cotton was regarded as an impartial authority on matters of history and record.

Writing from Cambridge University, on the 23rd of July 1622, William Lysle informed Cotton that he had dealt effectively for a book that 'was engaged for Trinity College: that you may have it'. Cotton was to exchange a 'Grosted' for this particular manuscript, which happened to be a description, with excellent maps, of a Portuguese Red Sea voyage. Lysle went on to ask Cotton to make up his mind concerning Mr. Legate, (presumably the printer to Cambridge University), 'because he desires nothing more than to do you service, and is importunate with me for an answer . . .' [2] Such statements as these are by no means unique. John Borough, later to become Keeper of the Tower Records and Garter King of Arms, wrote to Cotton in 1622 from Venice to discuss the purchase of a famous Italian library; William Bolde wrote to Cotton offering to be of service while travelling in Europe; and the names of a score or more of European scholars and librarians were to be found at the bottom of letters addressed to Cotton. The extent of Cotton's influence and patronage need be insisted upon no further. Diverse men of learning, of the arts, and of public life knew Cotton and were indebted to him for the use of his library—'Helicon's fountain', as it was called by John Barkham in proper antiquarian fashion. [3]

The important question is how Cotton used his influence to further historical scholarship. Granted that his library was a 'magazine of history', and further, that it was the source of much of his influence, what made Cotton an outstanding figure in the history of English historiography? The answer lies partly in the record of Cotton's dealings with the lesser government officials, the men who controlled and used the public records of England.

(d) Royal Officials

The bureaucracy of royal officials in Stuart England conformed to

[1] B.M. Cotton MS., Julius Caesar III, f. 23.
[2] B.M. Harley MS. 7000, f. 92. Legate, the younger, printer 1650.
[3] These letters are from B.M. Cotton MS., Julius Caesar III, fols. 36-6b (Burroughs); f. 16 (Barkham); fols. 26-7b (Bolde).

the familiar system of patronage and fees; the formal structure and 'rationalistic' character of the modern civil service emerged only after the administrative revolution of the nineteenth century. The hallmarks of the Tudor–Stuart bureaucracy (or of the medieval bureaucracy, for that matter) were continuity and the division of labour, not to mention the mass-production of records. Although record keeping in the Elizabethan and Jacobean period has already been described, something must be said about the general working of the state bureaucracy, in which the record keepers held their minor yet important posts.

What had distinguished the Tudor administrative revolution of the 1530's was national bureaucratic organization: '. . . in every sphere of the central government "household" methods and instruments were replaced by national bureaucratic methods and instruments. . . . Every reorganization that took place was in the direction of greater definition, of specialization, of bureaucratic order.' [1] This new bureaucracy was a powerful and reasonably efficient instrument of Tudor government. The system of bureaucratic patronage and clientage as it emerged during the Reformation decade was to remain typical of English administrative practice through the seventeenth and eighteenth centuries. And the commission of 1786–8, which investigated 'Fees, Gratuities, Perquisites, and Emoluments in Public Offices' came directly to the point: increasing fees and perquisites were the painful symptoms of the increasing complexity of administration. [2]

The abuses of the unreformed bureaucratic system provoked frequent complaints, and frequent, if ineffectual, attempts at reform. It has been said that during the latter part of Elizabeth's reign the Tudor bureaucracy threatened to become hereditary, and that control of the government was in the hands of perhaps no more than forty or fifty men. [3] Of course, the Elizabethan bureaucracy did not

[1] G. R. Elton, *The Tudor Revolution in Government* (Cambridge, 1953), 415; cf. p. 308. The civil service of Charles I has been studied in great detail by G. E. Aylmer, *The King's Servants, The Civil Service of Charles I, 1625–1642* (London, 1961). The definition of the words 'bureaucracy' and 'bureaucratic' in this chapter and elsewhere is consistent with Aylmer's discussion—see pp. 453–63.

[2] Quoted by Elton, *Tudor Revolution in Government*, 422.

[3] See Edward P. Cheney, *A History of England from the Defeat of the Armada to the Death of Elizabeth*, 2 vols. (New York, 1948), I, 49–50. There is a good deal of information in Cheney's chapters on institutions,

become hereditary, and the worst evils of the French *ancien régime* were avoided. Nevertheless, fees and red tape were on the increase; and, as R. H. Tawney recently put it, in the seventeenth century, 'the principal paths to an official career were patronage, patrimony, and purchase'.[1] Public servants in general were paid by fees extracted from the pockets of everyone, including other government officials, who had to do business with them. Under the circumstances, scholarly research in the public records had to depend on favour or influence—few scholars commanded fortunes. It was in this context that Sir Robert Cotton exerted his influence on behalf of England's men of learning.

An impressive list could be drawn up of the names of bureaucratic officials who wrote friendly letters to Cotton, or who borrowed from his library. In addition to the highest officers of state, the list would include the names of important secretaries and clerks, officials of the King's Household (for example, Sir George Buck, Master of the Revels, and Sir Frances Crane, Chancellor of the Order of the Garter), members of the College of Arms, and many others. Exchequer and other financial officials were prominent, of course, and almost without exception, Cotton knew the men directly charged with the keeping of public records. Arthur Agarde, John Bradshaw, and Thomas Fauconberge were the deputy Chamberlains of the Exchequer who held office during Cotton's lifetime. Every one of them was personally known to Cotton. Agarde, who held the office from 1570 until his death in 1615 left his historical collections to Cotton—strong testimony to the strength of their friendship. Upon Agarde's death Thomas Wilson, head of the State Paper Office, recorded his fears that Cotton would manage to control the appointment of Agarde's successor and thereby be in a position to appropriate or suppress records at a time 'when we may have most need of them'.[2]

The keepers of the state papers at the State Paper Office from 1603 to 1629 were Thomas Lake, Levinus Munck, Thomas Wilson,

especially on fees for office. The student will want to consult the appropriate volumes of W. S. Holdsworth, *A History of English Law*, 9 vols. (London, 1922–7). See also note 1, p. 140.

[1] R. H. Tawney, *Business and Politics Under James I, Lionel Cranfield as Merchant and Minister* (Cambridge, 1958), 123.

[2] S.P. 14/81, no. 69, dated Aug. 24, 1615. The information on bureaucratic officials comes mainly from B.M. Harley MS. 6018. There is some information in the letters, B.M. Cotton MS., Julius Caesar III, *passim*.

Wilson's son-in-law, Ambrose Randolph, and William Boswell—
every one of them known to Cotton. True, Thomas Wilson distrusted
and probably disliked Cotton, whose influence interfered with his
own bureaucratic empire building. Upon the news of Agarde's death
he wrote to his son-in-law, Randolf, urging him to apply for Agarde's
place 'for thereby we may make our own office perfect and do the
King and state general service by it'.[1] Among the deputy keepers or
clerks of the Records in the Tower during Cotton's lifetime were
William Bowyer, Robert Bowyer, Henry Elsynge, Sir John Borough,
and Nicholas Parker. These men were all indebted to Cotton for
some favour. And, like many other scholarly officials, Sir Henry
Fanshawe, Remembrancer of the Exchequer, made frequent use of
Cotton's library, presumably in order to pursue his Italian studies.
Whether they applied to Cotton for help in their official duties, or
in connection with their private scholarly pursuits—and often the
line was not very clearly drawn—these bureaucratic officials could
count on Cotton's generosity. In return, such men could help Cotton,
or those whom Cotton might choose to help.

(e) The Scholars, Historians, and Others

By the end of Elizabeth's reign Cotton's library had become one of
the great roadsteads of the learned world. All kinds of scholarly
cargoes could be loaded there; information was freely exchanged,
and Cotton, like a good factor, knew how to smooth the way through
customs. That Cotton did, in fact, help scholars to gain access to the
public records is clear from the case of Ferdinando Pulton, the
Elizabethan editor of the Statutes of the Realm. Toward the end of a
long life, Pulton began work on his most famous book, the *Statutes
at Large*. His plans for this ambitious undertaking were to set forth
a complete scholarly edition of known English statutes. For this
purpose he required free access at all times to the records in the
Tower. Possibly because this threatened their search fees, Bowyer
and Elsynge, the Keepers of the Tower records, threw difficulties in
Pulton's way. In a letter to Cotton, Pulton admitted that he had had
differences with Bowyer, but stated his willingness to let Cotton be
the judge between them. He went on to request Cotton's aid in
getting Bowyer to help him in working with the statutes and records
in the Tower, promising not only to do whatever Cotton asked, but
also to give any reasonable satisfaction to Bowyer for his help.

[1] Quoted by Wernham in Fox, *English Historical Scholarship*, 22-3.

Finally, he offered to submit his manuscript to Cotton or to the judges before publication. The result was that the opposition of the record keepers was overruled. Cotton intervened on behalf of Pulton, and the requisite access was granted by the Council in 1611.[1]

This evidence, as far as it goes, is conclusive. Pulton's case may indeed have been an isolated one, but in all probability it was not. Cotton was the recipient of many other letters asking that he exert his influence in official circles. Edmund Bolton, the Catholic historian and poet, wrote to Cotton to solicit his favour; and, in praising Cotton's generosity, observed truly enough, that 'we that are privy to the truth of things, do also know that without your assistance it is vain to pretend to weighty work in the antiquities of this kingdom'.[2] Dorothy Starkey, the wife of Ralph Starkey whose antiquarian zeal had led him to acquire Elizabethan state papers (which were finally confiscated by order of the Privy Council in 1619), wrote to Cotton as early as 1612 to ask for his assistance against her husband's enemies.[3] Whether or not such written entreaties were typical is ultimately unimportant; the fact remains that Cotton's position and influence did enable him to gain free access to official records. History hangs on written documents, but it is always well to remember that a few words spoken in the right ears could open doors quietly then as now.

From all over the British Isles and the continent letters discussing books, manuscripts, and antiquities found their way to Cotton's library in London. A very few examples must suffice to illustrate this rich scholarly correspondence. From Sir Symon Archer, the antiquary who amassed much of the material used in Dugdale's *History of Warwickshire*, came letters asking for 'a copy of Rouse's books concerning the antiquities of Warwickshire', and for information concerning the whereabouts of the rent rolls and court rolls of the earl of Warwick's lands.[4] From John Barkham in Essex came inquiries about the derivation of place names, and a promise to send Cotton some antique statues. In 1624, William Boswell wrote to ask Cotton for Lord Ellesmere's book of 'the last session of

[1] Pulton's letter to Cotton, dated Mar. 8, 1612, is in B.M. Cotton MS., Julius Caesar III, f. 78. See also Faith Thompson, *Magna Carta, Its Role in the Making of the English Constitution* (Minneapolis, 1948), 235; Holdsworth, *History of English Law*, IV, 309–10.

[2] B.M. Cotton MS., Julius Caesar III, f. 29.

[3] B.M. Harley MS. 7002, f. 205.

[4] B.M. Cotton MS., Julius Caesar III, f. 3.

Parliament', since the Lord Keeper had asked him for a copy of it and 'we know not where in Mr. Ellesmere's absence to ask, but of yourself whose favour on all occasions we have formerly had experience of'.[1] From the earl of Devonshire in 1629 came a letter praising Cotton for his industrious preservation of antiquity and thanking him for favours done. The French historian, Pierre Dupuy, wrote in 1630 to request a catalogue of Cotton's library and to ask his aid in points of history. Similarly, Richard Knolles, historian of the Turks, requested Cotton's assistance in 1610 in a note which reveals earlier acquaintance with the library. From Derbyshire Oswald Dykes wrote to give antiquarian and topographical information which he asked Cotton to pass on to Camden. John Selden, a frequent correspondent, wrote in a letter, dated July 24, 1624, to say that he had been working in the library of Bennet College and that he would keep a lookout for anything that might interest Cotton. In the meantime he was sending material on the reign of Queen Elizabeth touching the borders of Scotland. Perhaps this was in reply to a request from Cotton, who had just been given the responsibility of correcting the new edition of Camden's *Annales*.[2]

Cotton was not only an antiquary, but also an expert on Elizabethan history, as Camden himself had acknowledged. It is worth noting that Richard Rowlands, *alias* Verstegan, who had published a work against Queen Elizabeth's treatment of the Roman Catholics, wrote to Cotton on the 15th of June 1609, to inform him that he was at work on a book of antiquities of the English nation. As a gift from one antiquary to another he enclosed the tongue of a petrified fish. When Augustine Vincent, Rouge Croix pursuivant, began his work on the baronetage, he naturally wrote to ask Cotton's help, especially in order to procure Camden's and Francis Thynne's notes, which Cotton had told him about.[3] Sir Simonds D'Ewes was much indebted to Cotton, not only for materials for his work on the journals of Parliament during the reign of Queen Elizabeth, but also

[1] B.M. Cotton MS., Julius Caesar III, f. 37; on Barkham, *ibid.*, f. 15.

[2] On Camden's *Annals*, S.P. 14/168, no. 41. The correspondence mentioned in this paragraph is all taken from B.M. Cotton MS., Julius Caesar III, fols. 161 (Dupuy), 164 (Dykes), 225 (Knolles), 341-3 (Selden). Other letters are in B.M. Harley MS. 7002, *passim*.

[3] B.M. Cotton MS., Julius Caesar III, f. 379. Verstegan's letter, *ibid.*, 376. D'Ewes and Cotton were careful in their dealings with one another (B.M. Harley MS. 7002, no. 446).

for his social introduction to John Selden. It was D'Ewes, further-more, who joined Cotton in establishing the claim of Robert Vere to the earldom of Oxford in 1626.

The names of many more scholars could be added to the list of those who owed Cotton both footnotes and thanks. In general, it may be said that Cotton supplied advice and information; he seldom wrote sections of other men's books, although he naturally acquired the reputation for this. Cotton collaborated amicably with Camden, Speed, and other scholars. The division of labour in historiography was an accepted fact.

Cotton's collecting habits, as might be expected, were much criticized by some of his contemporaries. Sir Thomas Wilson was particularly vexed by Cotton's assiduous efforts to gain control of ancient manuscripts and state papers. The aldermen of the City of London had tried for years to regain possession of manuscripts alienated from their own archives in the sixteenth century, a number of which had subsequently come into Cotton's keeping. John Stow was at one time appointed to negotiate with Cotton for their return, and the negotiations were continued after Stow's death in 1605. The fact is that Cotton did acquire papers and manuscripts which had once belonged to the state, to the Corporation of the City of London, and doubtless to other corporate bodies. There can be no question that Cotton performed a service to historiography by acquiring such records for his library. Cotton appropriated public records by means which may appear suspect and devious, but there was no need to steal what could be bought or borrowed, and his reputation for unprincipled behaviour was largely undeserved.

At the Guildhall, indifference and inertia (not to mention possible corruption) made it extremely difficult for the aldermen to keep their records intact, and prevent them from being illegally copied or alienated. The *Liber Custumarum* and other manuscripts formerly at the Guildhall were, naturally, of great interest to the antiquaries of the sixteenth century.[1] It is not surprising, in view of the frequent unsuccessful attempts at regulation early in the seventeenth century, that these manuscripts had been acquired by private collectors. Cotton, however, had acquired his share from Francis Tate, not from the City. The probable history of these transactions has been traced, and the conclusion reached that there is no evidence that

[1] See Neil B. Ker, 'Liber Custumarum and Other Manuscripts formerly at the Guildhall', *The Guildhall Miscellany* (III, 1954), 37-45.

either Tate or Cotton was under any obligation to return Guildhall manuscripts and that Cotton perhaps acted generously in restoring parts of them to the City.[1] Certainly it is clear from the Repertory books of the City of London that London records were often indifferently kept. On the 19th of September 1609, while negotiations with Cotton went on, an entry reads as follows:

> That order may be newly taken and better observed than the former that the City's books be not carried abroad that they be lost as formerly divers have been, or if the court shall be pleased to allow of the carriage of them abroad that then whosoever shall deliver any book cause notice to be given thereof at the next court of aldermen after the delivery thereof to whom the same shall be delivered to the end an entry may be made into the Repertory where the same remaineth.[2]

In 1622, a decade after the Cotton episode was settled, the aldermen were still testily ordering that their records be more strictly kept.

The unparalleled richness of Cotton's historical and antiquarian collections can still excite the scholar's imagination. Long after Cotton's death, Thomas Fuller noted in *The Worthies of England* that Cotton's library was equally famous for the rarity, variety, and number of its manuscripts, as well as for the manner of their shelving: 'some libraries are labyrinths, not for the multitude, but confusion of volumes, where a stranger seeking for a book may quickly lose himself; whereas these are so exactly methodized (under the heads of the twelve Roman emperors) that it is harder for one to miss than to hit any author he desires'.[3]

It would be extremely difficult to overestimate the significance of Cotton's library for the growth of historical scholarship. In one field alone—the political and religious history of England from the reign of Henry VIII through Elizabeth and James I—the library contained nearly 100 volumes of original state papers and exact

[1] Ker, *The Guildhall Miscellany* (III, 1954), 37–45.

[2] Through the kindness of Professor Wallace MacCaffrey of Haverford College I was supplied with transcripts of entries in the 'Repertory Books' of the Court of Aldermen of London. This entry is Repertory, XXIX, f. 87. The entry for Oct. 15, 1622 (Repertory, XXXVI, f. 273b) continues a series of complaints which began when Stow was appointed to negotiate with Cotton for the return of manuscripts. On Stow's role, see Kingsford's introduction to John Stow's *Survey*, I, xxxii.

[3] Thomas Fuller, *The Worthies of England*, ed. by John Freeman (London, 1952), 247.

transcripts. An astonishing amount of state papers from the reigns of Henry VIII and Elizabeth rested on Cotton's shelves. One press contained 43 volumes relating to domestic and foreign affairs, some bearing notes by Cecil; another press contained 50 volumes of such papers bearing on England's relations with Portugal, Spain, Russia, Poland, the Scandinavian countries, the Hanseatic League, Holland, Turkey, and the Near East.[1] Nearly every English historian of note in the seventeenth century made some use of the great library by the Thames. And Fuller testified to the fact that Sir Thomas Cotton inherited the courtesy as well as the estates of his father, Sir Robert. The policy of free access continued more or less throughout the century; and in 1702, Sir Robert's grandson presented the entire collection to the nation.

Nearly all the great monuments of seventeenth-century English historical scholarship were constructed from materials found in Cotton's library. Sir Henry Spelman, Roger Dodsworth, William Dugdale, Thomas Rymer—men 'whose works have remained of such importance that they still continue to be used in almost every serious work devoted to the antiquities of medieval England'—worked long hours in Cotton's library.[2] Not until the eighteenth century was the supremacy of the Cottonian collection challenged by the Harleys, whose collecting was done through the agency of Humphrey Wanley. But the first great charter of scholarship bore the name of Cotton; and, as Professor David Douglas has observed:

> To assess the debt of medieval scholarship to the families of Cotton and Harley would be to trace the course of English historical research from the foundation of those collections to the present day when they repose in the British Museum. . . . The correspondence of the age, and the diaries of such as Humphrey Wanley, show a long succession of scholars seeking admission to those libraries, and very seldom being turned away. Formed as private ventures, maintained often with difficulty, those great collections seem always to have been regarded by their possessors as something of a public trust to be held in the interests of learning, and in both cases their final and hazardous transference into the hands of the nation seems to have conferred little immediate benefit on scholars since the transition had long been prepared by the generous way in which they were conducted. . . . It only remains for the modern commentator to add that without their [i.e. the Cotton's

[1] See C. E. Wright in *The English Library*, 194–7.
[2] D. Douglas, *English Scholars*, 17.

and Harley's] openhanded encouragement of learning the whole development of medieval scholarship would have proceeded on other and far less advantageous lines.[1]

To this it might only be added that research in Tudor and early Stuart history was equally benefited, especially by Cotton's inventory of state papers.

The worst of the losses suffered by Cotton's library occurred during the great fire of 1731 which marked almost exactly the centenary of Sir Robert's death. Although he was spared such losses by fire, Sir Robert learned other sharp lessons of adversity during the last two years of his life. His library remained closed and sealed from 1629 through 1631; his petitions to the King and to the Council were ignored; and the Royal displeasure had vicious effects. In 1630, attracted by Sir Robert's difficulties, a small group of conspirators tried to extort money from the old baronet by threatening him with blackmail and murder. The leader of the conspiracy, a man named Stevenson, set the stage for scandal and chose to play the unlikely role of injured husband in the farce. Cotton was expected to remain closeted with Mrs. Stevenson long enough for the blackmailer to accuse Cotton of having been 'lecherous with his wife'. The antiquary was not so obliging, however, for, as Cotton wryly observed, 'Sir Robert Cotton and the rest came down into the dining room, the space being so short of his staying in the upper room that no such act could be done as is surmised'.

The rest of the plot was a good deal less risible. The conspirators determined to get money from Cotton by raising a fear in him that they would kill him 'by land or water'. Asserting that they themselves were friends of two great lords, Cotton's enemies, who would secure their pardon if murder were committed, they added, more realistically, that since Cotton was in trouble already he would be undone 'if he ended not this matter'. In a final and scarcely less ominous exchange, they threatened to sue Cotton in the Court of High Commission and beg his fine. Fortunately, they had not taken the measure of their man. Cotton was a tough-minded antagonist who might have appreciated Pascal's remark—'that presumption should be joined to meanness is extreme injustice'. He set about proving that the conspirators were untrustworthy men and women with criminal histories. In his 'Abstract of all the Proofs of the Conspiracy of Stevenson and

[1] D. Douglas, *English Scholars*, 263–4.

others against Sir Robert Cotton', he put his long historical training to use for the benefit of 'Mr. Attorney General and my Counsel'.[1] His counter-attack succeeded; nothing more was heard of the affair. Its importance lies only in what it tells of Cotton's character, and of the seamy side of London life.

Why Cotton's name should be honoured as one of the founders of modern English historiography should by now be clear. The scattered contents of monastic libraries were preserved for use largely by Cotton's efforts. In an age given to drawing morals and precedents from history, Cotton provided not only what was expected, but also the indispensable means and support for critical, scholarly historiography. Thanks in large part to Cotton's exemplary patronage, the standards of English historical writing and thought were redefined. The debt of good scholarship to good librarianship cannot be too heavily emphasized; the danger to both from political irresponsibility is quite readily apparent. Cotton exercised his influence wisely on behalf of liberal learning, and did his best to maintain the precarious alliance that sometimes exists between politics and scholarship.

[1] This entire episode is based on 'Notes and Remembrances on the Stevenson Conspiracy Against Sir Robert Cotton', B.M. Add. MS. 14049, fols. 21–36.

6

THE VARIETIES OF HISTORY

MANY ATTEMPTS HAVE BEEN MADE to define the genera and species of history, but none has gained scientific standing. The historian may properly conclude that the right divisions of his subject are those which best suit his own purposes. To indicate the range and variety of seventeenth-century English historical literature, a classification of works by their titles would suffice. To make provision for the importance of philosophical theory and environmental influence in the development of historiography, a classification in terms of purpose and content is needed. In order to evaluate change and progress in the writing of history, methodological problems must be considered, even though few contemporary historians wrote essays on method. In selecting historical works to illustrate the varieties of history, arbitrary choices have been made, for as Ralegh rightly observed, 'the sea of examples hath no bottom'.

i TITLES: PROBLEMS OF CLASSIFICATION

It is a tribute to Sir Francis Bacon that the divisions of history which he proposed are still useful starting points for any discussion of the varieties of modern historical writing and thought. In his last major work, *De Dignitate et Augmentis Scientiarum* (1623), Bacon divided history into two major areas of study: natural history, which was concerned primarily with the deeds and actions of nature; and civil history, which was concerned primarily with the deeds and actions of men. Ultimately, both types of history, when properly

150

conceived and executed, would provide the subject matter of Baconian philosophy. All human learning, Bacon insisted, could be divided into history, poesy, and philosophy, with reference to the three intellectual faculties of memory, imagination, and reason; and the same divisions held for theology. The Baconian divisions of civil history are, however, the only ones immediately relevant to this study of seventeenth-century historiography.

Bacon divided civil history into three broad classes; sacred or ecclesiastical history; civil history proper; and history of learning and the arts, which he designated as lacking. He discussed civil history at some length, asserting that it was pre-eminent among human writings in dignity and authority, and that the difficulty of civil history was no less than the dignity. Memorials, antiquities, and perfect history were the three subdivisions of civil history. Memorials consisted of 'history unfinished, or the first rough draughts of history'.[1] Antiquities were 'remnants of histories'. Perfect history dealt with a portion of time, or with persons worthy of mention, or with 'exploits of the nobler sort'. The appropriate stylistic forms of perfect history were: chronicles or annals; lives; and narrations or relations. The divisions of ecclesiastical history were nearly the same as those of civil history, 'for there are Ecclesiastical Chronicles, there are Lives of the Fathers, there are Relations of Synods and other things pertaining to the Church'.[2] However, Bacon went on to make separate subject matter divisions of sacred history, which he designated as history ecclesiastical, history of prophecy, and history of divine judgments or providence.

Bacon formulated his divisions of civil history primarily in terms of style and subject matter (or content), rather than in terms of purpose or method. He recognized the stylistic deficiencies of civil history as it existed in his own day, and emphasized the need for new histories which would contribute to the advancement of learning. Nevertheless, Bacon was limited by his own lack of knowledge of the problems of contemporary scholarship; he was a brilliant critic, but not an expert judge of early seventeenth-century historical writing and thought. Bacon acknowledged that the study of antiquities

[1] Bacon, *Works*, VIII, 423. All references are to the Spedding, Ellis, and Heath editions published in Boston. All references in this and in the following paragraph occur in the Second Book of *De Augmentis*. See *Works*, VIII, 407–39, *passim*.

[2] Bacon, *Works*, VIII, 435.

was properly a part of civil history, but he was loath to admit that the techniques and special skills of antiquaries might be necessary to the writer of perfect history. His definition of antiquities was informative not only because of what it said, but also because of what it omitted:

> *Antiquities*, or remnants of histories, are . . . like the spars of a shipwreck; when, though the memory of things be decayed and almost lost, yet acute and industrious persons, by a certain per-severing and scrupulous diligence, contrive out of genealogies, annals, titles, monuments, coins, proper names and styles, ety-mologies of words, proverbs, traditions, archives and instruments as well public as private, fragments of histories scattered about in books not historical,—contrive, I say, from all these things or some of them, to recover somewhat from the deluge of time: a work laborious indeed, but agreeable to men, and joined with a kind of reverence; and well worthy to supersede the fabulous accounts of the origins of nations, and to be substituted for fictions of that kind; entitled however to the less authority, because in things which few people concern themselves about, the few have it their own way.[1]

Bacon thought that writers of universal history, seeking 'that compendious brevity', would be inclined to 'take up with rumours and popular reports', and thus write history from relations which were not authentic.[2] But nowhere did Bacon stress the importance of careful collation of manuscripts, or the comparison of chronicles and annals with public records. Meticulous and specialized research in source materials did not appeal to Bacon, who was willing to entrust the collection and ascertaining of facts to others.

Source materials Bacon considered under the heading of *memorials*, which he referred to as 'preparatory history'. *Memorials* contained the facts and information which writers of perfect history would presumably make use of in their work. Under *memorials* Bacon included commentaries and registers, edicts and decrees, titles of things and persons, and annals as well as chronologies. Since Bacon himself seldom cited examples it is difficult to know exactly how he would have classified particular works. What is certain is that Bacon did not distinguish clearly between primary sources and secondary authorities in his discussion of memorials. The utility of such a distinction was, however, coming to be more and more widely

[1] Bacon, *Works*, *VII*, 423–4.   [2] *Ibid.*, 431.

recognized by Bacon's scholarly contemporaries. Although it has never been an absolutely clear-cut distinction, it was essential to historical criticism, and Bacon was remiss in ignoring it.

The subdivisions of civil history proper contained a wide variety of historiographical types, but Bacon failed to discuss some titles which he ought to have recognized as historical. The *survey*, for example, Bacon ignored although most local history was written in survey form. The fact is that Bacon's rigid outline of civil history created a misleading impression of accuracy and precision of definition. No exact boundaries separated the shires of civil history; and this Bacon himself recognized in the case of cosmography, an example of 'mixed' history, containing elements of both civil and natural history. It is evident that in his discussion of historical writing Bacon made use of conventional terms and titles, which he merely arranged in a formal hierarchy. An examination of the terms and titles themselves will provide a more realistic idea of the richness of contemporary historiography.

The word *history* was used indiscriminately by seventeenth-century writers to apply to all kinds of works about the past. In dramatic literature, for example, histories had a prominent place, as the title page of Shakespeare's First Folio made clear: 'Mr. William Shakespeares Comedies, Histories, & Tragedies'. After 1588 history plays, especially those dealing with English subjects, became very popular. The historiographical importance of Elizabethan drama requires no comment—Shakespeare's Histories have been studied in detail.[1]

The humanist ideal of history as a narrative of important events, written according to classical models, had not been fulfilled in England when Bacon wrote. Poems, novels, plays, and political tracts carried the title of *history* in the seventeenth century, as did

---

[1] Amid this vast literature two books are outstanding: Lily B. Campbell, *Shakespeare's Histories Mirrors of Elizabethan Policy* (San Marino, 1958), and E. M. W. Tillyard, *Shakespeare's History Plays* (London, 1948). Two recent books are Irving Ribner, *The English History Play in the Age of Shakespeare* (Princeton, 1957), and Tom F. Driver, *The Sense of History in Greek and Shakespearean Drama* (New York, 1960). A very useful comment on the nature of the rules which governed the writing of history plays is in George Lyman Kittredge's edition of *The First Part of King Henry the Fourth* (Boston, 1940), ix. Narrative histories in verse were written, but they were unusual. William Slatyer, *The Historie of Great Britanie* (London, 1622), is an example of a lengthy history in doggerel verse. In 1595, Samuel Daniel wrote a verse history of the civil wars between Lancaster and York.

religious and scientific tracts. Many *histories* might equally well have been called annals or chronicles—terms which Bacon used, in fact, to designate types of perfect history. Historians continued to praise the method and style of the classical writers—Thucydides, Livy, Tacitus, and Polybius in particular—but few Englishmen attained to anything like the literary distinction and narrative power of the Greek and Roman historians.

Annals may be defined somewhat more precisely than *chronicles*. The annalistic form, whether classical or medieval, was one in which the events of each year were recorded serially. Generally speaking, English annals were bare recitals only of the events of each year. Tacitus had written annals which were supple works of art, but most English writers lacked Tacitus' gifts. Camden wrote his annals of Elizabeth's reign in accordance with classical models, as will be shown, and he was perhaps the first Englishman who thus achieved a masterpiece of interpretation; even so, he was frustrated in his efforts to achieve smooth narrative by the staccato requirements of an annual account.

According to the standard modern authority, a chronicle was 'a detailed and continuous register of events in order of time; a historical record, especially one in which the facts are narrated without philosophic treatment, or any attempt at literary style'.[1] This definition accurately describes most sixteenth- and seventeenth-century English chronicles. However, the word *chronicle* was also used as a loose synonym for history—Edmund Campion referred to his own *Historie of Ireland* (1571) as 'this Chronicle', although the work combined elements of the *survey*, with a narrative based on the reigns of English kings.[2] By the middle of the seventeenth century the word *history* was gaining currency as a title at the expense of *chronicles* and *annals*. On the one hand, this was simply because *history* was a more dignified title, which promised to sell better than the old-fashioned *chronicles* or *annals* in black-letter type. On the other hand, scholarly histories, and literary histories based on classical models were being written in ever greater numbers, as more and more Englishmen sought enlightenment from the past.

---

[1] *A New English Dictionary on Historical Principles* (Oxford, 1888 ff.), *sub.* 'Chronicle'.

[2] See *A Historie of Ireland* by Edmund Campion, with an introduction by Rudolf Gottfreid (Scholars Facsimiles and Reprints, New York, 1940), 'Epistle Dedicatory', n.p.

In 1633 James Ware published *The Historie of Ireland, Collected By Three Learned Authors*, which he dedicated to Thomas, Lord Viscount Wentworth. In the opening sentence of the dedication he observed that these histories contained 'Annales and other worthy memorialls of this Kingdom . . .', and went on to remark, in the Preface, that anyone wishing to reconstruct the history of Ireland might do so from original sources including 'the ancient and moderne recordes, both in this Kingdome and in England, as also out of diverse manuscript Annales and Chartularies, which are yet extant among us . . .'[1] Annals were in this case identified with memorials, and both were treated as source materials. Ware was an Irish historian, biographer, and antiquary of note, who was sensible of the difference between historical compilation and historical criticism and synthesis. Nevertheless, he used the terms *history, annals* and *memorials* almost interchangeably. This linguistic confusion was characteristic—in the seventeenth century there was a far greater latitude in the meaning of such words than exists today. The modern reader must therefore be prepared to accept a terminology which was often suggestive rather than exact.

Registers and *catalogues* were *memorials*, which might be either 'primary' sources—that is, manuscript compilations made by contemporaries who were either eye-witnesses, or charged with recording the events or facts listed—or they might be 'original' only in the sense that they were underived, being compilations made up by later historians or antiquaries. The word *register* was applied especially to compilations containing the forms of writs of common law, as cited by English lawyers in the sixteenth and seventeenth centuries. Bacon, however, pointed out that *registers* contained not only titles of things and persons, but also 'collections of public acts, such as edicts of princes, decrees of councils, judicial proceedings, public speeches, letters of state, and the like, without a perfect continuance or contexture of the thread of the narration'.[2] Although Bacon did not mention them, parish registers were also important sources, frequently used by seventeenth-century historians. Thomas Fuller, after discussing the records he had consulted in preparing *The Worthies of England* (1662), wrote, 'to these authentic records

---

[1] Ware's *Historie of Ireland* is included in the same volume cited in the previous note. See 'Preface', 4.

[2] Bacon, *Works*, VIII, 423. See also W. S. Holdsworth, *Sources and Literature of English Law* (Oxford, 1925), 116–17.

let me add the Church Registers in several parishes, denied indeed by our common lawyers, but stickled for by some canonists to be records-fellows at least, and having, though not the formality in law, the force thereof in history, very useful to help us in many nativities'.[1]

The seventeenth-century concern with secular and ecclesiastical antiquities produced a vast number of *catalogues* which proved remarkably useful to later historians. As might be expected, some *catalogues* were mere lists, while others were extended historical essays, based on meticulous research. Ralph Brooke's *Catalogue of English Kings, Princes and Peers* (1617) served some of the purposes of the modern *Complete Peerage*, although it was strongly criticized after its publication by Augustine Vincent in his *Discoverie of Errors in the first Edition of the Catalogue of Nobility Published by Ralph Brooke, York Herald* (1622).[2] Francis Godwin's *Catalogue of the Bishops of England* (1601), containing brief lives, satisfied the desire for information about the spiritual peerage. The book proved useful enough to be edited and continued by William Richardson in 1643. John Selden's *Titles of Honour* (1614) was one of the great historical works of the early seventeenth century. In a series of brilliant essays explaining and interpreting a catalogue of titles, Selden defined, and traced the history of, the titles of honour of his day. The work showed what could be done to make a *catalogue* a work of historical scholarship.

Monuments, views and *surveys* were commonly recognized as historical titles. In general, the word *monument* meant anything that by its survival commemorated a person, action, period, or event. The legal pedigree of the word revealed a more precise meaning: *monuments* were legal instruments, or written documents or records; and, by extension, information given in writing. The term was sometimes used as a synonym for *memorials* or source materials by antiquaries and historians. John Weever's *Ancient Funerall Monuments* (1631), for

---

[1] Thomas Fuller, *Worthies* (ed. Freeman), 12. Also John Selden, *Titles of Honour* (1631 ed.), 'Preface', Sig. b. 3v.

[2] Books which are mentioned in this chapter, but not quoted from, do not appear in the notes. The editions I have used are not necessarily first editions, although the dates given in the text are those of the first edition unless otherwise noted. In all cases the place of publication was London. The *Short Title Catalogue* provides the best bibliography of editions, and I have not thought it necessary to add to the notes on an already lengthy chapter.

example, described, with a wealth of learned detail, the burial customs and monuments of the 'Royal Progenie, the Nobilitie, Gentrie, and Commonaltie, of these his Majesties Dominions'.[1]

Views and *surveys* were terms which had been derived from the practices, recognized in law, of viewing and surveying land. A *survey* usually implied a comprehensive examination, discussion, or description of a particular area.[2] Stow's *Survey of London* was perhaps the best example of the type, although Richard Carew's *Survey of Cornwall* (1602) deserves more than passing mention. A great number of local *surveys* and *histories* of towns, counties, ecclesiastical sees, and the like were written in the seventeenth century, many of which, however, remained in manuscript. Taken together, they provide convincing evidence of the growth of interest in historical studies at the local level. Camden's *Britannia* and Speed's *Theatre of Empire* could be considered forms of the *survey*, written on a national scale.

Lives, memoirs, and *characters* were among the more popular forms of historical writing of the seventeenth century. Bacon rightly insisted that *lives* were consonant with perfect history; and his own *History of the Reign of King Henry VII* (1622) was one of the best early examples of the type. Sir Robert Naunton's *Fragmentia Regalia*, compiled about 1630, was little more than a series of character sketches of the Elizabethan great, but Fuller's *The Worthies of England* was a full-scale historical effort. Fuller organized his book in terms of counties—'seeing *where* is as important as *when* to a man's being', as he put it. Fuller described manners, customs, and landmarks in addition to writing brief lives of famous Englishmen. He distinguished sharply between what he called real and personal matters—real referring to 'the commodities and observables of every county'; personal to 'the characters of those worthy men who were natives thereof'.[3]

Sir John Spelman's *Life of Alfred the Great*, although written in the mid-seventeenth century, was not printed until 1709 when

---

[1] John Weever, *Ancient Funerall Monuments* (London, 1631), title page. Weever defines a monument on p. 1 as 'a thing erected, made, or written, for a memoriall of some remarkable action, fit to be transferred to future posterities'.

[2] A 'view' technically meant looking at a piece of land whereas a 'survey' implied actual measurement by surveyors appointed by commissioners or by a court. See Robert Callis, *Of Sewers* (London, 1647), 105–6.

[3] Fuller, *Worthies*, 10.

Thomas Hearne edited and published the manuscript. Spelman had deliberately sought to reconstruct the spirit of an age through the biography of its leading statesman:

> In Representation by Picture, though the outward Lineaments of the Feature be exactly hit, yet is there ever some Fail in the Expression of the Life it Selfe; because the Pencil, following the Exterior, can go no further than that is able to carry it. And the same defect is always in History, especially when, for want of Discovery of the Reasons and Affections whereupon the things and Actions moved, the bare done Deed represents not the Spirit nor Genius that was the Powerful Agent in them . . .[1]

Sir John Spelman had some of his father's historical gifts; and in the text of the work he showed that he had a talented biographer's instinctive feeling for his subject.

Not only did the younger Spelman attempt to depict Alfred's character, he also tried to show that the spirit of Alfred's age was very different from the age in which he himself lived. 'We must not expect', he wrote, 'such a solemne and steddy manage of Affaires then, as now in a full grown state, furnished with the ministry of all her necessary members . . .' This was, indeed, an important historical generalization, the significance of which was not always understood even by learned writers.[2] Bacon himself was inclined to ignore it in writing his *History of Henry VII*, although elsewhere he wrote brilliantly of the need for a history of learning which would charm 'the Literary Spirit of each age as it were from the dead'.[3]

The Life and Reign of Henry VIII by Lord Herbert of Cherbury was a work conceived in the Baconian spirit of *perfect history*. Lord Herbert began research for the biography as early as 1632, aided by a staff of clerks, but progress was delayed, and the title did not appear in print until 1649, a year after Lord Herbert's death. It was one of the most ambitious *lives* of the early seventeenth century, being, in fact, a general history of the times of Henry VIII. As a work of scholarship it still has some value, for Herbert quoted extensively from original records (translations of which he provided in the text), and he essayed interpretation as well as description. The literary defects of

---

[1] Sir John Spelman, *The Life of Alfred the Great* (London, 1709), 'Author's Dedication'.

[2] *Ibid.*

[3] Bacon, *Works*, VIII, 420.

the book were those typical of the times: a glut of quotations, and failure to break through the limitations of the annalistic form. The scholarly defects resulted in part from Lord Herbert's attempt to follow classical precedents; he freely interpolated speeches which had no basis in fact. Even though S. J. Brewer, the editor of the *Letters and Papers of Henry VIII*, was inclined to accept the content of some of these speeches on the ground that Lord Herbert might have had access to documents which had since disappeared, there is every reason to believe that Herbert was simply inventing, in the manner of Thucydides and Tacitus, what he thought would be appropriate to the occasion.[1]

Lord Herbert was by no means the only historian to make use of such invented speeches. Bacon, and a number of lesser writers, also followed classical precedents in this, as in other matters. Classical influences were undoubtedly still very strong in the early seventeenth century, when English historiography was evolving its own tradition. The influence of classical models on English historiography is a subject about which too little is known to justify broad generalization. One fact, however, seems clear: English historians sometimes equalled their chief master, Tacitus, in the writing of characters. The sharply defined characters inserted into seventeenth-century histories were remarkable literary achievements; and the further domestication of classical literary forms may have been rendered somewhat easier by the successful imitation of the Tacitean character.

Having become a native literary genre in the course of the seventeenth century, the *character* declined toward the end of the century with the steady development of biography. An observation made by Lord Herbert of Cherbury in the conclusion of his *Life and Reign of Henry VIII* suggests the stylistic problems of combining a *life* and a *character*; and, incidentally, it sums up Lord Herbert's attitude toward history:

> And now if the reader (according to my manner in other great personages) do expect some character of this prince, I must affirm (as in the beginning) that the course of his life being commonly held various and diverse from it self, he will hardly suffer any, and that his history will be his best character and description. Howbeit, since others have so much defam'd him, as will appear by the

---

[1] See H. A. L. Fisher, 'The Speeches in Lord Herbert of Cherbury's "Life and Reign of Henry VIII",' *English Historical Review* (XX, 1905), 498.

following objections, I shall strive to rectify their understandings who are impartial lovers of truth; without either presuming audaciously to condemn a prince, heretofore sovereign of our kingdom, or omitting the just freedom of an historian.[1]

The character had to be short, impressionistic, and direct. It expressed a clear and unqualified historical judgment or interpretation of motives. A life, on the other hand, was more detailed, thorough, and factual. Good historical biography required extensive research and depended for its effect on the accumulation of details.[2]

Lord Clarendon's *History of the Rebellion and Civil Wars in England* has been often praised for its characters, and often criticized for its partiality. This is not the place to dispute the virtues and vices of Clarendon's *History*; what is pertinent here is that the work illustrates Bacon's third division of perfect history, namely, *relations*. According to Bacon, *narrations* or *relations* of actions (such as the Peloponnesian War) were superior to *perfect histories* of times, because *relations* contained 'a manageable and definite argument, whereof a perfect knowledge and certainty and full information may be had; whereas the story of a time (especially if it be of a period much before the age of the writer) is sure to meet with many gaps in the records, and to contain empty spaces which must be filled up and supplied at pleasure by wit and conjecture'.[3] Bacon was much too sanguine about the possibility of attaining perfect knowledge and full information about recent historical events; and certainly Clarendon's work was lacking in adequate documentation. Still Clarendon's *History of the Rebellion* was the best (and, after its publication in 1702-4, the best known) history of the English revolution. It was the kind of historical relation which Bacon would have commended, not only for the sake of its superb characters, but because it could provide the basis for later histories of that time.

The lesser varieties and hybrids of history may be treated more briefly, for they present fewer problems of stylistic definition. *Breviaries, epitomes,* and *abridgments* were either short outlines of

---

[1] Lord Herbert of Cherbury, *The Life and Reign of Henry VIII*, reprinted from Kennet's folio edition of 1719 (London, 1870), 743-4.
[2] See David Nichol Smith, *Characters from the Histories & Memoirs of the 17th Century* (Oxford, 1918), x, li, and 'Introduction', *passim*.
[3] Bacon, *Works*, VIII, 425.

history, or condensations of longer works. According to Bacon's aphoristic phrase, epitomes were 'the corruptions and moths of history'.[1] The popularity of such epitomes and digests was at least understandable. The Elizabethan book-buying public included many men and women who could neither afford nor profit from longer historical works. John Stow's *A Summarie of Englishe Chronicles* (1565), although in fact an original work, set the pattern for simplified history. Countless later writers, lacking Stow's integrity, published epitomes which were little more than outlines of Stow's work. Grub Street was indifferent to scholarship, but not to books which would sell; and such books sold.

Cosmography was a hybrid or mixed history which was more common in the early seventeenth century than in later times. Bacon defined history of cosmography as 'indeed mixed of many things; of Natural History, in respect of the regions themselves, their sites and products; of History Civil, in respect of the habitations, governments, and manners of the people, and of Mathematics, in respect of the climates and configurations of the heavens, beneath which the regions of the world be'.[2] Peter Heylyn's *Microcosmus* was one of the best-known examples of the type; it went through many editions and grew finally to a folio cosmogony. Heylyn wrote in the preface 'To the Reader', in the 1621 edition, that 'At the first, there went into this *Little World* these six integrall parts, *History*, *Geography*, *Politics*, *Theologie*, *Chronologie*, and *Heraldrie*'. Cosmography was not unlike a large-scale *survey*. Heylyn's work contained no 'mathematics', but then Bacon himself had not stickled about the meaning of the word.

Many collections of historical documents were made early in the seventeenth century, although few were published until the second half of the century. John Selden complained in 1619 that England was behind other countries in publishing records, chronicles, and other historical materials:

But for *England*; howsoever wee have indeede in Print some good and select old Authors of our storie, through the benefit of a few worthy men that have affected that way to appeare beneficiall to their Countrie, yet the number of our *Historical materials*, which, being of singular use, remains still only in *Manuscript*, makes them

---

[1] *Ibid,*, VI, 189, from 'The Advancement of Learning'.
[2] *Ibid.*, VIII, 434.

all, that are publique, seem little more than a handfull well gather'd, where there might be a plentiful harvest . . .[1]

Acts of Parliament, legal documents, and similar memorials had, of course, been printed; and sixteenth-century scholars had begun to provide more or less competent editions of medieval chronicles. However, until 1655, when Dugdale completed and published Dodsworth's *Monasticon*, there was nothing to compare in scope and scholarship with Thomas Rymer's *Foedera*, published in twenty volumes between 1704 and 1735. The *Foedera* was indeed a 'plentiful harvest', being one of the greatest collections of English historical documents published in modern times.

It was not until the decades after 1660 that students and writers of history could begin to rely on printed source collections. The subsequent development of English historiography was profoundly influenced by the availability of printed sources. Elizabethan and early Stuart scholars had established the tradition of manuscript learning; their successors helped to make such learning available to a much wider public.

In fields allied to history, such as heraldry, genealogy, philology, and bibliography, considerable progress was made during the early seventeenth century. The scope of the present essay forbids discussion of these subjects, but attention must be called to the variety and significance of historical works in translation.

Englishmen were well-served by the Elizabethan translators. Most of the great works of classical history were made available to English readers before 1630, in translations which were readable, if not always exact. Sir Henry Savile's translation of Tacitus, published in 1591, was a remarkably accurate text—unlike North's better known and more popular translation of Plutarch's *Lives*. The literary qualities and scholarly virtues of Thomas Hobbes' translation of Thucydides (1629) won the admiration of contemporaries and of posterity. Modern historical works in Latin, Italian, French, and other languages were also translated; and the demand for such translation continued to grow as the mercantilist English state extended its interest in the old world and the new.[2]

---

[1] See Augustine Vincent, *A Discoverie of Errors* (London, 1622), which contains Selden's preface, 'To My Singular Good Friend, Mr. Augustine Vincent', from which the extract is taken.

[2] In addition to the works already cited in Chapter II, see H. B. Lathrop, *Translations from the Classics into English* (Madison, 1933).

Bacon early called attention to the stylistic inadequacies of English historiography. In matters of literary style and organization, most English writers were inferior to Machiavelli and Guicciardini, not to mention Thucydides or Livy or Tacitus. Translations made English readers aware of how much was lacking in the history of their own country and no doubt this awareness of deficiencies acted as a stimulus to improvement. But contemporary criticism of English writers should not be over-emphasized. In method and content, as well in style, the progress of English historical writing and thought was rapid and decisive after the beginning of the seventeenth century.

Reflecting on the different kinds of history which he had made use of in writing his *Titles of Honour* John Selden summed up the problem of defining the varieties of history:

> Under *Histories*, I comprehend here not only the Numerous store of *Histories* and *Annals* of Several States and Ages, wherein the Actions of them are put together in some continued discourse or thred of time, but those also that otherwise, being written for some narrow particulars, and sometimes under other names, so shew us in example what was done in *erecting* and *granting* or otherwise, concerning the *Titles* here medled with, that we may thence extract what conduces to the representation of the *Forms* and *Patents of Erections* and *Grants* and of the *Circumstances* and *Nature* of *the Being of them*.[1]

The value of a work of history, whatever its title, had to be determined on the basis of its content and the purposes which it could be made to serve.

ii CONTENT AND PURPOSE

A three-fold division of history—universal, territorial, and problematic—corresponds to ends, or norms, in terms of which historical work was accomplished.[2] Universal history may be taken

---

[1] John Selden, *Titles of Honour*, 3rd ed. (London, 1631), 'Preface', Sig. b. 3.

[2] My use of the word 'problematic' differs from that of Richard McKeon, whose work, however, is quite illuminating. See Richard McKeon, *Freedom and History* (New York, 1952), *passim*. The norms of work and history are discussed by Paul Schrecker in *Work and History* (Princeton, 1948), Chapters 1, 10 and 'Introduction', *passim*.

to include not only histories which, like Ralegh's *History of the World*, were universal in scope, but also speculations about history, that is, all general theories, philosophies, or theologies of history. The controlling assumptions of territorial history were those which derived ultimately from the nation state. Thus, historical works which dealt with affairs of state, or with local, biographical or episodic history primarily from a territorial point of view can be classed as territorial history. Problematic history was most often monographic, dealing with particular institutions, customs, or disciplines. The range of problematic history was as great as that of either universal or territorial history. Works of pure scholarship stood at one end of the spectrum; works of pure propaganda stood at the other. In general, titles which illustrate any one of the three divisions also illustrate the others, for the norms of work and history are not independent of, or unrelated to, one another.

Since the purpose of the present chapter is to provide a general view of the main contours of historical thought in early seventeenth-century England, primary emphasis will be placed on writers who were representative of the thought and expression of the age. Scholarship without a broad social and intellectual base soon declines—the decline of the Roman empire in the west synchronized exactly with the decline in scholarly standards. In England in the early seventeenth century scholars seldom became wealthy, but they were respected, and their works were read. And leagued with the scholars were many lesser historical writers and theorists who bridged the gap between the erudite and the popular taste for history.

The Christian interpretation of history remained dominant in the seventeenth century, yet most historians and commentators were becoming more concerned with the mundane problems of secular history; secularism insinuated itself gently into the minds and hearts of men.[1] Admonitions to read and study history came from all kinds

---

[1] As Professor Haskins pointed out, Christian Europe took its philosophy of history from Augustine and its chronology from Eusebius until quite modern times. See Charles Homer Haskins, *The Renaissance of the Twelfth Century* (New York, Meridian Books, 1957), 227. This of course does not mean that providence itself was not secularized in the course of time. The discussion in the text should make it clear that significant changes were taking place despite the frequent appeals to providence.

of writers, most of whom were not scholars. In the long run, however, it was the broadening of the social basis for historical studies that made possible continuing advances in scholarship. The historical revolution reached fulfilment after the Restoration, but the underlying causes of the rapid progress in scholarship at that time are to be sought in the slower shifts of educated opinion, as well as in the original contributions of individual historians.

(a) Universal History

Foreign influences played an important role in shaping English historical thought in the late sixteenth century. Many English historians were influenced by Jean Bodin's *Methodus ad Facilem Historiarum Cognitionem* (1566).[1] This work even provided Degory Wheare with the model for his *De Ratione . . . Legendi Historias* (1623). Thomas Blundeville's *The True Order and Method of Wryting and Reading Histories* (1574) was a translation of parts of two Italian treatises, one by Acontius, the other by Patrizzi.[2] Secular in tone, it was the direct outgrowth of an enthusiasm for the study of history on the part of an important group of men at court who had come to appreciate the value of historical learning. Without a doubt, however, the most characteristic expression of late sixteenth-century historical thought in England (and perhaps on the continent) was Pierre Amyot's preface to Plutarch's *Lives*. Amyot's 'To the Reader' was familiar to a number of English readers in North's translation, which appeared in 1579. Equalling even the Tudor chroniclers in his fondness for rhetorical platitudes, Amyot expressed perfectly the prudential theory of history's uses: 'For it is a certain rule and instruction which by examples past teacheth us to judge of

[1] The best modern edition of Bodin in translation is that published as no. XXXVII in the Columbia University Records of Civilization Series, with a good introduction. See John Bodin, *Method for the Easy Comprehension of History*, translated by Beatrice Reynolds (New York, 1945). On Bodin and his influence, see John L. Brown, *The Methodus ad facilem historiarum, A Critical Study* (Washington, D.C., 1939), and Leonard F. Dean, 'Bodin's *Methodus* in England before 1625', *Studies in Philology* (XXXIX, 1942), 160–6.

[2] See Hugh G. Dick, 'Thomas Blundeville's The True Order and Methode of Wryting and Reading Histories (1574)', *Huntington Library Quarterly* (II, 1940), 149–70. Lewis Einstein, *The Italian Renaissance in England* (New York, 1907), contains some comment on the influence of Italian historiographers.

things present and to foresee things to come, so as we may know what to like of, and what to follow, what to mislike, and what to eschew.' [1]

Bodin's *Methodus*, by contrast, was scholarly and highly original. Bodin rejected the Christian framework of universal history, sought to discover historical general laws, and emphasized the importance of climate and geography in determining the course of history. In his critical account of ancient and modern historians he gave one of the best early surveys of the history of historiography. English historians assimilated many of Bodin's ideas, but the long-range influence of Bodin was perhaps greatest on readers who sought bibliographical guidance and helps toward an understanding of historical theory.

The conventional ideas and attitudes toward history of the reading public found ample expression in the conduct books of the early seventeenth century. Henry Peacham's *The Compleat Gentleman* (1622) appealed to ambitious middle-class families, and probably to many others whose gentility was recent. Peacham asserted that gentlemen should not devote themselves to scholarship, but should read history for the sake of its lessons. Experience was a better teacher than books, and gentlemen should not waste their lives in libraries. Peacham recommended Camden's *Britannia* and Selden's *Anelecton Anglo-Britannicon* as the best introductory works on British history; in his choice of books, at least, Peacham showed discrimination. Bodin was cited as authority for the belief that history was even useful in curing the sick; and Plutarch's *Lives* was recommended to readers who sought an understanding of morality and the rules of 'well-being'. [2]

Richard Brathwaite's *The Scholler's Medley, Or, An Intermixt Discourse Upon Historical and Poetical Relations* (1614), dealt with the educational benefits of history, especially for the English gentry. When Brathwaite brought out an enlarged edition of the work in 1638 he changed the title to *A Survey of History, Or, A Nursery for Gentry*. Brathwaite wrote (in *The Scholler's Medley*) that he would be concerned with the 'several uses and fruits of Histories', and with the 'profit which redounds to every state, either Aristocraticke,

[1] See *The Lives of the Noble Grecians and Romans* (New York, Limited Editions Club edition, 1941), xxxiii.

[2] See Henry Peacham, *The Compleat Gentleman*, ed. by G. S. Gordon (Oxford, 1906), 51–3 and xiv–xv.

Democraticke, or Monarchicke, by the true understanding and use of histories'.[1]

There was nothing unusual about Brathwaite's treatment of these themes. Brathwaite was primarily concerned with the supposed benefits of history, rather than with first causes, or with a philosophical interpretation of history. He believed in the same ideas that Ralegh expressed in his *History of the World*, even asserting that 'a good historian teacheth thus: things (saith he) are purposed by Man, but disposed and moderated by God'.[2] Having served as Deputy Lieutenant, Justice of the Peace, and Captain of the trained bands in Westmoreland, Brathwaite was no doubt entitled to his opinion that knowledge of history was useful in disciplining soldiers. His faith in the therapeutic value of history must have been sorely tried, however, for it is unlikely that he ever actually encountered a drunkard who had been cured by reading history.[3]

A favourite analogy of early seventeenth-century writers was that between history and the theatre. The idea that history was a drama or spectacle was often the complement of the idea that God was 'the author of all our tragedies'. Brathwaite expressed this literary convention when he wrote that 'History's scope is not only to personate the acts of men upon the theatre of this world, but likewise to call out such Lawes, Orders, and Precepts, as well Morall as Divine, which may benefit their present state'.[4]

Although Brathwaite attempted to discuss historical evidence, he had no idea of the importance of research in original records, and could suggest only trivial methodological rules. 'The principall cause why so manie discordancies & meere oppositions in Histories arise', Brathwaite thought, was that historians failed to compare historical accounts; probability was the test of truth, and 'by the nature of the Agent, conjecturall events or reasons of events may be drawne'.[5]

Brathwaite wrote primarily for the majority of the gentry who,

---

[1] Richard Brathwaite, *The Scholler's Medley* (London, 1614), 1.

[2] *Ibid.*, 109.

[3] *Ibid.*, 89–105, 113. Brathwaite, like many other writers, was strongly influenced by the Tudor conception of history found in the *Mirror for Magistrates*. See Lily B. Campbell, *Tudor Conceptions of History and Tragedy in 'A Mirror for Magistrates'* (Berkeley, 1936), *passim*. See *Scholler's Medley*, 110–16.

[4] Brathwaite, *Scholler's Medley*, 6–7.

[5] *Ibid.*, 71, 74. Brathwaite valued moral history above all other kinds (see pp. 38–44).

167

while interested in history, were not interested in becoming scholars. Like many other middling landowners of his day, Brathwaite was inclined to be opinionated and a little pompous. Yet he had redeeming qualities; it is to him that we owe the witty lines on Puritanism:

> To Banbury came I, O profane one!
> Where I met a puritane one
> Hanging of his cat on Monday
> For killing of a mouse on Sunday.

The promoter of the scheme for an 'Academe Roial', Edmund Bolton, was a student of history who had travelled both in England and Ireland in search of antiquities. Like Brathwaite, he had received some legal training, but had never practised. Being a Catholic, Bolton was subject to the recusancy laws and was perhaps therefore overly anxious to avoid giving offence to the Crown. In his *Hypercritica, or a Rule of Judgement For Writing or Reading Our Histories* (1618?) he betrayed an excessive diffidence toward monarchical authority, but this did not prevent him from making some telling criticisms of contemporary styles of written history.

Bolton had no use for chroniclers who merely related events 'without their Premises and Circumstances'.[1] He was hypercritical of legendary history, and of etymological conjectures, although he admitted that without them the history of England would be almost a blank from the creation to the time of Julius Caesar. After pointing out the political uses of legendary history, he allowed his prejudices to overcome his perspicacity:

> Out of that very Story (let it be what it will) have titles been framed in open Parliament, both in *England* and *Ireland*, for the Rights of the Crown of England, even to entire Kingdoms. And though no parliament can make that to be a truth which is not such in the nature thereof, nor that much Autority is added thereby to the traditional Monument, because Parliament men are not alwaies Antiquaries, yet are we somewhat the more, and rather ty'd to look with favour on the case. Thereof it pleased me well, what once I did read in a great Divine, that *in Apochryphis non omnia esse Apochrypha.*[2]

Bolton went on to condemn the 'Vast Vulgar Tomes procured for the most part by the husbandry of Printers . . .' At the conclusion of his

[1] See Joel Elias Spingarn, *Critical Essays of the 17th Century*, 3 vols. (Oxford, 1908), I, 84. All references are to this edition.
[2] *Ibid.*, I, 86.

essay he listed the four main duties of a historian: as a 'Christian cosmopolite', to discover God's interventions in history; as a Christian patriot, to disclose the causes and authors of his country's good and evil; as a Christian subject, to show the benefits of obedience; and as a Christian *paterfamilias* to look after his own interests, since history might bring renown but never riches.[1]

Degory Wheare's published lectures on the study of history became a standard seventeenth-century work on historical writing and thought. *De Ratione . . . Legendi Historias* was in use as a textbook at Cambridge even at the beginning of the eighteenth century. A translation by Edmund Bohun was published in 1685 under the title *The Method and Order of Reading both Civil and Ecclesiastical Histories. In which the most Excellent Historians are Reduced into the Order in which they are Successively to be Read; and the Judgements, concerning each of them, Subjoined.* This translation included an Appendix of particular historians, both ancient and modern, compiled by Wheare's contemporary, Nicholas Horseman. In translation the book reached a wide English audience.

In the 'Antelogium', or introductory oration (which was actually delivered in 1635) Wheare gave a definition of history which pointed up the common belief that history confirmed universals:

> The definition . . . which I will stand by is this, *History is the Register and Explanation of particular affairs, undertaken to the end that the memory of them may be preserved, and so Universals may be the more evidently confirmed, by which we may be instructed how to live well and Happily.*[2]

Wheare went on to say that 'out of Particulars, general Precepts may be deduced, and Confirmed . . .', but he did not believe that students should come to the study of history until they already had a firm grounding in moral philosophy.[3]

---

[1] *Ibid.*, I, 114. Bolton's own attempt to write history was a conspicuous failure. *Nero Caesar, Or Monarchie Depraved* (London, 1627), was 'An Historical Worke' only in name. According to Bolton, Nero's villainy was detested by King James, but notwithstanding, Bolton thought the life of Nero taught the precious secret that 'No Prince is so bad as not to make monarkie seeme the best forme of government'. See *Nero Caesar*, 'Dedication', and pp. 24, 43, 91, 97–101, 116.

[2] Degory Wheare, *The Method and Order of Reading Histories*, translated by Edmund Bohun (London, 1685), 15.

[3] *Ibid.*, 16–30, 361.

Wheare's outlook was conservative; he maintained a rigid distinction between civil and ecclesiastical history. Rightly insisting that each required a separate scheme of periodization, he went on to argue that the study of ecclesiastical, and especially of sacred history would be most profitable, because sacred history alone 'makes no mistakes'.

In outlining the proper course of historical study Wheare advocated that readers begin by acquainting themselves with universal history. For this purpose he recommended that epitomes be read first, and singled out Sleidan's epitome of universal history for special praise. He urged the reading of ancient historians, and finally recommended the best modern writers, 'amongst which, Sir Walter Rawleigh, our countrey-man deserves the first place . . .' [1]

The central thesis of Wheare's theory of history was that history illustrated providence, and was 'nothing but Moral Philosophy cloathed in Examples'. Wheare saw the hand of God even in the writing of history: Herodotus had, by divine providence, begun his history where biblical accounts left off. The principal end of history, however, was 'Practice, and not Contemplation'. The historian was thus essentially a moralist, and historical truth depended not just on the validity of the historian's evidence, but also on the validity of the historian's moral philosophy. [2]

Despite its shortcomings as an *ars historica*, Wheare's work served a useful purpose; it remained for many years the best general introduction to modern historiography. The only work of comparable importance (aside from Bodin's outdated *Methodus*) was Peter Heylyn's *Microcosmus*, which contained no radically different ideas, and no fresh insights.

The historical thought of Thomas Hobbes was more original than has been generally supposed. It is a mistake to see in Hobbes only the deductive philosopher and psychologist of sovereignty. In the years before 1629, when he published his translation of Thucydides, he had bestowed his studies 'for the most part, in that kind of

[1] Degory Wheare, *The Method and Order of Reading Histories*, 40.

[2] *Ibid.*, 298. See also pp. 299–322. Wheare is discussed by William H. Allison, 'The First Endowed Professorship of History and Its First Incumbent', *American Historical Review* (XXVII, 1922), 733–7. See also *Remarks and Collections of Thomas Hearne*, 11 vols., edited by C. E. Doble, *et al.* (Oxford, 1885–1918), vii, 125–6, discussing the later history of this professorship and the controversy about teaching ecclesiastical subject matter.

Learning which best deserveth the paines and houres of Great Persons, *History*, and *Civill Knowledge*.[1] To trace the development of Hobbes' philosophy in relation to his ideas of history would require a separate work. In his *Behemoth* he applied to recent history the theories which he had developed in the *Leviathan*. Like his younger contemporary, Harrington, Hobbes wrote a 'problematic' interpretation of English history using ideas of explanation which could be applied to much wider historical fields.

It was as a translator of Thucydides that Hobbes first began to develop his ideas about history. The reasons which Hobbes gave for admiring Thucydides were not simply the conventional ones, although Hobbes did not disdain to repeat commonplaces in praising the uses of history. And, in his refutations of the criticism of Dionysius of Halicarnassus, Hobbes showed scholarly judgment and insight. Although he was mainly concerned with discussing Thucydides' methods, Hobbes in fact outlined a theory of history.

Hobbes quickly disposed of the problem of translation in his preface 'To the Readers'. He would make use of the best Greek text of Aemilius Porta—'not neglecting any version, or other helpe I could come by'. He went on to point out the need for maps in order to understand the history of the Peloponnesian War. A general map of Sicily he found extant, done by Philip Cluverius; a general map of Greece was lacking, and Hobbes therefore drew one as best he could. The importance of good maps was better understood by Hobbes than by many professed historians.

In his introductory essay on the 'Life and History of Thucydides', Hobbes dealt with various problems of method, style, and purpose in history. It is a pity that Hobbes did not develop some of the arguments he briefly outlined. The distinction he drew between truth and elocution was conventional: truth was the soul; elocution the body of history. 'The latter without the former is but a picture of history,' Hobbes wrote, 'and the former without the latter, unapt to instruct.' Thucydides supposedly combined the virtues of truth and of rhetoric. But Hobbes made it clear that rhetoric had no claims against truth. Unlike Bolton, Hobbes would not tolerate absurdity

[1] See Thomas Hobbes, editor and translator, *Eight Bookes Of The Peloponnesian Warre, Written by Thucydides The Son of Olorus* (London, 1629), 'Dedication'. A very valuable discussion of Hobbes' historical thought is Leo Strauss, *The Political Philosophy of Thomas Hobbes*, translated by Elsa M. Sinclair (Oxford, 1936), Chapter VI, *passim*, and p. 79.

in the name of patriotism. He obviously approved of Thucydides' suspicions of democracy, but he approved even more of his objectivity. Quoting Lucian, Hobbes reminded his readers 'that a writer of History, ought in his writings, to be a forraigner, without Countrey, living under his owne Lawe onely, subject to no King, nor caring what any man will like, or dislike, but laying out the matter as it is'. By implication, Hobbes repudiated this view in his later writings, but it must be remembered that the Greek civil war did not terrify Hobbes, whereas the English civil war did.

Hobbes considered Thucydides to be 'the most Politique Historiographer that ever writ'. He defended the style and method of Thucydides by pointing out that the annalistic form had advantages for a writer capable of blending analysis and narrative; and he argued that the speeches of Thucydides were one means of handling problems of causation:

> The grounds and motives of every action, he [Thucydides] setteth down before the action it selfe, either narratively, or else contriveth them into the forme of *Deliberative Orations*, in the persons of such as from time to time bare sway in the Common-Wealthe. After the actions, when there is just occasion, he giveth his own judgement of them, shewing by what means the successe came either to be furthered or hindered. Digressions for instructions cause, and other such open conveyance of Precepts (which is the Philosophers part) he never useth, as having so cleerly set before men's eyes, the wayes and events, of good and evill counsels, that the Narration it selfe doth secretly instruct the reader, and more effectually then could possibly be done by Precept.[1]

Hobbes touched on many other points of interpretation, often displaying an accurate understanding of the purposes served by Thucydidean conventions. He knew that the lessons of history could not be learned easily, by memorizing the precepts of philosophy. History had its own purposes and methods, and Hobbes even suggested that the proof of Thucydidean history was its coherence: 'In summe, if the truth of a History did ever appeare by the manner of relating, it doth in this History; So coherent, perspicuous and perswasive is the whole Narration, and every part thereof.' The

---

[1] Hobbes. *Thucydides*, 'Of The Life And History'. All quotations are from one or the other of the short prefaces which Hobbes wrote, which are without pagination.

172

Hobbesian idea of history, even as it appeared in his later work, bore the stamp of this early Thucydidean influence.

A historical theorist of striking originality and intellectual power was George Hakewill, whose major work, *An Apologie or Declaration of the Power and Providence of God*, precipitated a minor historical tempest when it first appeared in 1627. Bearing the subtitle, 'An Examination and Censure of the Common Errours touching Nature's perpetuall Decay', Hakewill's book successfully challenged the widely held belief in the corruption of nature.[1] Taking issue with Bishop Goodman, who had attempted to show that the great world and the little world of man had decayed and grown weaker in the course of time, Hakewill denied both the premises and the conclusions of his opponent. The literary and philosophical issues at stake were those having to do with man's place in the universe, and with the relative merits of the ancients as opposed to the moderns. Hakewill was a man of his time who accepted the conventions of seventeenth-century discourse, yet he was also an original thinker; and, in contrast to Goodman, who appealed to reason and theology, Hakewill appealed to history and empirical evidence. Although Hakewill naturally sought the safety of authority, the real strength of his argument was historical: evidence became a fundamental test of truth.

Hakewill knew that his ideas were not those held by most of his contemporaries: 'I have walked (I confesse) in an untrodden path, neither can I trace the prints of any foot steppes that have gone before mee, but onely as it led them to some other way ...'[2] In order to prove his thesis that the world had not decayed, but had, in many ways, progressed since the coming of Christianity, he had to refute the conventional arguments of analogy, which Goodman

---

[1] See George Hakewill, *An Apologie Or Declaration Of the Power And Providence Of God* ..., 3rd ed. (London, 1635). The 3rd edition contains additions and is the best one to consult. Hakewill dedicated the book to Oxford University. The best discussion of this whole controversy is Victor Harris, *All Coherence Gone* (Chicago, 1949). The conventional attitudes of Hakewill are rightly stressed (see Harris, p. 60), but as a historical theorist Hakewill seems to me to be rather more original, and less dependent on the appeal to authority than Professor Harris makes out. J. B. Bury, *The Idea of Progress* (New York, 1932), at pp. 88 ff., found Hakewill anything but original, but he was perhaps the first modern historian to stress Hakewill's importance.

[2] Hakewill, *Apologie*, 'Preface'.

and many other historians and theologians had used. The doctrine of symmetry or analogy was explicit in Goodman's idea that man, the microcosm, was analogous to nature, the macrocosm. Goodman, by invoking the argument of analogy, was able to assert that evidence of corruption in modern man necessarily implied evidence of decay. And the corruption or decay of man and nature he explained as the consequence of Adam's sin.

In denying the relevance of analogy, Hakewill contributed to historical thought in two ways: he called attention to the problem of establishing evidence for analogy, and he asserted that proof of progress or decay must rest on comparative history. The comparative method was valid, moreover, only if it involved induction from a number of instances.[1] The symmetry between past and present was inexact, according to Hakewill, and ultimately it was unhistorical:

> I do not believe that all Regions of the world, or all ages in the same Region afford wits always alike: but this I thinke, neither is it my opinion alone, but of *Scaliger*, *Vives*, *Budaeus*, *Bodine*, and other *great Clearks*, that the wits of these later ages . . . may be as capable of deepe speculations; and produce as *masculine*, and lasting birthes, as any of the ancientes times have done.[2]

Hakewill went on to criticize Bacon's idea of progress, and especially Bacon's metaphor of modern man as a dwarf standing on the shoulders of a giant. Modern men were as capable and as strong as the ancients—the only differences were owing to historical circumstances. Hakewill therefore proposed to 'looke backe into *Histories*, and compare time with time . . .' in order to discover the nature and extent of progress. There was, Hakewill concluded, 'a kinde of *circular progresse*' in all things, including the arts. Hakewill failed to develop the implications of his idea of progress, and rested his case on the old doctrine of mutability, yet he developed an acute insight into historical differences. No age, he wrote, 'but hath exceeded all others in some respects, and againe in other respects hath beene exceeded by others'.[3]

In his attack on the doctrine of analogy Hakewill had the support of scholars, notably the eminent Hebraist, John Spencer. Scientific thinkers were also growing sceptical of the doctrine of nature's

---

[1] Cf. Harris, *All Coherence Gone*, 58.
[2] Hakewill, *Apologie*, 'Epistle Dedicatory'.
[3] Quoted by Harris, *All Coherence Gone*, 80.

decay, and Hobbes was to deny that there had ever been a golden age from which man had declined. After about 1635 the doctrine of nature's decay was no longer seriously held. History and science were both against it. To believe in Christian providence, as Hakewill and his contemporaries did, was one thing; to proportion one's beliefs to the evidence of secular history was another. Hakewill admired the man who,

> . . . as a part of mankinde in generall takes a view of the *universall*, compares person with person, family with family, corporation with corporation, nation with nation, age with age, suspends his judgement, and upon examination clearly finds, *that all things work together for the best to them that love God*: and that though some members suffer, yet the whole is no way thereby damaged at any time . . .[1]

The historical evidence which Hakewill collected to support his main thesis was impressive in its variety. In his treatment of the history of scholarship and learning, he devoted space to a discussion of historiography. Quoting Bodin, Hakewill observed that all ages 'have their proper *genius*, which inclines the mindes of men to certain studies . . .' [2] He believed that his own age was inclining more and more toward historical studies.

(b) Territorial History

Works of territorial history may be divided into four main groups: national, local, biographical and episodic. In the early seventeenth century the most significant advances were being made in the field of local history. Camden was by far the most eminent national historian, although his *Britannia* was essentially a survey of local antiquities and history. In general, national historians were popularizers, not original scholars; most of their ideas about history were adequately summarized by the lesser historical theorists.

Two reasons help to account for the relative mediocrity of national histories written in the early seventeenth century. In the first place, the compendious works of Hall, Stow, Grafton, Holinshed, and Camden satisfied the immediate need for historical information. In the second place, English scholars had begun to realize that only by advancing knowledge of particular institutions, customs, and

---

[1] Hakewill, *Apologie*, 'Preface', Sig. b. 2.
[2] *Ibid.*, 38. See also pp. 259, 283–6.

disciplines could general historical knowledge be advanced. The anti-quarian movement therefore attracted the best scholars; and the tendency on the part of most national historians of the early seventeenth century was to write brief and, if possible, readable histories. Only Camden produced a gracefully written national history based on thorough and meticulous scholarship.[1]

Richard Knolles' *General Historie of the Turks* (1603) was one of the most popular national histories written in the early seventeenth century. Although Dr. Johnson praised Knolles for his style, he lamented that 'the nation which produced this great historian, has the grief of seeing his genius employed upon a foreign and uninteresting subject . . .' It was Johnson's opinion in 1751 that Knolles had recounted enterprises and revolutions 'of which none desire to be informed'.[2] Needless to say, this was a singularly mistaken judgment, for at a time when the Ottoman empire was still a great power, many Englishmen with mercantile or political interests in the near east desired to be informed about the history of the Turks. In fact, trade and travel in the early seventeenth century virtually insured a market for all kinds of territorial histories.

Although Knolles expressed conventional ideas about the purpose and meaning of history, he did attempt to specify reasons for the rise of Turkish power. Ultimately, Knolles referred all historical changes to the judgments of God, but 'next to these causes from above (without offence be it said) is the small care of Christian princes . . .' The disunity of Christendom was one cause of the rise of Turkish power; the virtues of the Turks another. The Turks had an 'infinite desire for soveraigntie' as well as 'rare unitie and agreement amongst themselves'; and they showed courage, temperance, and care for 'the two strongest sinews of every well governed commonweale, Reward propounded to the good, and Punishment threatened unto the offender . . .'[3]

Knolles divided his work into two main sections. The first was a

---

[1] Cf. Louis B. Wright, *Middle Class Culture*, 321.

[2] Samuel Johnson, *The Rambler*, 4 vols. (London, 1767), II, 95; No. 122, Saturday, May 18, 1751. Knolles' *History* was continued in various editions by other writers, some of whom made use of the reports of English ambassadors in Turkey. The work also served to provide plots for several of the heroic plays of the Restoration. Knolles published a translation of Bodin's *Methodus* in 1606.

[3] Knolles discussed his ideas about history at some length in the '*Induction*' to his History. Quotations are from this. See also *Historie*, 131.

narrative history of the rise of the Saracen and Turkish power; the second was a series of lives of the various Ottoman rulers. The book was largely a record of the crimes and military successes of the Turks, with the centre of interest on great men. The territorial state, symbolized in its rulers, was the basic unit of Knolles' study.

The scholarly value of Knolles' work was slight. He made use of various secondary authorities, notably Venetian histories, and Boisard's *Icones Sultanorum Turcicorum* (1596), but he lacked a good grounding in modern European history, and was content to rely on his own 'simple judgement to make choice of that [which] was most probable . . .' He interpolated speeches, quoted the 'purport' of letters (although he did not have the actual documents to work with), and set few limits on his use of conjecture. On the other hand, his *Historie* was readable and—considering the limited number of available sources—it was a considerable achievement.[1]

Most of the territorial histories of England written during the earlier seventeenth century were popularizations of earlier chronicles, with some additions from the works of antiquaries. Aside from Camden's *Annales*, these histories contained few original ideas or new facts. The works of Samuel Daniel, John Speed, and Sir Richard Baker were justifiably popular, however, for each wrote interesting narrative, and, in general, displayed good judgment. Some of the Tudor chroniclers continued to be reprinted, and Anthony Munday imitated their worst features in his *Brief Chronicle* (1611). Bishop Godwin's *Annals* were written in the modest hope that they might encourage better historians to study the Tudor period.

Samuel Daniel published *The First Part of the Historie of England* in 1612, long after he had established his reputation as a poet. The avowed purpose of the book was to provide a 'true history' of England in readable form. He asserted, however, that he would 'tread as tenderlie on the graves of his [King James'] magnificent Progenitors, as possibly I can: knowing there may (in a kind) be *Laesa Maiestas*, even against dead Princes'. He would deliver 'nothing but what is fit for the world to know' and would harbour no 'stubborn opinions'.

In the first few pages of his history Daniel announced his belief in providence, and drew the analogy between past and present:

We shall find still the same correspondencies to hold in the action

---

[1] Knolles, *Historie*. '*Induction*'.

of men: Virtues and Vices the same, though rising and falling according to the worth, or weaknesse of Governors: the causes of the ruines, and mutations of states to be alike: and the trayne of affaires, carried by precedent, in a course of succession under the like colours.[1]

This was a perfectly clear statement of the dominant seventeenth-century attitude toward historical change.

John Speed's historical writings have been favourably compared with Stow's, often for no better reason than that both men were tailors by profession. Literary historians have been inclined to praise Stow for his industry and Speed for his critical ability, but the truth is that Speed was inferior to Stow in almost every respect. Speed was perhaps best known in the seventeenth century for his Biblical genealogies, which were prefixed to many early editions of the King James Bible. These genealogies were little more than pious guess-work. Speed's *Theatre of the Empire of Great Britaine* and the *Historie of Great Britaine* (1611) were undeniably useful works, containing sensible observations on history. But Speed's critical acumen was limited: he objected to the Brute Legend not just on historical grounds, but also (and this was perhaps equally important to Speed) because Brute debased the English—Brute was guilty of adultery.

The *Theatre of the Empire* was actually a descriptive commentary on Speed's great series of folio maps of Great Britain. As a cartographer Speed deserved the reputation which he held in the seventeenth century; the maps in the *Theatre* were clear, detailed, and reasonably exact. In view of the fact that they were not based on new surveys, they were as accurate as could be expected. Certainly they served historians well. The value of Speed's historical work was slight for the medieval period, although when he reached the Tudors he made some use of manuscript materials; for such help he was indebted to Cotton, Spelman, and Bacon. Speed's work had little independent value, but it demonstrated more than just a conventional attitude toward history. Speed was a pioneer in maps, and one of the first English historians to include good reproductions of coins in his

---

[1] This, and the quotations in the preceding paragraph, are from the 'Epistle Dedicatory' in Samuel Daniel, *The First Part of the History of England* (London, 1613). There is a good short study of Daniel; see May McKisack, 'Samuel Daniel as Historian', *Review of English Studies* (XXIII, 1947), 226–43.

work. In its content, Speed's *Theatre* was for these reasons a landmark in English historiography.[1]

Sir Richard Baker's *Chronicle of the Kings of England* (1643) was eminently readable and retained its popularity in the later seventeenth century. Baker had published his *Chronicle* while still a prisoner for debt in the Fleet. He did not pretend to write from original sources, but he fortunately displayed more common sense about history than he did about his own affairs. He rejected the story of Brute and began with the coming of Julius Caesar to England. In the course of his work Baker attempted to give brief accounts of the men of learning, including the historiographers who graced each king's reign.

Lesser works, which were completely derivative in content and purpose, were Munday's *Brief Chronicle of the Successe of Times from the Creation of the World to this Instant* (1611), and Edward Ayscue's *Historie Conteyning the Warres, Treaties, Marriages, and other Occurents betweene England and Scotland* (1607). These were typical of the hack work of the age. Anthony Munday wrote expressly for the middle-class London public, dedicating his book to the Lord Mayor and 'all the Knights, Aldermen, and worshipful Brethren, the carefull Fathers and Governours of this Honourable Estate', as well as to the Merchant Taylors and to the Goldsmiths.[2] The only worthwhile parts of Munday's book were those he plagiarized from John Stow. Ayscue similarly plagiarized from Camden's *Britannia*. But then, as he admitted, his entire scholarly travel consisted only in reducing other men's works to a coherent whole, whereby the reader might 'carry the matter better in memory'.

Local histories were either of counties or of towns in the earlier seventeenth century; parish history had to await the publication of

[1] Speed's limited critical ability is apparent in the *Historie* (London, 1611). See, for examples, pp. 153, 291, 295, 316–17, 771–3. On Brute, see p. 165. Speed's *A Cloud of Witnesses* (London, 1616), contains his genealogies, and is reprinted in the anonymous commonplace book, *The Rich Cabinet* (London, 1616). Some of Speed's maps are conveniently reprinted in a Penguin book, with an introduction by E. G. R. Taylor, *An Atlas of Tudor England and Wales* (London, 1951).

[2] See Anthony Munday, *A Brief Chronicle* [etc.] (London, 1611); there are three separate dedications. Munday accepted the Brute legend (p. 477) and plagiarized freely from Stow's *Survey* (see pp. 526–72). William Fulbecke's *An Historicall Collection of the Continnal Factions . . . Of the Romans and Italians* (London, 1601) was a similarly uninspired work.

White Kennett's *Parochial Antiquities* in 1695. It was during the 1570's that local history and topography first began to be written independently by scholars. The first and most influential county history was William Lambarde's *A Perambulation of Kent: Conteining the Description, Hystorie, and Customes of that Shire* (1576). Lambarde was thorough and he was readable. His work contained much valuable information about the Kentish gentry, for whom the book was primarily intended. Lambarde's knowledge of local history and topography was impressive by any standards: he set out to describe the cities and markets, ports and liberties, religious houses and schools, civil customs and ecclesiastical foundations of the county, in addition to its topographical features and whatever else he considered to be its 'singularities'.[1] Lambarde's *Kent* inspired Richard Carew to undertake his *Survey of Cornwall*, which he began to write in the 1580's; in the 1590's John Norden began writing his surveys of particular counties, and the stream of county histories continued to grow rapidly thereafter.[2]

Carew's *Survey of Cornwall* (1602) was a delightfully written account of local customs, families and antiquities by a gentleman-scholar who took as active an interest in the present as he did in the past. Like Lambarde and other local historians, Carew was indebted to Camden for information, particularly about local government. He described gentry genealogies and listed Cornish worthies according to their ranks in society, but he was not indifferent to the wider economic problems of local history. An apt observer of changes in the economic and social terrain (as many local historians were), Carew speculated intelligently about why feudal dues were still enforced on tenants, why the value of land was increasing, and about the effects of the truck system at the tin-mines.[3] Occasionally, Carew

[1] See William Lambarde, *A Perambulation Of Kent: Conteining the Description, Hystorie, and Customes of That Shire* (London, 1826). This reprints the 1576 edition, including manuscript notes by the author. See esp. pp. 1–6.

[2] The best general survey of problems of local history is W. G. Hoskins, *Local History in England* (London, 1959); Chapter II deals with 'English Local Historians'. In the British Museum and elsewhere there are manuscript collections on local history as well as manuscript histories. See, for example, B.M. Stowe MS. 811, f. 2, *et seq.*; Harley MS. 793; Harley MS. 1944. The scholarly correspondence of the age abounds in references to the study of local history.

[3] See Richard Carew, *A Survey of Cornwall*, ed. F. E. Halliday (London, 1953), 123–8. This edition omits certain genealogical passages of interest

would describe some incident which he thought called for an apology. Touched by the story of a dog who had carried meat to a blind mastiff, Carew excused the reference by saying that Pliny would have found room for such a story. These details may have affronted the 'Dignity of History', but few Tudor or Stuart historians could resist them.

The revolution that took place in the study and writing of local history in the early seventeenth century was clearly marked, even though many important works remained in manuscript for a century or more. The new interest in local history was apparent in nearly every shire. Sampson Erdeswicke, Camden's friend, began work on his *Survey of Staffordshire* in 1593. When the work was published in 1723, in response to the continuing popularity of local histories, the editor pointed out that 'this Piece was so highly esteemed by the Gentry of this County, that many copies were taken of it, and preserved as valuable Rarities by Them'.[1] Percy Enderbie, the historian of Wales, noted in the preface to his *Cambria Triumphans* (1661) that the civilities of the gentry of Wales, 'and the help of a good library of Sir Edward Morgans of Lantarnam, encouraged me to bring this Embrion to maturity . . .'[2] Sir John Doderidge's *History of the Ancient and Modern Principality of Wales, Collected from Records in the Tower* (1630) was an even greater work. The massive manuscript collections of Dodsworth on Yorkshire history, the volumes of letters written by local antiquaries to one another, and the still unexplored manuscript histories of English towns and counties, all testify to the ferment of ideas about local history.[3]

In 1656, Sir William Dugdale published his *Antiquities of Warwickshire, Illustrated; From Records, Leiger Books, Manuscripts, Charters, Evidences, Tombs, and Armes: Beautified with Maps,*

to historians, but contains a useful introduction, and reprints some of Carew's letters. Carew distrusted the Brute legend (p. 82), but apparently refused to reject it. The episode of the blind mastiff is described on p. 182.

[1] Sampson Erdeswicke, *A Survey of Staffordshire* (London, 1723), 'Preface', by Sir Simon Degge. A great part of this *Survey* was devoted to genealogies of the gentry; at the end there is a short essay by Degge, 'Observations upon the Possessors of Monastary Lands', which contains interesting material on the fortunes of some gentry families.

[2] Percy Enderbie, *Cambria Triumphans, Or Brittain In Its Perfect Lustre* (London, 1661), 'To the Reader', Sig. B1.

[3] Dodsworth's Collections on Yorkshire, in transcript, are B.M. Harley MSS. 793–805.

Prospects, and Portraictures. In this work county history came of age. Dugdale dedicated the book to his patron, Sir Christopher Hatton, who had procured for him access to the public records and had supported him throughout his labours. Although scarcely readable as a narrative, *The Antiquities of Warwickshire* was an exhaustive and eminently scholarly work which defined new standards for county history, as Stow's *Survey* had for town history.

In 1697 when William Nicolson brought out his *English Historical Library*, he devoted several pages to local history. The book was by no means exhaustive, but it did show which books and manuscripts were reasonably well known. For a few counties little or no work had been accomplished. For several, manuscript histories were extant, and for at least a dozen counties, substantial works had been published. In the writing of town histories, Nicolson rightly said that 'Industrious *John Stow* leads the van in the present Century . . .' [1] The work of William Somner on *The Antiquities of Canterbury* (1640) was in form and content a *survey*, which closely followed the pattern set by Stow. Few histories of other towns were published before 1660, and most English towns had to wait until the eighteenth century for anything like adequate histories.

In general, local ecclesiastical histories were not undertaken, although Stow and Somner included a considerable amount of information on parish and church antiquities in their surveys. Dugdale's *The History of Saint Paul's Cathedral in London* (1658) was not a conspicuously successful attempt to write such history, although it set a valuable precedent. In the eighteenth century, when parish history became a favourite hobby of the country parson, much useful work was done, but even then the writing of local history was dominated by the interests of the squires. In fact, as Mr. W. G. Hoskins has recently observed, 'The dead hand of the seventeenth-century squire still guided, until recently, the hand of the living antiquary.' [2]

Biographical history was likewise closely related to the genealogical and heraldic interests of the English nobility and gentry. A steady stream of books, both popular and scholarly, conveyed information

[1] William Nicolson, *The English Historical Library*, 3 vols. (London, 1697), I, 191. This book and its later enlarged editions contain much valuable information on all phases of seventeenth-century historiography. On county histories, see Vol. I, 24–70, *passim*.

[2] Hoskins, *Local History*, 23.

about titles of honour and families of importance. A few examples must suffice to show that Selden's *Titles of Honour* was not isolated from the main currents of seventeenth-century learning.

In 1642 Sir John Doderidge's *The Magazine of Honour: Or a Treatise of the severall Degrees of the Nobility of this Kingdome . . . Collected by Master Bird* was published, the chief merit of which was that it provided legalistic definitions of ranks. Dugdale's *The Ancient Usage in Bearing of such Ensigns of Honour as are Commonly call'd Arms* (1682) was in fact an essay on heraldry, which contained also a catalogue of the present nobility of England. Other works having less obvious titles, also testified to the interest in noble pedigrees. Peter Heylyn's *A Help to English History*, for example, described the succession of the kings, nobility, and bishops of the kingdom.[1]

Dodsworth's *Monasticon* (1655–61–73) and Dugdale's *Baronage* (1675–6) were two of the greatest and most influential works written in this broad tradition of medieval documentary history. Of the *Monasticon*, Nicolson wrote 'Great and many are the Advantages which all the several Branches of our History (not only in Ecclesiastical, but Civil and Martial Occurrences) will derive from this Work: And hardly a private Family (of any Consideration) in the Kingdom, but will meet with something of its Genealogy and Pedigree.'[2] Robert Dale, writing also in 1697, observed that his own *Exact Catalogue of the Nobility of England and Lords Spiritual* was meant for those who had neither the leisure nor convenience to consult Dugdale's *Baronage* and other works.

Family histories were being written in the earlier seventeenth century, but most of these, including Gervase Holles' *Memorials of the Holles Family*, remained in manuscript.[3] Most biographical history at the popular level was concerned with the deeds of kings. William Martyn's *The Historie and Lives of Twentie Kings of England* (1615) was dedicated to 'the Gallant Gentrie of England', and was

[1] It is worth noting that Heylyn was obliged to deposit £200 for the privilege of using Cotton's library and borrowing books therefrom. See *The Historical and Miscellaneous Tracts of the Reverend and Learned Peter Heylyn, D.D.* (London, 1681), which contains a brief life of Heylyn by George Vernon, who makes this statement. Heylyn wrote several historical works, mainly on church history.

[2] Nicolson, *English Historical Library*, II, 187 (1697 ed.).

[3] See Gervase Holles, *Memorials of the Holles Family*, ed. by A. C. Wood (Camden Society, 3rd ser. LV). Holles claimed to 'affect nothing but truth and plainnes . . .' (p. 9).

not meant for the learned. Sir John Hayward's later works, *The Lives of Three Norman Kings* (1613), and his useful *Life of Edward VI* (1630), were more respectable—possibly Hayward had profited from his examinations following the Essex conspiracy.

Thomas Heywood, the dramatist, was in many ways the most interesting and successful of all the popularizers of history writing in the early seventeenth century. Elizabethan drama had helped to sustain the demand for popular biographical history, and Heywood exploited the moralizing conventions of Tudor poetry and drama in his *Nine Bookes of Various History Concerninge Women* (1624). In addressing himself to the reader, Heywood wrote:

> I only present thee with a Collection of Histories, which touch the generalitie of Women, such as have either beene illustrated for their virtues, and Noble Actions, or contrarily branded for their Vices, and baser conditions; in all which I have not exceeded the bounds of goode and sufficient Authoritie.[1]

He went on to stress the utility of his history as a means of promoting happiness in marriage, and as a guide to widows, but he knew better than to write a book of moral platitudes. He included jesting tales on the ground that 'they that write for all must strive to please all'.[2] And this he did, including throughout his history stories which were as bawdy as any to be found in the dramatic literature of the day. Heywood was simply a more able and amusing writer than most who catered to the popular taste for gossip in the plain wrapper of history.

Episodic history was not unknown in the earlier seventeenth century, but most of the great works of this type dated from the civil wars. Clarendon's *History* excelled all others which dealt with particular episodes; it owed something to classical models, and to the early influence of Selden on Clarendon. Writing as one who had 'been present as a member of Parliament in those councils before and till the breaking out of the Rebellion, and having since had the honour to be near two great kings in some trust', Clarendon was able to write contemporary history in the fullest sense. Far more than Camden, he wrote about men and events from first-hand know-

---

[1] Thomas Heywood, *TUNAIKEION: Or Nine Bookes Of Various History Concerninge Women* (London, 1624), 'To the Reader'.
[2] *Ibid.*, p. 430.

ledge; and his book still has some value as a source, although even so great a scholar as S. R. Gardiner made mistakes in interpreting some of Clarendon's statements. Thanks to Professor B. W. G. Wormald, it is now possible to read Clarendon in perspective; and no further attempt need be made here to assess his significance.[1]

The earlier English examples of episodic history were, for the most part, undistinguished. Bacon's category of *narrations or relations of actions* was (if narrowly conceived) identical with episodic history. But Bacon could hardly have been thinking of English *narrations*, for there were few narrative accounts of historical 'actions' written by Englishmen. The real stimulus to such writing came from the civil wars; and only after the Restoration was it possible to realize Bacon's hope that a collection of such narrations and relations 'would be a nursery whereby to plant a fair and stately garden when time should serve'.[2] Narrations were not generally used in writing a 'complete history of Times' until the eighteenth century.

(c) *Problematic History*

Problematic history was concerned with institutions, customs, laws, and scholarly disciplines related to history. Varying in purpose and content from the scholarly to the vulgar, works of problematic history were usually monographs on isolated topics, or else histories of particular institutions. In territorial history the unit of study was the state, or its land areas. In problematic history the unit of study was defined by the particular social, political, religious, or scholarly interests of the writer. In this chapter only a few samples of work in problematic history can be given.[3] Relevant methodological questions

[1] The quotation from Clarendon is from Edward, Earl of Clarendon, *The History of the Rebellion and Civil Wars in England*, W. Dunn Macray, ed., 6 vols. (Oxford, 1888), I, 5. See also B. H. G. Wormald, *Clarendon, Politics, History & Religion* (Cambridge, 1951), for comment. Bibliographical references having to do with the history of the manuscript may be found in Wormald's preface.

[2] Bacon, *Works*, VIII, 430.

[3] An extended commentary on the way in which historical ideas about the French religious wars of the sixteenth century influenced English political thought may be found in J. H. M. Salmon, *The French Religious Wars in English Political Thought* (Oxford, 1959). English reference to the French wars of religion, as Mr. Salmon observes, formed a significant part of the English attempt to explain the present by reference to historical

must be reserved for discussion in the following chapters, which examine the representative works of major historians.

The institutions whose histories and records were most often studied in the seventeenth century were Parliament, the Church, and the Courts of Law. Henry Elsynge, Clerk of Parliaments from 1621 to 1636, wrote a purely institutional history of Parliament, parts of which were incorporated into Cotton's tract, 'That the King's of England Have Been Pleased . . . to Consult with their Peers'. Elsynge was little swayed by contemporary controversy. Being free of the present-mindedness of the common lawyers, he succeeded in writing a book in which seventeenth-century ideas of Parliamentary rights and liberties were not pushed back into the fourteenth and fifteenth centuries, or into immemorial antiquity.[1] By comparison, even Sir Simonds D'Ewes was a less painstaking scholar, although his *Journals of All the Parliaments during the Reign of Queen Elizabeth* was a far more important work. It is worth noting that, although many Elizabethan and Stuart antiquaries were concerned with the history of Parliament, few works dealing specifically with Parliamentary history were published before the 1640's. Doubtless this was a tribute to the censorship laws.

Ecclesiastical history was almost inevitably partisan if not quarrelsome in the seventeenth century.[2] The foremost English Church historian of the century, James Ussher, was a formidable opponent of Catholicism, although he was noted for his moderation as well as for his learning. Ussher's definition of the English Church rested on historical foundations, and Ussher was too much of a scholar to seek easy triumphs by suppressing or distorting evidence. Peter Heylyn, on the other hand, was an Anglican extremist, most of whose historical works satisfied, at best, tractarian standards. His

experience (p. 3). The book not only suggests the importance of problematic history, but also indicates how important French legal thought was for the development of English historiography and legal theory.

[1] See Catharine Strathman Sims, ed., *Expedicio Billarum Antiquas* (Louvain, 1954), xvii–li, *passim*; also p. 157.

[2] One of the fullest and best discussions of English seventeenth-century ecclesiastical and legal history is Heinrich Arneke, *Kirchengeschichte Und Rechtsgeschichte in England (Von Der Reformation Bis zum 18. Jahrhundert)* (Halle, 1937); Arneke also argues that the late sixteenth and early seventeenth centuries mark a radical turning point in English historiography (see pp. 301–19). On Ussher's definition of the church, see W. K. Jordan, *Religious Toleration*, II, 143–69.

History of the Sabbath (1636) was typical of much problematic history, being written to show the Sabbatarians 'how much they have deceived themselves and others . . .' [1] Heylyn could not even tolerate the moderate Anglicanism of Fuller, whom he accused of giving grounds for 'inconformity and sedition' in his *Church History of Britain*. Although a few of Heylyn's criticisms were justified, his scholarship was incapable of sustaining his angry clerical absolutism. His criticism of Fuller served mainly, as he himself wrote, 'to make it clear and evident that there is too little of the Church or Ecclesiastical History in our Author's Book; And that there is too much of the State or Civil History, will be easily seen, by that unnecessary intermixture of State-Concernments, not pertinent to the business which he [Fuller] hath in hand . . .' [2]

Like most Anglican historians, Thomas Fuller argued against Roman Catholicism and denied or cast doubt on monkish miracles. Quoting Sir John Davies with approval, Fuller asserted that the papacy had usurped its power at the time of the Norman conquest. Fuller was not a profound antiquary, and some of his mistakes—such as dating the foundation of Cambridge University in the seventh century—would have been avoided by a more cautious writer. Yet there was much wit, learning, and common sense in Fuller's work. After comparing the various accounts of the date of King Lucius' conversion he noted that there was 'more than a grand jury of writers, which neither agree in their verdicts with their foreman, nor one with another . . .', and rightly attributed this to 'an anarchy' in authors' reckoning of years at this time. [3]

In the general secularization of thought which was taking place in

[1] Peter Heylyn, *The History of the Sabbath* (London, 1636), 'Epistle Dedicatorie'; also 'Preface', *passim*.

[2] See Peter Heylyn, *Examen Historicum: Or A Discovery and Examination of the Mistakes, Falsities, and Defects In Some Modern History* (London, 1659), 'Introduction to the Animadversions', esp. Sig. b v; Sig. b 4; Sig. b 6v. Heylyn's absolutist political views appear in his *Helps to English History*, p. 12 (1709 ed.).

[3] Thomas Fuller, *The Church History of Britain from the Birth of Christ Until the Year MDCXLVIII*, 3 vols. (London, 1837), I, 18–19. On miracles see, for example, I, 124 and 140. See Edwin Sandys, *Europae Speculum, Or A View or Survey of the State of Religion in The Westerne Parts of the World* (Oxford, 1629), 96, 119, 126, and *passim*. This is an excellent survey of the subject from the Protestant point of view. Although not strictly a history it contains much scattered historical information on different churches.

the seventeenth century, religious quarrels played an important part, especially after the outbreak of the civil wars. The Puritan preachers had brought history to the support of scripture in their contentions against prelacy; and the Leveller, John Lilburne, went on to discover in secular history arguments for political and religious liberty. In spite of all the differences of opinion among Puritans, there was widespread agreement that history itself proved the need for reformation without tarrying. And the Puritan belief in the progressive revelation of truth conceded the importance of historical investigation, especially into church affairs. After the Restoration of the monarchy and the Anglican church in 1660, controversy about church history was extended, for although institutions could be restored, older attitudes toward authority could not. Problematic history, therefore, flourished after the Restoration, when clerics in controversy explored the history of nearly every policy and precedent which affected the English Church.

The learned churchmen of the Restoration decades fought hard to explain and defend Anglican episcopacy, but they were powerless to halt the slow decay of the political powers of the Church. The revolution of 1688 brought to power a group of historical-minded moderates, who were prepared to recognize the changes which had taken place in both church and state. Professor Douglas has drawn attention to the importance of the historical attitudes of churchmen at this time of crisis:

> It was characteristic of the English Revolution—it was symptomatic of a permanent quality in the English mind—that an age of change should thus have conferred authority on men zealous for precedent and learned in its exposition. And it deserves emphasis that the Anglican Church when convulsed by the greatest threat to its historic continuity since the Reformation should at such a time have accepted the control of men who were before all else students of history.[1]

The significance of the historical revolution which had occurred in the preceding hundred years could not be better illustrated.

The history of the English courts of law was long subordinated to studies in the records and literature of the law. Lambarde's *Archeion* (1635), although important as a contemporary description of the legal institutions of England toward the end of Elizabeth's

[1] David Douglas, *English Scholars*, 209.

reign, was little more than an epitome of the history of the various courts. During the first half of the seventeenth century (which Maitland regarded as the heroic age of English legal scholarship), most historians, including Selden and Spelman, were mainly interested in the constitutional problems of legal history. The significance of Spelman's work on feudalism has already been pointed out. Selden was equally devoted to the problematic approach to history, and may be regarded as an equally great representative of the scholarly tradition. Although the bulk of Selden's work on legal history was small in comparison with the bulk of his work on ecclesiastical, oriental, and general historical topics, Selden's talents and industry were applied in accordance with the best and most modern standards of historical scholarship.[1]

The techniques and special skills which made possible advances in historical knowledge and in the canons of scholarship were cultivated by historians and antiquaries as a part of their work. Books on paleography, philology, and chronology came from the pens of some of the most eminent historical scholars of the day. Spelman's short essay on ancient handwriting—'Archaismus Graphicus' (1606)—was as indicative, in its own way, of this stirring of interest in technical studies as any of his later, more famous books. Written by Spelman primarily for the use of his son, 'Archaismus Graphicus' was not meant for publication. It was nevertheless the first important treatise on paleography written by an Englishman; and for all its faults, it did give 'Rules to judge the ancientness of MSS'.[2]

The scholars of the early seventeenth century were indeed innovators, and if much of the work of Selden, Ussher, Spelman, Camden, and other giants of historical learning was superseded later in the seventeenth century, much of the credit for the later advances must go to these men. They worked often by empirical, trial-and-error methods, for in many fields there were no standard works to guide them. They succeeded in opening up as yet unexplored territories to historical research.

History achieved the status of a learned profession during the seventeenth century in England. The scholars who grew to maturity while the Elizabethan Society of Antiquaries was still meeting were

---

[1] See W. S. Holdsworth, *Sources and Literature of English Law*, 148–50.
[2] B.M. Stowe MS. 1059, f. 12. Parts of 'Archaismus Graphicus' are in Latin.

among the first to display the qualities of mind which present-day historians would recognize and respect as professional. The facile Mathias Prideaux, writing in the mid-seventeenth century, listed philologists and historians, along with mathematicians, philosophers, physicians, lawyers, and divines, as men who deserved mention in 'The History of Professions'.[1] This was a significant recognition of the rising prestige of history as a learned discipline. Long before university chairs of history were common, the conviction had spread that history should be regarded as a profession as well as an art. The best medieval and Tudor chroniclers and historians were industrious, honest, and perceptive. The best seventeenth-century historical scholars—such men as Spelman, Camden, Ussher, Selden, and their successors—developed the tools of analysis and wrote the books which still arm modern historical scholarship.

[1] Mathias Prideaux, *An Easy and Compendious Introduction For Reading All Sorts Of Histories*, 4th ed. (Oxford, 1664), 345; see also 'Preface'. Prideaux was a hack in most respects, but this fact in itself gives point to his classification.

7

SIR WALTER RALEGH AND UNIVERSAL HISTORY

SIR WALTER RALEGH was under sentence of death for high treason, a man 'civilly dead' when he began work on his *History of the World*. The long days in prison in the Tower were a challenge to the pride and spirit of the middle-aged adventurer. History became, for Ralegh, another voyage, with its own triumphs and adversities. Having long ago learned to bear the world's adversities 'manlike, and resolvedly', he would write with uncompromising fidelity to what he understood to be timeless truth.

Thanks to the efforts of his wife and friends Ralegh did not long remain a close prisoner.[1] As soon as he was able to secure some privileges he began to occupy his time with studies. Soon after 1604 he was given better quarters accessible to the rampart walk overlooking the Thames, and was allowed to keep a servant and to employ assistants in his work. Friends began to visit him freely, bringing him books and the conversation which he enjoyed. He thus lived without freedom, but with sufficient liberty to write a history which reflected the learning of many ages, and the experience of his own unquiet life.

How much help he received in writing his *History* is a question

[1] See Sir Charles Firth, 'Sir Walter Raleigh's History of the World', *Proceedings of the British Academy*, VIII (London, Oxford University Press, n.d.), p. 16, and *passim*. Also T. N. Brushfield, 'Sir Walter Ralegh and his "History of the World",' *Reports and Transactions of the Devonshire Association for the Advancement of Science, Literature, and Art* (XIX, 1887), 387–418.

which need not detain the reader. Robert Burhill, Ben Jonson, and others helped Ralegh, but Jonson's clumsy boast that 'the best wits of England were employed for making of his history' was hardly worthy of repetition.[1] The *History of the World* was Ralegh's throughout in style and spirit; whatever he borrowed he made his own. Ralegh did most of the research himself, and probably all of the writing. The recent discovery of Ralegh's manuscript notebook only confirms the judgment of earlier historians: Ralegh was in command of his own *History*. His library in the Tower contained books on geography, chronology and theology, as well as standard works on the history and antiquities of England and many other countries. Ralegh had at hand the printed sources he needed to write a universal history—his notebook catalogues a historian's working library. It also reveals Ralegh's intense interest in historical maps, and proves that he had struggled as a historian to acquaint himself with unfamiliar problems of Hebrew philology.[2] Some of the books on Ralegh's shelves were undoubtedly borrowed, as were many of the ideas which informed his work, but these facts do not make Ralegh a thief.

No more need be said of Ralegh's life than is necessary to dispel a common misunderstanding of his thought. The legend of Ralegh's atheism was spread by his enemies; if accepted, it would make nonsense of his *History*. Ralegh was a confirmed believer in Christianity and in the Christian doctrine of providence. His scepticism was academic—and, by Montaigne's standards, shallow. Except as it strengthened his defence of faith it was of minor importance in his historical thought. Ralegh was sceptical of men's promises and of their capacity for self-government. Being 'damnably proud', he despised the rabble, and was contemptuous of vulgar forms of

[1] This was reported by William Drummond, whose reliability is somewhat open to question. See Ben Jonson's 'Conversations with Drummond' in *Works*, ed. C. H. Herford and Percy Simpson (Oxford, 1925), I, 138.

[2] Mr. Walter Oakeshott, Rector of Lincoln College, Oxford, very kindly made available to me in 1954 the manuscript copy of Ralegh's 'Notebook'. See also Newman T. Reed, 'The Philosophical Background of Sir Walter Ralegh's History of the World', *Northwestern University Summaries of Dissertations*, 1934, II, 14-19; and Ernest A. Strathmann, *Sir Walter Ralegh, A Study in Elizabethan Scepticism* (New York, 1951), Chapter I, *passim*. Edward Edwards, *The Life of Sir Walter Ralegh*, 2 vols. (London, 1868), II, 321-2, reproduces a letter from Ralegh to Sir Robert Cotton requesting books.

worship. Yet even when he appeared most sceptical he subordinated reason to faith, and deferred to the authority of the Bible.[1] Ralegh accounted it 'an impiety monstrous to confound God and nature: be it but in terms'.[2] His *History* was esteemed by Puritans above almost any other secular book. They liked it not just because Ralegh had dared to criticize kings, but because he justified the ways of God to man, not in poetic fiction, but in sober fact.[3]

Ralegh's historical synthesis was original in its overall conception, not in its details. It was transitional in the sense that it reasserted medieval ideas of universal history in terms which were meaningful to seventeenth-century Christians. A work of history which went through more editions in the seventeenth century than the collected works of Shakespeare may be assumed to have aroused deep responses. Yet early in the eighteenth century even Henry Felton, the divine who argued against deism, would laud Ralegh primarily as a stylist rather than as a philosopher of history.[4] The ebb tide in religious enthusiasm left Ralegh's *History* on a dry beach. His proud greatship became in time merely an object of literary curiosity—an anachronism in the age of reason.

In the chronology of historical writing and thought Ralegh's *History* marked the ending, not the beginning, of an epoch. It is clear, in retrospect, that Ralegh summed up earlier ideas and attitudes, many of which, of course, continued to be vigorously

[1] Strathmann, *Ralegh*, Chapter VII, *passim*. Ralegh was a literalist who rejected the allegorical interpretation of Genesis. See Ralegh, *History*, I, iii, iii, 73. All quotations are taken from *The Works of Sir Walter Ralegh*, ed. by William Oldys and Thomas Birch (Oxford, 1829), but in order to facilitate reference to other editions all citations will be to book, chapter, section, and page, as above.

[2] Ralegh, *History*, Preface, lvii.

[3] See Brushfield, 'Sir Walter Ralegh . . .', *Devonshire Association*, 404; E. Strathmann, 'The History of the World and Ralegh's Scepticism', *Huntington Library Quarterly* (III, 1940), 265–87. The *History* went through ten distinct editions between 1614 and 1687; abridged versions also were printed in the seventeenth century. It is tempting to identify Ralegh's historical thought with Calvinism, but it would be difficult to prove that Ralegh owed more to Calvin than he did to Augustine. The significance of the Calvinist reformation, and especially of Calvinist theology for Elizabethan intellectual history, has been amply demonstrated by modern scholars. Ralegh's thought, however, is too eclectic to be called 'Calvinist' in any very precise sense; and I have therefore avoided this ambiguous and possibly misleading term.

[4] See Strathmann, *Ralegh*, 256–7.

asserted by scholars of great learning and reputation. Ralegh made no original contribution to scholarship, for that was not his purpose; and in any case he lacked both the necessary materials and training. No doubt he would never have attempted so vast a work had he had the trained historian's sense of the difficulties. Nevertheless, his prose can still quicken his dead philosophy into moving life. His *History* remains one of the most characteristic expressions of the English Renaissance; no other work comes as close to defining the early seventeenth-century idea of history.

Ralegh expressed his theory of history most clearly in his Preface, in Book I, and in his digression on the use of conjecture in history. Scattered throughout the *History of the World* were aphorisms, observations, and *obiter dicta* which were occasionally at variance with his considered opinions, but for the most part Ralegh revealed himself as a remarkably consistent writer. It may seem strange that Augustine and Machiavelli could each find a place in Ralegh's scheme of history, but it must be remembered that Ralegh saw the hand of Providence even in Reason of State.[1]

The traditional character of Ralegh's historical thought may be gathered from the allegorical frontispiece that Ralegh used to illustrate the first edition of his work. History as *Magistra Vitae* stands triumphant over death and oblivion; and Cicero's other phrases, *Testis Temporum, Nuncia Vetustatis, Lux Veritatis*, and *Vita Memoriae* are written on the bases of the four columns which flank the central figure of *Magistra Vitae*.[2] In the preface Ralegh paraphrased the familiar Ciceronian text in the course of his elaborate essay describing the purpose and end of written history.

Ralegh was conscious of following a 'common and approved custom' in praising history, yet he did not simply borrow other men's thought.[3] In giving his own account he began as follows:

> True it is that among many other benefits, for which it [History] hath been honoured, in this one it triumpheth over all human knowledge, that it hath given us life in our understanding, since the world itself had life and beginning, even to this day: yea, it hath triumphed over time, which besides it nothing but eternity hath

[1] See Strathmann, *Ralegh*, 169.
[2] This illustration is conveniently reproduced in Lily B. Campbell, *Shakespeare's 'Histories', Mirrors of Elizabethan Policy* (San Marino, 1947), as the frontispiece.
[3] Ralegh, *History*, Preface, v.

triumphed over: for it hath carried our knowledge over the vast and devouring space of so many thousands of years, and given so fair and piercing eyes to our mind, that we plainly behold living now, as if we had lived then, that great world, *Magni Dei sapiens opus*, 'the wise work', saith Hermes, 'of a great God', as it was then, when but new to itself. By it, I say it is that we live in the very time when it was created; we behold how it was governed; how it was covered with waters; and again repeopled; how kings and kingdoms have flourished and fallen; and for what virtue and piety God made prosperous, and for what vice and deformity he made wretched, both the one and the other. And it is not the least debt which we owe unto history that it hath made us acquainted with our dead ancestors; and out of the depth and darkness of the earth, delivered us their memory and fame. In a word, we may gather out of history a policy no less wise than eternal; by the comparison and application of other men's forepassed miseries with our own like errors and ill deservings.[1]

How conventional this all was is readily apparent; the ideas were redeemed from the commonplace by the imaginative music of Ralegh's prose.

The primary purpose of history, as the foregoing passage indicates, was to provide the means for leading a good life. In history men could see and understand God's judgments, which 'are forever unchangeable'. The symmetry between past and present was fearful and exact—hence one might frame policies which were politic as well as eternal. Wise men would discern 'the bitter fruits of irreligious policy', but Ralegh was careful to add that ignorance of history was no excuse for the wicked, since the justice of God 'doth require none other accuser than our own consciences'.[2]

Ralegh gave numerous instances of the bitter fruits of irreligious policy, drawing his examples in the preface from English and European history. His condemnation of Henry VIII was one reason why James I thought Ralegh 'too saucy in censuring princes'. But Ralegh's attitude toward history was such that princes least of all were exempt from judgment and censure. One of the first duties of the historian was to note God's judgments in particular; and, although God's judgments fell upon those of all degrees who trifled with his mercy,

---

[1] *Ibid.*, v–vi.
[2] *Ibid.*, viii, and vi (in the 1829 edition p. vi was incorrectly numbered p. iv).

history itself was the narration of 'actions which were memorable'.[1] The historian was to describe great public events and the actors who took part in them. For this view Ralegh found good precedents: God's judgments 'upon the greater and greatest have been left to posterity: first by those happy hands which the Holy Ghost hath guided; and secondly, by their virtue who have gathered the acts and ends of men, mighty and remarkable in the world'.[2]

Ralegh was writing universal history in the tradition of Augustine, Orosius and Otto of Freising. He was concerned, however, not with the problem of the two cities, but with the moral lessons of history. Ralegh wrote universal history from a layman's point of view and with a layman's interest in theology. He was not concerned with the church, but with temporal events in human societies. His medieval philosophy of history was tempered by his anti-Aristotelian secular humanism.

The first cause of all things was God; nature, including man, was meaningless without God. Ralegh's scepticism reinforced his faith, for he could discover nothing in man's mere existence to justify being mindful of him. Although man was prone to worship nature—the created instead of the creator—there was no 'working power' at all in nature. God alone was the source of all power, and he operated in nature through the medium of second causes. Ralegh attributed 'no more self ability' to creatures than 'a clock after it is wound up by a man's hand hath'. He compared second causes to the action of a ship's rudder; and also, since he had the Elizabethan fondness for piling up metaphors, he spoke of 'all second causes whatsoever . . . [as] but instruments, conduits and pipes, which carry and displace what they have received from the head and fountain of the universal'. Ralegh confessed that he did not understand exactly how God might be said to work in this process. But then the mystery was one which should not be inquired into too deeply: 'certain scholastical distinctions worst and pervert the truth of all things'.[3]

Reproving those writers and politicians who taught that the fall of empires was the result of inward dissensions or outward and foreign force, Ralegh asserted that such second causes were merely

---

[1] See 'The Life of Sir Walter Ralegh' by William Oldys in his edition of *The History of the World*, 2 vols. (London, 1736), I, clxxxvi–cxc, for discussion of Ralegh's difficulties with King James.

[2] Ralegh, *History*, Preface, vi–viii.

[3] *Ibid.*, I, i, x, 24, 25, 26; cf. also Preface, li.

of secondary importance. The only determinant in history was divine providence. Ralegh was careful to define what he meant by providence, but his definition, while clear enough, was not one that eliminated the practical difficulties which the historian had to face.[1]

Providence Ralegh defined as God's ordering of events in accordance with his natural loving care of men. Since God existed in eternity, while men existed in time, God had foreknowledge of human history. God was, so to speak, a spectator of the whole of human history, as well as the author of the historical script. All creatures, from the angels to 'the unworthiest worms of the earth', were subject to God's providence. Unlike predestination, which only referred to the theological ends of man, providence was a theological principle of unlimited applicability.[2]

Since providence was a force operating on history from the outside it was unverifiable in any historical sense. It could be used indiscriminately to explain anything or everything. Moreover, Ralegh was trapped in inconsistency when he attempted to discriminate between the causal and the accidental in history. The problem of 'deserving well and receiving ill' was an obvious one to Ralegh, but he was unable to solve it without resorting to sophisms. Machiavelli had at least suggested that *virtu* and *fortuna* were related to the circumstances of the times. Ralegh, translating these terms into an alien language, observed that 'it is a thing exceedingly difficult to distinguish between virtue and fortune', and went on to proclaim that the distinction was meaningless in any case, since fortune 'was only a kind of idolatry and god of fools'.[3]

Like Augustine, Ralegh repudiated such words as fate, fortune, chance, and hazard in history—yet Ralegh was inconsistent enough to use them in practice. He probably felt that such terms were permissible when events were being discussed at the level of second causes, but he failed to make this clear, just as he failed to establish a meaningful hierarchy among second causes. The problem of historical inevitability was posed by the very fact that Ralegh's theory of providence left no room for the contingent in history.

Only by resorting to Augustinian paradox could man's freedom be reconciled with man's fate. Ralegh was not concerned with the

---

[1] See Ralegh's discussion of the fall of empires in the Preface, vii–viii.
[2] On the definition of providence, cf. Ralegh, *History*, I, i. xiii, 34–6; also I, i. xiv, 36.
[3] *Ibid.*, I, i, xv, 39; on virtue and fortune, cf. Preface, xxxiv.

relationship between free will and predestination in theology, but he was deeply concerned with man's responsibility for evil. The essential problem was how to avoid a kind of universal necessity which would bind God and man alike, and make nonsense of all moral judgments. That Ralegh was aware of the problem and of its implications may be inferred from the fact that he gave a brief résumé of the history of the idea of fate or destiny. He concluded, significantly enough, that fate and destiny were admissible in theory, provided that they were not used to deny freedom of the will:

> ... such is the dispute concerning fate or destiny, of which the opinions of those learned men that have written thereof may be safely received, had they not thereunto annexed and fastened on an inevitable necessity, and made it more general, and universal than it is, by giving it dominion over the mind of man, and over his will.[1]

This was much less straightforward than Augustine's statement concerning free will and foreknowledge—'the religious mind chooses both, confesses both, and maintains both by the faith of piety'.[2]

Ralegh attempted to steer 'the middle course' in discussing the paradox of God's foreknowledge and man's responsibility. Only his literary skill kept him from running aground on logical sandbars. He suggested that the working of fate might be explained by man's inherent tendency to put himself 'altogether under the power of his sensual appetite'.[3] In his digression on astrology he identified fate with the commonplace Elizabethan notion that the stars incline but do not compel the will. The condition of man and the course of his life on earth were plotted out for him, although he was free to choose another, better course. Yet Ralegh could on one page say that God's providence operated through celestial bodies and on the next imply that the stars were somehow responsible for inclining the will of man to wickedness.[4] Ralegh's theory of history was thus an eclectic one, which he supported by invoking, as the occasion demanded, unhistorical or even anti-historical explanatory concepts.

[1] Ralegh, *History*, I, i, xi, 27.

[2] Saint Augustine, *The City of God*, transl. by Marcus Dods (New York, Modern Library, 1950), Book V, p. 153.

[3] Ralegh, *History*, I, i, xi, 29–30.

[4] Ralegh defended his digressions on the ground that 'the life of man is nothing else but digression' (*History*, Preface, lxi); the best remedy against fate, Ralegh believed, was a 'religious education'; on the influence of the stars, see *History*, I, i, xi, 31–2.

Ralegh discussed his idea of evidence in a digression in which he defended the use of conjecture in writing history. Elsewhere in the *History of the World* he commented on particular problems of evidence as they arose. Taken altogether his statements provide a remarkably full account of the assumptions which he and other contemporary historians made when they approached the study of universal history.[1]

Ralegh's defence of conjecture was neither an irrelevant aside, nor was it a total denial of the ideal of scientific inquiry. Ralegh was familiar with contemporary arguments against the use of conjecture but deliberately rejected them. His reasons for doing so have bearing on nearly all aspects of his historical thought. Obviously, he perceived that the ancient historians whose works he admired had filled out their own narratives with conjecture. He probably realized that the line between valid inference and conjecture was often exceedingly thin, and that, to deal honestly with his readers, he ought not to pretend to certainty. But Ralegh was driven to defend conjecture for a different reason. The uncertainty of all second causes whatsoever was sharply contrasted by Ralegh with the certainty of the first cause, known by faith. He could not afford to admit that verifiability was the test of truth. Ralegh had thought this question through more carefully than most of his contemporaries, who were inclined to praise Truth and Providence in the same breath.

By the time Ralegh wrote his *History* the criticism of Aristotle had become almost fashionable outside the universities. Ralegh's objections to Aristotle were not the same as Bacon's, for Ralegh was mainly interested in showing that an Aristotelian analysis of causes hindered the understanding of providential history. Ralegh believed firmly that faith was as essential to the historian as knowledge—'for all histories do give us information of human counsels and events as far forth as the knowledge and faith of the writers can afford, but of God's will, by which all things are ordered, they speak only at random, and many times falsely'.[2]

Ralegh sometimes used Aristotelian categories, but he had no use for what he took to be Aristotelian or scholastic explanations:

> That these and these be the causes of these and these effects, time hath taught us and not reason; and so hath experience without art.

---

[1] Cf. Strathmann, *Ralegh*, 249–50. On Conjecture, *History*, II, xxi, vi.
[2] Ralegh, *History*, II, xxi, vi, 612.

The cheesewife knoweth it as well as the philosopher that sour runnet doth coagulate her milk into a curd. But if we ask her a reason of this cause, why the sourness doth it? whereby it doth it? and the manner how? I think that there is nothing to be found in vulgar philosophy to satisfy this and the like vulgar questions.[1]

Ralegh went on to criticize Aristotle's theory of causation in some detail. He distrusted any elaborate intellectual analysis of the causes of events, whether in nature or in history. Experience was more important than scholastic disputation in arriving at useful knowledge of second causes.[2] The validity of conjecture followed from Ralegh's assumption that history was an empirical study which could not be raised to the level of an exact 'science' except by transcending the historical process.

Only by referring to the truths of revelation could the historian overcome the inherent faults of secular historical method. The greatest merit of his own history, Ralegh thought, was that it did just this:

> But this history of the kings of Israel and Juda hath herein this singular prerogative above all that have been written by the most sufficient of merely human authors: it setteth down expressly the true and first causes of all that happened; not imputing the death of Ahab to his over-forwardness in battle . . . but referring all unto the will of God, I mean, to his revealed will: from which, that his hidden purposes do not vary, this story, by many great examples, gives most notable proof.[3]

All historians who explained events in terms of second causes were indulging in conjecture; and, as he observed, even the best historians were never able to give assurance, although they might give satisfaction: 'informations are often false, records not always true, and notorious actions commonly insufficient to discover the passions which did set them first on foot'.[4] In terms of second causes, all history was the history of accidents: '. . . matters of much consequence, founded in all seeming upon substantial reasons, have issued from such petty trifles as no historian would either think upon, or could well search out'.[5] Conjecture was, in short, a necessary evil. Ralegh's words recall Pascal's—'Cleopatra's nose:

---

[1] Ralegh, *History*, Preface, xlv.   [2] Cf. Strathmann, *Ralegh*, 240-53.
[3] Ralegh, *History*, II, xxi, vi, 613.   [4] *Ibid.*
[5] *Ibid.*, II, xxi, vi, 615.

had it been shorter, the whole aspect of the world would have been altered'.[1]

Conjecture was, however, not just a necessary evil: it became a virtue when put to proper use. Since the end and scope of all history was 'to teach by examples of times past such wisdom as may guide our actions', the historian was free to make use of conjecture for worthy purposes. 'For he doth not feign', Ralegh wrote, 'that rehearseth probabilities as bare conjectures; neither doth he deprive the text, that seeketh to illustrate, and make good in human reason, those things which authority alone, without further circumstance, ought to have confirmed in every man's belief.' [2]

The source of the authority to which Ralegh referred was the Bible. Although the historian was at liberty to interpret obscure passages in the Bible, and was under an obligation to try to reconcile divergent accounts of the same event, he was not free to contradict scriptural statements. The authority of the Bible was absolute; it took precedence over all secular accounts. Lying behind this belief was a tradition going back to the Church fathers, especially to St. Augustine, whom Ralegh often quoted. From Augustine Ralegh got his argument that Plato and other pagan philosophers who seemed to anticipate in their writings the loftier ethics of Christianity had in fact stolen their ideas from 'divine letters'—that is, from the Bible.[3] Ralegh expressed the very essence of his creed when he wrote that it was 'needless trouble' to search out the truth 'as it were by candlelight, in the uncertain fragments of lost authors, which we might have found by daylight, had we adhered only to Scriptures'.[4]

Ralegh anchored his chronology in biblical history, and based his reckonings on a system which he himself devised, after a careful study of other chronologers from Eusebius to Ussher. Ralegh's reputation as a chronologer was at its height in the seventeenth century, when the exact year of the creation of the world was a matter fit for learned controversy.[5] His method of procedure was

---

[1] Blaise Pascal, *Pensees* (New York, Modern Library, 1941), 59.

[2] Ralegh, *History*, II, xxi, vi, 616–17.

[3] *Ibid.*, I, iii, iii, 74; cf. I, vi, i, 163, and I, vi, *passim*.

[4] *Ibid.*, III, i, xiii, 43.

[5] Ralegh's date for the creation of the world was (by inference) the year 4032 B.C. Ussher, the standard authority in England, placed it in 4004 B.C. Scaliger favoured 3949, Luther 4000, G. J. Voss 3946. See Preserved Smith, *A History of Modern Culture*, 2 vols. (New York, 1934), I, 289–92. Ralegh's reputation as a chronologer was mentioned by Anthony

the usual one: comparison of authorities. The uncertainty and disagreement of historians in all 'questions and disputes of time' was
such, however, that Ralegh was often obliged to defend his own
views in some detail. But whatever the occasion, his argument was
fundamentally the same: 'let us build upon the scriptures themselves
and after them, upon reason and nature'.[1]

The importance of establishing a connection between sacred and
profane history, so that the concurrent histories of Greece, Persia,
Israel, and Rome could be dated with some accuracy in a common
chronological system, had been recognized by the earliest chronologers. Ralegh devoted a long chapter to the discussion of this
problem. He centred his attention on the dating of the Babylonian
captivity, since this was, in his opinion, the key to all subsequent
chronology. Although he confessed that he could not 'find how the
seventy years of captivity are to be divided among them which
reigned in Babylon', he skilfully defended his own conjectures. In
particular, he attempted to show why Scaliger's arguments were unacceptable. The details of his criticism of Scaliger (for whom Ralegh
expressed the highest respect) are of little interest at present. What
is significant is that, within the framework of scriptural argument,
Ralegh was by no means deficient in critical sense.

When Ralegh came to deal with problems of evidence and proof
in secular history his acumen did not desert him. The fact that he
flatly rejected the account of 'Nabuchodonosor's' invasion of Egypt,
as given in Herodotus and Diodorus, in favour of the stories of the
biblical prophets, Isaiah, Jeremiah, and Ezekiel, is not really to the
point.[2] Even the prophetic books of the Bible took precedence over
profane histories. In investigating the history of Rome he took pains
to find contradictory accounts of the same events; by allowing for
the bias of his authorities he hoped to make his own narrative
impartial. After Polybius Ralegh complained that the Roman
historians were in general partisan and untrustworthy. 'We shall,'
Ralegh wrote, 'have cause to wish that either they were somewhat

---

À Wood in *Athenae Oxonienses*: 'Authors are perplexed, as some are
pleased to say, under what topic to place him, whether of statesman,
seaman, soldier, chemist, or chronologer; for in all these he did excel.'

[1] Ralegh, *History*, I, viii, ii, 251; cf. viii, x, 300; also on disagreements
among historians, II, xvi, vii, 497; and cf. II, ii, i, 37, and Chapter I,
passim; II, vii, i, 216–17.

[2] *Ibid.*, III, i, viii, 27 and ff.

less Roman, or else that some works of their opposite writers were extant, that so we might at least hear both sides speak . . .'[1]

This weighing and comparing of authorities in order to determine their relative credibility was, of course, by no means a satisfactory method of finding out what actually happened.[2] It must be remembered, however, that Ralegh had no alternative, that this was still the approved method of writing ancient history, and that few historians yet understood its limitations. Ralegh at least did not claim to be describing certainties, except when he followed scriptural accounts; when he dealt with secular affairs he admitted that he could describe only probabilities. His basic misconception appeared, appropriately enough, in his discussion of Annius of Viterbo. He knew that Annius was untrustworthy, yet Annius was still an authority to be reckoned with; Ralegh did not simply dismiss him, but attempted to determine whether or not particular statements in Annius were more or less plausible, more or less agreeable to reason, to nature, or to scripture. Ralegh boasted that he believed nothing 'that Annius's Berosus, Metasthenes, and others of that stamp affirm, in respect of their bare authority', but he went on to say that 'where other histories are silent, or speak not enough, there may we without shame borrow of these, as much as agrees with that little which elsewhere we find, and serveth to explain or enlarge it without improbabilities'.[3]

The key phrase—to explain or enlarge without improbabilities— suggests the general procedure which Ralegh followed in handling problems of evidence and proof. On the surface this phrase might appear to be an anticipation of the coherence theory of historical truth, but what Ralegh meant by it was something much more elementary, namely, an extension of the idea of conjecture. Any statement of historical fact was conjecturally true, provided that it did not contradict statements found in a superior authority. The initial problem was to determine the relative standing of different authorities. Once this was done the only other question was what statements would serve best to clothe or adorn the narrative. Ralegh

---

[1] *Ibid.*, V, iii, ix, 284. Cf. Ralegh's criticism of Livy, V, iii, x, 293–303, and 309–11.

[2] For example, he chose to follow Vergil on one point because he thought that Vergil was an upright man, 'who surely followed good authority' (II, xiv, i, 446; cf. 441–4).

[3] Ralegh, *History*, II, xxiii, iv, 676; cf. II, xiv, i, 446.

showed his discrimination in judging probabilities, and in ranking authors according to the credibility of their testimony. His method served to illustrate his interpretations, but not to verify particular, empirical facts.

No reader of the *History of the World* can fail to be impressed by difference in tone, in attitude, and in treatment between the earlier and later books, or between the parts which deal with secular history and those which deal with sacred history. The distinction between sacred and secular history was, of course, accepted in principle by most historians, but in practice it was falling to disuse—like a carelessly observed rule of grammar. Ralegh's historical orthodoxy was apparent, yet even in his work the transition toward a more secular viewpoint was clearly marked.

Ralegh was too good a writer of narrative history to make God the cause of every event in his *History*. In speculating about the causes that had prevented a reunion between Israel and Judah, Ralegh admitted that 'to say that God was pleased to have it so, were a true, but an idle answer (for his secret will is the cause of all things) . . .' [1] He went on to assert that he would boldly look into second causes. These proved, upon examination, to be that the people were unruly and their governors unwise. So tame a conclusion was not necessarily characteristic, but Ralegh was inclined to explain events in terms of very general political or psychological principles.

Ralegh could on occasion refer to the effects of climate and geography, or to the pressure of population (in the case of the Cimmerian invasions of Lydia), but his mind was most sensitive to the personal—to motives rather than to environing conditions. He criticized other historians' accounts of the causes of the Trojan war, but his own explanation was hardly original: 'Thus did all Greece, either as bound by oath, or led by the reputation and power of the two brethren, Agamemnon and Menelaus, or desirous to partake of the profit and honour in that great enterprise, take arms against the Trojans . . .' [2] Only in his dour opinion of Paris did Ralegh excel his predecessors: 'Whereupon I think that Paris had not regard either to the rape of Europa, Medea, or Hesione; but was merely incited by Venus, that is, by his lust, to do that which in those days was very common.' [3]

In general, Ralegh gave whatever *ad hoc* explanations he thought

[1] Ralegh, *History*, II, xix, v, 570.
[2] *Ibid.*, II, xiv, ii, 450; cf. V, i, iii, 20.   [3] *Ibid.*, II, xiv, ii, 449.

fitted the facts. Rome and Greece both fell because they were corrupted by riches and sensuality; God worked through the medium of various (but for the most part very general) second causes, to bring about the ruin of each state. Unless a sudden catastrophe suggested God's direct intervention and judgment, Ralegh assumed that God worked mysteriously; when God intervened more directly it was by temporarily depriving the governors of understanding when some punishment was intended for the multitude.[1] Ralegh occasionally referred to hazard and to fortune, but these words were used as common figures of speech.[2]

As a good Christian and a good Elizabethan Ralegh believed that the devil was an industrious enemy of mankind. Satan was the arch-deceiver who, having once played upon the open stage of the world, now laboured more diligently than ever in the minds and hearts of men. The scandalous religious beliefs of the heathen were attributable to the workings of Satan, who also became the world's first sophist by practising the art of making the worse appear the better cause. Above all, the devil was a black magician, a teacher of sorcery, poisoning, and witchcraft. Yet for all his power Satan remained in the shadows of history. Nothing in Ralegh's cosmology could deflect the beams of providence.[3]

In the later books of the *History of the World* Ralegh devoted more space to the narrative of events, made fewer moral judgments, and referred less often to God's—or the devil's—interventions in history. Ralegh never lost sight of his purpose in writing a universal history, but he apparently felt more at ease with the captains and kings of the classical world. He became more concerned with the content of secular, territorial history as he went further into the histories of Greece and Rome. Under scrutiny, his work shows the characteristic qualities and emphases of secular historiography in the Tudor age.

Ralegh's general approach to classical history can be defined with respect to three significant problems: (1) the role of the individual in history, (2) the relation of continuity to change in history, and (3) the derivation of political lessons from history. Although these problems were not unrelated to one another, they each involved separate assumptions about the relation of past to present. Like

---

[1] *Ibid.*, III, viii, viii, 179–80; IV, ii, iv, 321; IV, v, ix, 489.

[2] Cf. *Ibid.*, Preface, xv; IV, v, x, 491.

[3] See, for examples, *ibid.*, I, vi, ix, 186–7; I, xi, iii–viii, 390-405.

most of his contemporaries, Ralegh was inclined to assume that the past was a spectacle witnessed from the present, that mutability did not reign, either in nature or in history, and that lessons valid for all time could be drawn from few or singular historical examples.

In the *History of the World* Ralegh consistently emphasized the dramatic and spectacular aspects of history. History was the record of conflicts involving leadership and the use or abuse of power. The military career of Alexander the Great was far more interesting to Ralegh than the effects of Alexander's victories on Greek and Asiatic society. Although it is true that Ralegh had few sources to work with, this fact does not explain why he chose to emphasize the deeds of great men rather than the social history of states.[1] It does not explain, for example, why Ralegh devoted more space to Xenophon and the 'March of the Ten Thousand' than he did to the entire history of the Peloponnesian War. No doubt Ralegh admired men who took risks, as he himself had done, but he was not for this reason committed to a 'great man' theory of history.

Leaders like Alexander the Great and Caesar were, according to Ralegh, the makers of history, even though they unknowingly fulfilled God's purposes:

For so much hath the spirit of some one man excelled as it hath undertaken and effected the alteration of the greatest states and commonweals, the erection of monarchies, the conquest of kingdoms and empires, [etc.] . . .; such spirits have been stirred up in sundry ages of the world and in divers parts thereof, to erect and cast down again, to establish and destroy, and to bring all things, persons, and states, to the same certain ends, which the infinite spirit of the Universal . . . hath ordained.[2]

To Ralegh's way of thinking, history was a drama, or spectacle, in which different actors played their assigned parts until they were borne off the stage. Ralegh himself frequently used the image of the theatre; in a revealing passage he wrote: 'But the name which he [Cassander] forbore, his sons after him were bold to usurp, though with ill success as will appear when they shall enter upon the stage whereon these old tragedians, under new habits, as no

---

[1] For his character sketch of Alexander, see *History*, IV, ii, xiii; Ralegh thought that Alexander was the man referred to in Daniel's prophecy (IV, ii, vii, 327). This led him to accept the late Hellenistic historians' adverse accounts of Alexander.

[2] Ralegh, *History*, IV, ii, iii, 310–11.

longer now the same persons, begin to play their parts, with bigger looks and more boistrous actions, not with greater grace and judgment than in the scenes already past.' [1] This was perhaps more revealing than Ralegh realized—he was looking at history from the outside, watching scenes which might be laid in Athens or Rome or Babylon, but which were played by actors who spoke an English idiom. The difference between past and present was at best an illusion, a matter of costume. [2]

The problem of continuity and change in history was thus one which Ralegh was at a loss to understand. On the one hand, there was 'nothing wherein nature so much triumpheth as in dissimilitude', but on the other hand, 'of the great similitude found in world events, the limitation of matter hath been assigned as a probable cause'. [3] Ralegh saw the life of man as constantly changing—'either increasing toward ripeness and perfection, or declining and decreasing toward rottenness and dissolution'. [4] He was nevertheless inclined to stress the similitude between past and present, and the constancy of human nature. It has already been suggested that Ralegh thought of change as somehow external and illusory—a matter of costuming. Edmund Spenser in the Mutability Cantos of the *Faerie Queene* had given clear expression to an analogous idea. Mutability, having asserted her claim to sovereignty in the world, was answered by Nature:

> I well consider all that ye have sayd,
> And find that all things stedfastnes doe hate
> And changed be: yet being rightly way'd
> They are not changed from their first estate;
> But by their change their being doe dilate:
> And turning to themselves at length againe,
> Doe worke their own perfection so by fate:
> Then over them Change doth not rule and raigne;
> But they raigne over Change, and doe their States maintaine. [5]

---

[1] *Ibid.*, IV, v, x, 497; cf. Preface xiii, xxxii, xlii–xliii.

[2] *Ibid.*, V, i, vi, *passim* on sea-fighting; II, xxii, ix, 646, the plight of Joash compared with that of Charles VIII in Florence; I, v, v, 151–2, the longevity of the patriarchs compared with the Elizabethans; V, ii, ix, 136–7, Carthaginian and Dutch mercenaries compared; also Preface, *passim*.

[3] *Ibid.*, Preface, iii; V, iv, i, 535.

[4] *Ibid.*, I, ii, v, 61.

[5] Edmund Spenser, *The Complete Poetical Works*, ed. R. E. N. Dodge (Cambridge, Mass., 1908), Canto LVIII, p. 676.

In some ways, Ralegh's *History of the World* was the historical counterpart of Spenser's allegorical epic; and Ralegh's idea of historical change answered to Spenser's idea of mutability—the enduring substance of human nature belied the accident of change.

How far Ralegh was influenced by contemporary assumptions about the political uses of history is a question which does not admit of a simple answer. In many cases Ralegh merely followed his sources and described what happened. Yet when he did attempt to derive political lessons from history he betrayed a typical Elizabethan lack of understanding of historical contexts. Almost any historical event might serve as an example of a general political law or maxim of statecraft. Ralegh was not really interested, for example, in the specific historical question of how the Macedonian generals retained their hold on the Persian empire after Alexander's death. He was content to plagiarize from the fourth chapter of Machiavelli's *Prince*, adding a few comments of his own on why the kingdom of Darius did not rebel against Alexander's successors. The lessons of history interested Ralegh far more than questions of historical fact regarding the social structure of the Persian empire.[1] In so far as Ralegh was concerned with forms of government it was to assert a correspondence between the old Persian and the modern Turkish governments. He was intent on pointing out the strength and weakness of a form; as he observed, 'the cause why the Macedonians held so quietly the Persian empire is well set down by Machiavel and concerns all other kingdoms that are subject to the like form of government'.[2]

This tendency to jump from a particular, local, historical instance to a general political or philosophical statement was evident in many of Ralegh's digressions. The occasion for his digression on tyranny was the concrete case of Carthaginian tyranny.[3] Ralegh elsewhere attempted to make good his historical arguments by citing parallel, modern examples. He was often at his best when he drew on his own experience to illustrate some point about the strategy of a leader, or to show why an enterprise had failed. If he had shown comparable skill in suggesting points of difference between ancient and modern

[1] Cf. Ralegh, *History*, IV, v, viii, 476–81. Ralegh frequently borrowed (or plagiarized) from Machiavelli as well as other writers. His debts to Machiavelli are traced in Nadja Kempner, *Ralegh's Staatstheoretische Schriften* (Leipzig, 1928); this work ignores the *History*, but is otherwise most useful.

[2] Ralegh, *History*, IV, v, viii, 476.

[3] *Ibid.*, V, ii, ii, 142–4.

histories he would have been less representative of the climate of opinion, but more significant in the history of ideas.

To some extent Ralegh's uncompromising moral faith prevented him from understanding or even becoming curious about standards which were recognizably different from his own. Pagan customs and institutions were all too easily dismissed with contempt. The deification of Hellenistic monarchs during their own lifetimes Ralegh attributed to mere flattery and vanity; and having once judged the custom he showed no further interest in it. This was a curious failure —at least in one who had read his Machiavelli—yet it was characteristic of Ralegh that he could hold the most diverse, and often contradictory beliefs without being conscious of inconsistency. The world's presumed decay and degeneration did not suggest to Ralegh a significant idea of historical change; admiration for the Machiavellian analysis of 'reasons of state' did not keep Ralegh from being an outspoken critic of Machiavellian ethics; nor did respect for military virtue and success incline Ralegh toward a compromising acceptance of *realpolitick*.[1] Perhaps such considerations helped to prompt Lord Acton's remark—'I venerate that villainous old adventurer for his views on universal history'.[2]

In the seventeenth century, when the hand of providence was visible to the makers and to the writers of history, Ralegh's *History of the World* was held in highest esteem. Milton and Hampden and Cromwell could agree with Bishop Hall and Dr. Heylyn that Ralegh was a profound and exact writer of universal history. Few English historians of the seventeenth century failed to mention Ralegh's *History* 'without some epithet or sentence in its praise'.[3] But the work had no sequel; Ralegh had admirers, but no successors. The date at which Ralegh's narrative broke off was 130 B.C. No universal history, comparable to Ralegh's in purpose and content, carried on

---

[1] See Strathmann, *Ralegh*, 167–71. Ralegh, *History*, V, vii, xii, 898 on fall of Rome. Ralegh had contemplated prefacing his *History* with an essay on the theme of the Four Monarchies. His reason for choosing to write of ancient rather than modern history may have been simply his prudent belief that 'whosoever, in writing a modern history, shall follow truth too near the heels, it may happily strike out his teeth' (Preface, lxiii). On degeneration, see Ralegh, *History*, IV, vi, ix, 526, and *passim*.

[2] Quoted by Edward Thompson, *Sir Walter Ralegh, the Last of the Elizabethans* (London, 1935), 227.

[3] Oldys, 'Life of Sir Walter Ralegh' in Vol. I of his edition of the *History of the World*, clxxxiv.

the history of Rome's rise to power and developed the theme of why Rome, too, was destined to be cut down by 'a rabble of barbarian invaders'. One reason for this stillness was that the best seventeenth-century historians were primarily concerned, as were the scientists, with discoverable and verifiable facts. Ralegh's overall providential interpretation of history might still be accepted, but the methodological assumptions which sustained it were becoming obsolete.

Ralegh was not indifferent to the contemporary revolution in thought, yet the very eclecticism of his philosophy suggests that he was not one of the Moderns. His scientific interests, his pursuit of chronological accuracy and cartological exactness, even his scholarly digressions stand witness to the fact that he did not blindly defy intellectual change. However, the effect of Ralegh's art was to resolve the doubts and dissonances of human history. He appealed formally to an extravagant, if sublime providence, and attempted to make this preternatural power an integral part of historical composition. The result was a superb expression of the baroque style.[1] But Ralegh's *History of the World* had few affinities with exact scholarship; it was the philosophy of history, not history itself that triumphed over time.

[1] Cf. Wylie Sypher, *Four Stages of Renaissance Style* (New York, Doubleday Anchor Original, 1955), 180–5.

8

JOHN STOW AND LOCAL HISTORY

LABORIOUS JOHN STOW deserved a less condescending epithet. He was no mere tailor of antiquities, but one of the most accurate and businesslike of the English historians of the sixteenth century. Born about 1525, Stow was a younger contemporary of Archbishop Parker, and an older contemporary of William Camden. Both scholars recognized in Stow a man of great ability; both became his benefactors. An honoured colleague of the knights and gentlemen of the Society of Antiquaries, in which he served as secretary, Stow was never poor in the admiration of men of learning. Howes, in his edition of Stow's *Annales*, described him as tall of stature, lean of body and face, of a pleasant and cheerful countenance, and very 'sober, mild and courteous to any that required his instructions'. Howes went on to say that Stow 'always protested never to have written anything either for malice, fear, or favour, nor to seek his own particular gain or vainglory; and that his only pains and care was to write truth'.[1] Few historians could say this with greater honesty than Stow.

The fact that Stow was a self-educated man, who worked as a tailor in order to support himself as an antiquary, may help to explain why Stow was sometimes patronized as an 'honest and knowing man', but 'an indifferent scholar'.[2] His command of

---

[1] See Stow, *Survey*, I, xxvi, quoted by Kingsford. All references are to Kingsford's edition. The introduction contains the best biography of Stow, but there is also a sympathetic account of him in the *D.N.B.*, *sub* Stow.

[2] Thomas Hearne, quoted by Kingsford, *Survey*, I, xxxviii.

languages may have been imperfect, but this is captious criticism. Stow was a distinguished scholar whose *Survey of London* was nothing less than a definitive work on local history. The book was definitive not only because of the general accuracy of its information, but also because it helped to establish the way in which town history should be written. Works of historical scholarship can be definitive in no other sense—the historian can never ask, much less answer, all the questions which might be put to his materials. Stow provided a model worthy of imitation, and facts which are still usable—the longevity of his work is an index of its worth.

A Survey of London could only have been written by a man who had devoted his life to historical studies. Although Stow took justifiable pride in his other books, including his youthful editing of the works of Chaucer (1561), the *Survey* was the best justification for a lifetime devoted to patient and painstaking research. When he brought out the first edition of the *Survey* in 1598 he was already past seventy, and had been engaged in the study of English history and antiquities for over forty years. He had lived in London all his life, but had travelled as long and far in the city as most travellers had in the provinces of a wider world.

Stow knew London better than any man of his time. London streets, buildings, bridges, and customs were to him the living embodiment of London's history and greatness. He wrote, abridged, continued, and revised his Annals and Chronicles for years without making a significantly original contribution to historical knowledge. His *Survey of London*, however, was a masterpiece of clear, finished history. It was the deceptively simple product of a mature mind reflecting on innumerable facts about the past and present of a great city. Stow wrote in an attractive, simple style a thoroughly documented account of the greater London of his day. He called his book a *Survey*, but it was much more than a topographical description of the city.

Stow did not think of himself as having created a new form of history. He acknowledged that William Lambarde's *Perambulation of Kent* had suggested to him the idea of writing a local history. Yet Stow's *Survey* was in fact the first great history of any English town. Stow's other works were long ago worn out by time; his *Survey* is still the most accurate and complete reference book on Elizabethan London.

Town history has perhaps inevitably reflected bourgeois interests,

It was entirely appropriate that Ralegh, proud of command in voyages and in poetry, should have written a universal history, and that John Stow, proud of his plain London citizenship, should have memorialized the achievements of Londoners in a book packed with solid facts. Stow was not a philosopher of history, but an empirical historian who took pains to discover what actually happened. The utility of history he took for granted, believing that no facts were trivial in themselves or because they were facts about obscure men. All of Stow's works reflect something of the middle-class citizen's tastes and interests; and much can be learned about the viewpoints of middle-class Elizabethans from reading Stow's *Survey* alone. Yet when all allowance has been made for the mirroring of bourgeois attitudes, Stow's originality remains. In order to appreciate the nature of Stow's contribution to the study of local history, his middle-class assumptions must first be recognized—and not over-emphasized.

Nashe and other Elizabethan writers made sport of the 'lay chronigraphers that write of nothing but of Mayors and Sheriffs, and the dere yere, and the great frost'.[1] The bourgeois chroniclers of the sixteenth century, including Stow, wrote to please a middle-class reading public which was eager for all kinds of historical information. Some of the reasons for the growing popularity of history have already been given: a volume of history was expected to be a guide to moral, political, or financial success. Tudor chronicles sanctioned middle-class virtues, and condemned such vices as the middle class had most reason to fear. The temporal and spiritual utility of history, implied if not expressed by these writers, sometimes led to the frank inclusion of practical information in annals and chronicles. Thus in Stow's *Summarie* of 1604 (and in later editions) there was an almanac, a table of dates for the law terms, a table giving the distances and the best routes between London and various provincial towns, and the dates of fairs. Yet the utilitarian explanation of history's flourishing state does not disclose the deep psychological needs that made history both attractive and satisfying, especially to middle-class readers.

The middle-class concern with history was part of a much wider concern with the sanctions of tradition. The economic, social and religious upheavals of the sixteenth century created new opportunities, but at the same time created new, or intensified old,

<hr>

[1] Quoted by Kingsford, *Survey*, I, xxviii.

insecurities. Only in comparatively recent times have revolutionary changes been justified in the name of 'progress'. And even Marxian revolutionaries have discovered the sanctioning virtues of traditional nationalism. In the sixteenth century, when the Tudor dynasts were trying to transform the institutions of medieval England into more effective agencies of the central government, they repeatedly appealed to historical tradition.

The medieval English state, in which sovereignty was diffused by feudal law and custom, was transformed in the course of the sixteenth century into a strong, centralized, sovereign nation state. The bureaucratic machinery and power resources of a later age were unavailable to the Tudors, however, and they could achieve only a limited, Parliamentary 'absolutism'. It was therefore essential, at the time of the Reformation, to associate the nation with the monarch, and to establish the sovereignty of the King in Parliament. But at the same time the medieval sanctions of legal right and custom had to be upheld. Consequently, the apologists of the Henrician Reformation distorted history to their own purposes, urging that Henry VIII was the restorer of the true traditions of medieval English kingship and monarchy.[1]

The middle classes were both the beneficiaries and the victims of the changes that took place during and after the Reformation. On the one hand, they profited economically and socially, not only from speculation in monastic lands, but also from the greater opportunities for social mobility which the Tudor revolution in government provided. On the other hand, guild status was rendered less secure, especially in the later sixteenth century; and, naturally, all religious beliefs were subject to close political inspection after the Reformation. The Tudor monarchs were, however, the best guarantees against a return to the anarchy of the fifteenth century. It is hardly surprising, therefore, that the bulk of the middle class was vigorously loyal to the Tudors; even Mary Tudor could count on at least passive obedience.

Vestiges of the psychological insecurity which troubled even the articulate, intelligent, and wealthy merchant aristocracy appeared

---

[1] See Mathew A. Fitzsimons, 'Politics and Men of Learning in England, 1540-1640', *Review of Politics* (VII, 1944), 452-83. J. W. Allen, *History of Political Thought*, 162, and W. Gordon Zeeveld, 'Richard Morrison, Official Apologist of Henry VIII', *Publications of the Modern Language Association* (LV, 1940), 406-25.

as late as the mid-seventeenth century in the writings of Henry Robinson.[1] Psychological insecurity was more immediate and widespread in the sixteenth century, when society was adjusting to the changes of the Reformation, and men and women were still profoundly anxious about the maintenance of political stability and strong government. The danger of disobedience was one of the lessons of history which was therefore equally welcome to Tudor monarchs and to middle-class citizens. Beyond this, and even more indicative, perhaps, of the desire for reassurance was the general tendency of Tudor chroniclers and historians, including Stow, to stress continuity with the past and to reassert traditional values.

Whether or not John Stow was hired by the Privy Council to write governmental propaganda into his chronicles is ultimately unimportant.[2] Stow would probably have supported Elizabethan policy, just as Camden did, out of conviction, and because Elizabeth was a moderate. He had no use for fanatics. Like most antiquaries, Stow revered the past, and respected the achievements of Catholic generations. He was able to clear himself of the charges made against him in 1569 that he was a papist, but he never pretended to approve of Protestant iconoclasts. For the defacers of ancient monuments Stow felt real bitterness and contempt.

The first historical work that Stow published was *A Summarie of Englishe Chronicles* (1565). In his preface Stow acknowledged that he got most of his information from Fabian, Hardynge, and Hall. But he wrote that he would not be 'left naked' if these men claimed their own: 'For somewhat I have noted which I my selfe, partly by paynful searche, and partly by diligent experience, have found out.' [3] Stow began his book with a list of 'The Names of Authours in this Booke alledged', thus anticipating any objection that he had failed to acknowledge his sources. Although frankly a summary, the book was competently done and contained some original work. Stow brought it up to date from time to time, and made various additions

[1] See W. K. Jordan, *Men of Substance* (Chicago, 1942), 218.

[2] See Conyers Read, *Mr. Secretary Walsingham*, 3 vols. (Cambridge, Mass., 1925), III, 454–5. Professor Read sets a very high value on Stow's chronicles, and especially on Stow's chapter in Holinshed's *Chronicle*. He believes that the works of Stow and Camden have been consistently under-rated.

[3] John Stow, *A Summarie of Englishe Chronicles* (London, 1565), 'To the Reader'.

which indicate that he was becoming more aware of methodological problems. In the edition of 1570, for example, Stow included brief biographical and critical accounts of his various authorities. Of Galfridas Monumetensis (Geoffrey of Monmouth) Stow wrote: '. . . his chronicle of the Britons is of some: scornefully rejected: wherein they shewe their greate unthankfulness, not to embrace him, who painfully for their beholfe playeth only the part of an interpretour . . .' [1] Stow went on to say that historians ought to consider the times in which Galfridas lived; and he concluded that 'the true Histories may of a skillful Reader be well decerned from the false, and many things in him that seem strange are approved by the best Writers of al Ages . . .' [2] Stow was not unaware of the problems presented by Geoffrey's account. He acknowledged the superiority of William of Malmesbury as a scholar, but he refused to believe that all of Geoffrey's stories were necessarily false.

Stow himself grew to be more sceptical of legendary history as he grew older. In his *Annales* (1592) Stow rejected the forgeries of Berosus who had attempted to trace the descent of the native British as far back as the age of Noah's sons. He clearly indicated that he gave the story of Brute on the authority of Geoffrey of Monmouth, and that he delivered the story of the early kings of Britain 'after the common received opinion'. [3]

Stow informed his readers that the printer had insisted that he write Annals rather than a History. His *Annales* were not in a class with Camden's, for Stow did not attempt to relate events to their causes and he failed to solve the stylistic problems inherent in an annalistic presentation. Stow had already begun work on a history, however, and it is unfortunate that this 'farre larger volume' perished. Recognizing that his *Annales* were much less than the greater work of history he intended, Stow had to rely 'wholly upon this comfort, that the truth and credit of my Authors is in no point injured how simple and naked soever the stile may be judged'. [4] It is true that

[1] Stow, *Summarie* (London, 1570), no pagination.

[2] It is instructive to compare this statement with the long argument to the same effect in Acton Griscomb's preface to his edition of *The Historia Regum Britanniae of Geoffrey of Monmouth* (New York, 1929). Stow was mistaken about the date of Geoffrey's work.

[3] Unlike Stow, Edmund Howes attempted to defend the Brute legend in his continuation of Stow's *Annalls*. See Edmund Howes, *The Annals or General Chronicle of England* (London, 1615), 'A Historical Preface . . .'

[4] Quoted by Kingsford, *Survey*, I, xxi.

Stow described some natural history which to a sophisticated reader might appear comic—a 'strange worme found in the heart of a horse' in 1585 told readers little about English history. But it tells the modern scholar much about the vestiges of an ancient belief in natural omens, which still survived among Stow's contemporaries; Stow's worm was far more 'primitive' than Stow himself could possibly have imagined.[1]

Stow recorded the alterations of time—he was more alert to historical change than most writers, partly because he was enamoured of antiquity, and partly because he felt the insecurities of his generation. 'The sudden rising of some men causeth them to forget themselves,' he complained; and he clearly felt that the old ways were generally best.[2] The *Survey of London* is especially valuable to modern historians, however, because it preserves so much scattered information about changes in the economic and social environment. Stow's pages contain evidence of the decline in charitable bequests to religious foundations, evidence of the growing crisis in poor relief, of the increasing wealth of the merchants, of the expansion of London's population—evidence for all sorts of important developments which were taking place in Stow's time. Yet Stow drew very few of the conclusions which modern historians have drawn from his work. One reason for this was that Stow lacked a theoretical framework of explanation, and did not attempt to write problematic history. Another reason is simply that the force of local tradition was still very strong when Stow wrote. It was almost inevitable that Stow would tend to emphasize deviations from tradition, and reassert older values, rather than condone change. Analysis of the content of Stow's *Survey* will suggest why it appealed to middle-class readers. At the same time it should be emphasized that Stow's standards of relevance cannot simply be derived from his class or calling.

Stow pushed back the origins of London as far as he could into antiquity. He concentrated his attention, however, on the history

[1] John Stow, *A Summarie of The Chronicles of England* (London, 1604), 362.

[2] Stow, *Survey*, I, 179. On the alterations of time see, for example, I, 89–90, 104, 127; II, 36–7, 81. Stow's typical phrase was 'Thus farre Fitzstephen, of the estate of things in his time, whereunto may be added the present, by conference whereof, the alteration will easily appeare'. *Survey*, II, 81. Stow refused to record the names of the iconoclasts who later erected fine monuments for themselves. See *The Diary of John Manningham*, ed. by John Bruce, Camden Society (XCIX, 1868), 103.

of London from the medieval period, when the records began to be full and trustworthy. What he stressed was the time-honoured character of the city and the broad continuity of its traditions.

Stow was too careful a historian to make statements that he did not think he could prove with sound evidence. He made it quite clear that it was Fitzstephen's opinion that London had been founded by Brute and the Trojans.[1] For his part Stow was content to point out that London had traditions which extended back to the Romans. The Emperor Constantine had been a Londoner, and Stow insisted that London's spiritual governors had originally been Roman appointees.[2] Stow informed his readers that he had examined Roman burial urns, and other remains, which workmen had dug up while excavating a foundation.[3] But he believed that such Roman remains were slight and therefore refused to over-emphasize them. He realized that he was not a competent Anglo-Saxon scholar, and left the credit of his account of Anglo-Saxon history 'to the judgement of the learned'.[4] When he came to medieval and modern history, however, he was able to cite a wide variety of sources. He possessed a detailed knowledge of medieval chronicles and had, of course, consulted all sorts of original records. It was his knowledge of primary sources that enabled him to reconstruct the orders, customs, and activities of the London citizenry.

Stow's interests were secular, nothwithstanding the fact that he held a simple and dignified religious faith, which seems to have made him tolerant of all decent men. He was intolerant only of those who practised intolerance in the name of zeal for religion—they were, quite simply, 'bad people'.[5] Stow's *Survey* was, in essentials, a secular book which reflected the secular interests of the Elizabethan age.

Stow surveyed the structural features of London and the social life of its citizens. His secular interests were nowhere more apparent than in his descriptions of London churches. He had visited nearly every church in the city, and knew a great deal about the history of all the more important ones. What interested Stow was not the ecclesiastical history of a church, but its lay history and antiquities.

[1] Stow, *Survey*, I, 1–2; 81. [2] *Ibid.*, I, 170; II, 125.
[3] *Ibid.*, I, 168–70.
[4] *Ibid.*, II, 126. See Kingsford's notes, II, 380–1; Stow made several mistakes.
[5] *Ibid.*, I, 220.

He studied church registers and burial plaques to find out what the citizens had done for the churches; he did not concern himself with what religion might have done for the citizens. He wanted to know the names of the local men and women who were buried in the different churches, and what sort of contributions they had made toward the upkeep and repair of church buildings.

To Stow, churches were monuments of antiquity, and repositories of valuable records. No doubt churches were sacred to Stow, but whether in themselves or by virtue of their history it would be hard to say. The following passage fairly represents Stow's attitude and the nature of his interests:

> Then in Needelars Lane have yee the parrish church of *Saint Pancrate*, a proper small church, but divers rich Parishioners therein, and hath had of olde time many liberall benefactors, but of late such as (not regarding the order taken by her Maiesty) the least bell in their church being broken, have rather solde the same for halfe the value, then put the parish to charge with new casting: late experience hath proued this to bee true, besides the spoyle of monumentes there.[1]

Stow did not hesitate to criticize materialistic greed as this passage shows. Yet what he most regretted was the decay of worthy traditions. Fortunately, Stow's moral indignation seldom got the better of his interest in the material facts.

When he wrote about the dissolved monasteries in and about London, Stow took pains to find out their valuations, but said little about the provisions made for the monks and nuns. He may have avoided this subject for fear of becoming involved with the licensing authorities. Stow had in the past suppressed information which he thought would be likely to provoke the government, and he was perhaps never wholly free from suspicion of being an indifferent Protestant. After Bishop Grindal's chaplains had searched Stow's home in 1569 they reported that 'his bokes declare him to be a great favourer of papistrye'.[2] Although their sense of judgment was contemptible, and Cecil rightly decided to ignore Grindal's report, it is obvious that Stow had reasons for caution. That he was primarily

---

[1] *Ibid.*, I, 261.

[2] Quoted by Kingsford, *Survey*, I, xvii. On Stow's religious reputation, See James Gairdner, ed., *Three Fifteenth Century Chronicles*, Camden Society (XXVIII, 1880), xi. Stow's memoranda are interesting; see pp. 94–147.

interested in historical matters and not in religious controversy was perhaps his saving grace.

Stow was not the first writer to record London events. The city chronicles appeared as early as the reign of Edward I; and Fitzstephens, the biographer of Thomas À Becket, had written an account of London in the twelfth century, which Stow used to great advantage. Nevertheless, the honour of being the first historian of London belonged to Stow, who was the earliest writer to make use of the public records of the city and of the nation in a scholarly work.[1]

Modern historicism has insisted that custom and tradition are expressions of the organic growth of society; Stow and his contemporaries assumed that custom and tradition must be static norms. Nostalgia for the good old days and for the supposed purity of ancient virtue perhaps came more easily to the Elizabethan historians, who thought that it was their prerogative and duty to make moral judgments. Yet it is remarkable that Stow, while complaining of the 'new vanity of men's mindes, much unlike to the disposition of the ancient citizens', nevertheless sought to understand the causes of at least some of the social changes which he recorded.[2] It is true that he was primarily interested in description: the wealth, honours, charities, and diversions of generations of London citizens were carefully documented in Stow's pages. But if he noted with regret the decay of hospitality, the new enclosures, and much else, he also understood better than most of his contemporaries that history was a process of development.

No doubt every historian reveals something of his own time and place and personal circumstances in his writing. In this sense every work of history is a social document, or can be read as such. Like any other document, Stow's *Survey* bears the stamp and date of the age in which it was written. Unlike most documents, Stow's *Survey* was also a work of art—historical art of the highest competence. The elements which distinguish it are two: purity of scholar-

---

[1] There is a good discussion of the early chronicles of London in James Gairdner, *Early Chroniclers of Europe*, Vol. I, *England* (London, S.P.C.K., 1879), Chapter VII, *passim*. Stow refrained from writing about the city government of his own day in any detail, presumably because he believed that James Dalton was preparing such a work. See Valerie Pearl, *London and the Outbreak of the Puritan Revolution* (Oxford, 1961), 46.

[2] Stow, *Survey*, II, 78; see I, 27 (enclosures); II, 20 (the decay of hospitality); cf. I, 104.

ship, and originality of organization, or style. The former helped to make the latter possible. Stow spent the greater part of his life collecting material, learning the texture of facts, and discovering how to organize and compose a history.

Stow was a practical man, not given to theorizing about his work, but he understood that the basic requirement of all historical scholarship was the empirical verification of fact statements. The importance which Stow attached to verifiable facts can hardly be over-estimated. His manuscript notes contain an astonishing variety of historical materials, including copies of letters and proclamations, selections from medieval chronicles, lists of names, statistics compiled from various sources, accounts of sea voyages, and topographical observations. In some cases Stow copied out the divergent accounts of the same event which he found in different chronicles.[1] On the whole, Stow was careful to note where he got his information, although he sometimes made extracts without indicating a source.

In his *Survey* Stow perfected the methods he had used in his earlier works. As a matter of course he now cited the evidence which supported his statements of fact. If he had any reason to doubt the credibility of a witness he sought confirming evidence. In a typical passage Stow wrote:

> That Marchants of all nations had theyr Keyes and warfes at this Citty whereunto they brought their Marchandises before, and in the raigne of *Henry* the second, mine author [Fitzstephen] wrote of his owne knowledge to be true, though for the antiquity of the Citty, he tooke the common opinion. Also that this Citie was in his time and afore diuided into wards, had yearely Sherifs, Aldermen, generall courts, and assemblies, and such like notes by him set down . . . he wrote likewise of his owne experience, as being borne and brought up amongst them. And to confirme his opinion, concerning Marchandises then hither transported, whereof happily may bee some argument, *Thomas Clifford* (before *Fitzstephens* time) writing of *Edward* the Confessor, sayeth to this effect . . .[2]

Stow went on to cite William of Malmesbury, and concluded with a phrase which occurs again and again in the *Survey*: 'Also I reade in

[1] See B.M. Harley MS. 542, f. 10, on comparison of accounts. B.M. Harley MSS. 539, 540, 543, *passim*. Further lists of Stow's sources are given by Kingsford, *Survey*, I, lxxxvi-xciii.

[2] Stow, *Survey*, I, 82.

divers records that of olde time . . .' [1] When Stow knew, on the basis of records, that a common opinion was wrong he explained why, and also gave his sources. Moreover, he corrected his own mistakes when new evidence convinced him that he had been wrong.

The variety of sources Stow was actually able to make use of in his *Survey* may come as a surprise to anyone accustomed to thinking of Stow as a mere chronicler. Stow based his account on monastic and guild records, church registers, wills, patents, parliamentary records, and other records in the Tower and Rolls House, as well as chronicles, histories, poems, and the personal memories of the older inhabitants of London. He often referred his readers to Hall's *Chronicles* or to his own *Annales* for further information on particular points. But always he was concerned 'to put down some proofe' for what he said. [2] In the dedication which he prefixed to the *Summarie Abridged* for 1604 Stow summed up in simple, eloquent words his historical faith: 'I mean (God willing) so to trie all matters worthy of immortalitie by the certaine touchstone of the best allowed Historiographers and Sound records, that neither any bodie by me shalbe deceiued nor I forced to craue pardon if I do offend.' [3]

No historian is infallible. Stow made honest mistakes; and when he knew he was ignorant of something he said as much. It would be easy to criticize Stow for being unaware of methodological refinements and for being indifferent to the broad problems of historical explanation. The subtleties of present-day historical theory and practice were simply beyond Stow's vision. Modern historians have undoubtedly profited from philosophical inquiry into the problems of truth and fact in history. Differences of opinion about historical method, when restated in terms of the differences between a coherence and a correspondence theory of truth, can often be explained or at least clarified; and clarity is not the least virtue in a historian or philosopher. Yet the good historians of the past were less often deceived by the appearance of authority than has sometimes been

[1] Stow, *Survey*, I, 82. Stow was naturally proud of his record learning—see *ibid.*, II, 147–8. Stow's willingness to revise in the light of better evidence was evident throughout his work. See *ibid.*, I, 221; II, 40, 121 and notes, for examples.

[2] *Ibid.*, I, 156. The variety of Stow's sources and the use he made of them are discussed by Kingsford in his Introduction. Stow was credulous about some religious matters (I, 196), but much less gullible than his old enemy, Richard Grafton, the chronicler. See *ibid.*, II, 349–50.

[3] Quoted by Kingsford, *Survey*, I, lxxxi.

supposed, especially by philosophers who detect error or naïveté in nearly every version of the correspondence theory.[1]

It has been shown that Stow realized that facts must be *established*, that they do not exist simply because one finds them in so-called authorities. Moreover, Stow did not assign the same degree of probability to every historical statement—Brute was doubtful; Caesar was not. Stow obviously accepted public records as authoritative, but he was not therefore merely sublimating a simple correspondence theory of truth. In all historical writing and thought the historian's judgment is of more decisive importance than the logician's categories of criticism. The methods of evidence and proof which Stow used were on the whole appropriate to his subject matter. It would be rash to assume that Stow was lacking in judgment when he insisted '. . . that the perusing of auncient records & best approued histories of all times (not without great difficultie obtained) do not only moue me, but for their authoritie driue me to acknowledge both mine & other men's errors, & in acknowledging, to correct them . . .'[2]

Stow has thus far been considered primarily as a man of his time, and as a historian who believed that 'in hystories the chief thyng that is to be desyred is truthe'.[3] His methods of evidence and proof required common sense and judgment, but not great subtlety or originality. The Society of Antiquaries expected from its members the kind of documentation which Stow provided; and although Stow could take justifiable pride in the thoroughness of his scholarship, he did not originate new techniques of study. What he might justly have claimed (although he never did) was the right to be called the originator of town history and the founder of a new style in English historiography. The local historians who preceded Stow wrote county histories; and Camden's *Britannia* provided, at best, a large-scale survey which could not be reduced and made to apply to

[1] R. G. Collingwood in *The Idea of History* (Oxford, 1946) was contemptuous of much early historical writing largely on the grounds that it was not based on a coherence theory. The medieval chroniclers often were too inclined to accept authority, but cf. Marie Schultz, *Die Lehre von der Historischen Methode bei den Geschichtschreiberndes Mittelalters (VI–XIII Jahrhunderts)* (Berlin, 1909).

[2] Quoted by Kingsford from *Summarie Abridged* for 1604; see *Survey*, I, lxxxi.

[3] Quoted by Kingsford from Stow's earliest historical work (1565); see *Survey*, I, lxxxvi.

the circuit of a city. Stow found some hints on organization in Lambarde's *Perambulation of Kent*, but he had to depend on his own historical judgment and imagination in laying out the overall plans for his *Survey*.

The selection of facts in historiography is determined by ideas of relevance; and the organization of facts constitutes one aspect of historical style. Stow's ideas of relevance cannot be explained simply by reference to the climate of middle-class opinion, nor can the organization of the *Survey* be explained by earlier precedents. Although the *Survey of London* had much in common with other local histories —every genre is by definition made up of individuals sharing common characteristics—it was nevertheless unique, in the sense that it was not modelled on earlier town histories; and it was original, in the sense that it was the first book to reveal the kind of questions that a town historian should ask.

The ability to ask new and fruitful questions and to organize evidence skilfully, was (and still is) an attribute of the gifted historian no less than of the gifted scientist. To formulate a relevant hypothesis presupposed knowledge of the subject matter of inquiry, but knowledge by itself did not guarantee that the scientist or historian would perceive significant relationships. The procedure which Herodotus followed in formulating a significant hypothesis to explain the annual flooding of the Nile has been called a model of scientific reasoning.[1] Naturally, he did not use the vocabulary of science, but he did proceed in a scientific way to explain a physical event. As a historian Herodotus also selected and ordered his material so as to bring out significant relationships; and his ideas of relevance have proved remarkably durable.

John Stow was by no means as great a historian as Herodotus, but in his way he was no less 'scientific'. And, like Herodotus, he has often been criticized for being naïve, garrulous, and uncritical. While it is true that such criticism may appear to be justified in relation to Stow's early work, it is completely mistaken when applied to the *Survey*. Stow understood the importance of asking himself questions about his evidence; and he selected and ordered his materials to bring out significant relationships. By inverting some of his statements we may reconstruct the questions that he was trying to answer. On the whole, it may be said Stow showed discrimination

[1] See Morris R. Cohen and Ernest Nagel, *An Introduction to Logic and Scientific Method* (New York, 1934), 197–206.

and excellent critical sense about what was relevant to his purposes in writing a local history.

In studying Stow's *Survey*, it is particularly important to realize that Stow was attempting to answer questions which were not chosen at random, but which form a pattern. They were, in fact, the same questions which twentieth-century local historians must ask. Posterity, in this case, has much to learn from Stow about how to organize a town history, what questions are relevant, and what sources of information to seek. It is only necessary to consider how closely Stow's *Survey* agrees with the injunctions and suggestions of W. G. Hoskins in his *Local History in England* (1959) in order to recognize the intrinsic merits of Stow's approach.[1]

Stow described the general organization of the *Survey* in a paragraph which merits close examination:

> Having thus in generality handled the originall, the walles, gates, ditches, and fresh waters, the bridges, towers and castles, the schooles of learning, and houses of law, the orders and customes, sportes and pastimes, watchings, and martiall exercises, and lastly the honour and worthiness of the Cittizens: I am now to set down the distribution of this Citty into parts: and more especially to declare the antiquities note worthy in euery of the same: and how both the whole and partes haue beene from time to time ruled and gouerned.[2]

Stow began his *Survey* with a long introduction which might have been entitled 'The Face of the Town'. It provided an all-around picture of the city which Stow was going to write about; and it is still an amazingly clear and well-arranged picture of the essential features of Elizabethan London.

The significance of the site was not lost upon Stow, who, after a description of the walled circuit of London, immediately turned to the essential question of water supplies. Although the river may have sufficed for the earliest inhabitants, a primary factor in the growth of London (or of any other town) was the availability of good water supplies. Unlike many modern town historians who have ignored this problem, Stow recognized it and gave clear answers to the questions of how the city was served 'with sweete and freshe waters'

[1] See especially Chapters VI and VII of W. G. Hoskins, *Local History in England*. The book contains most valuable comments throughout, and I am heavily indebted to it for much of the following discussion.

[2] Stow, *Survey*, I, 117.

which, as he went on to say 'being since decaid, other meanes haue beene sought to supplie the want, as shall be shewed'.[1]

Stow dealt with the relations of London to the surrounding area at the end of the *Survey* in a chapter called 'An Apologie of the Cittie of London'. He began with a short discourse in defence of urban living, in which he defended London against the charge that it had become an over-mighty city, draining strength and prosperity away from the provincial towns. Stow went on to point out the military and economic reasons for London's growth and importance. The Thames, he observed, was admirably suited to commerce, for it 'openeth indifferently upon France and Flaunders, our mightiest neighbours . . . and this Citie standeth thereon in such convenient distance from the sea, as it is not onely neare enough for intelligence of the affayres of those Princes, and for the resistance of their attempts: but also sufficiently removed from the feare of any sodaine daungers that may be offered by them . . .'[2] The problem of supplying London with necessities—food, water, and fuel—could be met easily, again thanks to London's situation on the Thames. Coal could be shipped by sea, and food could come overland because London was near to the sources of supply.

The economic problem, as Stow realized, had two sides, for London not only drew supplies from the country, it also dispersed foreign wares to the countryside, and helped to maintain Norfolk, Suffolk, Essex, Kent, and Sussex—counties which 'stand not so much by the benefite of their owne soile, as by the neighbourhood and nearnes which they haue to London'.[3] Stow, in short, was very much concerned with the question of how London was related to England.

The layout and building materials of the city occupied Stow's attention throughout the *Survey*. Although he seldom described the architecture of buildings he usually noted the use of timber, stone, and lead, and carefully explained the gradual paving and building over of ancient watercourses, such as Walbrook, and the filling in of marshland, so that no signs remained other than the apparently irrelevant names of streets.[4] Stow was ever alert to the significance of place-names, and his questioning of such names usually led him back to ancient records or to descriptions of the city in which he found evidence for his hypothetical conjectures.

As a result of Stow's interrogations, the history of the extension

[1] Stow, *Survey*, I, 11.   [2] *Ibid.*, II, 200.
[3] *Ibid.*, II, 213.   [4] *Ibid.*, I, 14.

of London could be traced with considerable accuracy. Stow's historical curiosity was aroused by all kinds of incidents of London life. He recognized problems in small happenings which would have moved few other people to ask questions, much less search for historical answers. Consider, for example, Stow's account of the Galley men of Mincheon Lane:

> In this lane of olde time dwelled diuers strangers borne of Genoa and those parts, these were commonly called Galley men, as men that came vppe in the Gallies, brought vp wines and other merchandises which they landed in Thames Street, at a place called Galley key: they had a certain coin of silver amongst themselues which were halfe pence of Genoa, & were called Galley halfe pence: these halfe pence were forbidden in the thirteenth of *Henry* the fourth, and againe by Parliament in the fourth of *Henry* the fift, it was that if any person bring into this realme Galley halfe pence . . . hee should be punished as a Theefe . . . notwithstanding in my youth I haue seene them passe currant, but with some difficulty . . .[1]

Stow's authority was the Letter Book of the City of London, but the entry was one which he might easily have passed over had he not been curious to explain a youthful memory.

The gradual changes which took place in old streets was a theme which Stow handled to perfection. From movable stalls to sheds, to shops, and finally to tall houses was a characteristic development; the name alone might record an ancient use, or an ancient boundary.[2] Suburban growth and in-filling was another problem which Stow recognized as significant and important, not only from a topographical point of view, but also from the point of view of social and economic history.[3] As the wealthier classes began to vacate their large houses in the city, these were turned into tenements for a number of poorer families. The process was just beginning in London in the sixteenth century, but Stow took note of it.[4]

In his chapter 'Of Orders and Customs' Stow drew attention to economic questions, and throughout the *Survey* took note of occupational customs, prices, charitable bequests, and other indicators of economic change and development. Moreover, Stow was concerned

---

[1] *Ibid.*, I, 132–3. [2] See, for example, *ibid.*, I, 81, 119, 346.
[3] See, for example, *ibid.*, I, 127–9; II, 52, 66, 69–98, 367–8. Stow noted abuses, II, 74, 79–80, 367–9.
[4] *Ibid.*, 237, for example. Earlier there had been considerable movement; cf. I, 81.

with population problems, and with what historians today would call the problem of social mobility. Stow did not attempt to provide population statistics, and his demographic observations were admittedly fragmentary, but he recognized the significance of shifts in the social strata:

> . . . that the estate of London, in the persons of the Citizens, is so friendly enterlaced, and knit in league with the rest of the Realme, not onely at their beginning by birth and bloud as I haue shewed, but also verie commonly at their ending by life and conuersation (for that Marchants and rich men, being satisfyed with gaine, doe for the most part marry theyr Children into the Countrey, and conuey themselues after *Ciceroes* counsell, *veluti ex portu in agros & possessiones*): I doe inferre that there is not onely no danger towards the common quiet thereby, but also great occasion and cause of good loue and amitie . . .[1]

Stow was an intelligent observer, with a trained eye for significant detail. And he owed more than is perhaps commonly supposed to the fact that he surveyed in person the London of his own day.

Fieldwork gave Stow's *Survey* its solidity. Stow's work on records was remarkably good, but only by direct observation of every street and building could Stow have discovered the visual evidence of the past which explained what no written records could.[2] Stow walked because he could not afford to ride, but he did not lose by walking—the evidence before his eyes made the records come to life. Even today in reading the *Survey* one is struck by the immediacy of Stow's London; it is as though one were to walk slowly through the streets and alleys, and visit the landmarks of a city in which time had been idle. The sense of the present was no less an achievement in Stow's *Survey* than the sense of the past.

The differences between Stow's *Survey* and a good modern work on local history are differences in emphasis and in the degree of generality of the questions asked, not differences which reflect radical changes in standards of relevance. Stow was remorseless, and sometimes undiscriminating, in his collection of details, but as Mr. Hoskins has observed, 'it is detail, rightly selected, that finally illuminates the generalizations, all the talk about taxable wealth and social classes, wage-levels, and price movements'.[3] The fact that

[1] Stow, *Survey*, II, 208.

[2] See Stow's description of the dissolved Priory Hospital of St. Mary Spittle, *Survey*, I, 166-7.   [3] W. G. Hoskins, *Local History*, 105.

Camden and Dugdale and countless other good historians turned to Stow for enlightenment, and depended upon him for particular facts should dispel the notion (if it is still held) that Stow was a mere compiler and arranger of antiquarian notes. The details in Stow's work were 'rightly selected' to illuminate historical continuity and change. That is one reason why the book has proved so useful to scholars.

The ideas that order facts in many modern histories have been derived from disciplines which did not exist as such in Stow's day. The idea of discussing class structure in terms of the economic stratification of the community, or the idea that opportunities for social mobility might help to determine the attitude of the bourgeoisie toward an existing government, or the idea that capital accumulation and entrepreneurship might be related to the breakdown of social traditions—these were all concepts which could only have been understood long after Stow wrote. They all assume a relatively high degree of sophistication in economic or social theory. The questions which Stow asked were generally simpler ones.

What is significant is that Stow recognized certain kinds of facts as relevant to his purposes as a historian. These were facts which explained how the community worked through the centuries—how it solved problems of housing and provisioning and governing, what it did to supply the needs of the poor, what customs, pastimes, and memorials were peculiar to it. The lists of names of building donors and other worthy benefactors of London found in Stow's pages can only by implication be said to explain the changing pattern of social relations. Certainly Stow failed to understand the importance of formulating broad hypotheses of explanation. Yet it is no less certain that he understood the importance of organizing his *Survey* so as to illuminate the historical growth of the community.

The themes of local history have changed from time to time and from place to place, not only in response to differences in point of view and interest, but also because each community presents its own problems and its own historical surfaces. The historian of the parish or of the county could not simply copy the historian of the town, yet the general questions which historians would recognize as relevant to the history of any community were those which Stow was trying to answer. His work was a model of local history in the seventeenth century, and it has not lost all value as a model of style and method to practising local historians today.

9

WILLIAM CAMDEN AND
TERRITORIAL HISTORY

WILLIAM CAMDEN WAS BORN IN 1551 and died in 1623. At the time
of his birth English historiography was still largely medieval in
character. The best modern historian of England was the Italian
cleric and humanist, Polydore Vergil. The bourgeois chroniclers,
notably Fabyan, Hall, and Grafton, were transitional figures, who
drew upon the works of the great medieval chroniclers without
understanding the limitations of their own scissors-and-paste
methods. Sir Thomas More's *History of Richard III* was a superb
literary portrait, but not a work of historical scholarship. Except
for biographies, the early Tudor age produced no great native
historical literature. By the time of Camden's death the whole
character of English historiography had changed. The medieval
chronicle had been superseded by the modern history. Original
research, especially in the public records, had become the hallmark
of good historical writing. Camden's *Annales Rerum Anglicarum et
Hibernicarum Regnante Elizabethae*, written for an international
reading public, challenged comparison with the best territorial
histories produced on the continent. The *Annales*, along with the
Britannia, were a tribute to the intellectual expansion of Elizabethan
England.

As a national historian Camden had no equal among his English
contemporaries. The circumstances of his life, and the accident of
Burghley's patronage, gave him opportunities which no other his-

torian enjoyed—and he made the most of them. The *Annales* of Elizabeth's reign revealed the virtuosity of Camden's scholarship, but there is no reason to suppose that Camden was not a man of his time. He, too, accepted the moral, political, and religious assumptions upon which the Elizabethan state was founded. Whoever wants to understand those assumptions will want to read with care Camden's historical works.

Camden himself knew the satisfactions of a man of learning: his work was his pleasure; he enjoyed the company of many distinguished friends; and he achieved a deservedly high reputation as a historian, antiquary and teacher. Moreover, he showed dignity, courtesy, and restraint in nearly everything that he did. An intellectual aristocrat, conservative because he wished to preserve the best traditions of the past, Camden was able to write the history of the reign of Elizabeth with sympathy and understanding.

Critics who have impugned Camden's integrity have done so unjustly.[1] They have accused him, on the flimsiest evidence, of having suppressed his true opinion of Mary Stuart, and of having weakly submitted his manuscript to King James I for corrections. In fact, Camden was stauncher and wiser than his critics imagined. He shunned all prejudice 'forasmuch as it taketh away a man's judgement, and doth so blind the Minds of men in matters both of Religion and State, that like dim Eyes they can behold nothing clearly'.[2]

In submitting the supplement of his *Annales* of Queen Elizabeth to the king's 'judicious censure', Camden admitted that he might have offended in certain matters, such as his eulogy of Sir Francis Walsingham, but he ended the draft of his letter by asking for historical evidence, and expressing his willingness to forgo a popular reputation:

> I see that the Earl of Essex's affection in his later days was variable toward the King. I would know upon what grounds, if his Majesty

[1] Those charges, spread by Camden's envious enemies, are discussed and refuted by Camden's biographer in the *D.N.B.* Camden himself wrote: 'As for Danger, I feared none, no not from those who think the Memory of Succeeding Ages may be extinguished by present Power.' See William Camden, *The History of the Renowned Princess Elizabeth*, 4th ed. (London, 1688), 'The Author to the Reader', Sig. b. This is the best translation of the *Annales*, but the student should consult Thomas Hearne's edition (Oxford, 1727) of the original Latin work. Hereafter all footnote references to the *Annales* will be cited as *History*, referring to the 1688 edition.

[2] Camden, *History*, 'Author to Reader', Sig. b.

thinketh it fit that they may be particulated. As I do not dislike that they [the *Annales*] should be published in my life time: So I do not desire they should be set forth in English until after my death. Knowing how unjust carpers the unlearned readers are . . .[1]

In the light of Camden's scholarly achievements it would be unwise to impugn his integrity simply because he submitted his manuscript to his king.

Camden beheld clearly the high tragedy of Elizabeth and Mary; he understood the implacable necessities which drove the Catholic and the Protestant Queens ever further apart. He himself was content to let every man 'have his free liberty to judge according to his Fancy', but he would not, as a historian, compromise his integrity by pointing morals at the expense of truth: 'By inveighing against the Enemies of my Countrey, to aim at the Commendation of a good Commonwealths-man, and at the same time to get the Repute of a bad Historian, I held a thing ridiculous.' [2] It is unnecessary to defend Camden from the charge of servility; it is essential, however, to recognize the conventions of his thought in order to assess his contribution to English historiography.[3]

Classical influences shaped Camden's early career as a scholar.

[1] B.M. Cotton MS., Vespasian F IX, f. 125. The letter is unsigned and undated, obviously a first draft.

[2] Camden, *History*, 'Author to Reader', Sig. b 1.

[3] Camden's writings, including his letters, are more important, in this connection, than the details of his life. The best life of Camden is that in the *D.N.B.*, but the life by Richard Gough, in his edition of Camden's *Britannia*, is still of great value; Gough's notes are especially useful. See William Camden, *Britannia, or, a Chorographical Description of . . . England, Scotland, and Ireland*, translated by Richard Gough, 3 vol. (London, 1789), I, i–xxii. The first edition of the *Britannia* appeared, after ten years of work, in 1586; Camden made many corrections in later editions. Many local historians and antiquaries wrote to him, offering advice, corrections and additions. See Thoma Smitho, ed., V. Cl. *Gulielmo Camdeni . . . Epistolae* (London, 1691), letter XXX, 36–9; cf. letter XXII, Lambarde to Camden, 28–30. Hereafter I shall refer to this volume of letters as Camden, *Epistolae*. Thomas Smith reprinted in this work most of B.M. Cotton MS., Julius Caesar C V. Those letters were subsequently rearranged in correct chronological order; it should be noted that Smith's dates are sometimes inaccurate. B.M. Cotton MS., Julius Caesar F VI also contains Camden letters printed by Smith. A recent study is Fred Jacob Levy's 'William Camden as Historian'. Unpublished Ph.D. Dissertation, Harvard University, 1960.

He was a master of Greek as well as Latin; and he was known as a classicist long before he became famous as an antiquary. His Greek grammar was by far the most popular (or, perhaps, the most widely used) of his books. He was thoroughly familiar with the ancient historians, and when he began work on the history of Elizabeth's reign, he took as his counsellors Polybius and Tacitus.

Camden's knowledge of English antiquities was acquired over a long period of time. He not only learned Anglo-Saxon in order to pursue his research, but he travelled, as he tells us, 'over almost all England, and consulted the most experienced and learned persons in each county'.[1] In addition to writing the *Britannia*, Camden, like Stow, edited medieval chronicles.

The notebooks and collections of Camden afford some insight into his working habits, and reveal something of the prudence of his mind. He made careful transcripts of Leland's notes, and of countless other materials that he thought might prove useful to him in his antiquarian and historical work. He kept a kind of rough diary of events during Elizabeth's reign, and his account of events from 1603 until his own death in 1623 formed skeleton annals of King James' reign. When he wrote to describe the arguments for and against the proposed marriage of the Duke of Norfolk and Queen Mary, he did not merely depend on his own memory or invention. He had read carefully the contemporary pamphlets and paraphrased their arguments in his *Annales*.[2] Macaulay was certainly not the first historian

---

[1] Camden, *Britannia*, 'Mr. Camden's Preface to the Reader', I, i, in Gough's edition, 1789. All references to the *Britannia* are to this edition. Camden goes on to describe his research thus: 'I have carefully read over our own writers, and those among the Greek and Roman authors who made the least mention of Britain. I have consulted the public records, ecclesiastical registers, many libraries, the archieves [*sic*] of cities and churches, monuments, and old deeds and have made use of them as irrefrageable evidence, and when necessary quoted their very words however barbarous, that truth may have its full weight.' Camden also probably learned Welsh in order to carry on his research. See John Aubrey, *Brief Lives*, ed. Oliver Lawson Dick (London, 1950), 51.

[2] See B.M. Cotton MS., Julius Caesar F XI, *passim*; Camden's extracts from Leland's notes are in B.M. Cotton MS., Julius Caesar F X, fols. 103, 157b-9, 163-4b, and *passim* (see *English Historical Review*, LXV, 1950, p. 506). Camden's diary is in B.M. Harley MS. 36, fols. 493-4b. (See *English Historical Review*, LXVIII, 1953, pp. 234-58). Some of Camden's working notes are in B.M. Harley MS. 530, fols. 82-90b. Camden's correspondence with Spelman, Ussher, and the continental scholars was

to recognize the importance of popular literature as a source of information about current attitudes and opinions.

According to his own testimony, he first undertook the study of English antiquities at the request of a foreigner, Abraham Ortelius, 'that excellent reviver of ancient geography'.[1] The French historian, De Thou, was indebted to Camden for information concerning England and Ireland which he made use of in his own history; and Camden was encouraged by De Thou, and others, to continue his work, lest strangers be 'at a loss in the Affairs of our Country'.[2] Continental writers, in fact, exerted a steady influence on Camden's historical thought, for Camden, unlike Stow, Holinshed and other bourgeois annalists of the sixteenth century, corresponded directly with eminent continental men of letters.

Camden showed little of the provincialism that characterized these earlier Tudor chroniclers. Still, Camden knew the value of Stow's work, and he did not scorn the writings of lesser men. He never repudiated the historiographical traditions of his own country. Instead he enriched the English tradition by adapting classical and Renaissance ideas to the established English patterns of history writing.[3]

In all his works, Camden expressed strong feelings of patriotism. He undertook the task of writing the *Britannia*, he said, because he was prompted by the love of his country, as well as by friends who had confidence in him. In the *Britannia*, Camden included a stately panegyric on the British Isles, which he repeated in 'plaine english' in his *Remains of a Greater Work*. In this book he declared that Britain is 'well knowne to be the most flourishing and excellent, most renowned and famous Isle of the whole world: So rich in commodities, so beautiful in situation, so resplendent in all glorie, that if the Omnipotent had fashioned the world round like a ring, as he did like a globe, it might have been most worthily the only gemme

---

especially important. See especially B.M. Add. MS. 25384, f. 5. Some of Camden's papers for the *Britannia* are in B.M. Cotton MS., Titus F IX.

[1] Camden, *Britannia*, 'Mr. Camden's Preface', I, i.

[2] See J. Collinson, *The Life of Thaunus* (London, 1807), 136–55, *passim*, and 173.

[3] Cf. Edward Fueter, *Histoire de L'Historiographie Moderne*, translated by Emile Jeanmaire (Paris, 1914), 204; Fueter concludes that Camden followed the pattern of the Italian humanist historian, Blondus, both in the *Annales* and in the *Britannia*, and that Camden 'donne des Regests, non une Histoire'. Fueter is wrong on almost all counts.

therein'.[1] Camden showed greater restraint in his *Annales*, but he remained a scholarly patriot.

Camden felt strongly that he was writing for posterity, not just for his contemporaries.[2] When he invoked posterity, Camden was perhaps only voicing an Elizabethan commonplace, yet he was sensitive to currents of thought which were beginning to effect a reorientation in men's attitudes toward their ancestors and toward posterity. One of the uses of posterity was to consecrate the idea of progress. Camden did not, like Bacon, give philosophical expression to an idea of progress. He insisted, however, that the pursuit of antiquity was neither 'an impertinent inquiry into past things' nor a mere retreat from present realities. No educated man should lack knowledge of his country's history:

> I want not arguments to recommend this undertaking to honest and worthy men who wish to see their native country illustrated, or to prove that these studies afford the most agreeable and liberal entertainment. If there are any who wish to remain strangers in their own country and city, and children in knowledge, let them enjoy their dream.[3]

Camden was less victimized by the past than many of his contemporaries, because he knew more about it; he understood the presentness of the past and could be objective about historical continuities. Posterity, he knew, would improve on his work in the same way that he had improved on the works of his predecessors.

The man who first set Camden the task of compiling an historical account of Elizabeth's reign was Lord Burghley. Camden himself has described his difficulties and his hopes. Burghley had given him access to his own papers, 'and then the Queen's Rolls, Memorials,

---

[1] William Camden, *Remaines of a Greater Worke Concerning Britaine* (London, 1605), 1. The historical value of the *Britannia* is dealt with briefly in an article by Rudolf B. Gottfried, 'The Early Development of the Section on Ireland in Camden's *Britannia*', *English Literary History* (X, 1943), 117–30.

[2] See Camden, *Remaines*, 1, 7, 11. In the *Britannia* he wrote: 'Another age and other men will daily produce new discoveries. It is enough for me to have begun.' See *Britannia*, I, iii, and 'Mr. Camden's Preface', *passim*. Camden dedicated his *History* 'To God, my Countrey and Posterity, at the Altar of truth . . .' (Sig. C 1).

[3] Camden, *Britannia*, I, ii, 'Mr. Camden's Preface'. Cf. Carl Becker, *The Heavenly City of the Eighteenth Century Philosophers* (New Haven, 1932), 131.

and Records'; and Camden was confident that in these papers he would 'meet the real truth of Passages lodged, as it were, in so many Repositories'.[1] Camden laboured, sweating and covered with dust, to get his fit matter together, but he was interrupted, first by the death of Burghley, and then of Elizabeth. When he finally resumed his work he procured all the help he possibly could from Sir Robert Cotton. He also consulted with 'men who have been present at the transacting of Matters, and such as have been addicted to the Parties on both Sides in this contrariety of Religion'. Finally, he weighed and examined all the evidence in the 'balance of my own judgement'.[2]

Camden outlined his theory of history in a few short paragraphs. These merit close attention, for they show that Camden was making use of the best classical traditions in order to cope with the difficult problems of writing contemporary history. He adapted, but he did not imitate; he drew upon many traditions, but his ideas about history were his own. He knew that he was writing a new kind of history.

Camden realized how important it was for any historian to cultivate objectivity, and he doubted that he might 'lawfully' interpose any opinion of his own. The use of speeches and orations he rejected 'unless they be the very same *verbatim*, or else abbreviated', and he refused to adorn his discourse with 'animadverting observations'. Camden had defended the use of conjecture as indispensable to the study of etymology, and in the *Britannia* argued 'that we are obliged to recur to conjecture in every science'. This attitude toward conjecture was one which Camden modified considerably in his *Annales*, but it remained beneath the surface.[3]

Camden maintained that his entire business was to inform the

---

[1] Camden, *History*, 'Author to Reader', Sig. a 2.

[2] *Ibid.*, 'Author to Reader', Sig. b.

[3] *Ibid.*, 'Author to Reader' contains all the quotations used in this paragraph except the one from the *Britannia*. Cf. Camden's statement: 'My enqueries into the etymology and first inhabitants of Britain were conducted with hesitation; and in such uncertainty I have pronounced boldly on nothing, convinced that the origins of the nations of remote antiquity are necessarily obscure . . . I have investigated the antient divisions of Britain, and given a brief account of the orders and courts, and of the flourishing kingdoms of England, Scotland and Ireland. In the same brief manner I have described . . . the bounds and qualities of the soil, the places memorable in antiquity; the dukes, earles, barons, and the most antient and illustrious families.' *Britannia*, 'Mr. Camden's Preface', I, i.

mind; he trusted that his readers would not find him lacking in that 'ingenuous Freedom of Speech joyned with modesty which becometh a historian'. To him, affairs of war and policy were the proper subject matter of history, 'yet Ecclesiastical matters I neither could nor indeed ought I to omit', for 'Religion and the Commonwealth cannot be parted asunder'.[1]

Camden thus insisted on the essential unity of history. By emphasizing the importance of factors other than war and policy, he made a significant contribution to the theory and practice of English historiography. He still accepted the conventional distinction between the functions of the political and ecclesiastical historian, but he refused to write a mere political chronicle. The main difference between Camden and earlier writers lay in the fact that Camden applied disciplined scholarship to the problems of causation. More important than the fact that Camden took Polybius for his model was what he quoted from Polybius:

> Take away from History Why, How, and to What End, Things have been done, and Whether the thing done hath succeeded according to Reason; and all that remains will be an idle Sport and Foolery, than a profitable Instruction; and though for the present it may delight, for the future it cannot profit.[2]

By treating questions of 'How, Why, and to What End' as secular historical problems, Camden succeeded in writing a history which fulfilled modern rather than medieval norms.

The limits within which the historian was free to tell the whole truth were prescribed by the moral and political ideals of the state. Camden's own conservatism made him angry with 'those curious inquisitive people who seek to know more than by the Laws is permitted them'. The dividing line between freedom and licence was one which Camden would not try to cross. 'Things manifest and evident', he wrote, 'I have not concealed; things doubtful I have interpreted favourably; things secret and abstruse I have not pried into.'[3] Above all, the hidden meanings of Princes were not to be inquired into too deeply. Like Ralegh, Camden realized that if a modern historian pursued truth too near the heels, it might strike out his teeth. Yet it was not just fear of the censorship that made

[1] See Camden, *History*, 'Author to Reader', *passim*.
[2] Camden stressed his indebtedness to classical models in matters of style as well as purpose. See *ibid.*, 'Author to Reader', Sig. b 3.
[3] *Ibid.*, 'Author to Reader', Sig. b 1.

Camden an intellectual conservative. He respected the meaning of that Elizabethan phrase, 'mysteries of state'. Elizabeth had used it to shut off debate, and James used it to stifle criticism. The phrase offends ears accustomed to hearing the ideal of free inquiry praised. Nevertheless, the historian who would understand this Elizbathen phrase must begin by attempting to understand the mind of a man like Camden.

In the long introduction which he wrote as a prologue to the Annals of Elizabeth's reign, Camden reviewed the history of England from the beginning of the Reformation to the death of Queen Mary. The essay was a model of balance and restraint. Camden did not conceal things manifest and evident, and things doubtful he interpreted favourably. Most of the blame for Henry VIII's divorce he put upon Wolsey. Wolsey was 'the cause of divorce', by which Camden meant that Wolsey was the instigator. He depended on the arrangement of arguments to show the various causes of events. Henry's character he interpreted as favourably as the evident facts permitted, saying of him that he was a man of great virtues as well as great vices. Camden showed sympathy for Mary Tudor, attributing to her bishops responsibility for the persecutions and cruelties of her reign. Camden's sympathy for Mary Tudor helps to explain his sympathy for Mary Stuart: both women were sovereign Queens. Respect for the divinity that hedged a king or queen was still deeply felt by Camden and his contemporaries.

Camden's treatment of the dissolution of the monasteries was sane, although not entirely unprejudiced. Henry VIII was avaricious, but he had the excuse of human frailty in the monks. The responsibility for schism in the Church Camden placed squarely on the Pope, who 'constrained the king'. Henry was a man too full of spirit to tolerate constraint—had not the Churchmen themselves implored the Pope not to cut Henry off and thereby endanger the Church? Camden was pro-Protestant, but he did achieve, to a remarkable degree, impartiality and objectivity in his account of religious affairs. Even in his introduction Camden managed to convey a sense of the complexity of the historical process.

Camden's purpose in writing his *Annales* was to provide a general history of the Elizabethan state. He wrote in Latin in order that the book might circulate more freely, and abandoned the apparatus of footnotes, realizing that other scholars could not gain access to most of the State Papers he had used. Important documents he quoted at some length, always indicating in the text the source of a quotation.[1] The elaborate scholarly apparatus of the *Britannia* would have been out of place in a work of contemporary history which had at least semi-official sanction and support. The content of the *Annales* was appropriate to the broad purposes Camden had defined in the Preface. He risked offending against the 'Dignity of History' in order to be as comprehensive and thorough as possible.

Whatever was of importance to the Elizabethan state was of interest to Camden. He was concerned with social, political, economic, and religious history, with wars, rebellions, voyages, lives, even with the stars that inclined, and the weather that compelled, the wills of men. Yet, like every other historian, he had to choose what to emphasize and what to ignore. The projection of the state which Camden drew was a political one, because ultimately political policy was decisive in the mercantilist state. Relative power, one of the primary concerns of statesmen in the age of mercantilism, became the unifying concept in Camden's territorial history. The state, in its quest for internal unification and external power, regulated more and more the corporate bodies, local officials, and mighty subjects of the nation. Camden's *Annales* recorded the evolution of state policy in response to the changing circumstances of international power politics.

Camden based his narrative on national political history; he put special emphasis on foreign affairs, and his work is still an excellent guide through the very important and complicated marriage negotiations of Elizabeth's reign. He did not confine his interest to any one stratum of society, but he rightly focused attention on the doings of the Court and Council. There is much scattered information in Camden's work on such diverse subjects as farming, the navy, supplies for the royal household, English commercial relations, etc. But what still lends significance to Camden's treatment of these subjects is the fact that he wrote about them not merely to fill pages in a chronicle, but to shed light on the policies of the Elizabethan government.

Camden discussed currency manipulations, import-export regulations, the activities of the trading companies, and other economic

[1] The State Papers of Elizabeth's reign were not available to scholars except as they found their way into Cotton's library. Owing to the vagaries of seventeenth-century typographical practices the only sure guide to whether or not a document is being quoted is Camden's own statement in the text.

matters from the point of view of state policy. He sympathized completely with the mercantilist policies of Elizabeth, and he often stated the reasons and arguments which were used to justify particular decisions. He can be charged with a failure to give proper emphasis to some of the most important measures of Elizabethan social policy, notably the poor law legislation (to which he devoted only a paragraph), but, in general, his sense of proportion was admirable.[1] The practices and some of the controlling assumptions of English mercantilism stand revealed in the pages of Camden's *Annales*.

The general character of Camden's historical work has been described at some length in order to clarify Camden's role in the development of historiography. The traditional values of truth, objectivity, patriotism and morality in history were neither critically analysed nor questioned by Camden. His ideas of explanation were seldom original in the sense that Sir Henry Spelman's theory of feudalism was original. Camden derived most of his ideas of explanation from his study of Elizabethan statecraft and diplomacy. His work was significant not because he elaborated a general 'theorem' of explanation, but because he analysed the immediate causes of historical events in terms used by contemporaries.

The sixteenth-century struggle for power was formally dynastic, rather than national—and religious, rather than imperialistic. After Elizabeth came to the throne, Europe entered a period of religious conflict which reduced diplomacy at times to little more than subversive ideological warfare. The breakdown of international diplomacy under the weight of religious fanaticism had intensified distrust, and helped to turn even domestic religious differences into issues of power politics.[2] Camden could not avoid being influenced by the

---

[1] On the Russia company and its trade, see Camden, *History*, 1567, 103; 1569, 123–5; 1583, 285–6. Camden's praise of Elizabeth for her regulation of grain market, 1566, 82; 1600, 597. On the Hanse towns, 1595, 503–5. On manipulation of currency (debasement of coinage), 1560, 48–9. Commercial relations with Denmark, 1600, 593–6. East India Company, 1600, 596. These are only examples—others may easily be found. In general, Camden gives more space to economic matters in the second part of his *Annales*, the part which covers the years 1590–1603. This was published posthumously, at Camden's request, in 1625. The first part appeared in 1615.

[2] See Garret Mattingly, *Renaissance Diplomacy* (London, 1955), 121–210 *passim*.

fears and concerns of Elizabethan statesmen and politicians. Considering the gravity of the threats to Elizabeth's throne it is surprising that Camden could write with as much objectivity as he did. In achieving what he called 'an even and undistempered mind' Camden set an example of impartiality for all writers of contemporary history. It is a tribute to the professionalism of Camden's historical and antiquarian training that he was able to do this. The professional quality of Camden's historical thought emerges most clearly, however, in the details of his work.

Exactly what Camden meant by the word 'cause' he did not say. He seldom used the word, and when he did he obviously expected his readers to accept it without quibbling. When he referred to the reasons why Elizabeth admitted Murray and the Scottish Rebels into England, he meant the ostensible reasons which Elizabeth gave to justify herself. When he attributed the spread of drunkenness in England to the bad habits picked up by the soldiers in the Netherlands, he may have been guilty of shallowness, but he did not have the means to make a more searching analysis. Camden at least aimed at giving reasonable explanations of events. Even what he detested, he attempted to explain in terms of historical forces. Camden had no use for Puritans, but he did not resort to a theory of providential punishment to explain the rise of Puritanism.[1]

Camden was at his best in his explanations of English foreign policy. He grasped the principle of the balance of power and used it to explain Elizabeth's successful diplomacy:

> Thus sate she as an heroical Princess and Umpire betwixt the *Spaniards*, the *French*, and the Estates . . . And true it was which one hath written, that *France* and *Spain* are as it were Scales in the Balance of Europe, and England the Tongue or the Holder of the Balance.[2]

In general, however, Camden explained events indirectly, in terms of the particular considerations which motivated important individuals. He did not, in doing this, confuse pretexts with causes; he was perfectly aware that power politics determined the crucial decisions

---

[1] On Puritanism, see Camden, *History*, 1568, 107; see also 1583, 288-9. On Murray, 1565, 78; on the soldiers, 1581, 263.

[2] *Ibid.*, 1577, 223. That Camden worked out a detailed and coherent theory of the balance of power is not implied. See Mattingly, *Renaissance Diplomacy*, 163.

more often than the alleged 'glorious pretext of religion'. He never directly said that Elizabeth was guilty of using religion as a pretext for furthering her own ends, but he frequently charged that foreign politicians concealed their private ambitions under a pretended zeal for religion. In 1578, when the Pope and the Spaniards were plotting to invade England and Ireland, they were 'carrying on their own private ends under the Pretense of restoring Religion'. Murray stirred up Scotland 'under colour of preserving Religion', and in France, the commotions which began to flame forth during the minority of Charles IX were masked on both sides 'under the glorious Pretext of Religion'.[1]

Camden knew that the velvet glove was most fashionable on the iron fist. His understanding of the politics of power enabled him to distinguish between diplomatic means and ends. He was fully aware, for example, of the political importance of dynastic marriage schemes, and of the reasons of state which prompted royal courtships and hastened or delayed royal weddings.[2] What Camden lacked in the way of direct political experience he made up for in scholarship and in his determination to avoid unwary credulity. No doubt his training as a humanist and his experience as a teacher served him in good stead. Above all, he had been given access to the documents of men in power. What Camden could not do, of course, was to rid himself of his preconceptions.

Every historian who attempts to explain events must decide whether or not to use only those ideas of explanation that he finds expressed in his sources. To some extent, his preconceptions about the nature of historical explanation will enter into this decision: some modern historians try to explain events in terms of general covering laws; others try to explain them in terms of the issues that seemed relevant to contemporaries.[3] Camden was one of the latter, for he described and explained the events of Elizabeth's reign almost exclusively by referring to the ideas, questions, and issues which occupied the

---

[1] For these quotations, see Camden, *History*, 1578, 230; 1565, 78; 1562, 58; see also 1567, 89; 1564, 71, and *passim*.

[2] See Camden's treatment of the Darnly marriage proposals (1565, 79); Anjou proposals (1571, 160); and cf. John Seeley, *The Growth of British Policy*, 2 vols. (Cambridge, 1895), I, 37, and 1–250, *passim*.

[3] Cf. William Dray, *Laws and Explanation in History* (Oxford, 1957), 55, 74–5, 98–101, and *passim*. This is an illuminating study; it should be read in conjunction with Patrick Gardiner, *The Nature of Historical Explanation* (Oxford, 1952).

attention of contemporary statesmen. By carefully describing *how* things happened he sought to explain *why* they happened.

The danger was that Camden might too easily identify himself with the interests of the Elizabethan State. The fact that Camden was horrified by rebellion—as all contemporary statesmen were—meant that he tended to explain rebellion primarily from the point of view of those who had to cope with it. He did not attempt to examine the historical conditions under which rebellions occurred; instead, he tried to settle the question of who was to blame. Thus, it might be argued that Camden was unconsciously biased, and that his apparent impartiality was really nothing more than the calculated policy of the Elizabethan government.

According to this thesis, Camden wrote impartially about religion, for example, only in so far as he adopted the Erastian viewpoint of Elizabeth, who condemned the excesses of both Puritans and Catholics. Like his great Queen, Camden was rather more tolerant of native Catholics than of native Puritans, simply because native English Catholics represented less of a threat to royal power and prestige.[1] Camden achieved impartiality in writing about Mary and Elizabeth by never directly criticizing them. Instead, he placed the blame for all that happened on incompetent or wicked councillors, or on the conjunction of their stars.[2] Similarly, Camden's impartiality in dealing with Parliamentary and foreign affairs amounted to little more than giving both sides of every argument, and supplying 'all the facts' that seemed relevant to the English government.[3] The

[1] Camden's attitude might be summed up in his remark that 'persons whose Minds differ in Religion do too-much obscure the light of Honesty and Truth on both sides . . .' See Camden, *History*, 1578, 227. For typical examples of Camden's attitude toward Puritans, see *ibid.*, 1560, 42; 1573, 192–3; 1580, 247; 1583, 288; 1584, 301; 1588, 420–1. Camden's handling of Catholic problems: *ibid.*, 1559, 20–31; 1560, 48; 1563, 69–70; 1570, 148; 1571, 167–8; 1572, 187–8; 1577, 223–4; 1580, 246–7.

[2] Indicative of Camden's attitude toward royalty is his condemnation of Buchanan's works. See *History*, 1567, 95; also cf. 1565, 80; 1583, 282–4. Camden believed in astrology, but only suggested it to explain the mystery of Leicester's fascination for Elizabeth. See *ibid.*, 1588, 419. He also believed in magic and witchcraft; see 1589, 438; and in the mysterious climacterical year—see, for example, 1578, 227. On astrology generally, see Camden, *Epistolae*, Letter XC, 130–1.

[3] There were difficulties with the French translation of the *Annales* on the ground that Camden was unfair to the French. See Camden, *Epistolae*, Hotman to Camden, 1617, Letter CLXI, 201. Cf. Camden's treatment

difficulty with this thesis is not that it lacks coherence or support, but that it fails to account for Camden's originality in formulating sound explanations on the basis of the ideas and evidence available at the time.

Camden's treatment of rebellion furnishes a starting point for discussion of the limitations and virtues of Camden's historical method. When he described rebellion he did not point obvious morals, but he did assign responsibility, and by implication moral blame. Camden might be compared to a judge in a criminal court, who can weigh evidence impartially, but who nevertheless cannot understand what makes a criminal. When Camden summarized the causes of the rise and progress of the Irish rebellion he recited a number of separate counts: private ambition, Irish craft, papal intrigue, English irresoluteness, the avarice of old soldiers who made war a trade, and the accident of Irish successes in the field.[1] He described how the rebellion had taken place, not why it probably or necessarily would have taken place. Camden did not enter into a detailed analysis of Irish social conditions, such as Sir John Davies attempted in his *Discoverie of the True Causes Why Ireland was never entirely Subdued* (1612). For Camden, the relevant factors were those which had appeared relevant to the English government at the time.

Camden was inclined to assume that the multitude was always passive, and that the key to the problem of rebellion lay in the attitude of the great lords. Only once, when trying to explain why London citizens had responded to Essex, did Camden generalize about the social forces which forged rebels:

> For the Citizens, though, according to the temper and Disposition of the Vulgar, they were desirous of change and Innovation, yet by reason of their Wealth they were fearful withall, and unshaken in their untainted fidelity to their Prince. (And indeed Poverty, of all other things, is that which soonest plungeth the *English* into Rebellion.) [2]

The most serious limitation of Camden's method was that it failed, except by implication, to show the relative importance of the separate

of the confiscation of gold carried by Spanish ships driven ashore on England, *History*, 1568, 120-1.

[1] See Camden, *History*, 1603, 658; cf. 1599, 567.

[2] *Ibid.*, 1601, 609; cf. 1569, 134 (Norfolk rebellion); 1569, 136 (Dacres rising).

determinants of a given situation. On the other hand, Camden's method was not without its own virtues.

Camden sought the explanation of historical events in the written evidence, in the empirically given data. On a very few occasions Camden referred to divine justice or to providence, but the steady orientation of Camden's thought was toward a secular, empirical explanation of history.[1] In this sense, Camden was a true Baconian, a man who rejected scholasticism in all its forms, and Ralegh, for all his criticism of Aristotle, was the heir of a dying medieval tradition. Furthermore, Camden tried to suggest the historical necessities which limited human freedom of action and choice in nearly every historical situation. He saw that real historical dilemmas were seldom if ever resolved by good intentions. He sympathized with Elizabeth and on the whole upheld her decisions because he recognized how difficult it was for her to know what to do. The historical situation in which she was placed conditioned her actions. In the same way, Camden sympathized with Mary Stuart who, like Elizabeth, did not always have alternative choices. Camden's impartiality was, in this sense, the product of his historical understanding. He did not feel qualified to judge precisely because he realized how complicated the problems were.

This can be illustrated by examining Camden's narrative of the histories of Elizabeth and Mary. He understood Elizabeth better than he did Mary, but he knew that both women were under pressures of various kinds, that neither could afford to be completely candid, or to act toward each other as kinswomen rather than as Queens. Elizabeth could not afford to take chances with Mary, however convincing Mary's arguments might seem; there were reasons of state to be considered, more important than reasons of heart. Camden presented Mary's very convincing arguments for an audience with Elizabeth, quoted at some length from Mary's letters, and

[1] For references to providence, see Camden, *History*, 1578, 231; 1583, 290; cf. 1561, 56; 1591, 454. The clearest and best statement of Camden's views on religion and on his own concept of religious impartiality is that contained in Camden's letter to Dr. Rives of July 3, 1618. Dr. Rives had been ordered by the government of Ireland to reply to a writer who had accused Camden of dissembling his religion and of questioning the miracles of St. Patrick. Dr. Rives got in touch with Ussher, who was a close friend of Camden; Ussher asked Camden to write a letter of reply to Rives. See Camden, *Epistolae*, Letters, CXCIV, CLXXXVII, CLXXXVIII, CXCV.

abridged Elizabeth's letter of reply; his own brief comment brought home the point:

> By means of these letters and *Heris* his Words, Queen Elizabeth seemed, (for who can dive into the secret meanings of Princes? and wise men do keep their thoughts locked up within the closet of their Breasts,) seriously to commiserate the most afflicted Princess her kinswoman.[1]

Camden was no doubt wise to keep his thoughts to himself, but Camden's modern readers would be wise not to read too much into Camden's silences. To Camden, the secrets of princes were in reality 'an inextricable labyrinth'.[2] Elizabeth was an extraordinarily subtle woman, and whether she sympathized with Mary, or only pretended to, was a question which no historian could confidently settle. The only sure fact was that Elizabeth was influenced by the arguments of her council to proceed with caution. It was a 'matter of state', a matter involving the safety of England. And this is what Camden always insisted on, in his discussion of the marriage schemes, and even in his discussions of the trial and execution of Mary. The trial was perhaps not fair to Mary, but it was inevitable, given the historical situation. Camden did not give his own opinion of the trial. He let the facts speak for themselves, and the facts described a situation, a dilemma, in which both Mary and Elizabeth were caught. Camden saw the drama of Mary and Elizabeth as a tragedy.[3] And he was too cautious a scholar to read his own opinions into the evidence.

What Camden sensed in the drama of Elizabeth and Mary, as well as in the broader movements of history, was a pattern of relationships. The unity of history consisted in the fact that historical events were not merely separate isolated phenomena, but were joined and twisted together. Thus Camden felt obliged to give the background of some of the important events on the continent, because they were a part of English history: 'And let it not seem from the purpose, if I give a brief touch from what Beginnings the *Netherlands War* brake forth at this time, whereof I must of necessity make mention, forasmuch as it is joyned and twisted with English matters and Counsels.'[4]

---

[1] Camden, *History*, 1568, 110.
[2] *Ibid.*, 1579, 233.
[3] Camden refers to this affair as a tragedy; *ibid.*, 1587, 392.
[4] *Ibid.*, 1568, 120.

The year 1575 was a critical one for the Dutch, and Camden gave a masterly analysis of the dilemma in which the Prince of Orange found himself. Camden, as usual, presented the arguments of the different Dutch factions in order to convey the complexity of the situation. His method was not unlike that of the classical historians who used speeches and arguments for the purpose of analysis. But just as Thucydides could be criticized for inventing arguments which were at best 'appropriate to the occasion', so Camden can be criticized for inventing arguments which he could not have known in detail.[1] This raises the whole question of what Camden's standards of proof were.

Camden seldom documented statements in his *Annales*, and therefore it is impossible to tell in most cases what evidence he was using, or how much he was inferring from his evidence. He specifically stated that he did not make things up out of his head, and certainly he did not forge, conceal, or deliberately distort evidence. Nevertheless, he was sometimes forced to *re-create* arguments on the basis of information which was by no means sufficiently detailed to justify all of his statements. This was especially true when he dealt with the affairs of a foreign power. For instance, Camden was acquainted with only a few of the Spanish documents relating to the Armada. In order to explain the reasons behind the projected Spanish invasion, Camden attempted to re-create the arguments that would have impelled a foreign monarch to make war on England. The defence of Camden must essentially be that of Thucydides, who adhered 'as closely as possible' to the general sense of what was really said.[2]

There are, however, good reasons for believing that Camden did not permit his imagination to roam far beyond the facts. He refused to guess at the intent of secret instructions, such as those which the Papal emissary, Vincentio Parpalia, brought with him to England in 1560. 'What matters were propounded', Camden noted, 'I find not, for I do not think they were put in writing; and to roave at them, with the common sort of historians, I list not.' [3] He did report what the

[1] For example, Camden could not have known in detail what arguments were used by the Dutch in 1575. See *ibid.*, 1575, 209 ff. Most likely Camden borrowed from De Thou, and inferred the rest from English sources.

[2] Crawley's translation; see Thucydides, *The Peloponnesian War* (New York, Modern Library, 1934), 14. On Spanish reasons for invasion, see Camden, *History*, 1588, 402–11.

[3] *Ibid.*, 1560, 47.

Pope was rumoured to have said. When he reported rumours he was usually careful to label them as such. Naturally, Camden had to decide which witnesses or documents were lying and which were telling the truth. When he asserted that Sir Edward Bayham had paid Ralegh for his pardon after being arrested as a supporter of Essex in 1601, he did not say why he accepted this current rumour. Three centuries later, when the manuscripts of the Earl of Leicester were catalogued at Holkham Hall, confirmation of Camden's statement was found in a signed letter of Ralegh, addressed to Sir Edward Coke. Camden's critical judgment was vindicated, although it is still impossible to tell what authority Camden had for making the statement.[1]

Whether he was dealing with rumours or with state papers Camden did what he said he would do—he weighed the evidence in the balance of his own judgment. He assessed the credibility of different witnesses, compared the stories told by both sides in a dispute, and set down nothing in malice. For some events, he could rely in part on his own memory and notes. For most events he had documents to work with; and when he quoted from these he usually quoted verbatim, even though he felt that this was perhaps an offence against 'the Laws of History'.[2]

Camden obviously felt that it was somehow beneath the dignity of a historian to include such irrelevant details as Stow had included in his *Annals*. Yet Camden described a good many trivial events which had no bearing on his history. In a typical passage he wrote, 'I know not whether it be worth the while to mention that which all Historiographers of our time have recorded, to wit, that in the month of *November*, a new Star, or, if you will a *Phenomenon* . . . [appeared].'[3] Camden was not sure that even his account of Drake's expedition might not 'seem too light, and to proceed from an idle Brain, and not

---

[1] See *Historical Manuscripts Commission Reports, Various.* Vol. IV, 1907, 325.

[2] See Camden, *History*, 1560, 46; 1572, 176 (Norfolk's trial, which Camden had witnessed). Camden probably did not have access to the records of the Court of Star Chamber. In some instances, notably in his treatment of the Essex conspiracy, he made serious mistakes. See *The Egerton Papers*, ed. by J. Payne Collier (Camden Society, 1840), 321. On Camden's judgment of the credibility of Buchanan's statements, see *History*, 1567, 88–90, 95, 97.

[3] Camden, *History*, 1572, 190. See also 1561, 57; 1571, 158–9; 1574, 206; 1580, 244; 1581, 265; 1582, 273; 1583, 285–6; 1594, 489–90.

beseeming the Gravity of an History'.[1] He was torn between his respect for the classical laws of history and his antiquarian interest in the phenomena of history. And, like most of his contemporaries, Camden doubted the propriety of intruding on the preserves of sacred history. He was therefore hesitant to proceed without asking leave of the ecclesiastical historians to touch upon 'some few things which are linked with matters which concern the Commonwealth'.[2]

Camden seldom commented in his own words on the events that he thought were most important. He tried to make the facts speak for themselves, by quoting documents or by describing at length a situation as it appeared to contemporary actors responsible for making critical decisions. Camden, however, recognized the decisive moments of history as well as any historian of his time—the space devoted to an event was the measure of its importance. Circumstances, as he warned his readers, were the means whereby the events of affairs, as well as the reasons and causes thereof, would be revealed, and he doubted that he might lawfully interpose his own opinions.[3]

The stylistic problems which Camden had to overcome were inherent in the annalistic form. The chapters in a modern general History are likely to bear topical rather than chronological titles. However lamentable the results may be of separating art and literature from economics, economics from politics, and religion from everything else, the results of following an annalistic pattern were likely to be even worse. Fortunately, Camden strove to imitate Tacitus rather than his own contemporaries. On occasion he abandoned the attempt to maintain a strict chronological sequence, and turned back when necessary to give the history of affairs which at a particular time engaged the attention of English statesmen. Thus, in discussing the Irish rebellion of 1580, which had been preparing for

---

[1] *Ibid.*, 1580, 255. Camden also thought it was not 'expedient for the public good, that all manner of Villanies . . . be made known and publisht; for he that relateth such things doth as good as teach them'. *Ibid.*, 1579, 235.

[2] *Ibid.*, 1581, 271–2.

[3] See Camden's comments in his preface to the *History*, 'Author to Reader'. Professor Collingwood defined critical history in such a way that Camden would have to be considered a 'critical' historian, but Collingwood's further argument—that this was still just a version of scissors and paste—is hardly fair to Camden, or to any of his learned contemporaries. See R. G. Collingwood, *The Idea of History* (Oxford, 1946), 258–61.

some time, Camden treated it as a historical unit: 'Thus much of matters in *Ireland*, which I have mentioned all together, that the series of the story might not be interrupted, though other things fell out in the mean while, which in respect of their time, should have been mentioned first.' [1]

It was as a writer of contemporary history that Camden put later historians most deeply in his debt. His *Annales* contained not only facts and interpretations, but also shrewd estimates of character, made by a contemporary who had questioned men present at the transacting of great affairs. Camden was the first major English historian to write 'classical' character studies of his contemporaries. His portraits of Elizabeth, Mary, Burghley, and other officials were well drawn and revealing. It is doubtful that Camden was ever 'basted by a courtier of the Queen's in the Cloysters at Westminster for denigrating Queen Elizabeth in his History', as John Aubrey asserted. [2] Nevertheless, the story indicates that Camden's seventeenth-century reputation was not that of a mere panegyrist. Camden's characters ranged in length from a few sentences to a paragraph or two. Most of them were in the nature of epitaphs, written to commemorate the names of notable men and women who had died in the course of the year. However, Camden's summation of Mary Stuart's personality anticipated the kind of character that Clarendon wrote. [3]

The character of Queen Elizabeth as it emerged in the pages of Camden's history was that of a moderate who ruled her heart with her head, and who sought the good of her country above all other felicities. Camden admired Elizabeth's prudence, respected her judgment, and never underestimated the responsibility that she ultimately bore for the security and prosperity of England. The likeness of Camden's portrait of Elizabeth has, in general, been borne out by modern historical research. Camden never doubted Elizabeth's greatness. And although he was sympathetic, he was not adulatory; some practices he condoned as necessary, but without approving them. Many later historians have drawn on Camden's account of Elizabeth. Few have shown themselves superior to Camden in good judgment, impartiality, and respect for truth.

[1] Camden, *History*, 1580, 243. Also 1562, 59; 1567, 103; 1571, 158; 1574, 205, and *passim*.

[2] Aubrey, *Brief Lives* (ed. Dick), 51.

[3] For the character of Mary, see Camden, *History*, 1587, 385–6; for Burghley, 1598, 557–9.

The significance of Camden's historical work might be estimated in many ways. The founding of the Camden Society in 1840 honoured the man whose name had become a synonym for learning. When Froude wrote his lengthy history of the reign of Queen Elizabeth he treated Camden's work with the respect due to all authoritative accounts. Speaking of his own methods of revealing Elizabeth's character, Froude wrote what Camden might equally well have written: 'Her character I have left to be gathered from her actions, from her letters, from the communications between herself and her ministers, and from the opinions expressed freely to one another in private by those ministers themselves.' [1] Froude differed from Camden in matters of emphasis, and in the organization of his work: he still, however, made essentially the same methodological assumptions that Camden made.

A second great revolution in historiography took place in the nineteenth century, the results of which are still being felt. Modern historiography acquired new tools of analysis, developed different theories of relevance, and submitted its own and all previous methods to critical examination. Philosophers, economists, psychologists, and all kinds of historical specialists have subsequently probed, analysed, examined, and argued about the idea of history and the methods of historians. Froude's scholarship was long ago censured by historians; and there can be no question but that knowledge of Elizabeth's reign had been greatly advanced by methods which were unknown in Froude's day. To stress the modernity of Camden's thought is not to say that he wrote as a twentieth-century historian would write. It is to insist that modern historians can benefit from Camden's work, that Camden was one of them. And, as Professor Butterfield has shown, it is possible for retrogression to take place in historical scholarship unless historians continue to hold conference with their predecessors. [2]

Modern historicism, extending far beyond the immediate territory of the historians, has profoundly altered our sense of the past. Intellectuals as diverse in outlook as Burke and Ranke, Hegel and Marx, the Göttingen professors and the English Darwinians contributed to the overthrow of the older notions of historical continuity.

[1] See James Anthony Froude, *The Reign of Elizabeth*, 5 vols. (London, Everyman, 1912), V, 473. See also III, 175; V, 315.

[2] See Herbert Butterfield, *Man on His Past* (Cambridge, 1955), 169–70, and *passim*.

The principles of contextualism, the quest for general laws of social development, *geistesgeschichte*, and historical relativism are only a few of the legacies of modern historicist thought. Signs of this new attitude toward historical change began to appear in a few books written in the seventeenth century, but our modern historical consciousness was not fully developed and defined before the nineteenth and twentieth centuries. Today we are almost painfully sensitive to historical change, aware of the constant rushing of the present into the past, and of how much we differ in ideas and outlook from our ancestors. It is well to be reminded that the qualities of mind and spirit which produce good work are much the same in every age.

Looking back on the seventeenth century we may recognize the origins of the modern profession of history. It was entirely appropriate that William Camden should have founded the first endowed professorship of history at an English university. He was both a teacher and a scholar; and he sensed that the study of history belonged properly in the modern university.

10

SIR FRANCIS BACON AND THE IDEA OF HISTORY

A PRIMARY OBJECTIVE of Baconian policy in the field of learning was to secure a closer alliance between the experimental and the rational faculties. Aristotle's logic was dead—killed by scholasticism. Bacon's philosophy was premised on change. Bacon called for a complete reappraisal of the strategy of science and scholarship. Nothing short of a revolutionary purge of traditional modes of thought would suffice for the conquest of nature. The philosopher-scientist would have to compel himself 'to sweep away all theories and common notions, and to apply the understanding, thus made fair and even, to the examination of particulars'.[1]

The loose analogy between science and statecraft was one which Bacon himself favoured, and it reveals an essential quality of his mind. He was a writer, a critic, a framer of policies, not a professional scientist or scholar.[2] Erudite, brilliant, and always persuasive in setting forth schemes for the advancement of learning, Bacon recognized problems and formulated long-range policies, but he did not implement these policies himself. At best, he provided illustrations, or smoothly written models, like the *History of Henry VII*, which was a brilliant 'prize essay', but not a Thucydidean 'possession for all time'.

[1] Bacon, *Works*, 'Novum Organum', VIII, 132. Cf. F. H. Anderson, *The Philosophy of Francis Bacon* (Chicago, 1948), 300.

[2] The analogy was used, for example, in 'Novum Organum', *Works*, VIII, 133.

To discover a new passage from facts to axioms in science required more time and patience than Bacon could command. He was not unaware of the deficiency of evidence in his own works, but he could not take the time to verify details. He compared himself appropriately to Alexander the Great who, according to Titus Livius, 'had done no more than take courage to despise vain apprehensions'. A like judgment, Bacon supposed, might be passed on himself in future ages: 'that I did no great things, but simply made less account of things that were accounted great'.[1]

Perhaps Bacon was, for once, too modest. His work was significant and important in helping to bring about changes in the climate of seventeenth-century opinion. As a promoter of the ideal of scientific inquiry in all fields of knowledge Bacon exerted an influence that was out of all proportion to his knowledge of contemporary science. The gap between theory and practice, so evident in his scientific writing, was also evident in his historical thought. Moreover, to some extent Bacon's presuppositions about history seriously distorted his understanding of science. Natural history was closer to civil history in Bacon's intellectual perspective than it was to the logico-experimental science being developed by some of Bacon's contemporaries. Nevertheless, Baconian naturalism was thoroughly 'Modern' in its purposes; and the very fact that Bacon brought history and scientific philosophy together made him an important figure in the development of British empiricism. His first outstanding descendant was John Locke, with his 'historical, plain' method of treating knowledge. Both Locke and Hume came close to accepting the Baconian argument that all philosophy must proceed from the study of empirical or historical particulars.

The advancement of learning depended on the advancement of history. Bacon thought that good hopes might be conceived of natural philosophy 'when natural history which is the basis and foundation of it, has been drawn up on a better plan; but not till then'.[2] As in natural philosophy, so in political, and in all other varieties—historical deeds and actions were to be the stuff and matter of induction.[3] It will not be feasible to detail the similarities between Bacon's idea of natural history and his idea of civil history, nor to

[1] Bacon, *Works*, 'Novum Organum', VIII, 133.

[2] *Ibid.*, 'Novum Organum', VIII, 134

[3] See *ibid.*, 'Novum Organum', VIII, 136. Cf. 'Descriptio Globis Intellectualis', *Works*, X, 409–10; also 'De Augmentis', *passim.*

argue the extent to which his philosophy was rational or empirical, mechanical or scientific. It is apparent that Bacon had an inadequate understanding of the role of hypotheses in scientific work. He nevertheless saw that the road to scientific knowledge 'does not lie on a level, but ascends and descends; first ascending to axioms, then descending to works'.[1] In this way, Baconian philosophy returned continually to historical particulars. The purpose of the present chapter will be to examine some of the relationships between theory and practice in Bacon's works. First, his philosophical opinions about the nature and purpose of history in general must be examined; only then will it be possible to evaluate his contributions to English historiography.

In choosing a military metaphor to illustrate his idea of how historical particulars should be marshalled in order to arrive at axioms, Bacon revealed his point of view.[2] Like a general, he was more interested in the strategy of knowledge than in the tactical problems of particular sectors; he was also more aware than most writers of the connections and similarities between the different fronts of knowledge. History, as opposed to philosophy, was most often associated in Bacon's mind with the idea of concrete, individual instances. In the *Descriptio Globis Intellectualis*, which he probably wrote some time in 1612, Bacon observed that 'History is properly concerned with individuals, the impressions whereof are the first and most ancient guests of the human mind and are the primary material of knowledge'.[3] He went on to say that under philosophy he would include all 'arts and sciences and in a word whatever has been from the occurrence of individual objects collected and digested by the mind into general notions'.[4] In this work Bacon's ideas about history, and even his classification of the types of history, were substantially complete; he made no major changes in his later works.

When Bacon identified history with individual instances he did not suggest that history was the study of the unique; nor did he believe (as Professor Collingwood maintained) that history should

---

[1] *Ibid.*, 'Novum Organum', VIII, 137; also VII, 138–9; cf. Anderson, *Philosophy of Bacon, passim.*

[2] Bacon, *Works*, 'Novum Organum', VIII, 136.

[3] *Ibid.*, X, 403; cf. 'De Augmentis' (1623), in *ibid.*, VIII, 407.

[4] *Ibid.*, X, 405; see also 'Novum Organum', VIII, 159. History was a kind of general category for political and other kinds of philosophy. See 'De Augmentis', *Works*, VIII, 408.

be studied for its own sake.[1] The very fact that he identified all history with experience and insisted that experience must be ordered by inductive philosophy should dispel the notion that Bacon was interested in the past for its own sake. 'The empire of man over things depends wholly on the arts and sciences,' Bacon wrote, and he firmly believed that the utility of history consisted in providing the material means to extend this empire.[2]

In the *Advancement of Learning* (1605) the primary division of history was quadripartite. Literary and ecclesiastical history were made co-ordinate with civil and natural history. In the *Descriptio Globis Intellectualis*, and in all works written after 1612, history was divided into natural and civil, civil history including not only ecclesiastical and literary history, but also the subordinate varieties of history. Bacon's new two-fold division of history represented an important advance in historical theory, for by implication it deprived ecclesiastical history of the special privileges which had hitherto been accorded it. Bacon was in no sense challenging the prerogatives of divinity, but his shift of emphasis, although slight, was significant. Matter of divinity might still show itself in both natural and civil history—principally in the latter—but 'History Ecclesiastical' was no longer thought of a having independent status. Bacon meant that church history (although not necessarily the history of prophecy, or of providence) should be written in accordance with the same rules which governed the writing of other kinds of civil history. The relevance of theology to civil history was thus restricted.[3]

By 1623, when Bacon undertook the Latin translation and revision of the *Advancement of Learning*, he had published his *History of Henry VII*, and his historical thought was fully developed. The *De Augmentis* summed up and elaborated Bacon's arguments, yet (1) history still corresponded to the faculty of memory; (2) history was the same thing as experience; and (3) history was properly concerned only with individuals circumscribed by time and place.[4] It is true that Bacon elsewhere in the *De Augmentis* saw fit to question the ancient

[1] See R. G. Collingwood, *The Idea of History*, 58. Cf. Bacon, *Works*, 'Novum Organum', VIII, 115, 134; 'De Augmentis', VIII, 407–8, 415–16.

[2] Bacon, *Works*, 'Novum Organum', VIII, 162–3; 'Advancement of Learning', VI, 347.

[3] See *Ibid.*, 'Advancement of Learning', VI, 199–200; 393–412; 'De Augmentis', VIII, 435–7 and IX, 345–57.

[4] See *Ibid.*, VIII, 407–8.

identification of history with memory, but he did not reject this basic proposition in his formal definition of history.[1]

The problem raised by Bacon's definition was simply this: how could history be a mere matter of memory, and at the same time a discipline or 'knowledge'? Civil history in particular Bacon regarded as a form of knowledge, capable of instructing the mind; and natural history was to 'inform the intellect' by drawing in part upon the liberal sciences.[2] Moreover, Bacon had urged historians to 'set down sound and true distributions and descriptions of the several characters and tempers of men's natures and dispositions, especially having regard to those differences which are most radical in being the fountains and causes of the rest, or most frequent in concurrence and comixture . . .'[3] Here Bacon was advocating that history should become a broad social study, akin to scientific anthropology.

It is apparent that Bacon was less consistent in his definitions than might at first sight appear. His method of laying everything out in systematic form had the effect of giving his investigations, as Spedding noted, 'an appearance, though a superficial and delusive one, of exact and delicate discrimination'.[4] In fact, Bacon was flatly inconsistent in his assertions about the nature of history. If history was a matter of individual instances and pure memory—not involving imagination or judgment—then civil history could hardly be 'preeminent' among human writings. But history, and especially civil history, did require judgment, as Bacon himself insisted.[5] This contradiction, or inconsistency, was fundamental. Bacon subordinated history to philosophy in the interest of his scientific strategy. In theory, history was nothing more than raw experience; in actual fact, it was a form of knowledge, which obviously required the use of reason and imagination.

[1] See *ibid.*, 'De Augmentis', VIII, 408, 453. Also, Leonard F. Dean, 'Sir Francis Bacon's Theory of Civil History Writing', *English Literary History* (VIII, 1941), 161–83; especially 163.

[2] Cf. Bacon, *Works*, 'De Augmentis', VIII, 410, 415–16.

[3] *Ibid.*, 'Advancement of Learning', VI, 332. See also VI, 101–2; XI, 43; XIII, 183; IX, 216–17, 300. Cf. L. F. Dean, 'Bacon's Theory of Civil History Writing', *English Literary History* (VIII, 1941), 172.

[4] From Spedding's preface to 'De Interpretatione Naturae Proemium', *Works*, VI, 439.

[5] See Bacon, *Works*, 'De Augmentis', VIII, 453. Hume was far more consistent. See David Hume, *A Treatise of Human Nature*, ed. L. A. Selby-Bigge (Oxford, 1888), 107–8.

In the history of the rise of the inductive method in the social sciences Bacon's dilemma defined a recurrent problem. To arrive at axioms of civil knowledge by generalizing from historical particulars was a Baconian ideal.[1] Yet the fulfilment of the ideal depended on the initial historical investigation. This meant that history would have to be informed by relevant ideas of explanation. Bacon tended to assume that the philosopher was capable of providing these without necessarily engaging in historical research himself. The 'wiser sort of historians', according to Bacon, had described the different characters of human natures and dispositions in their works. From these he thought a scientific treatise on character might be written. Yet the difficulty was evaded, not solved, by saying that 'the wiser sort' of historians had provided information and some of the general axioms which the philosopher, as social scientist, could use.[2]

The Baconian dilemma followed inevitably every attempt to make historical description—history as mere experience—serve the interests of anthropological or sociological synthesis. At least Bacon had realized that the mere gathering of information, (i.e. research in the most restricted sense) was not 'perfect history', and that good historians did make some use of axioms, theorems, or ideas of explanation which ordered the facts in a meaningful way. Unfortunately, he did not explain how this was done by historians, nor did he attempt to show precisely how philosophical axioms could be derived by induction from written histories. If history was a separate discipline with its own methods, purposes, and significance, then its relevance to philosophy was a problem requiring much more intensive study. If history was nothing but 'the primary matter of philosophy', then the problem for philosophy was how written histories were related to experience. The new Baconian philosophy perforce called in doubt the old history.[3]

In the *Parasceve* Bacon set forth his ideas of a natural and experimental history such as might serve for the foundation of a true philosophy. Although this work dealt with natural history it nevertheless described quite accurately Bacon's method of procedure in writing civil history, especially the *History of Henry VII*. The dis-

[1] See Bacon, *Works*, 'Advancement', VI, 347 ff.
[2] See *ibid.*, 'De Augmentis', IX, 216 ff.
[3] *Ibid.*, 'De Augmentis', VIII, 416; cf. Anderson, *Philosophy of Bacon*, 181-9.

tinction between research and interpretation, sharply drawn in the *Parasceve*, was characteristic:

> For as much as relates to the work itself of the intellect, I shall perhaps be able to master that by myself; but the materials on which the intellect has to work are so widely spread, that one must employ factors and merchants to go everywhere in search of them and bring them in. Besides, I hold it to be somewhat beneath the dignity of an undertaking like mine that I should spend my own time in a matter which is open to almost every man's industry. That however which is the main part of the matter I will myself now supply by diligently and exactly setting forth the method and description of a history of this kind, such as shall satisfy my intention.[1]

The essential point, for Bacon, was that in such a primary history as he envisaged 'the end rules the method'.[2] The historian—as opposed to the research assistant—would be required to understand the philosophical end, or purpose, which the new history would serve. Thus, in organizing and presenting historical facts, the true historian would bear in mind the needs of 'the Interpreter'.[3] In fact, until historians became philosophers, or philosophers historians, there presumably could be no advancement of learning. Although Bacon never directly said this, it was the conclusion toward which his work pointed.[4]

Much of the ambiguity in Bacon's treatment of the relationship between history and other branches of knowledge, including philosophy, can be traced to semantic confusion. In particular, the word 'history' was a source of confusion. Bacon used the word history to mean at least three different things: (1) the 'facts' of experience; (2) written historical collections or narratives; and (3) the judgments of relevance made by the historian.[5] With respect to civil history, the first usage implied the perished past in its entirety, which was known only by memory. Records and other traces of this past formed the raw material of all historical investigation. The second usage was

[1] Bacon, *Works*, 'Parasceve', VIII, 354–5.

[2] *Ibid.*, 'Parasceve', VIII, 358.

[3] *Ibid.*, 'Parasceve', VIII, 360.

[4] Bacon issued a few warnings against applying his method to unsuitable subject matter, but these do not invalidate the present argument. Cf. *ibid.*, VI, 292–3; IX, 126, 232.

[5] Cf. *ibid.*, 'Descriptio Globis Intellectualis', X, 414, 463; 'Advancement', VI, 182, 184–8, 218.

more ambiguous. It implied not only the collections of evidence made by the 'factors and merchants' of history, but also the organized narratives of the true historian. The third usage was implicit in Bacon's statement that 'the end rules the method'; the wiser sort of historian had always, Bacon thought, had in mind the utility of history for civil knowledge.[1] What Bacon failed to make clear was the difference between the facts of experience and historical facts. He failed to realize that every historical fact had to be 'established', and that consequently there was no interval between research and interpretation. It was a misfortune that Bacon took seriously the ancient identification of history and memory.

Had Bacon been more inclined to use the word history to denote a particular discipline or knowledge, he might have recognized the importance of investigating in greater detail the relationship between historiography and philosophy. In the *Advancement of Learning* he commented suggestively on the relationship between the different branches of knowledge:

> . . . every knowledge may be fitly said, besides the profundity (which is the truth and substance of it, which makes it solid,) to have a longitude and a latitude; accounting the latitude towards other sciences and the longitude towards action; that is, from the greatest generality to the most particular precept . . .[2]

He went on to observe that the latitude ruled how far one branch of knowledge should meddle with another, while the longitude ruled 'unto what degree of particularity a knowledge should descend'.

This statement was entirely in keeping with his idea of a proper relationship between history, as a branch of knowledge, and philosophy. History was far more deeply immersed in matter, far more conversant with particulars than philosophy; but history nevertheless had a latitude toward philosophy, and toward poesy as well.

In all fields Bacon wanted to segregate truth which was humanly discoverable from the dogmas of philosophy or revealed theology. Bacon's theory of natural history differed from his theory of civil history in one important respect, for he sought to free science, or natural history, from the dead hand of academic scholarship. His influence in promoting 'experimental philosophy' outside the univer-

---

[1] See Bacon, *Works*, 'Advancement', VI, 288, 347 ff.; also cf. 'De Augmentis', IX, 217 ff.
[2] *Ibid.*, VI, 295.

sity curriculum was immense.[1] Nevertheless, the purpose of the new history and philosophy, whether natural or civil, was the same. Bacon sought to define the purpose of all learning in terms of high utility—the advancement of that knowledge which would contribute to the happiness and well-being of mankind.

In a passage which deserves to be quoted at some length Bacon identified ultimate truth with ultimate utility. Against the objection that he was building a system which ignored abstract wisdom, Bacon wrote as follows:

> For I am building in the human understanding a true model of the world, such as it is in fact, not such as a man's own reason would have it to be; a thing which cannot be done without a very diligent dissection and anatomy of the world. But I say that those foolish and apish images of worlds which the fancies of men have created in philosophical systems must be utterly scattered to the winds. Be it known then how vast a difference there is . . . between the Idols of the human mind and the Ideas of the divine. The former are nothing more than arbitrary abstractions; the latter are the Creator's own stamp upon creation, impressed and defined in matter by true and exquisite lines. Truth therefore and utility are here the very same things: and works themselves are of greater value as pledges of truth than as contributing to the comforts of life.[2]

To benefit the whole human race was, however, Bacon's express purpose in devising his new philosophy. Utility and progress became the twin ideals of Baconian doctrine. 'All knowledge is to be limited by religion, and referred to use and action', he wrote in the *Valerius Terminus* (1603); and he added that the end of knowledge was the restoration of man to the sovereignty and power he enjoyed before the fall.[3] Returning to the same theme in the *Novum Organum* (1620) he insisted that the true and lawful goal of the sciences was none other than this: 'that human life be endowed with new discoveries and powers'.[4]

Bacon believed that only by investigating second causes could these great ends be achieved—secularism was perhaps the most

---

[1] See Anderson, *Philosophy of Bacon*, 292–303. Cf. Bacon, *Works*, 'Novum Organum', VIII, 124–7.
[2] Bacon, *Works*, 'Novum Organum', VIII, 156–7. On 'idols', see VIII, 76–90.
[3] *Ibid.*, VI, 34–5.   [4] *Ibid.*, VII, 113; cf. VIII, 53, 68.

obvious characteristic of his philosophy. Hence, Bacon proclaimed the need for a thorough reformation in historiography; civil history, no less than natural history, ought to be written with a view to its high utility. Bacon's brilliant proposals for a history of learning and the arts must be read in this context.

Without the History of Learning 'the history of the world seems to me as the statue of Polyphemus without the eye'.[1] Bacon's proposals for a complete and universal history of learning appear most striking and original when compared with the unimaginative redactions of contemporary historical theorists. The modern reader finds it easy to forget that Bacon was primarily interested in the philosophical 'arguments' and uses of such a history, not in the historical methods by which it could be properly written. Bacon was certainly correct, however, in his analysis of the general requirements of a history of learning and the arts:

> Above all things (for this is the ornament and life of Civil History), I wish events to be coupled with their causes. I mean that an account should be given of the characters of the several regions and peoples; their natural dispositions . . . emulations and diffusions of religions . . . [etc.] Now all this I would have handled in a historical way, not wasting time, after the manner of critics, in praise and blame, but simply narrating the fact historically, with but slight admixture of private judgment.[2]

When completed, this history would assist 'the wisdom and skill of learned men in the use and administration of learning'; and the learned might then be able to derive and establish 'the best form of government'.[3] Bacon was obviously at his best when describing what was needful, in pointing out the kinds of questions which the historian of ideas should ask. But like many other intellectual reformers, Bacon was somewhat vague about how his theory should be translated into practice. Undoubtedly he justified his reputation as a theorist and critic by providing original and suggestive ideas. However, nothing can be accomplished by praising him for the wrong reasons. Bacon contributed to the advancement of history by making available and explicit the insights of a philosopher of science and of history.

As a philosopher of science Bacon had some influence even on the

---

[1] Bacon, *Works*, 'De Augmentis', VIII, 418.
[2] *Ibid.*, 'De Augmentis', VIII, 419–20.
[3] *Ibid.*, 'De Augmentis', VIII, 420.

research of the Royal Society. As a philosopher of history and social science Bacon was no less influential, although his programme for research had fewer direct issues. Bacon demanded that civil history be made the basis of a science of man. Instead of repeating the old cliché that history was 'philosophy teaching by examples', Bacon had tried to show that history could be made to serve the purposes of true induction. Convinced that civil history was capable of yielding exact knowledge, that it could contribute to a scientific understanding of man in society (just as natural history could contribute to a scientific understanding of the powers of nature), Bacon was one of the first to proclaim that history belonged with the sciences.[1]

In theory, Bacon's programme represented a radical break from both the humanistic and scholastic traditions. Bacon repudiated the moral and historical philosophy of humanism almost as completely as he rejected medieval Aristotelianism. To Bacon the whole bent of the times of humanism had been 'more towards copy than weight'.[2] By following the authority of antiquity men had forgotten how to progress: 'men have been kept back as by a kind of enchantment from progress in the sciences by reverence for antiquity, by the authority of men accounted great in philosophy, and then by general consent'.[3] The old age of the world was its true antiquity, and the present was thus logically of greater authority than the past. But the essential point was that truth was the daughter of time, not of authority. The errors of the ancients, especially the error of flying from a few examples to the most general conclusions, had to be avoided. Not only in natural philosophy, but in the other sciences—including logic, ethics, and politics—Bacon called for a new approach: 'a total reconstruction of sciences, arts, and all human knowledge'.[4]

Bacon thought he saw examples of the new approach in Machiavelli and Guicciardini. He admired the Florentine political historiographers for what he thought was their scientific analysis of character. Not realizing how impressionistic they really were, Bacon praised them for accuracy and objectivity. He was, of course, much more interested in extending the scope and application of inductive

[1] See *ibid.*, VIII, 112, 159; VI, 332-47, 359, 367, 389. Cf. Leonard Dean, 'Bacon's Theory of Civil History Writing', *English Literary History* (VIII, 1941), 165.

[2] Bacon, *Works*, 'Advancement', VI, 120.

[3] *Ibid.*, 'Novum Organum', VIII, 116.

[4] From the Proemium to 'Magna Instauratio', *ibid.*, VIII, 18; see also *ibid.*, 'Novum Organum', 156-60.

philosophy than he was in attacking the problem of how history could be scientific. 'We are much beholden to Machiavelli and other writers of that class,' Bacon wrote, 'who openly and unfeignedly declare or describe what men do, and not what they ought to do.' [1] Bacon wanted to found a new kind of history on objective scientific observation. The fact that Machiavelli appeared to be writing in this way was enough for Bacon, who was anxious to point out the direction in which historiography could progress. [2]

By integrating history into the scientific movement of his day, Bacon lent the weight of his authority to progressive historical practice. [3] He swept away much of the uncertainty and doubt that had troubled even historians like Camden, who were reluctant to impeach tradition. And with the publication of his *History of Henry VII* (1622) Bacon appeared to close the gap between theory and practice in his philosophy. Ironically, the literary brilliance of the work effectively hid Bacon's errors of fact and faults of method. The book was a tribute to the humanism which Bacon supposedly despised. In following his own precepts for the composition of a history Bacon revealed (perhaps without knowing it) the ambiguity of his historical theory. In writing his historical narrative Bacon excelled most of the Renaissance masters of literary style. From a comparison of Bacon's historical theory and his historical works an invidious conclusion must be drawn: Bacon contributed to the advancement of history by telling historians what and how they ought to write, not by writing a scientific history.

In style and purpose Bacon's *History of Henry VII* was a masterpiece which challenged comparison with the historical works of Machiavelli or Guicciardini, but in content, it was less trustworthy than the 'barren and commonplace narratives' which Bacon used, and uncharitably dismissed as 'a very reproach to history'. [4] In method, it was an apt illustration of Sir John Harrington's epigram: 'Treason doth never prosper: What's the reason? Why, if it prosper none dare call it treason.' The methods that Bacon used were

[1] Bacon, *Works*, 'De Augmentis', IX, 211.

[2] See *ibid.*, VI, 332–8; VIII, 420. Also L. F. Dean, 'Bacon's Theory of Civil History Writing', *English Literary History* (VIII, 1941), 165.

[3] Cf. Bacon's attempted reconstruction of the meaning of ancient myths in 'De Sapientia Veterum' (1609) in *Works*, XII, 405–54. There is a valuable commentary in Anderson, *Philosophy of Bacon*, 48–79.

[4] Bacon, *Works*, 'De Augmentis', VIII, 421.

treason to objective history, but the treason prospered for more than two centuries. The sheer virtuosity of the *History of Henry VII* convinced generations of historians that Bacon was an original authority for the reign. Bacon was a professed critic of those historians who were 'no good witnesses as to facts'; and if Bacon provided information which was not to be found in other sources it was generally assumed that Bacon must have had access to sources which were afterwards destroyed or lost.[1]

It was not until the nineteenth century, when Wilhelm Busch undertook a most un-Baconian examination of the *History of Henry VII*, sentence by sentence, that the extent of Bacon's treason to history began to be realized. 'We possess', Busch wrote, 'almost all the direct and indirect sources of information from which he [Bacon] drew, and he shows, in the use he made of them, such indifference as regards simple historical truth, that he must, as a voucher for facts, appear to us in a very dubious light.'[2] The main points of Busch's indictment were these: (1) Bacon's most important authority was Hall's *Chronicle*, which Bacon handled much more freely than Hall had handled his authority, Polydore Vergil; (2) Bacon made use of the Rolls of Parliament and a few other records, but did not always reproduce their contents accurately; (3) he made only incidental use of Cotton's collections; (4) he dealt with most of his secondary authorities in an arbitrary and superficial way, allowing free play to his own imagination; and (5) haste was no excuse, since Bacon went out of his way to give an appearance of substantive fact to his opinions and additions.

As a consequence of nineteenth-century source analysis Bacon lost his reputation as an original authority for the reign of Henry VII. Unfortunately, the plodding Wilhelm Busch was inclined to belabour the obvious (Bacon did not claim to be reproducing his sources word for word), and to miss the significance of Bacon's historical interpretation. The insights and ideas of an experienced politician, which Bacon certainly was, had as much to do with the success of the *History of Henry VII* as did literary skill.

[1] Even Spedding, who edited and corrected Bacon's *History*, made this mistake. See Bacon, *Works*, XI, 65-6, 116, 165-7, 178, 306-7. Cf. Notes, pp. 234, 245, 251-3.

[2] See Wilhelm Busch, *England Under the Tudors, King Henry VII*, Vol. I, translated by Alice M. Todd (London, 1895), 416-23. The quotation is from p. 423.

Bacon wrote the *History of Henry VII* during the months from June to October 1621, immediately after his downfall. He had begun to collect material for such a history at least as early as 1611. John Speed made some use of Bacon's notes and collections in writing his own *History* (1613). Bacon, in turn, may have borrowed material from Speed. Both writers repeated the same errors, but any general estimate of Bacon would not be materially changed if a few errors could be ascribed to Speed.[1] The important point is simply that Bacon, like Speed and other historians, was willing to accept on authority statements made by earlier chroniclers. The need for an inquisition of historical sources, analogous to the 'inquisition of nature', was not recognized by Bacon. It is most instructive to trace Bacon's discussion of the problems of evidence and proof from his early work through the *De Augmentis*. The lack of any significant revision of opinion, especially in the *De Augmentis*, suggests that Bacon was fundamentally insensitive to the need for explicit procedures of verification.

In his fragmentary *History of the Reigns of K. Henry VIII, K. Edward, Q. Mary, and part of Elizabeth*, which Bacon began some time in Elizabeth's reign, he observed that besides memory and tradition, 'the acts, instruments, and negotiations of states themselves, together with glances at foreign histories' were the best originals and instructions out of which to write a history. This was commendable enough, but Bacon went on to say that the historian would not have so far to travel 'if there had been already digested any tolerable chronicle as a simple narration of the actions themselves, which should only have needed out of the former helps to be enriched with the councils and speeches and notable particularities'.[2] He implied that the good historian performed his job—using scissors, paste, and pencil—by rewriting existing narratives, and adding apt or impressive detail from original sources. Bacon believed that 'the best of the ancient histories were contrived out of divers particular Commentaries, Relations and Narrations, which it was not hard to digest with ornament, and thereof to compound one entire story'.[3]

Bacon was perfectly correct in pointing out that a lack of previous research made his own task much more difficult. Earlier chronicles and accounts obviously were indispensable to historians; the public records could not, by themselves, provide answers to all historical

[1] See Busch, *Henry VII*, 418. [2] Bacon, *Works*, XI, 35.
[3] *Ibid.*, XI, 34.

problems. But Bacon was also advancing the highly dubious proposition that research and interpretation were distinctly separate operations. In this early work Bacon's error was understandable, but in the *De Augmentis* he did little to correct it; his ideas were for the most part entirely consistent with those he had expressed twenty years earlier. Bacon may have been confirmed in his opinions by the immediate success of his *Henry VII*, which was praised by no less a scholar than Selden.[1] In any case, he did not attempt to elucidate methodological problems on the basis of his experience in writing civil history. In order to see how Bacon used his sources, what his standards of evidence and proof really were, we must turn directly to the *History of Henry VII*.

One of the chief sources of error in Bacon's *History* was an inadequate and inaccurate chronology of events. This became obvious in Bacon's treatment of the policy which Henry pursued in order to keep Britanny from being absorbed by France. Bacon connected events which were separate—the seige of Nantes by Charles VIII, and his sending of ambassadors to England, and separated actions which were part of one plan—Henry's sending aid to Brittany and also to Maximilian in Flanders. Similarly, Bacon mistook the date of the meeting of Henry's second Parliament, which took place during the Brittany crisis. Following the authority of Polydore Vergil, Bacon gave the date as 1488, whereas the Parliament actually met in November 1487. Had he used the Rolls of Parliament he would have been able to provide the correct date. Spedding argued that Bacon used some transcript or partial copy of the Rolls which did not provide the date; Busch assumed that Bacon had made use of the Rolls themselves. In either case, Bacon was remiss, for he might have asked someone to check the date for him. And only extreme carelessness could account for Bacon's mistaking the date of Henry VII's death. The king died on the 21st of April 1509, not on the 22nd of April 1508, as Bacon, following Speed, confidently asserted.[2]

Bacon's willingness to take his chronology on trust is indicative

---

[1] See Selden's 'Preface' in Augustine Vincent, *A Discoverie of Errors* (1622).

[2] See Bacon, *Works*, XI, 354; Busch, *Henry VII*, 418; and Spedding's note, *Works*, XI, 117n. Spedding and Busch point out that Bacon was following Speed. There was, however, some question about the exact day of death.

of his general attitude toward questions of evidence and proof.
He would use original sources to illustrate or enrich his narrative,
but he would not take the trouble to use them systematically to verify
the accuracy of statements of fact. He quoted extracts from Perkin
Warbeck's proclamation almost verbatim from Speed's *History*, but
gave the 'tenor' of the rest of it from memory. He might easily have
secured an accurate copy from Cotton, for as he pointed out, the
original was in Cotton's library and he had had 'much light for the
furnishing of this work' from Cotton.[1]

There is no need to multiply examples of Bacon's carelessness—
he was simply not interested in doing the spadework of history. What
fascinated Bacon was historical interpretation. He could, on occasion,
use historical evidence quite effectively to demolish an improbable or
mistaken interpretation. He was able to prove, for example, that
Perkin Warbeck had taken the title of Duke of York from the first,
and had not had it forced upon him by the Irish after his landing in
Ireland.[2] Being an astute lawyer as well as a most intelligent observer
of human nature—as his *Essays* prove—Bacon had a highly developed
sense of what was probable. This helped him to get at the 'bottoms of
pretences'. Probability, however, became more than a critical tool
in Bacon's hands. It became the basis for many of his historical
explanations.[3]

That Bacon did not always distinguish carefully between probability and proof was a fault which few of his contemporaries were in
a position to criticize. Bacon must be criticized in terms of his own
standards. He castigated those men of learning who 'have taken for
the construction or for the confirmation of their philosophy certain
rumours and vague fames or airs of experience, and allowed to these
the lawful weight of evidence'.[4] Bacon sometimes invented details
in the manner of a historical novelist, going far beyond the statements found in his sources; on one occasion he misread a Latin
word and then inferred details from his own mistaken reading.[5]
When Bacon invented speeches for his characters he was following
one of the well-established classical and humanist traditions. Here
again, however, probability was the basis of interpretation. He

[1] See Bacon, *Works*, XI, 251; cf. 250–7, *passim*.
[2] See *ibid.*, XI, 206–7.
[3] For examples, see *ibid.*, XI, 70 ff., 230, 301–2, 320–1, 348–9.
[4] *Ibid.*, 'Novum Organum', VIII, 133.
[5] Cf. *ibid.*, XI, 53; Busch, *Henry VII*, 419.

depended too much on the accuracy of his insights into men's characters.

Bacon has been criticized by some modern historians for neglecting to mention economic and social causes, and for concentrating on personal motives and power politics.[1] To some extent this criticism is unjustified, for Bacon was deliberately writing a particular kind of history, restricted to political affairs. Moreover, he did not entirely neglect economic and social matters. Certainly he was aware of the need for economic histories, as his 'Catalogue of Particular Histories' proves.[2] It is true that he concentrated on the analysis of character in the *History of Henry VII*, but it was character in relation to situation. Bacon had definite ideas about the relevance of economics to early Tudor politics. The psychology of the individual in politics was only one of the factors, albeit the most important one, which Bacon took into account.

Most of Bacon's historical explanations were conceived in terms of Bacon's experience with seventeenth-century politics and statecraft. Some of his ideas he owed to Machiavelli and Guicciardini, and some he discovered in his various authorities, but once Bacon had made an idea his own he did not question its relevance to past conditions. Fortune and providence Bacon considered out of place in civil history, and when he used these terms he obviously did so mainly for literary effect. Richard III was overthrown by divine revenge; the Scottish marriage, which eventually led to the union of the two crowns, was brought about 'by God's wonderful providence'; and the marriage contract between Prince Henry and Catherine was similarly by 'the secret providence of God' ordained to be the occasion of great events and changes. This was the extent of Bacon's concern with first causes.[3]

Bacon's concern with economic policy was a remarkable feature of his *History*. The problem of enclosures could hardly escape notice, and Bacon used this as an occasion to comment on one of his favourite topics—the desirability of maintaining able-bodied yeomen as the backbone of a strong army.[4] Professor Heckscher quoted with

---

[1] See Leonard Dean, 'Bacon's Theory of Civil History Writing', *English Literary History* (VIII, 1941), 182.

[2] See Bacon, *Works*, VIII, 373–81.

[3] See *ibid.*, XI, 45, 297, 322. On fortune (which Bacon did not use in a deterministic sense), see *ibid.*, XI, 79, 353–4. Cf. 'Of Fortune', XII, 215.

[4] *Ibid.*, XI, 144–5.

approval Bacon's formulation of Henry's commercial policy: 'bowing the ancient policy of this estate, from consideration of plenty to consideration of power'.[1] Bacon was a thoroughgoing mercantilist in his stress on considerations of power. State power as an end in itself dominated economic policy, Bacon thought; it was for this reason that economic and political history had to be considered together.

Just as Bacon assumed that contemporary mercantilist doctrine was relevant to late fifteenth-century conditions, so he believed that 'reason of state' was the hidden consideration in all the diplomatic crises of Henry's reign. By the use of conjecture Bacon sought to discover the truth behind the pretences of the King. In discussing the imposture of Lambert Simnell, Bacon argued that the chief instigator of the plot, judged by the 'precedent and subsequent acts', was probably the Queen Dowager. And 'that which doth chiefly fortify this conjecture is, that as soon as the matter broke forth in any strength, it was one of the King's first acts to cloister the Queen Dowager in the nunnery of Bermondsey, and to take away her lands and estates . . .'[2] Here Bacon frankly admitted that conjecture was the basis of his interpretation. Actually, he proceeded in the same way when he disregarded the ostensible reasons for the seven-year delay in the marriage between Catherine and Prince Arthur and reconstructed the considerations which were probably decisive in terms of 'reason of state'.[3]

This was a perfectly legitimate method of procedure (many examples of it can be found in the *History*), but it was liable to objection on the ground that Bacon did not always bother to distinguish between his conjectural hypotheses, and the fortifying evidence or proof. A more careful historian, William Camden, had refused to pry into things secret and abstruse. Bacon might have provided historians with a useful tool of analysis had he pointed out the importance of reconstructing episodes in the light of a hypothesis. Spelman's 'theorem' of feudalism would doubtless have appealed to Bacon as an example of the use of scientific historical method.[4] Unfortunately, Bacon himself appeared to disregard the difference between an idea of explanation and the facts and inferences which served to verify or disprove it.

When he inferred hidden motives, reasons or plans Bacon was

---

[1] E. Heckscher, *Mercantilism*, II, 16; cf. Bacon, *Works*, XI, 145.
[2] Bacon, *Works*, XI, 73.
[3] *Ibid.*, XI, 317–19.   [4] Cf. Pocock, *Ancient Constitution*, 103.

often extremely persuasive. The analysis of character in relation to situation called for imaginative insight; and here, Bacon thought, political experience offered better guidance to the historian than books. In his short essay 'On the Fortunate Memory of Elizabeth' Bacon observed that it was not to 'monks or closet penmen' that one should look for guidance in past politics. It was rather 'for ministers and great officers to judge of these things, and those who have handled the helm of government, and been acquainted with the difficulties and mysteries of state business'.[1] The experienced statesman could not only read between the lines and discover causes hidden by deliberate design, he could also point out the political lessons of history.

Bacon was careful to stress the importance of beginning with the known facts of a situation, especially an unusual one such as that which Henry VII faced when he had to deal with Lambert Simnell. 'Therefore we shall make our judgment upon the things themselves, as they give light one to another, and (as we can) dig truth out of the mine', Bacon wrote.[2] Nevertheless, he was, as always, primarily concerned with the question of interpretation. The 'things themselves' defined a problem, and it was up to the historian to make the proper inferences, to explain or interpret the facts in terms of what was most probably true. The test of truth, in this case, was the historian's judgment, enlightened by his political and philosophical experience.

The similarities between Bacon's approach to history and Machiavelli's require some comment. Both writers emphasized the role of the individual in history, both tried to show that character and intellect had to be adaptable for the individual to succeed, and both assumed that the analogy between past and present was in no need of demonstration. Bacon's analysis of character and situation was unusually cogent, but he did not ask himself a question which modern historians have come to regard as fundamental: is the present being read back into the past? For a variety of reasons Bacon was insensitive to the problem of the relationship between past and present. As a lawyer, as a scientist, and as a seventeenth-century historian he tended to look for analogies rather than differences.[3]

---

[1] Bacon, *Works*, XI, 443. [2] *Ibid.*, XI, 70.
[3] Bacon believed that in natural history, 'men's labour therefore should be turned to the investigation and observation of the resemblances and analogies of Things, as well in wholes as in parts'. *Ibid.*, 'Novum Organum', VIII, 234.

Since human nature did tend to remain the same Bacon's characterizations were often accurate and revealing. When historical changes had destroyed the basis for analogy, then Bacon was likely to be as much in error as Coke. Bacon dwelt at greater length than most historians on legal history, chiefly because he believed that such history served to inform the judgment of kings, councillors, and persons of estate.[1] When he discussed Henry's 'De Facto' Act, which declared that subjects should not be held guilty of treason for rendering obedience to a king in fact (whatever he was in right), Bacon fell into error. Some of the legal complexities of this act, and the political calculations which led up to it, may be found in Bacon's text. The important point is that Bacon commented on the law in a way which was quite foreign to the fifteenth century. 'For a supreme and absolute power cannot conclude itself', Bacon wrote, arguing that Parliament was such a power, and that a precedent act of Parliament could, therefore, never bind or frustrate a future.[2]

Bacon was, as Professor Kenneth Pickthorne pointed out, quite wrong in his conception of the power of statute-making as supreme and absolute in the early Tudor period. The change that had taken place in the sixteenth century was far more radical than Bacon realized; indeed it was almost revolutionary with respect to constitutional history. Bacon was no doubt more realistic than Coke in his comments on the 'De Facto' Act; and he anticipated in his comments a theory which was to emerge later in the seventeenth century. But Bacon was still guilty of reading his own seventeenth-century opinion back into late fifteenth-century history.[3]

The limitations of Bacon's historical method in the *History of Henry VII* can be summed up by saying that Bacon disregarded important problems of relevance. He distinguished between the social, economic and intellectual conditions which defined a situation, and the human acts which set in motion particular events.[4] A distinction between immediate and long-term causes was, how-

[1] Bacon, *Works*, XI, 147-8. Major laws were described in some detail. See 129-34, 140-8, 182-6, 240-3, 263, 332-5.

[2] *Ibid.*, XI, 241.

[3] See Kenneth Pickthorne, *Early Tudor Government, Henry VII* (Cambridge, 1949), 151-6. But cf. Bacon, *Works*, XI, 141, where Bacon suggests that there might have been a problem involved because of the 'difference of times'.

[4] Bacon used the old analogy of the spark and the fuel in discussing the Lambert Simnell episode, *Works*, XI, 71.

ever, as old as Thucydides. The fundamental mistake Bacon made was in thinking that causal explanations could be divorced from detailed original research. The relevance of an idea of explanation to a given body of 'facts' could not be taken for granted, as the French legal humanists had shown. Bacon, intent on interpreting the complex interplay between character and situation, was unaware of two perils: (1) that his own experience might prove misleading; and (2) that his analysis of character might prematurely shut off inquiry.

Bacon's analysis of the character of Henry VII illustrates the latter point. The portrait of Henry as an avaricious, stubborn, overly suspicious monarch was accepted by generations of historians. That Henry's suppression of the Yorkists might have been wise, though harsh, policy, or that Henry's financial measures might have been calculated to strengthen the crown and control the nobles rather than satisfy Henry's desire for full coffers—these explanations were ruled out by Bacon, who was arrogant enough to think he could calculate probabilities more precisely than Henry.[1] Bacon was far from 'scientific' in his approach to political history; and few of his ideas were derived inductively from the study of history. This is not to say that Bacon's methodology was inferior to that of most seventeenth-century historians. Bacon's faults were, however, more discordant, because he was more explicit about his historical theory.

The virtues of Bacon's *Henry VII* were far more obvious to contemporaries and to posterity than were the faults of the work. Bacon was a very great historical stylist, writing in the best humanistic tradition. What his work lacked in the way of thorough research and methodological refinement it made up for in style and content of ideas. It was no mean achievement to write a history which eliminated the irrelevant detail of the chronicles and provided a thematic structure for the history of a reign. The organization of the *History of Henry VII* was so far superior to the annalistic methods used by earlier historians, including Camden, that the work may be said to be the first modern classic of English history.

[1] On Henry's character, see *ibid.*, XI, 37–40, 65, 197, 229, 234, 324, 336, 355–65, and Appendix II. For modern estimates, see K. Pickthorne, *Early Tudor Government, Henry VII*, 152–3; J. D. Mackie, *The Earlier Tudors 1485–1558* (Oxford, 1952), 212–18 sums up modern opinion. To some extent Bacon's character of Henry VII may have been distorted in order to point up political lessons.

Bacon organized his narrative around general themes or topics, each of which he treated chronologically to reveal different stages of development. Apart from the character sketch of Henry at the end of the book, there were four major themes which formed the structural unity of the work. The first was the theme of dynastic succession, or how Henry gained and kept the throne. The second was the theme of statecraft, or how the King dealt with a problem of foreign affairs. The third was the theme of attempted usurpation, centred on the political machinations of Perkin Warbeck. Finally, the less clear-cut theme of the last part was the politics of power, or how Henry consolidated his position at home and abroad. The Perkin Warbeck episode admirably illustrated Bacon's care and deliberation in arranging his material. Instead of following a strict chronological sequence Bacon allowed the demands of his argument to determine his discussion of particular points. Only a careful reading of Bacon's text can reveal the subtlety of Bacon's style.[1]

To estimate the significance of Bacon's contribution to English historical writing and thought in the seventeenth century one must compare Bacon's works with those of other historians and philosophers. Bacon was aware of the revolution in learning in his own day. Science, not religion, was the new and revolutionary force in human society.[2] Bacon was a superb propagandist for the scientific revolution; and not the least of his services to learning was to bring history and science closer together. In calling for new and better civil histories Bacon was speaking for the best historians of the age. If he misunderstood some of the methodological principles of civil history, as he did those of natural history and science, this did not greatly lessen his influence. Among Bacon's contemporaries there were better scientists and better historians, but no one else could write, argue, and persuade as effectively as Bacon could.

[1] I wish to express my gratitude to Frank West, a former thesis student at Reed College, for helpful discussion on this and other points in this chapter, and for calling attention to some references which I would otherwise have overlooked.

[2] See Bacon, *Works*, 'Novum Organum', VIII, 110. On Bacon's distrust of religious obscurantism, see *ibid.*, VI, 421; VIII, 124–6. See also H. Arnecke, *Kirchengeschichte und Rechtsgeschischte*, 315–16.

11

JOHN SELDEN AND
PROBLEMATIC HISTORY

JOHN SELDEN WAS ONE OF ENGLAND's most learned men. His contemporaries in the long Parliament seem to have regarded him
'somewhat in the light of a valuable piece of national property, like
a museum, or a great public library'.[1] Scholars and statesmen, both
in and out of Parliament, sought his advice on questions which
covered the whole compass of legal and historical learning. The
range of Selden's scholarship was impressive even to his close friends,
who were themselves giants of erudition. Archbishop Ussher
eulogized Selden in his funeral sermon by declaring that he himself
felt scarce worthy to carry Selden's books after him. Men as diverse
in temperament as Dr. Johnson and Coleridge found in his *Table
Talk* enduring wisdom behind the chisel edge of wit. The *Table Talk*

[1] Quoted from an anonymous source by S. W. Singer, in the preface to
his edition of Selden's *Table Talk*. See *The Table Talk of John Selden*, ed.
S. W. Singer, 2nd ed. (London, 1856), lxxvi. I have quoted from Singer's
text because it is, on the whole, accurate and clear, but all quotations have
been collated with the definitive text, edited from manuscript copy by
Sir Frederick Pollock for the *Selden Society* (1927). The account of Selden's
life by Sir Edward Fry in the *D.N.B.* should be checked against the unpublished doctoral dissertation of David S. Berkowitz, 'Young Mr. Selden,
Essays in Seventeenth Century Learning and Politics' (Harvard Univ.,
1946), which corrects, for example, the mistaken idea that Selden took an
active part in the Protestation of the Commons in 1621. This dissertation
is especially helpful in providing a detailed chronology of Selden's writings;
it is the fullest account of Selden's work that I know of.

275

was, indeed, an incomparable expression of Selden's profoundly rational and disciplined intelligence.

Selden was said to have taken as his motto 'Above all, Liberty', to show that he would examine things and not take them on trust.[1] Fundamentally conservative and moderate in his political beliefs— a man who wanted to enjoy the peace and quiet of ordered society— he was nevertheless prepared to fight stubbornly to preserve liberty. His deepest conviction was that liberty could only be preserved by knowledge of law, custom, and history. The ancient liberties of Englishmen were the only inalienable rights in which Selden believed; he had no use for abstract mythologies, for the divine right of kings, for the natural rights of man, or for 'Pretending Religion and the Law of God', which he thought was a sure way to set all things loose.[2]

In the House of Commons where Selden spoke against able and practised opponents he was known as a distinguished debater. In conversation he was polished, incisive and urbane. Written history, however, he regarded essentially as a means to an end, not as an art. His books contained sentences which clarified and summed up brilliantly whole paragraphs of argument, but he did not write graceful narrative prose. He built his historical works in an almost Cyclopean fashion, with quotations piled upon quotations, most of them still in the languages in which he found them. History was the study of problems; and historical method was as scientific as Selden could make his procedures of verification and proof. Purpose and method defined the style of Selden's work—the very virtues of his scholarship worked against any fluency of style.

Selden took an active part in politics, serving 'as burgess in several Parliaments, both in those which had a King, and which had none'.[3] He was the most remarkable of those common lawyers who formed the core of the Parliamentary opposition to the early Stuarts. The intimate connection between politics and historical scholarship is evident in nearly all of Selden's work.[4] Although he studied history in the spirit of an inquirer he believed that history

---

[1] See Anthony À Wood, *Athenae Oxonienses*, 5 vols. (London, 1817), III, 368. This statement was, however, disputed by the eighteenth-century editor of this edition.

[2] See *Table Talk*, 145, and *sub* 'Religion' and 'Preaching', *passim*.

[3] Quoted from a translation of Selden's epitaph (written by himself) by Singer, *Table Talk*, lxix.

[4] The best studies of this aspect of Selden's work are Heinrich Arneke, *Kirchengeschichte und Rechtsgeschichte*, 258–84, and Berkowitz, 'Young

should provide light for the 'practice and doubts of the present'—
that is, historical inquiry should be directed toward the clarification
of present problems. To be of use to the present, however, written
history had to be true to the evidence. Selden was willing to compromise on the issues of his own day, but not on the truths of history.
He realized that historical argument would be meaningless if the
facts could not be established with certainty, or at least beyond
reasonable doubt.

It was entirely characteristic of Selden that he published his
Historie of Tithes without deleting a single paragraph in it, as Cotton
apparently had advised. When the book was suppressed, and he
himself called upon to answer for the passages which offended the
clergy, he confessed that he was sorry for publishing it, but not sorry
for having written it. In reply to the animadversions of Dr. Tillesley
he asked, 'Is there a syllable in it of less truth because I am sorry for
publishing it?' [1]

Selden's command of languages, his knowledge of philology,
diplomatics, and palaeography enabled him to carry out a programme of historical research which few scholars in any age could
duplicate. He was one of England's best orientalists; as a Christian
Hebraist he had few superiors either in England or on the continent.
He knew Arabic, some Ethiopian, and could read Persian as well as
other near eastern languages. His knowledge of Latin as it was
written in all periods from classical times to his own provided him
with a means to verify the dates of documents and to detect forgeries. Greek, Anglo-Saxon, old French, German, and Spanish were
among the other European languages he knew. The French legal
humanists, notably Cujas, Budé, Alciat, and Brisson strongly influenced his historical thought. Yet his cosmopolitan learning in no
way diminished his respect for English common law. To the end of

Mr. Selden' (Harvard doctoral dissertation), Chapters IV, VI, and VII,
passim.

[1] John Selden, *Opera Omnia*, 3 vols., ed. by David Wilkins (London,
1726), 'A Reply to Dr. Tillesley's Animadversions Upon the *History of
Tythes*', III, 1371. This is the standard edition of Selden's works and I
have quoted from it whenever necessary although it is by no means a
definitive text. The arrangement of the volumes is poor, and some pages
are misnumbered. Page references are to the numbered columns, or
'pages', and volume references to the volume number, not to the parts
into which the volumes are divided. My quotations from the *Historie of
Tithes* are from the first edition, London, 1618.

his life he was proud of his calling as a common lawyer; his erudition buttressed his belief in the rule of law.

With the founding of the Selden Society in the nineteenth century, Selden's work in legal history won deserved recognition. As an editor of texts, and as a writer on English as well as on international law, he helped to lay the foundation of modern legal studies in England. Modern historians have corrected his errors of fact and interpretation, but the methods they have used are essentially the same as those which he helped to develop. Realizing that history involves comparison, and that legal history in particular should be based on the comparative study of legal institutions, Selden overcame most of the limitations of the common law approach to history.[1]

Some acquaintance with Selden's intellectual biography is indispensable to an understanding of his historical writing and thought. He brought to bear on his subject matter a mind superbly trained in history, law, and political debate. The importance of breadth as well as depth of scholarship was explicitly recognized by Selden, who had travelled in a far wider world than most of his contemporaries:

> It is said that all isles and continents (which are indeed but greater isles) are so seated, that there is none but that, from some shore of it, another may be discovered. . . . Certainly the several parts of good arts and learning have that kind of site. And, as all are to be diligently sought to be possessed by mankind, so every one hath so much relation to some other, that it hath not only use often of the aid of what is next it, but, through that, also of what is out of ken to it.[2]

The purpose of the present chapter will be to examine Selden's historical thought as revealed in the *Historie of Tithes*. Some of his other works may have brought him greater prestige among the learned, but none was more characteristic, none better illustrates

---

[1] Cf. W. S. Holdsworth, *Sources and Literature of English Law* (Oxford, 1925), 147–50; Pocock, *Ancient Constitution and Feudal Law*, 89, 100, 135, 137–8, 154–5; and David Ogg's introduction to his edition of Selden's *Ad Fletam* in the 'Cambridge Studies in English Legal History' series. Ogg is more critical of Selden, pointing out his mistakes of fact and emphasis. See *Ioanis Seldini: Ad Fletam Dissertatio*, ed. David Ogg (Cambridge, 1925), xix–lxvi. Selden's knowledge of Hebrew was perhaps less satisfactory than he realized. It should also be noted that he did not entirely overcome the common law doctrine of 'custom and the immemorial' (cf. 'Notes on Fortescues de Laudibus' in *Opera*, III, 1890–3).

[2] Selden, *Titles of Honour*, in *Opera*, III, 99.

seventeenth-century problematic history, and none raised more significant questions of relevance. As an example of ecclesiastical history it was far from typical; indeed, by posing the question of how history was related to religion it forced a reconsideration of the very nature of church history. Selden did not provoke the tithes controversy, but his *Historie* defined the intellectual alternatives: one might argue either from history or from divinity, but there should be no question of appealing to divinity when the historical evidence proved weak.

In his early essay on the *Duello* (1610) Selden epitomized the enduring features of his historical thought: '*Historical traditions of use, and succinct description of ceremony* are my ends; both deduced from the ancients, but without proselenick affectation.' [1] The *Historie of Tithes* was also written to examine a tradition of use, and was based on hard-headed examination of the evidence. Antiquarian affectation was meaningless to Selden, who made every historical fact count.

The economic problems of the Church provided Selden with the starting point for his investigation of the history of tithes. The Puritan attack on the hierarchy was symptomatic of a far wider and more serious attack on the economic practices and policies of the Church. Land-hungry magnates, driving businessmen, the secular-minded in all walks of life had reason to join in the attack. Profiting from lay patronage and impropriated tithes, men of substance were not prepared to fight for the financial independence of the ministry. The alternatives to lay patronage (i.e. the right of a layman to present to a church living) were episcopal nomination or popular election. The former was unacceptable to the gentry, who clung tenaciously to their inherited advowsons and impropriated tithes; the latter was unacceptable to the bishops. The opportunities for nepotism—not to mention the opportunities for simony—inherent in lay patronage effectively smothered efforts at reform. Since lay patronage was regarded as a form of property right, suits concerning patronage were usually decided in the common law courts. This only exacerbated the feelings of hostility on the part of many churchmen toward lay patrons and their defenders, the common lawyers.

From the point of view of the clergy at large, the problem of tithes was of fundamental importance: in an era of rising prices and declining opportunities for advancement, the rank and file of the clergy were becoming victims of the economic scissors. They were therefore desperately anxious to find a means—other than civil litigation—to

---

[1] Selden, *Opera*, III, 55–6.

compel the payment of tithes. The system of lay patronage was not seriously attacked until Laud began his reforms in the 1630's. Long before this, however, clergymen had bitterly complained about impropriated tithes, non-payment of tithes, and the general decay in the maintenance of the Church.

The problem of tithe payments had been vastly complicated by the revolutionary changes which took place in the sixteenth century. Former monastic lands were exempt from tithes even when they had passed into lay hands. Some tithes had been commuted to money payments, the value of which declined sharply with the rise in prices. The leasing of tithes by clergymen in return for ready cash or annuities often resulted in parishes which provided no living for the minister; and, in the case of one lease of 2000 years' duration, this involved nothing less than the outright transfer of tithes into lay hands. Such leasing, even on a lesser scale, became a profitable and safe form of investment. Perhaps the most serious problem was simply that the Church found itself unable to tap the new sources of wealth which were opening up in trade, commerce, mining, and improved farming based on enclosures.

In traditional agricultural societies tithes were normally paid out of the natural yearly increase of crops and animals. Production for use involved no complicated bookkeeping, and the products of the fields and the barns could be readily counted by the local priest. With the coming of early modern capitalism, and urban growth, the opportunities for evading payment of tithes increased along with the incentives to evade. Many clergymen, seeking clear title to their income, consequently tried to argue that tithes were due and payable by divine moral law, which was eternal and superior to any human positive law.

From the point of view of the businessman, whether he was engaged in industry, commerce, or farming, the absolute claim of the Church to tithes of one-tenth of his property was a denial of just those property rights which he regarded as essential to his welfare; the sanctity of contract and the constitutional liberties of the individual were equally threatened by clerical divine right theory. Furthermore, to a considerable segment of the landowning and commercial classes, tithe payments literally meant the difference between solvency and economic ruin. The struggle over tithes was waged not only between clergymen and laymen, but also between laymen who held impropriated tithes and those who did not. Few laymen, however, were prepared to acknowledge that tithes were an absolute obligation, imposed by God in the form of divine moral law; the clerical claim threatened both the economic and the social privileges of the lay classes of the nation. It was infinitely preferable to maintain that tithes were wholly subject to determination by the secular common law. In these circumstances, as Christopher Hill has observed, 'the Church's failure to win victory outright was equivalent to defeat, since the whole trend of development of society was against it'.[1]

Selden intended his *Historie of Tithes* to be a direct contribution to the problem under discussion: the historical question was how tithes had in practice been paid. He denied any intention of meddling with the question of divinity, which had nothing to do with history. Yet Selden was obviously aware of the implications of his argument. If he could show that in practice tithes had been paid for reasons which had nothing to do with divine right theory, he would have forced his clerical opponents to admit that history did not support their claims—fact could be historically proved; divine right could not. Moreover, Selden knew that historical traditions determined legal rights, and that even the meaning of the words in the Bible was known by nothing but tradition. History was the matrix of thought.

Clearly Selden was engaged in a dangerous controversy, which involved issues of even greater consequence to the Church than the immediate question of tithes. At stake was the whole Reformation thesis that historical precedents were relevant to the doctrine and organization of the Church. Few men realized how devastating the full implications of Selden's arguments were, but many sensed danger in Selden's firm insistence that his *Historie* could only be criticized on secular historical grounds.

In reply to a demand made by Buckingham in 1620 that he express his own opinion touching the divine right of tithes, Selden wrote a letter of explanation that was a studied, ironic insult. Begging leave to keep his opinions to himself, Selden pointed out some of the consequences of rash expression:

And I trust your Lordship doth not wish that I should chuse my side before I studied it, and were also able to defend it. If then, my

[1] Christopher Hill, *Economic Problems of the Church* (Oxford, 1956), 131. The preceding four paragraphs are directly based on the first five chapters of Mr. Hill's admirable book. Anyone who wishes to understand the issues at stake in the tithes controversy will want to read this work.

Lord, I should so upon study of it chance to conclude, through my own collection, that they [tithes] were due *jure divino*, I should notwithstanding much doubt of my own judgment; when I find, that not only in the churches of *France*, *Spain*, *Italy*, and *Germany*, and of all other foreign Christian commonwealths, whose practice I have read in their laws and decisions, but also in the laws and practice of this his majesty's great monarchy, that no tythes are at all, or have been for many ages since, paid or to be recovered as due *jure divino*, but only according as the secular laws made for tythes, or local customs, ordain or permit them. Good my lord, then think but what it would be for me, a private man, and bred in the studies of secular laws, to determine the question on this side, and so accuse both the whole state I live in, and all other churches of Christendom, of an universally established practice against the law of God.[1]

Selden went on to observe that in a book printed by public authority in Elizabeth's reign, it was expressly stated that the *jure divino* theory of tithes was one of the greatest and grossest errors of the papists. As in a game of chess, Selden played deliberately, and protected his key pieces by defences in depth. The critical problem was the relevance of the content of his *Historie* to the political struggle over tithes. The significance of his book may be inferred from a bare outline of the thesis.

Selden began his *Historie* by discussing the customs of tithing in antiquity, paying particular attention to the practices of the Jews. 'It is no news', he wrote, 'to have the eldest of Jewish customs usurped, though according to time and place diversely varied among the Gentiles.'[2] Among all nations of the ancient world Selden demonstrated that tithes had been determined, in cases of dispute, by the secular authority. Among the early Christians, voluntary oblations had taken the place of tithes. The maintenance of the clergy presented few problems until the Church became a universal institution, embracing the wicked and the devout of many nations. Selden could

---

[1] Selden, *Opera*, III, 1394. For Selden's view of tradition, see *Table Talk*, 155, *sub* 'Tradition'. Selden's 'To the Reader of Sir James Sempil's Appendix' (*Opera*, III, 1350–64), and his 'To the Reader of Dr. Tillesley's Animadversions' (*ibid.*, III, 1370–86), contain pertinent information about his attitudes. On his express purpose in writing see also, 'Of my Purpose and End in Writing the History of Tythes' (*ibid.*, III, 1451–8), and the 'Preface' and 'Review' in the *Historie of Tithes, passim*.

[2] Selden, *Opera*, III, 1095.

find no evidence that tenths were paid, or offered to the Church for holy uses, until toward the end of the fourth century.

The scheme of periodization which Selden adopted was based on a quadripartite division of the Christian era. He sought to discover the known use, opinions, and constitutions of every four hundred years, touching the duty or payment of tithes. In each period, new and characteristic developments were described. Thus, the period from 800 to 1200 was marked by the emergence of infeodations, advowsons, and certain other practices which were not to be found in earlier centuries.

In the eighth chapter, Selden began his 'review and comparative history of tithes' in different countries. The fact or practice of tithing could not be affirmatively concluded from what was ordained for tithes in any of the canons of the Church. The essence of Selden's argument appeared in his comment on a petition of the clergy dating from the fiftieth year of the reign of Edward III: '. . . the practised Common Law (for by that name, as *common* is distinguished from *sacred*, are the Ciuil or Municipall Laws of all Nations to be stiled) hath never given way herein to the Canons, but hath allowed customes, and made them subject to all ciuill titles, Infeodations, discharges, compositions and the like'.[1] This was, in fact, the re-iterated argument of the book. What made it so unfuriating to the clergy was that Selden documented it in detail, using evidence and proofs that they could not refute. Moreover, he deliberately explained the origin and development of particular laws, practices, and opinions entirely in secular terms.

Selden's ideas of explanation were perfectly integrated with the purpose and content of the work: he explained continuity and change by reference to power politics, economic interests, and legal traditions of use. He might have agreed with Ranke that the relationship between church and state is the content of history. In discussing the history of tithes, he treated the Church exactly like any other human institution; there was not even a vestige of the supernatural in Selden's historical thought.

According to Selden, the first general council of the Church to command the payment of all tithes as a Christian duty was the Lateran Council of 1215, under Innocent the Third: '. . . about which time Ecclesiasticall Autoritie became more powerfull, the Canons

[1] See Selden, *Historie of Tithes* (London, 1618), 176–7 and 155, 359, 390, 402, 405–9, 471, 475.

were more receiud into practice (that before were little, especially herein obeyed) and Parochiall right to Tithes grew to be more established'.[1] Selden stressed the fact again and again that it was the political power of the Church that determined how far the canon law was accepted in England and elsewhere.[2]

As an Erastian Selden saw no reason to trust the Church, especially in the light of its historical record. He pointed out, for example, that after about 1200, it seemed certain that churches and religious houses had deliberately concealed the titles to tithes that had originated in arbitrary lay consecrations (i.e. specific grants of tithes made arbitrarily by laymen to a particular church or monastery).[3] Fearing loss of revenue in the event of suits for the recovery of such tithes at canon law (which shortly after 1200 prohibited arbitrary consecrations), the religious houses attempted to hide the evidence of previous lay bounty. The legal technicalities of Selden's arguments did not obscure his main point, which was that churchmen were no less subject to economic motivation than were laymen.

The amount of economic interpretation in the *Historie of Tithes* suggests that the common lawyer's concern with profit and property was not detrimental to his understanding of ecclesiastical history. Selden pointed out that early in the Middle Ages laymen had begun to build and endow churches, and invest chaplains, partly with a view to increasing their own income. The 'profits that rose out of Christian deuotion' were now divided between the clergyman and the lay patron. Thus, in these early times 'erecting of churches became, amongst some, to bee rather gainful than deuout, for the Patron would arbitrarily diuide to the Incumbent, and take the rest to his own vse'.[4]

The faults of the laity were, however, compounded by the clergy. Secular priests would instruct the laity in the most ridiculous falsehoods, and even abuse God's name, in order to secure their own gain. The regular clergy, on the other hand, were not unwilling to argue that every man might dispose of his tithes at pleasure to charitable uses—that is, to a monastic order. Under Henry VI a Franciscan friar was condemned as a heretic for insisting on this argument—but then, as Selden observed, the friar was in good company.[5] In a later chapter Selden quoted Wycliffe's explanation

[1] Seldon, *Historie of Tithes*, 137–8.
[2] See *ibid.*, 290–2, 362, 468–9, 472–3, 489.
[3] *Ibid.*, 469–70.   [4] *Ibid.*, 83, 84.   [5] *Ibid.*, 171–4.

of why laymen were justified in conveying tithes to what church or monastery they made choice of: it was that the laity might thereby give to the best priests and not have to suffer the rich, evil, parasitic priests to batten on their tithes.[1]

In England, most infeodations into lay hands had occurred as a result of the dissolution of the monasteries. The payment of tithes to laymen who purchased monastic lands was provided for by the Statute of 32, Henry VIII, cap. 7, which defined the remedies at common law for the recovery of tithes. In effect, infeodated tithes were held like any other inheritable properties or rents.[2] Selden was concerned to show not only what the law was, but also that history did not lend support to the canonists' claim that infeodations had originated in voluntary grants made by the clergy or the Pope to the secular power. The Church, in other words, could claim no title to infeodated tithes by right of former possession.[3] The immediate question of historical origins obviously involved the much broader questions of rights of jurisdiction, and Selden therefore devoted the last chapter of his book to a history of the jurisdiction of tithes in England.

Selden readily admitted that by the practised common law of his own day, and according to the most ancient year books, the regular jurisdiction of spiritual tithes belonged by right to the ecclesiastical courts. Even the statutes which dealt with infeodated tithes left this ancient right intact. What Selden sought to prove was that the common law courts had from the earliest times exercised jurisdiction in cases involving lay property rights in tithes. He was directly concerned with the legal tradition which derived, on the one hand from feudal law, and on the other from canon and civil law.[4] It was only necessary for him to show that common law writs had served to remove cases from the ecclesiastical courts, for he had earlier demonstrated that such writs had not been challenged until about 1200, when the canon law was extended as a result of the insolent power politics of the Papacy.

[1] *Ibid.*, 290-2. The practice had been recognized before the time of Innocent III, both in canon and in common law. See *ibid.*, 458.

[2] *Ibid.*, 395-7.

[3] *Ibid.*, 475.

[4] See especially *ibid.*, 411-13, 488-91. Chapter XIV (on jurisdiction) is too technical to be readily summarized—as, although to a lesser degree, are most of Selden's chapters. The paragraph in the text represents only the main point of Selden's elaborate argument.

Common law governed and limited canon law except in spiritual matters; and 'before about the time of *Henrie* the second, the King's secular Courts of Iustice originally held plea of the right of tithes'.[1] The key to Selden's argument was that 'tithes alone could neuer have been collated like a Benefice, had they not been first founded or created as a Benefice'.[2] Canon law to the contrary—and in spite of what the Pope might write from Rome—'we know the truth by a cloud of home-bred witnesses'.[3] The common law tradition was of more ancient authority than any other in England; and, as he showed in his final chapter, there was no break in the continuity of common law tradition. Whatever might be the use of canon or civil law in controversy, the governing authority of the common law was a matter of historical record.[4]

Since Selden claimed to be writing about fact and not about right he was obliged to discuss questions of relevance almost exclusively in terms of historical method. The proof of any argument from history depended on exact knowledge of the facts and on awareness of 'the difference of Ages'.[5] From the law courts Selden took his terminology of historical proof, and from the study of philology he derived the first principles of scientific history. True philology, he thought, 'establishes principles to euery Facultie that could not of it selfe alone know how to get them'.[6] In writing of evidence, of witnesses and testimonies, and of examinations he revealed his common law training. But, like the French legal humanists whom he admired, he held that a common lawyer had every reason to study philology; and in consequence he could ask 'to whom it belongs more to write the *Historie of Tithes*, than to a *Common Lawyer*?'[7]

Examples of Selden's mastery of the techniques and special skills required for the writing of exact history could be fetched from every chapter of his *Historie*. He chose his testimonies by weight rather than number, preferring what was 'Autoritie enough' to what was merely various.[8] It goes without saying that he preferred manuscripts to printed texts, the language of the original to any translation, and

---

[1] Selden, *Historie of Tithes*, 415. [2] *Ibid.*, 355.
[3] *Ibid.*, 359.
[4] On feudal tithes, see *ibid.*, 475; also (on tradition of common law), 478–9.
[5] *Ibid.*, 411. [6] *Ibid.*, 'Preface', xix. [7] *Ibid.*, 'Preface', xx, xvii.
[8] *Ibid.*, 'Preface', xxi. See also 195–6, and Selden's 'Letter to Mr. Augustine Vincent', *Opera*, 1692–1705.

the full account to any paraphrase or gloss. The philological problems which Selden had to overcome in writing his *Historie of Tithes* were indeed formidable, and his opponents naturally attempted to discredit his interpretations on philological grounds. Yet, since few were his equals in linguistic knowledge, and none in general learning, they found it virtually impossible to prove mistakes against him. Philology itself was a historical study; and Selden was heavily armed with original historical manuscripts.

One of the best introductions to Selden's concept of historical method is a passage which occurs in the 'Review', which he appended to the *Historie of Tithes* to justify and explain the content of the various chapters. Referring to laws which had been discussed at length in the text itself, Selden wrote:

> The *force of the words* of all those Laws; the Autoritie that made them; and the *Territories to which they were extended,* are especially to be observed by euerie one that here looks after humane positiue Law. For manie talk and write of that, and tell vs here of *ius Ecclesiasticum* (at least if they fail in their Arguments from *Ius Diuinum*) but whence that *Ius Ecclesiasticum* is, and where or when made, they little enough know. For what hath a *Prouinciall Councell* of one Nation to doe with another? What hath the *Imperialls* of the old *French* Empire to doe with England? Nay, what hath the *Popes* Decrees to do here? But because there was a time when their autority was more largely acknowledged; their Decrees that bred much of what now iustly continues in some States (which also iustly now denie their autoritie) remain most obseruable, and wee haue giuen them their places.[1]

Four principles of evidence and proof may be deduced from this passage. First, Selden stressed the importance of establishing facts within specific historical contexts; second, he argued that historical comparisons should be made only on the basis of precise definitions; third, it was necessary to consider how precedents were related to particular historical traditions—in short, he raised the crucial issue of relevance; finally, he indicated that chronological discrimination was essential. It should be obvious that Selden had a far better understanding of historical method than most seventeenth-century historians. In practice, each of his methodological principles supported the others; his concept of method was rationally coherent—

---

[1] Selden, *Tithes*, 477.

and scientifically grounded in that he sought empirical verification
for all fact statements.

i CONTEXTUALISM AND COMPARISON

Selden was careful to protect himself from the elementary objection
that he had quoted words out of context. He pointed out, for
example, that he did not give Cyprian's words alone and then his own
gloss, 'but I haue carefully and shortly exprest also the occasion of
his passages; and so, that an vnderstanding Reader may collect
as much out of them as he might do if he had the whole context
of *Cyprian* by him'.[1] But Selden went much further than this.
Instead of simply setting out to collect precedents he tried to discover
how particular practices and opinions were related to the circumstances of the times in which they appeared, and to the historical
traditions of which they were a part.

Comparative history was the means of establishing events in
context; and by broadening the basis of comparison Selden was able
to overcome most of the errors of inexact analogy. In *Titles of Honour*
he described in some detail his idea of comparative history, observing
that 'there is nothing more conduces to a right judgment than the
careful examination of constitutions and customs, their received
interpretations and their force, in the state and age of which any
civil disquisition is raised'.[2] In the *Historie of Tithes*, he compared
(and above all contrasted) the theory and practice of tithing in different ages and countries. In feudal societies Selden showed that feudal
tithes were determined by feudal law; if canon laws had governed, it
was only 'as farre forth as the Clergie could make the Laitie subject
to them'.[3] Throughout the book Selden sledge-hammered this point:
the claims set forth by the old canonists had to be interpreted in the
light of the nature of the times.

If the canons expressed nothing more than the opinions current at
a particular time in the Church, they could obviously not be used as
proof of how tithes were in practice paid.[4] But having disposed of an

[1] Selden, *Tithes*, 460.

[2] See Selden, *Opera*, III, 103 ff. The passage should be read in full. It is
also cited by Arneke, *Kirchengeschichte und Rechtsgeschichte*, 268–9.

[3] Selden, *Tithes*, 489.

[4] B.M. Lansdowne MS. 173 contains a number of papers, some by
Selden, relating to liberty of the subject. Selden argued (f. 52b) that law

inferential error in the argument from precedents of canon law, Selden could not very well substitute another one, based on the common law myth of Custom and the Immemorial. He was obliged, therefore, to ground his argument on 'the historical understanding of documents'. When he referred to the 'immemorial customs and old ordinances that are against the Canons' he meant such customs or traditions of payment as could be verified on the basis of contemporary records.[1]

The error of those who insisted that all tithes were due by Mosaic law was that they either did not define their terms, or did not distinguish the practices of different ages. Tithes were paid by the laity to the priesthood of the Gospel, but by earlier custom tithes were paid by the laity to the Levites who in turn paid to the son of Aaron: 'But these considerations can only be where the knowledge of fact preceeds, for without exact Distinction of their seuerall Tithes, any argument drawn from them, may soon be found a grosse fallacie, that may both deceiue him which makes it and those whom he teaches.'[2] Comparison, in short, required exact definition and distinction of terms; and also it involved considerations of relevance.

ii RELEVANCE AND PROOF

In his 'Preface' Selden declared that he sought nothing but truth; he would not 'make or creat Premisses for a chosen Conclusion, that I rather would then could proue'.[3] He wanted to provide his readers with the grounds for a free judgment, but he realized that it was not enough merely to observe the proprieties of academic scholarship.[4] Accurate references and quotations verbatim did not insure sound historical conclusions. The problem of relevance was inseparable from the problem of proof. That Selden was thoroughly aware of this, his critics discovered to their chagrin when they attacked him on the ground that his *Historie* was written to disprove

---

is superior to precedent, which is nothing more than the interpretation of the law by judges. The idea that precedents represented nothing more than opinions was basic to Selden's historical argument.

[1] Selden, *Tithes*, 'Preface', v. Cf. *Opera*, III, 1150, and *Tithes*, 475. Of the Bible: 'The Text serves only to guess by; we must satisfy ourselves fully out of the Authors that lived about those times.' See *Table Talk*, *sub* 'Bible, Scripture', 7.

[2] Selden, *Tithes*, 456; see also 62–3 for Selden's views on the importance of accurate distinctions.

[3] *Ibid.*, 'Preface', xii.   [4] See *ibid.*, 196.

a divine right to tithes. In reply, Selden carefully pointed out that they misunderstood what he had and had not proved.

In order to substantiate his argument that tithes had been paid in all societies because of human positive laws Selden had to show (1) why the history of opinion was not relevant to the history of practice, and (2) that his documentary evidence for the history of practice outweighed negative objections.[1] He revealed his concern with the first point directly, in his attacks on all unsupported inferences from biblical or canon law precedents, and indirectly, in his purely secular explanations of why different tithing practices prevailed at different times in the Church. Moreover, especially in the 'Review', he tried to inform his readers why the practices of one age or nation did not necessarily have relevance to those of another.[2] In short, Selden exposed and condemned the *ignoratio elenchi* fallacy in its historical forms.

It was relatively easy to detect error, and criticize the logic of clergymen; it was much more difficult—and more important—to establish historical truth. Selden took his stand on the principle that history was not 'whatever had actually happened in the past', but rather what could be proved with evidence. In commenting on his failure to find any evidence for the payment of tithes in the Christian church until about A.D. 400, he wrote, 'I was not so bold to make the negatiue, that *no Tithes were paid*, but that *it could not be proued that any were*'.[3] The negative objection that some tithes might have been paid (or perhaps were paid) did not count against the evidence which he had presented, that oblations and other forms of maintenance of the clergy were not the same thing as tithes. Clearly, the various tests by which Selden established the meaning of statements found in documents, and the truth or falsehood of them, were of decisive importance in probating historical truth.

Selden thought that the old sceptics who would never profess that they had found a truth, 'shewed yet the best way to search for any'. He was firmly convinced, however, that the 'inmost Sanctuarie of Truth' could be reached by a good historian provided he had sufficient evidence and liberty of inquiry.[4]

[1] Cf. Selden, *Tithes*, 156–7. See also 260, and Chapter IX, *passim*, for examples.
[2] See *ibid.*, 460; cf. 'Preface', iii.
[3] *Ibid.*, 460 (Selden's italics).   [4] *Ibid.*, 'Preface', xiii.

iii COHERENCE AND SYNCHRONISM

Selden's basic methodological principles can be described accurately in terms of a coherence theory of historical truth. He was one of the first English historians to abandon completely scissors and paste methods; not authority, but internal coherence became the criterion for judging historical truth. Like most lawyers and historians (past and present), Selden was sure that there was a correspondence between his historical statements and a past reality, that his facts were not simply imaginative reconstructions. Or, to put it another way, Selden rejected the relativistic implications of the coherence theory.[1] Nevertheless, the tests which he applied to determine the meaning and significance of particular statements found in his sources indicate that he had grasped the essential point, that facts are conclusions reached only after a process of thought.

The opening sentences of the *Historie of Tithes* stated the problem: how was Holy Writ to be interpreted? Abraham, upon his return from redeeming Lot with his substance, and all the substance of Sodom and Gomorrah, was blessed by Melchizedeck, to whom he gave tithe of all—according to Holy Writ. 'But what that *all* was, is not clearly agreed vpon,' Selden observed.[2] He then proceeded to show what the passage must have meant by developing a coherent picture of the available philological evidence. Greek, Arabic, Hebrew, and Latin versions of the same passage were compared in order to arrive at the conclusion that Abraham had paid nothing more than customary tithes of the spoils of war. Other instances as well show that Selden interpreted obscure passages in his sources, and confidently rejected falsehoods on the basis of the internal coherence of his web of evidence.[3]

Most of Selden's arguments depended in one way or another on philological tests. It is true that he did not invent these, any more than he invented the test of coherence, which sanctions truth in all varieties of factual knowledge. The important point is that he was able to apply these tests methodically to the subject matter of history. The detection of medieval forgeries obviously called for something

[1] There is an excellent short discussion of the difference between the coherence and correspondence theories of historical truth in W. H. Walsh, *An Introduction to the Philosophy of History* (London, 1951), Chapter IV.

[2] Selden, *Tithes*, 1.

[3] See, for a good example, *ibid.*, 29.

291

more than mere conjectures about the credibility of monkish tales. Selden noted that the legends of Popes and others were often stuffed with falsehoods, 'as being bred in the middle ages among idle Monks', but he did not reject them for this reason. Instead, he argued that the evidence presented, for example, by Cardinal Baronius, purporting to show that Pope Damasus had, in about 380, published decrees concerning tithes, was supposititious. It could not be made to fit with a coherent picture of those times, based on the analysis of other evidence.[1]

Selden used the word 'synchronism' to mean simple chronological coherence—the test of sequence or continuity. To examine a document 'by storie and Synchronisme' was to find out first how it fitted the historical context in which it was supposedly written, and second to discover whether or not it was chronologically possible for the events described to have taken place at the stated time.[2] Narrowly defined, synchronism was little more than a self-evident proposition: historical events or personages must be grouped together according to their dates. King Kenulph of West Saxony cannot be attending a certain synod because he is dead—therefore the document asserting that Kenulph was at the synod must be suspect. In a broader sense, however, synchronism might be said to describe the whole range of chronological tests based on knowledge of palaeography and diplomatics (the words were of course not yet in current use), by which Selden distinguished historical truth from falsehood and error. Exact chronology supported—indeed, made possible—exact history. The facts of time, place, and circumstance had to agree with one another; if they did not, explanations were called for. History was thus a succession of problems in the interpretation of evidence.

History had, for this very reason, implications for divinity and other fields of knowledge. The farther the historian extended his jurisdiction over matters of fact, the more he encroached on the traditional beliefs of churchmen, statesmen, and all others who were concerned, directly or indirectly, with matters of fact as opposed to relations of ideas. Selden maintained that he had written a mere

---

[1] Selden, *Tithes*, 43–5. See also 159–60, 197, 463. It is not my contention that *all* of Selden's arguments can be explained in terms of a coherence theory. Selden rejected miracles largely on the basis of improbability. See *ibid.*, 273, 456. Most of Selden's conjectures, however, were based on philological principles, not on apparent probability.

[2] *Ibid.*, 202; see 200–3, *passim*, on Kenulph.

narration and was in no way responsible for the sacrilegious uses to which his facts might be put.[1] Yet the real problem was not so simple: what ethical or political decision did not depend ultimately on knowledge of tradition? and who but the historian could define the purpose, meaning, and significance of the various historical documents which recorded these traditions? The opinions and practices of one age differed from those of another, as Selden demonstrated; and to infer practice from opinion was as gross and ridiculous as to make abstract right the test of fact. 'The Clergy', he observed in private, 'would have us believe them against our own Reason, as the Woman would have had her Husband Against his own Eyes: What! will you believe your own Eyes before your own sweet Wife?'[2]

The 'inferences and arguments' which were brought against Selden's 'express testimonies of history' were more revealing than anyone realized at the time.[3] Selden had probed to the quick: to proportion one's belief to the evidence was to doubt most if not all of the clerical arguments in favour of a historical divine right to tithes. Selden had certainly not written against the maintenance of the clergy, nor against divine right theory as such; he had, however, shown that the historical precedents for such a theory were either false or irrelevant.

The storm over the *Historie of Tithes* proved to be no minor disturbance: it brought to the surface all kinds of submerged problems of bias, inference, and relevance. Selden's scholarship revealed problems which have been of concern to historians and philosophers to the present day. In the seventeenth century, the controversy was important for another reason as well; the disparity between historical reason and historical faith was openly revealed for the first time.[4]

The book which best summed up the clerical objections to Selden's *Historie* was Richard Mountague's *Diatribae Upon the First Part of*

[1] See Selden, 'To the Reader of Sir James Sempil's Appendix', *Opera*, III, 1349–64; 'Of my Purpose and End in Writing the History of Tythes', *Opera*, III, 1451–8; 'To The Reader of Dr. Tillesley's Animadversions', *Opera*, III, 1369–86.

[2] Selden, *Table Talk, sub* 'Clergy', 33.

[3] Selden, 'Purpose and End', *Opera*, III, 1452.

[4] The problem of reason and faith will be discussed in the following chapter. The main issue was simply to what extent historical reasons supported the 'truths' of revelation. The phrase 'historical faith', as here used, does not imply that faith was necessarily dependent on such historical

the Late History of Tithes (1621). 'The cause is of importance,'
Mountague wrote, 'for which you [Selden] are suspected: God's
right, *Melchizedeck's* portion, the Patrimony and inheritance of
the Church.' [1] Selden, being a man who had searched out what few
had ever heard of, had the power to do great mischief, especially
by stirring up the ignorant and unlearned. According to Mountague,
he was a vicious hypocrite who, like the water men on the Thames,
would 'looke one way and row another'.[2] Selden's protestations
of innocence were not to be believed: 'Protest what you list upon
some after-claps, which peradventure you looked not for: no man
will beleeve your protestations, having read your *History* with
consideration . . .' [3]

Mountague struck immediately at the weak point in Selden's
line of defence. On the one hand Selden had claimed that his *Historie*
was a mere narration and nothing else; on the other, he had asserted
that antiquity was related in it to give other light to the practice
and doubts of the present. According to Mountague's relativistic
interpretation of these statements, Selden could not be an impartial
historian since he admitted that he wrote with an ulterior, even
utilitarian purpose.[4] Mountague took every opportunity to discredit
Selden's *Historie* by discrediting his motives, but he realized that this
tactic was by no means sufficient. He therefore tried to show, first,
that the logical implications of Selden's premises were subversive of
God's law, and second, that Selden's facts were inaccurate.

The crucial issue was whether or not Selden was justified in separating history from ethics and divinity. Mountague stressed the consequences of Selden's historical argument:

> . . . either you must disavow the *Ius Divinum*, or, as your selfe con-
> fesse, set that, and *Ius Positivum* together by the eares: viz. That
> *The Lawes and practice both of this Kingdome, and all Christen-*
> *dome, are against God's Law.* Avoyd the sequell, and then make
> your selfe master of your owne Words, if you can. I wonder, a man

proofs, but merely that the main tenets of the Christian faith were known
by tradition. Christianity was a historical religion in that Christ the Son of
God had directly intervened in the historical process.

[1] Richard Mountague, *Diatribae Upon The First Part of the Late History
of Tithes* (London, 1621), 6. I have changed the original punctuation to a
full colon. See also pp. 3–7, *passim.*

[2] Mountague, *Diatribae*, 13; cf. 13–15, *passim.*

[3] *Ibid.*, 15.   [4] *Ibid.*, 16–17.

that thus writeth can so protest, as you do, against maine and indeniable consequences; in and from his writings as you *have shewed*, by your owne confession, the one; therefore you have determined, by your owne supposition, the other.[1]

This was rhetorically excellent, but it of course did not meet the objection that, on historical grounds, facts were facts—whether subversive of God's law or not. Hence, Mountague had to proceed to a criticism of Selden's testimony. And here Mountague revealed himself for what he was—a clever, unscrupulous and somewhat fearful clergyman, who respected authority more than he respected facts.[2]

Early in the *Diatribae* Mountague betrayed his fear of Selden by alleging that if the clergy had set out to write history instead of divinity, then Selden would never have dared to publish a history of tithes.[3] This was but one example of the way in which Mountague tried to keep his general offensive from stalling before Selden's fortified positions—it mattered not how ridiculous an argument was as long as it served as propaganda to disparage Selden's scholarship. Mountague's attack on the factual accuracy of the *Historie of Tithes* failed; and there is no need to recount the wordy details of that failure.[4] His diatribes were seldom effective against Selden's proofs. When grammar or philology seemed to support Mountague, he was for grammar and philology; when they did not he dismissed them as irrelevant. Appealing to the authority of scripture, antiquity, and the Church, Mountague failed to answer the historian's question: how do you know you are right?[5]

By limiting historical research to questions that were empirically verifiable Selden forced every one of his opponents to accept the historical challenge: justification by the evidence. As he informed

---

[1] *Ibid.*, 80. See also 119: 'And may it not be answered here to purpose, *Thus you have made the Law of God of no force by your own traditions*?'

[2] Mountague wrote the following: 'Nor can you [Selden] give condigne Satisfaction to God and his Church, so much by you wronged, though you plucke out your eyes, split your tongue in pieces, lop off that right hand which put pen to paper to doe us wrong . . .' *ibid.*, 20.

[3] *Ibid.*, 33–4.

[4] See, for example, *ibid.*, 24–5, 73, 117 ff., where Mountague attempts to discredit Selden's authorities, Budé, Scaliger, etc.; 123 ff., where Mountague attacks Selden's humane learning; and cf. 137–8.

[5] See *ibid.*, 181, 217, 320–41, 497 ff. Cf. Selden, *Table Talk*, *sub* 'Bible' and 'Preaching'.

another opponent, Sir James Sempil, 'My *title* is *history* only, so are all the three parts of it, so is every line of the whole. Now to offer to disprove any thing in my *history* must be either by shewing that I have *false quotations*, or that I *falsely* relate the *words*, or *sense*, of my authors, or that I have omitted *testimonies* for other sides, that are of better credit.'[1] In the course of the seventeenth century this idea was to win general acceptance among the intellectual leaders of the nation.

Viewed from a greater distance of time, and against a broader intellectual background, the whole controversy over the *Historie of Tithes* appears to turn on disagreements about the relevance of history to divinity. Selden did not lack defenders in the Church, nor among the most devout of the laity. William Sclater, in *The Quaestion of Tithes Revised* (1623), wrote that he could find nothing in Selden to justify the Seldenists, who inferred a right to commit sacrilege from mere previous fact.[2] A far greater scholar, Sir Henry Spelman, approved of Selden as an authority for history, although he himself believed in a divine right to tithes, and even wrote *De Non Temerandis Ecclesias* to prove that sacrilegious impropriations had always been followed by divine retribution.[3] Clearly, these men accepted Selden's distinction between historical fact and abstract divine right, yet they also believed that history was somehow relevant to religion. The question was how? and to this question there was no easy answer.

Spelman, like most seventeenth-century historians, took comfort in a providential interpretation of history. But providence was a value, not a fact; and its relevance to history was entirely a matter of faith, which could neither be proved nor disproved. Indirectly, the tithes controversy opened up the whole question of the place of values in a world of facts. Christianity was above all a historical religion based on tradition. Was divinity then nothing but history

---

[1] Selden, *Opera*, III, 1350.

[2] William Sclater, *The Quaestion of Tithes Revised* (London, 1623), 197–226 *passim*.

[3] See *The English Works of Sir Henry Spelman, Published in his Life-Time; Together with his Posthumous Works*, ed. by Edmund, Lord Bishop of London, 2nd ed. (London, 1727), especially the 'Larger Work of Tythes', 121; and cf. the comments of Clement Spelman (Sir Henry's grandson) in his Preface to 'De Non Temerandis', xi.

dully taken up?[1] Could any of the 'truths' of revelation or of moral philosophy be verified by the methods of history? Everything depended on what principles and what evidence one was prepared to accept as relevant. As Selden said: 'When a Protestant and a Papist dispute, they talk like two Madmen, because they do not agree upon their Principles.' [2] Unless historians and divines agreed upon their principles, including their principles of relevance and of proof, there would be no end to their disputes.

The progressive secularization of learning was one of the unforeseen consequences of the historical and scientific revolutions of the seventeenth century. The significance of the historical revolution will be considered in the final chapter; here, all that need be said is that Selden contributed to a new understanding of, and respect for, history as an autonomous and scientific method of inquiry. History was to become scientific in its own way, however, and it should be obvious that Selden could not have written 'scientific' history if he had not been a master of humanistic culture. He made mistakes—sometimes very surprising and avoidable mistakes—which distorted parts of his interpretation of legal history. Moreover, his pioneering works, including *Ad Fletam, Titles of Honour*, and the *Historie of Tithes*, made demands even on the learned reader; and a harsh style did not simplify difficult subject matter. Yet these books can still instruct the understanding; the main outlines of Selden's historical interpretations remain valid. Modern scholarship has been revisionist only in details.[3]

Selden was sometimes deceived by 'the fountains', and mistook false texts for original sources. If Bacon was victimized by his philosophy, Selden was victimized, in ways far more subtle, by his historical techniques.[4] He agreed with Bacon, however, in thinking that little history worthy of the name had been written in England

---

[1] See Selden, *Table Talk*, *sub* 'Learning', 85: 'Most Men's Learning is nothing but History dully taken up. If I quote *Thomas Aquinas* for some tenet, and believe it, because the School-Men say so, that is but History. Few men make themselves Masters of the things they write or speak.' I have corrected the text of Singer, who writes 'duly taken up . . .', on the basis of Pollock's edition.

[2] Selden, *Table Talk*, *sub* 'Pope', 117–18.

[3] Cf. David Ogg, *Ad Fletam*, 'Introduction', xxvi–xxviii and lxv–lxvi.

[4] See Arnecke, *Kirchengeschichte und Rechtsgeschichte*, 276–84; Berkowitz, 'Young Mr. Selden', (unpublished Ph.D., Harvard), IV, 56; cf. 'De Laudibus', *Opera*, III, 1890.

before his time. He had no use for the '*Postils, Polyantheas*, common place books or any of the rest of such excellent Instruments for the aduancement of Ignorance and Lazinesse'.[1] The proper study of history was use: the actual traditions and practices which had governed social relations in the past. Knowledge of history provided the basis for an accurate appraisal of present problems. The true historian was not interested in providing parables of virtue and vice for Everyman.

Selden's ideal judicious reader would have recognized the folly of trying to reduce his methods to a set of rules and precepts. The skill, knowledge and self-discipline of the professional scholar could not be epitomized; understanding history was the work of a lifetime. Selden could state the general principles of sound scholarship clearly enough: 'Ay, or no, never answered any Question,' and, equally, 'The Reason of a Thing is not to be enquired after, till you are sure the Thing itself be so.' [2] But such observations were, he thought, most appropriate in table talk.

[1] Selden, *Tithes*, 'Preface', ii.
[2] Selden, *Table Talk*, *sub* 'Question', and 'Reason', 138-9.

12

THE HISTORICAL REVOLUTION: CONCLUSIONS AND CONJECTURES

IN MEDIEVAL EUROPE, as in other traditional societies, short-term changes occurred rapidly, violently, and unpredictably. Fire, famine, pestilence, or war might destroy in one locality with the suddenness of a judgment of God, while in another all remained peaceful. The uncertainties of life in the world were accepted as natural; the rituals of the Church gave meaning to the accidents of nature or of history. No one supposed that the present differed radically from the past; mutability in the realm of nature resolved itself into cycles, and God's providence determined the fall of empires no less than the yield of the earth. Medieval historiography reflected the fact that chronological change did not necessarily imply fundamental historical change.

The transition from traditional to modern industrial society was everywhere accompanied by a new secular idea of progress, which was both a symptom and a cause of change. As long as life remained relatively static, history appeared to repeat itself; progress, however, implied an awareness of process in history, and a determination not to repeat the errors of the past. The gradual acceptance of an ideal of progressive change, based on the conquest of nature, marks a decisive turning point in the history of modern states.[1]

[1] On the distinction between 'traditional' and modern industrial societies, see especially W. W. Rostow, *The Stages of Economic Growth* (Cambridge, 1960), Chapters I–III. H. Butterfield, *The Origins of Modern Science 1300–1800* (London, 1951), 171, calls attention to the connection between an essentially static economy and a correspondingly static view

That the seventeenth century was the critical period of transition in England, France, and Holland would not be disputed by most modern historians. During the lifetime of Sir Isaac Newton (1642–1727) the intellectual revolution which orients the modern world attained decisive power. The history of that intellectual revolution has yet to be written; its causes stretch back farther than the Renaissance; its effects will be felt everywhere tomorrow.[1] The historical revolution was a part of the whole revolutionary transition of the seventeenth century.

The nature of the historical revolution in England, and its significant dates, emerge as conclusions from the evidence presented in earlier chapters. Why and how history was new-modelled, and with what results, can only be related conjecturally, in the hope that further research will resolve the problems raised by interpretation. 'In conjectures I durst not be too bold,' Selden once observed, '. . . but when they seem to offer themselves, they deserve the choice of judgment.'[2] The conjectures presented immediately after the review of conclusions are not mere fancies; they direct attention to significant problems. How well they deserve the choice of judgment the reader must decide for himself.

The historical revolution denotes a whole complex of changes in the purpose, content, method, and style of historical writing in the period between about 1580 and 1660. While there is no doubt that the Reformation stimulated all kinds of historical inquiry (much of it based on previous Renaissance scholarship), the significant changes in English historiography did not occur until the 1580's, when more adequate facilities for research became available, and the antiquaries began to question their medieval authorities. The contrast between John Leland and William Camden expressed much more than a difference of some forty years in their ages. Leland, for all his learning, was medieval; Camden, in spite of what he owed to Leland, was modern. The style and method of the *Britannia* (1586) were original, serviceable, and characteristic of the new scholarship.[3]

of history. This book is extremely useful to the lay student of the history of science.

[1] See A. C. Crombie, *Augustine to Galileo, The History of Science A.D. 400–1650* (Cambridge, Mass., 1953), 276–7, and Chapter VI, *passim*.

[2] John Selden, *Opera Omnia*, III, 96.

[3] See T. Kendrick, *British Antiquity*, Chapters IV and VIII, *passim*, especially p. 150.

In the decades after 1660 English scholars were reputed among the best in Europe. The output of historical works more than kept pace with the general increase in the publication of books; libraries grew rapidly in size, and the institutional arrangements of scholarship took on a recognizably modern form. By 1707, when the modern Society of Antiquaries was founded, the outcome of the historical revolution was beyond dispute: massive works of erudition were available; major historical generalizations about the nature of feudalism had been formulated; sound methodological principles had been elaborated and put to use. The publication of Clarendon's *History of the Rebellion and Civil Wars in England* left no doubt that modern history had become a part of modern literature.

All this, however, points to the fact that the critical period of transition occurred some time before the end of the century. Exact dates are, of course, no more than convenient parentheses to enclose periods in intellectual history. Obviously, the English Rebellion acted as a stimulus to historical inquiry—as the Reformation had in the preceding century. Yet no great cluster of English historical scholars appeared immediately after the Reformation. It was not until Camden, Spelman, Stow, Cotton, and their contemporaries began to study history—roughly a generation after the Reformation —that we can discern significant qualitative and quantitative changes in the English historical tradition. After 1660 there was nothing like a reorientation of historical scholarship, partly because there was no longer any need for a thorough reform of the theory and practice of historiography. Continuity was far more significant than change.

The historical revolution may be defined briefly, provided that important qualifications are kept in mind. The persistence of medieval ideas, attitudes, and methods was apparent throughout the seventeenth century, and beyond. Secularism was seldom truly atheistical (charges of 'atheism' were common enough, but were seldom substantiated); and few scholars were openly hostile to a providential theory of history. Religion played a part—often a decisive part—in directing historical inquiry. The established Church, the Universities, and the Inns of Court encouraged the study of history and related subjects, for the most part, by unofficial means. Class distinctions were recognized by contemporaries, but English society was not divided by the shibboleths that have sometimes characterized modern historical and sociological controversy. No formula satisfactorily expresses the relationship between Calvinism, capitalism, and middle-class culture; this, however, does not excuse the historian from the duty of interpretation.[1]

The variety of purposes that history served increased as the reading public grew in size and influence. The middle-class passion for utilitarian knowledge was nothing new, but in the sixteenth century the ideal of high utility came to have more and more power to sanction change. While the chroniclers continued to stress the moral lessons of history, the apologists of church and state were busy developing the techniques of problematic history. Common lawyers, churchmen, government officials, and Parliament-men all studied the past in order to judge the policies and problems of the present. The rise of problematic history brought about a lessening of respect for the mere voice of authority, especially as the records of tradition were exposed to critical scrutiny. Bacon, Hakewill, and other writers began to question the doctrine of the world's decay and degeneration. An idea of progress began gradually to make its way into historical thought.

The proliferation of new types of history was the most obvious characteristic of the historical revolution. The growing secularism of the age inevitably found expression in the content of history books. Equally, religious warfare was extended into the realms of history; and both the Church and the state took an interest in historical polemics. From the dialectic of controversy came the impetus to collect quantities of information, especially transcripts from the public records. And the founding of Sir Robert Cotton's great library was a pledge for the future of the whole antiquarian movement.

The content of legal and constitutional history was greatly enriched as a result of continuing research into the origins of disputed political authority. Bacon advocated a universal history of learning and the arts, and although no such history was written in the seventeenth century, much preliminary work was done. Territorial history, extending knowledge of lands beyond the British Isles, reflected the growing cosmopolitanism of the Jacobean age: the folklore and customs of primitive peoples proved fascinating, and

[1] The most recent contribution to the problem of definition is Sidney A. Burrell, 'Calvinism, Capitalism and the Middle Classes: Some Afterthoughts on an Old Problem', *Journal of Modern History* (XXXII, June 1960), 129–41.

foreign histories in translation found interested readers. Scholars like Spelman, Ussher, and Selden helped to establish a sound tradition of comparative history. Heraldry and genealogy had stimulated interest in local history. By 1660 English local historians had no reason to complain of any lack of native models worthy of imitation.

The revolution in historical method had, of course, to await the fulfilment of certain conditions. First, studies in philology had to be far enough advanced to serve as tools for historical research. The break-through in knowledge of Anglo-Saxon, which occurred in the mid-sixteenth century, opened the way to far-reaching reinterpretations of English history. Until the meaning and authenticity of ancient documents could be established with some degree of assurance, historians could not develop higher standards of evidence and proof. Philology was therefore essential to sound scholarship; in every field of history this came to be recognized.

The existence of adequate facilities for research, as well as better means of access to the public records, was the second precondition for sustained advances in historical method. International scholarly communication was a third; seventeenth-century English historians had much to learn, especially from the French legal humanists. Finally, it was essential that the best antiquaries and historians should begin to recognize the importance of a theory of historical process.[1]

As historians developed more adequate tests for dating their sources they began to see that the total historical context was important, and to realize that fact and opinion were often at odds. It took a long time, however, for most of them to realize that their basic assumptions might be faulty, that the remote past might have few continuants into the present, and that the problem of relevance was therefore crucial. Persistent disagreements about relevance marked the literature of controversy.

Original thinking had more to do with the revolution in historiography than the discovery of new facts. The ability to ask the right questions, to make new relevant connections, and to provide ideas which would illuminate some of the dark tracts of time, was as rare in the seventeenth century as it is today. Each of the five historians discussed in the preceding chapters was representative of a trend in English historiography; and each had something to say that was

---

[1] In science a theory of impetus was of comparable though even greater importance. See Butterfield, *Origins of Modern Science*, Chapter I.

original. From the point of view of method alone, however, the significant advances were being made by the historians who sought 'the fountains', who set limits on the use of conjecture in history, and who insisted that verifiability was the test of truth.

New ideas of historical explanation never came as sudden revelations to ignorant men. A great deal of study and experience was required to produce a new interpretation. The best English historians were all in debt to Classical and Renaissance writers for help in understanding the past. English historiography was also profoundly influenced by ideas drawn from other fields of knowledge. The economic theory of mercantilism provided new historical insights; and if the common law myth of Custom and the Immemorial proved to be an obstacle to understanding, at least the common lawyers' devotion to research provided a corrective.

Changes in the purpose, content, and method of written history inevitably brought about changes in style. The ordering of evidence in terms of ideas called for more flexible forms of organization than the old annals and chronicles could provide. Valid historical generalizations could be made only by historians who compared events, not by those who were content merely to place them in a chronological sequence. Meaningful periodization in history was very slowly achieved, however, for this demanded that historians be able to explain how and why successive ages differed from one another. From the Greek and Latin historians of antiquity, English historians learned how to organize their narratives; and as imitation gave way to originality, the splendid series of historical characters of the seventeenth century began to appear.

English prose style acquired many of its modern characteristics during the Elizabethan Renaissance. Bacon's language was clear, precise, and expressive—admirably suited to the needs of a new scientific age. Changes in style were closely related to changes in content, and, less closely, to changes in the social and economic environment. It was not until after the Restoration that 'mathematical plainness' became a literary virtue, but long before this the ideals of middle-class culture had penetrated former strongholds of the aristocratic tradition in literature. The baroque magnificence of Ralegh's prose was appropriate to a work that discovered the meaning of history in a continuing act of faith. Ralegh conveyed a sense of the poetry of history better than any of his contemporaries, but even he could not sustain the grand manner throughout. As the century wore on, the working prose of historians approached closer and closer to the norm of rational simplicity, or in a word, utility.

English historiography benefited immeasurably from the fact that great literary artists from Shakespeare to Dryden dealt with the themes and passions of political power. The state, as the arena of power, was the setting for high tragedy, in which the protagonists acted out historical reality. Political odes and satires, characters, lampoons, pamphlets, and news letters also contributed something to the Englishman's awareness of history. If the scholarly tradition in historiography failed to maintain contact with the literary tradition, it was not because scholars lacked imagination. Rather, it was because there were increasingly difficult, technical problems to be solved, and scholars were turning more and more toward specialized research.[1]

The historical revolution, unlike the scientific, resulted in no great Newtonian synthesis. It was obvious enough to contemporaries that there were profound differences between natural science and history, but it was also true that scholars had learned only too well a hard lesson of scientific method—not to frame general hypotheses on the basis of unverified facts.

Revolutions in thought proceed no more evenly or peacefully than economic or political revolutions. The old order survives, to a greater or lesser extent, along with the new. Only in retrospect is it possible to recognize overall patterns of development, and to correlate significant happenings in one area with those in another. The socio-economic conditions which made possible a general advancement of learning in the sixteenth and seventeenth centuries cannot be dealt with apart from the intellectual and scientific advances themselves. The historical revolution was analogous to the scientific revolution in that both were influenced, directly and indirectly, by what was taking place in other sectors of learning, and by changes in the fundamental structure of society.

The eighty years preceding the Restoration were crucial for the future development of an industrial civilization in England. This is not to say that the conditions for a 'take-off' into self-sustained economic growth were achieved in England at this time. It does mean,

[1] There is an excellent brief discussion of the literary conventions of the seventeenth century in G. N. Clark, *The Seventeenth Century* (Oxford, 1929), Chapter XIX.

however, that a more or less marginal, static, and therefore vulnerable, economic society was rapidly being transformed into one which created within itself the dynamics of change. The fact that this economic revolution coincided with the historical revolution, and with equally significant developments in literature, philosophy, religion, politics, and science suggests the futility of trying to isolate individual causes from the total historical situation. The influence of historical writing and thought on other fields of knowledge took place in a cultural context that was favourable to analogous and reciprocal influences. Before we can go ahead to examine the influence of history on other fields, we must briefly describe some of the features of the cultural context itself, as it developed in the course of the sixteenth and seventeenth centuries.

The overall patterns of intellectual development in which the idea of history figured prominently were: (1) the attack on authority; (2) the appeal to experience; (3) the rationalization of utility; and (4) the extension of the quantative method. Such terms as these are not important in themselves; they mark—like arrows on a map—some of the main routes of intellectual advance. What matters in each case is the actual movement of ideas along each of these broad routes.

The attack on authority took many forms in the sixteenth and seventeenth centuries. In religion it was directed against the authority of the Roman pontiff; in philosophy, against the authority of Aristotle and the scholastics; in science, against the authority of traditional metaphysics, which had created a closed hierarchical world, logically ordered, but scaled more to human values than to observed facts. The destruction of the medieval cosmos was the most immediate and alarming consequence of the scientific revolution. An infinite universe, characterized not by the striving of its elements toward perfection, but rather by mathematical laws of motion, was the creation of the New Philosophy. It quite literally called all in doubt—all considerations of meaning, purpose, and harmony, all authority for the view that the world of facts and the world of values were one.[1]

---

[1] No attempt can be made to provide even a brief list of books dealing with these questions. Alexander Koryé, *From the Closed World to the Infinite Universe* (New York, Harper Torchbook ed., 1958), proved particularly illuminating. See also Herschel Baker, *The Wars of Truth*, 235, and *passim*. Cf. Strathmann, *Sir Walter Ralegh*, 240-1.

The scientific revolution had reached all forms of culture by the beginning of the seventeenth century. Religion, philosophy, art, and history were forced to take account of the fact that the earth was no longer the unmoving centre around which revolved the spheres of heaven. Instead of being confident of his place in a unified scheme of things, thinking man became an observer, desperately trying to invent new theories which would 'save the appearances'. It was only natural that scepticism, subjectivism, and relativism should come to have new significance—the concepts and methods of natural science were subversive of all kinds of traditional beliefs. Pascal summed it up in a sentence: 'The eternal silence of these infinite spaces frightens me.' [1]

The failure of Protestantism to establish any clear authority for the interpretation of Scripture contributed to the sense of confusion. Truth could not rest on authority; reason was an inadequate test of revelation. But the extreme doctrine—that intensity of belief was a guarantee of truth—finally discredited itself. Only by segregating natural truth from supernatural truth could men make the best of both worlds—the religious world of the spirit, and the secular world of money-making, science, and politics.[2] Bacon advocated segregation in the interests of a scientific naturalism; Calvin in the interests of dogmatic theology—each in his own way may be said to have rationalized the principle of utility.

The historical attack on authority was scarcely less devastating than the scientific. The tithes controversy revealed how ominous were the implications of secular history for divinity; questions of fact were subject to historical determination; questions of divine right were (to put it bluntly) subject to arbitrary determination by ecclesiastical authority. However, since all questions of right emerged from the facts of particular historical situations, and since the Church, by its very nature, stood on historical foundations, it was evident that history could not be completely segregated from divinity. As long as history was a relatively undeveloped discipline, with its own weakness for authority, it presented no problems. When it became, in the course of the seventeenth century, independent and fully capable of proving cases against authority, it was no longer the submissive servant of faith.

The attack on authority in science nearly always involved an appeal to experience. New hypotheses had to be tested in one way or

[1] Pascal, *Pensees* (Modern Library), no. 206, p. 75.
[2] See Baker, *Wars of Truth*, 205–6, and 156–62, 167–9.

307

another against the evidence of the senses; the experimental method was grounded in the idea of verifiability. New observations were less important, at first, than new ways of putting old questions. What mattered was not so much a willingness to experiment—the alchemists had done little else—but constructive ideas of what experiments to make. The ordering of experience, and the factual verification of the intellectual order, were essential components of scientific method in every field. In the course of a very different intellectual development, the new history arrived at methodological conclusions which were remarkably similar to those of the new science.

In most branches of humane learning the appeal to experience took the form of an appeal to historical knowledge—that is, to the verified facts of human experience, as opposed to the values and beliefs inherited from the past. Evidence, comparison, and verification were the reference points for the appeal to experience. In philosophy, theology, and law historical knowledge was profoundly important in shaping new ideas.

Human values, however, were not subject to verification in the same way that matters of fact were. Hence, continuing appeals were made to Reason or to Revelation, but in the course of the seventeenth century both Reason and Revelation tended to acquire historical connotations. The apparent triumph of Reason in eighteenth-century thought can easily be misunderstood unless one realizes the extent to which Reason had already been redefined so as to include knowledge derived not from the internal operations of the mind but from history.

Perhaps the clearest definition of Reason as a kind of history was given by Jeremy Taylor, who maintained that one of the three kinds of Reason was *pistis*, 'that is, such things which the understanding assents to upon the report, testimony and affirmation of others, viz., by arguments, extrinsecal [*sic*] to the nature of the thing, and by collateral and indirect principles'.[1] Locke was to use a similar definition of Reason when he attempted to redraw the boundary between Reason and Faith. Locke's argument will be considered later; here, it is only necessary to observe that empiricism resting on historical fact became a distinctive feature of British philosophy. And, broadly speaking, both the rationalists and the empiricists made good use of historical facts and historical generalizations.

[1] Quoted by Baker, *Wars of Truth*, 234. See also S. L. Bethell, *The Cultural Revolution of the Seventeenth Century* (New York, 1951), 57–68.

As early as 1660, when Jeremy Taylor dedicated his *Ductor Dubitantium* to Charles II, he had moved far in the direction of denying natural law or indeed any universally recognized moral principles. He argued that Ulpian's maxim—*Jus Naturale est quod natura omnia animalia docuit*—was contradicted by the observed facts of history, as the researches of 'this last age' had shown.[1] This was only one example, albeit an important one, of the way in which historical research tended to become a solvent of traditional beliefs.

The rationalization of utility began at an early date and took many forms. The praise of useful learning went along with the actual production of utilitarian goods for a wider market. As Professor Nef has pointed out, 'By the mid-seventeenth century, partly as a result of the growing use of cast and pig iron and coal, England had obtained a lead over all other countries in the production of common commodities, in which quantity and utility rather than quality and elegance were the main concern of the makers and consumers.'[2] Between 1570 and 1660 England became a major producing area for such goods; and English writers tended more and more to rationalize new beliefs and new experiments in science and society on utilitarian grounds. Continuing material progress depended to a large extent on this favourable intellectual environment.

The protestant segregation of nature and grace, like the Baconian segregation of secular and religious knowledge, served the utilitarian purpose of minimizing social strife. The flow of English philanthropy into more secular channels was indicative of the many changes in thought and feeling which helped to bring about an industrial revolution in England during the late sixteenth century. The moderate Anglicanism of Hooker appealed to nearly everyone who respected reason, learning, and tradition, but the pragmatic strain in Hooker's argument was significant: civil and ecclesiastical laws were to be formulated by rational men, who would take into consideration history and the needs of the time.[3] The more radical Puritans of the seventeenth century were biased toward an act of faith that was beyond or contrary to Reason and evidence, but even they were

---

[1] Quoted by Baker, *Wars of Truth*, 236.

[2] John U. Nef, *Cultural Foundations of Industrial Civilization* (Cambridge, 1958), 53. The controversy raised by Professor Nef's interpretation of the industrial revolution in this period does not, in my opinion, invalidate this point. However, it should be realized that the argument here is conjectural.

[3] See Baker, *Wars of Truth*, 199.

forced to extend the limits of secular liberty, if only to protect them-selves: to save religion Roger Williams secularized politics. The growth of the ideal of toleration, in response to political necessities in seventeenth-century England, was itself favourable to the progress of science, scholarship, and economic enterprise.

The rationalization of utility was seldom a deliberate, self-conscious act, yet it is remarkable how well suited to the needs of the time was the tenor of thought of the intellectuals. It has been said that changes of feeling were the subtle basis for the scientific revolution, and that our modern industrial civilization was built up on cultural founda-tions.[1] Certainly the early industrial revolution had much in common with the intellectual revolution; and both were closely related to the contemporary revolution in science. What was perhaps most signi-ficant was the extension of the quantitative method of reasoning—and the commitment, on the part of the scientists, to quantitative values, to the principle of verifiability, and to mathematical language.

The precise observation of nature in Renaissance art was part of the pre-scientific interest in the identification of organic form. Scientific biology, which scarcely began before the seventeenth century, owed much to the artists, who were the first to observe and record with precision the world of natural forms.[2] From the point of view of the modern intellectual historian, science and art were parts of a single creative activity. Although art and biology and history relied less on quantitative and mathematical methods than did the physical sciences, it is nevertheless clear that the quantitative approach to problems was dependent to a high degree on precision of observation.[3] Allowing for obvious differences between the various fields of thought, we may without impropriety speak of advances in precision, and even of an extension of the quantitative method.

The quantitative methods of science did not necessarily have any-thing to do with the mere quantity of available data—quantification, in the strict scientific sense, was a purely methodological procedure, implying mathematical measurement. The methods of the historian were not quantitative in this scientific sense, but historical research in a wide variety of original sources did call for new techniques and

[1] See Butterfield, *Origins of Modern Science*, 104; and Nef, *Cultural Foundations*, 64 and *passim*.
[2] See Arthur David Ritchie, *Studies in the History and Methods of the Sciences* (Edinburgh, 1958), 128.
[3] Crombie, *Augustine to Galileo*, 368 and 274–380, *passim*.

skills, and for more readily available collections of documents and books. It may be said that quantitative methods were applied to the study of history in so far as historians deliberately sought to investigate in quantity the original records as well as the literary remains of the past. If this distinction is borne in mind, misunderstanding should not result from the ambiguity of the adjective 'quantitative'. To weigh, measure, and compare were scientific activities, yet the reasoning of the scientist about his evidence was not radically different from the reasoning of the scholar about his—both had to discover what was relevant amid the quantities of particular facts.

In the second half of the sixteenth century, advances in precision were made in almost all fields. The invention of new instruments (the telescope and microscope first appeared in Europe during the 1580's) only accelerated the rate of scientific advance. The exact measurement of time and place became increasingly important: the reform of the Julian calendar, and the new cartography were indicative of the European concern with exact quantitative measurement. A similar striving for quantitative accuracy may be discerned in many other fields. It was at this time that some of the first efforts were made to produce and use statistics.[1] But far more important—at least for the development of historiography—was the quantitative expansion of libraries, and the new emphasis on original research.

It was the lawyers and historians, including the antiquaries, who made the necessary first steps toward a science of finding out if information can be relied on. The methods of evidence and proof elaborated by the legal and historical scholars of the seventeenth century provided a sound technical basis for the emerging social sciences. And it has recently been suggested that even physical science owed something to this broad historiographical tradition.[2]

The remainder of this chapter will be devoted to exploring the ways in which history and historical thought influenced other fields of knowledge: religion, philosophy, science (including social science), literature, and law. Most of these influences are conjectural in the sense that the evidence for them is incomplete, and no attempt has been made to give detailed explanations. Nevertheless, there can be no doubt about the growing importance of historical attitudes in the

[1] See Nef, *Cultural Foundations*, 6–17. Medieval administrative officials had sometimes compiled statistical information and this precedent may have been important.

[2] Ritchie, *History and Methods of Sciences*, 172.

climate of opinion. The impact of science on the modern world has provided the theme for many excellent books, ranging from monographs on Augustan poetry to surveys of the European Enlightenment. How the idea of history shaped the thoughts and attitudes of modern generations has until recently been a curiously neglected subject.[1] There is a clear need for more detailed studies of the relationship between history and other fields of inquiry, especially comparative studies of method stressing the problem of relevance.

One of the central problems of philosophy and theology in the seventeenth century was the relationship between Reason and Faith. The rise of science had virtually transformed the study of this ancient problem. In general, the scientists themselves were concerned to prove that secular science was perfectly compatible with Christian faith. Boyle and others identified Reason with natural philosophy, and then tried to show that religious truth stood in no need of the verification or demonstration required in natural philosophy. This was another way of saying that there were different degrees of evidence and truth appropriate to different subject matters.[2] Boyle, as a Baconian, believed that actual experience was more authoritative than any theory, and this allowed him to invoke the evidence of historical experience in defence of Faith.

Unfortunately, such an argument cut both ways—there was historical testimony favouring Revelation, but how accurate was it? Could the historical evidence stand up under the scrutiny of men who had learned to demand a high degree of probability in historical proofs? Toward the end of the seventeenth century, when Locke tried to set the boundaries between Reason and Faith, he appealed to 'the clear and self-evident dictates of reason' as a superior test of truth.[3] Much of his argument, however, implied or presupposed an awareness of how difficult it is to prove divine revelation on the basis

---

[1] Among the first and best of the modern studies of this subject are the works of Paul Hazard. See especially Paul Hazard, *The European Mind 1680–1715*, translated from the original French, *La Crise de La Conscience Européenne* (Paris, 1935); cf. Butterfield, *Origins of Modern Science*, 197.

[2] See R. Westfall, *Science and Religion in Seventeenth Century England*, 164–85.

[3] John Locke, *An Essay Concerning Human Understanding*, abridged and edited by A. S. Pringle-Pattison (Oxford, 1924), IV, 10, p. 358. See also IV, 10–12, pp. 339–41 on degrees of assent to historical proofs.

of historical testimony. 'For the evidence that any proposition is true,' Locke wrote, '(except such as are self-evident) lying only in the proofs a man has of it, whatsoever degrees of assent he affords it beyond the degree of that evidence, it is plain that all the surplusage of assurance is owing to some other affection, and not to the love of truth.' [1] Scrupulously applied to the historical testimony for Christian revelation, Locke's principles would have subverted the authority of the Bible itself. [2]

Locke was too much devoted to Christianity, and to common sense compromises, to apply his arguments consistently to the subversion of faith. But it is worth noting that he felt obliged to defend himself against the charge that he had only 'an historical faith'. In *The Reasonableness of Christianity* (1695), he flatly denied the objections of some, 'that to believe only that Jesus of Nazareth is the Messiah, is but an historical, and not a justifying, or saving faith'. [3]

If Reason tended to replace Revelation as a final court of appeal in the eighteenth century it was at least in part because historical scepticism had undermined the authority of the Scriptures, as well as men's faith in the miracles and revelations of the Christian tradition. Rejecting the errors of the past in the name of Reason, some eighteenth-century writers, including Bolingbroke, were inclined to minimize the importance of exact methods of research. Still, the historical scepticism of the eighteenth century owed much to the historical scholarship of the seventeenth century.

The fideistic controversy of the later seventeenth century was quite obviously a case in point. Father Simon's *Histoire Critique du Vieux Testament* (an English translation of which appeared in 1682) was an early example of the 'higher criticism', based on historical argument and textual exegesis. The book, banned by Bossuet, was kept alive in more than forty refutations. Directed primarily against the bibliolatry of Protestantism, Father Simon's History shocked the Catholics, delighted the sceptics, and drove the Protestants to undertake an urgent study of biblical exegesis. [4]

The proliferation of sects during the civil wars in England had

[1] Locke, *Human Understanding*, IV, xix, p. 359.

[2] See Westfall, *Science and Religion*, 185.

[3] John Locke, *The Reasonableness of Christianity*, edited, abridged, and introduced by I. T. Ramsey (Stanford, 1958), 43.

[4] See Paul Hazard, *The European Mind*, Part II, 'The War on Tradition'; also Louis I. Bredvold, *The Intellectual Milieu of John Dryden* (Ann Arbor, 1934), Chapter IV.

directed attention to the same general problem: from whence do the Scriptures derive their authority? In the *Leviathan* (1651) Thomas Hobbes answered the question to his own satisfaction by observing that it was meaningless, and that 'the question truly stated is, *By What Authority they are made Law*'.[1] Hobbes carried his Erastianism to extremes, but the very fact that he wrote as a secular philosopher lent significance to his attack on Scriptural authority. He made only casual references to history, but he quoted from the Scriptures with devastating effect. In the fourth book he charged that the Church of Rome had brought all kinds of errors into religion 'from false, or uncertain History'.[2] This was Protestant doctrine, but it did not endear him to the Protestants who saw his argument for what it was—a far-reaching attack on the validity of all private testimony to revelation, past or present.

Historical scepticism could mean either scepticism about the possibility of any kind of historical knowledge—this being a form of extreme Pyrrhonism—or scepticism about particular facts and beliefs resulting from the application of critical historical methods to a body of evidence. The growth of both kinds of historical scepticism was more or less continuous in the later seventeenth century. In Pierre Bayle's *Dictionaire Historique et Critique* (1697) the critical part destroyed the historical.[3] Bayle himself stopped short of complete Pyrrhonism, but many rationalists and freethinkers were eager to proceed further, and to deny that history had any relevance to the present, or to the future. This development, sustained in part by Cartesian scepticism and by Spinoza's historical iconoclasm, was comparatively unimportant in British philosophy. Generally speaking, the British empiricists retained a far greater measure of respect for history, and for what Locke called the 'historical plain method'.[4]

The tradition of British empiricism probably owed something to the English respect for legal and historical precedents. In any case, it is clear that verified historical testimony came to be accepted as

---

[1] Hobbes, *Leviathan* (Modern Library ed.), III, xxxiii, p. 337.
[2] *Ibid.*, IV, xlvi, pp. 604–5.
[3] See Hazard, *European Mind*, 108, and Chapter V, *passim*.
[4] Locke, *Human Understanding*, 'Introduction', p. 10 and cf. note 4. Spinoza's essay, 'Of the Interpretation of Scripture' (see the *Tractatus Theologico-Politicus*, Chapter vii) is actually an essay on problems of historical method.

a part of Experience, and that historical scepticism (such as Hume displayed in his essay on miracles) did not involve the outright rejection of historical proofs. It is true that Hume's arguments against miracles were subject to logical criticism, especially since he arbitrarily ruled out historical testimony to all supernatural phenomena, but Hume did not attack historical testimony as such. Rather, he insisted that historical experience could not be used to *prove* miracles. And had he confined his argument to the case of the resurrection, it would have been virtually impossible to refute it.[1]

The importance of historical arguments in British philosophy could be demonstrated in a variety of ways, but one further example must suffice. Bishop Butler, writing under the influence of contemporary scientific thought, accepted the philosophical distinction between matters of fact and relations of ideas, and deliberately omitted all value-judgments from his arguments for Christianity. 'It is obvious', he wrote in the *Analogy of Religion* (1736), 'that Christianity, and the proof of it, are both historical. And even natural religion is, properly, a matter of fact.' [2]

The relationship between science and history was a great deal closer in the seventeenth century than it has since become. Bacon and Descartes illustrate this: both were comprehensive and influential historians of science; and between them they elaborated the conditions for future scientific progress. The historical element was more pronounced in Bacon's thought, but in the case of both it has been said that their views about the history of science provide the key to their conceptions of scientific method.[3] Our knowledge of the ways in which modern science was actuated from the outside—by economic life, by war, medicine, and the arts—has been vastly increased in recent decades. That history was also one of those

---

[1] This is not the place to defend this statement, or to enter into the controversy about Hume's philosophical ideas. The notion that Hume was somehow attacking human testimony as such in his essay on miracles is succinctly stated by Father Garraghan. See Gilbert J. Garraghan, S.J., *A Guide to Historical Method*, ed. by Jean DeLanglez, S.J. (New York, 1946), 301. For Hume's own views, see his *Enquiry Concerning Human Understanding*, Sections X and XI.

[2] Quoted by Bethell, *The Cultural Revolution*, 67, from Butler's *Analogy*, Part II, Chapter VIII.

[3] See A. C. Crombie, 'Historians and the Scientific Revolution', *Endeavour* (XIX, 1960), 9–13. Mr. Crombie stresses the importance of Descartes' views about the history of science; see especially p. 11.

forces, and an important one, is certainly a reasonable and useful hypothesis.[1]

There is no disputing the fact that science became the intellectual ideal of the eighteenth-century philosophers, and that the methods of science cast their reflections on literature and the social sciences. The question that must now be asked is, how exact was the correspondence between the methods of physical science and those of the humanities and social sciences? In borrowing the vocabulary of science writers did not necessarily change their habits of thought. Knowledge of history was more widespread in the seventeenth century than knowledge of science. As collectors and compilers of information the historians and antiquaries had been every bit as industrious as the scientists. The important distinction between matters of fact and judgments of value had been clearly drawn by Selden. Sound principles of evidence and proof had been developed in many fields. It is, indeed, often hard to tell whether science or history or some other discipline provided the basis for new ideas of how to deal with social problems.

The study of economics progressed rapidly in the later seventeenth century, and showed signs of being influenced by the scientific tendency to use quantitative methods. William Petty used the term 'political arithmetic' to describe his scientific or theoretical economics. Like other members of the Royal Society he thought that social truths might be discovered by applying the methods of physical science. The growth of statistical studies in the decades following the Restoration was a tribute to the scientific spirit. Nevertheless, it is also true that the study of economics owed much to the historiographical tradition.

From John Wheeler's *Treatise of Commerce* (1601) to William Fleetwood's *Cronicon Preciosum, Or An Account of English Gold and Silver Money* (1706), the historical element in English economic writing was pronounced. Fleetwood's book was the first attempt to write a full-scale history of prices. It was directly related to the earlier tithes controversy, which had come to a head in 1646. During that year Sir Henry Spelman's work on tithes, containing his views

---

[1] See G. N. Clark, *Science and Social Welfare in the Age of Newton*, 2nd ed. (Oxford, 1949), 74, and *passim*. This is probably the best short survey of the ways in which science was influenced by outside forces. There is a useful bibliographical essay in R. S. Westfall, *Science and Religion in Seventeenth Century England*.

on the importance of the price revolution, had been posthumously printed. Fleetwood picked up the relevant passages from Spelman in White Kennett's *Parochial Antiquities*. His purpose in quoting Kennett was to prove the utility of a historical study of prices, and to show how fatal it would be to commute tithes to fixed money payments. Fleetwood was, in short, continuing the historical studies of his predecessors. After the publication of his book, statistical studies of price history became an established part of economics.[1]

That history permeated the political thought of the seventeenth century is obvious. Nearly every English writer on political theory devoted some pages to a discussion of the antiquity of the constitution.[2] A good many historical myths were kept alive in this way; and it must be said that some of the historical passages were irrelevant to the political theories which they were meant to support. The historians and antiquaries themselves were all too often guilty of the vices of pedantry and prejudice, as Bolingbroke scornfully complained.[3] Yet even in eighteenth-century England the study of history remained the basis for the study of politics—Reason came to supplement, but not to supplant History.

Modern literary historians were among the first to recognize the importance of patterns of historical thought in the dramatic and critical literature of England during the sixteenth and seventeenth centuries. Shakespearean scholars, bent on tracking down the sources of plot and character, explored all the early chronicles and histories that provided Shakespeare with dramatic ideas. From such studies came a new understanding of the relationship between history and literature. And it is no accident that in modern universities literary professorships have often been held by men primarily concerned with socio-intellectual history.

As a branch of literature in its own right historiography became a subject for literary scrutiny during the Renaissance. Readers, writers, and publishers took a direct interest in written history, and as a result acquired a new sense of historical perspective. The formal

[1] All of the information on Fleetwood is taken from G. N. Clark, *Science and Social Welfare*, Chapter IV, and pp. 147–54. See also John Wheeler, *A Treatise on Commerce*, ed. by George Burton Hotchkiss (New York, 1931), 'Introduction', 10.

[2] See Pocock, *Ancient Constitution*, 46–7.

[3] See Henry St. John, Lord Viscount Bolingbroke, *Letters on the Study and Use of History*, a new edition, corrected (London, 1792), Letter III, *passim*.

structure of the eighteenth-century novel was to some extent an imitation of history—a facetious imitation in the case of Fielding's *Tom Jones*. English literary criticism, however, provides possibly the best example of the way in which historical ideas and attitudes were incorporated into the conventions of literature.

The quarrel between the Ancients and Moderns has been fully investigated, from its origins in the sixteenth century to its inconclusive ending in the eighteenth century. In spite of the fact that the quarrel was often conducted in rather abstract and unhistorical terms it is obvious that one of the crucial issues involved was the nature of historical progress. Directly related to this was the critical problem of relativism versus absolutism.

English critical relativism took shape in the seventeenth century, and its arguments became apparent in the writings of most critics after the Restoration. While it is true that both relativists and absolutists made use of historical argument, the significant fact is that the environmental approach of the early relativists, including Dryden, owed something to the historians and antiquaries, who had already begun to study the classics in the same way, stressing the importance of historical contexts.[1] Moreover, in a larger sense, there can be no doubt about the direct influence on Dryden's intellectual development of one work of history in particular—Father Simon's *Critical History of the Old Testament*.[2]

The close connection between English historiography and English law was not peculiar to the seventeenth century—the common law was too deeply rooted in history to be studied without reference to theories of historical development. It is true that lawyers, as such, were not necessarily concerned with legal history, yet the writings of Coke, Selden, Hale and many others bear witness to the close affinity between legal scholarship and historical writing and thought. The reciprocal influence of law on history, and of history on law, especially in the seventeenth century, has been amply demonstrated.[3] In the eighteenth century this reciprocal influence continued, and

[1] The most illuminating book on this aspect of the quarrel between the Ancients and Moderns is Emerson R. Marks, *Relativist & Absolutist, The Early Neoclassical Debate in England* (New Brunswick, N.J., 1955), especially pp. 84–5 and 127–30.

[2] L. Bredvold, *Intellectual Milieu of Dryden*, 106.

[3] In addition to the writings of Sir William Holdsworth, especially *A History of English Law*, 9 vols. (London, 1922–7), see the books of Arnecke and Pococke, already cited.

Blackstone provided a major synthesis of ideas drawn from history, law, and the social sciences.

Blackstone's *Commentaries on the Laws of England* encompassed an entire legal system. Not since Justinian's *Institutes* had there been a legal synthesis of greater historical significance. The complex ideas and institutions of the common law were reduced by Blackstone to a kind of rational order—an achievement of immense importance for the whole future development of law in the English-speaking world. In commenting on the laws of England Blackstone summed up the history of the law, and made the study of law a part of the general science of man. As an illustration of the way in which conflicting ideas of Reason and History, Nature and Faith, Fact and Value could be brought together to form an intellectual union, Blackstone's book remains in a class by itself; no other book of the century serves as well to reveal the historical origins and attributes of the Age of Reason.

Rational and scientific, but also mysterious—even religious—the Law stood above the particular rules and reasons found in individual English laws. Precedents 'contrary to reason' could not be admitted in the Science of Law, but the Mystery of Law was such that no man could doubt that 'the wisdom of our ancient law determined nothing in vain'.[1] In attempting to elucidate the Mysterious Science of the Law, Blackstone in practice made the study of law a branch of the study of history. The purpose of the *Commentaries* was to arrive at 'the general spirit of laws and principles of universal Jurisprudence' by a historical study of English laws.[2]

In seeking to discover constant and universal principles of Law by examining particular laws Blackstone was doing for the study of law what Hume and Robertson and Gibbon were doing for the study of history. Striving to make valid generalizations about human nature, the eighteenth-century historians, philosophers, and social scientists were all becoming deeply concerned with problems of relevance, with the relationship between present and past experience, and with the place of values in a world of facts. Obviously, such concerns were not exclusively historical. Many eighteenth-century writers have justly been accused of mistaking their own prejudices for history, yet the relevance of ideas of history to all forms of social thought is indisputable. Bolingbroke expressed a characteristic

[1] Quoted by Daniel J. Boorstin, *The Mysterious Science of the Law* (Boston, Beacon Press, 1958), 27–8.
[2] Quoted by Boorstin, *ibid.*, 35.

English belief when he declared that, 'as experience is conversant about the present, and the present enables us to guess at the future; so history is conversant about the past, and by knowing the things that have been, we become better able to judge of the things that are'.[1]

The main purpose of this book has been to examine the origins and nature of the historical revolution of the seventeenth century. The intellectual consequences of that revolution, sketched here in brief and necessarily simplified strokes, are still observable. Modern historicism and relativism began to develop in the favourable climate of seventeenth-century opinion; and the methods employed by modern historians and social scientists have, to a large extent, been developed from the working procedures of seventeenth-century scholars, who dealt with the facts of history whether or not they called themselves historians.

The scientific ideals that inform modern studies of man in society have always been derived ideals, which can only be realized indirectly. Only in so far as the methods of science are appropriate, or relevant to the study of human behaviour may it be said that social generalizations have the force of scientific general laws. The immediate problem faced by the historians and social scientists of the early eighteenth century was that of testing and judging the facts of historical experience. Science might provide ideals of mechanistic explanation, but by itself Science could not authenticate the facts of history, much less distinguish what was good from what was bad.

Reason, it was said, had established strict rules of criticism to try the truth of fact, but, after all, Reason was no more a scientific term than Nature, or any of the other resounding commonplaces of eighteenth-century thought. In practice, the methods of history were found to be more appropriate to the study of man than the methods of Newtonian mechanics. Reason became the grand passion of the philosophers, historians, and scientists (and of most lawyers and theologians as well), but the image of Reason was not necessarily the same in the minds of all reasonable men.

In a passage crammed with the great abstractions of the age, Bolingbroke explained the role of Reason in History:

What may have happened, is the matter of an ingenious fable; what has happened, is that of an authentic history: the impres-

---

[1] Bolingbroke, *Letters on Study of History*, Letter III, pp. 55–6.

sions which one or the other makes are in proportion. When imagination grows lawless and wild, rambles out of the precincts of nature, and tells of heroes and giants, fairies and enchanters, of events and phaenomena repugnant to universal experience, to our clearest and most distinct ideas, and to all the known laws of nature, reason does not connive a moment; but far from receiving such narrations as historical, she rejects them as unworthy even to be placed among the fabulous.[1]

This was high tribute to the importance of rational and scientific ideals. The only trouble with the statement was how to apply it in practice. So general as to be obvious to all, it could be interpreted differently by each of the students of the ways of man. In the long run, it was not by pursuing abstract universals such as Nature and Reason that scholars in various fields were to advance human knowledge and human understanding; it was by cultivating their own gardens, and by studying history.

[1] *Ibid.*, Letter III, p. 97.

INDEX

'Abreviate of Tower Records', William Lambarde, 135

Abridgments, defined, 160–1

Academe, Prince Henry's, 106

Academe Roial, Edmund Bolton's, 106, 168

Accedens of Armorye, Gerard Legh, 43

Acton, Lord (Sir John Dalberg), 209

Acton, Robert, Queen's secretary, letter to Cotton, 128

Acts and Monuments, John Foxe, 40

Ad Fletam, John Selden, 297

Advancement of Learning, Sir Francis Bacon, xv, 256, 260; *see also* Bacon, Sir Francis

Agarde, Arthur: collections of, 36; catalogue by, 73; ability, 75; member Soc. Antiquaries, 76; *Compendium*, 79, 82, 83; on records, 81; Deputy Chamberlain, 141

Aids to research, xviii; *see also* History, ancillary disciplines; Libraries; Record Offices

Albion Mareoticus (eponymous King), 16

Alciat, André, 277

Allen, Thomas, 138

Amyot, Pierre, 165

Analogy, doctrine of, *see* History, analogy

Analogy of Religion, Joseph Butler, bishop, 315

Ancient Constitution, 28–9, 122

Ancient Funerall Monuments, John Weever, 156

Ancients and Moderns, quarrel of, 100, 210, 318

Ancient Usage in Bearing such

Ensigns . . . as . . . Arms, Sir William Dugdale, 183

Andrewes, Launcelot, 93

Anelecton Anglo-Britannicon, John Selden, 166

Anglican Church, *see* Church, English

Anglicanism, Hooker's defence of, 22

Anglo-Saxon, studies of, 35, 100, 102–3, 110–11, 218, 233, 303

Annals, xxi; defined, 154

Annals, Francis Godwin, 177

Annales, William Camden, 187, 230–52

Annales, John Stow, 211, 216, 222

Annius of Viterbo, 16, 203

Antiquarianism: heritage of, 113–16; contribution to history, 113, 115; stylistic faults, 115; *see also* Antiquary; Soc. of Antiquaries; and names of antiquaries

Antiquaries, Society of, *see* Society of Antiquaries

Antiquary, as historian, 60–2, 114, 115; *see also* 92–116

Antiquas Rediviva, 66, 106

Antiquities: spread of interest in, xxii; European concern with, 15; reasons for study of, in England, 99; and history, 110–11; definitions of, 114, 151–2; examples, 181–2

Antiquities of Canterbury, William Somner, 182

Antiquities of Warwickshire, Sir William Dugdale, 181–2

Apologie or Declaration of the Power and Providence of God, George Hakewill, 173

Appeal to Experience, 306, 307–8

323

Arabic, study of, 57
Arcana imperii, 69, 71
Archaeologus, Sir Henry Spelman, 103
Archaeology, 48, 105
Archaionomia, William Lambarde, 31
Archeion, William Lambarde, 76, 188
Archer, Sir Symon, 143
Archives, importance of, 32, 60; definition of, 33; ecclesiastical, 34; *see also* Records
Areopagitica, John Milton, 41
Aristotle: on poetry and history, 46; criticism of, 199; logic of, 253; authority attacked, 306; *see also* Bacon; Ralegh; Scholasticism
Ars historica, 170
Arundel and Surrey (Thomas Howard), earl of, 64, 67, 130
Ashmole, Elias, 105
Attack on Authority, 306–7
Aubrey, John, 250
Augustine, Saint, 9, 194, 196, 201; idea of history, 10–12, 25, 197–8; *see also* History, theory
Authority, appeal to, 203, 295; attack on, 306–7
Averroists, 9
Ayscue, Edward, 179

Bacon, Sir Francis: 253–74, 307
    BIOGRAPHY: as stylist, xxi; on Hayward's case, 41; knowledge 48; a 'Modern', 100–1; as critic and framer of policies, 253; as philosopher, 262–3; as reformer, 262; reputation, 262; influenced by Machiavelli, 263–4, 269, 271–2; influence of, 263, 274; mercantilist, 269–70; as historian of science, 315
    History of the Reign of Henry VII: 157–8; a model, 253; style and purpose of, 264 ff.; Busch's criticism of, 265; use of sources,

265–8; sources of error in, 267; praised by Selden, 267; probability and proof, 268–9; economic interpretation in, 269; fortune, 269; ideas of explanation in, 270; problem of relevance in, 270, 272; reason of state in, 270; relationship of past to present in, 271–2; role of individual in, 271; limitations of method, 272; mistaken analogy bet. past and present, 272; character in, 273; style of, 273–4
    HISTORICAL WRITING AND THOUGHT: on the varieties of history, xiv, 150–3; primary objective of policy, 253–4; evidence and proof, 254, 266; idea of progress, 254, 256: induction, 254, 258; presuppositions, 254; relationship bet. civil and natural history, 254; bet. theory and practice, 255; scientific thought, 254, 263; significance of work, 254, 274; definition of history, 255–8, 259–60; history as study of particulars, 255; as experience, 258; types of history, 255; divinity, 256; memory and history, 256–7; providence, 256, 261, 269; relevance of theology to history, 256; of philosophy to history, 258; utility of history, 256, 261; views of history in different works, 256; history as form of knowledge, 257–8; distinction bet. research and interpretation, 258–9; dilemma of thought, 258; ideas of explanation, 258–69; ambiguity of use of word 'history', 259–60; history and other forms of knowledge, 259–60; segregation, idea of, 260; high utility, 261, 262; secularism, 261; truth and utility the same, 261; History of Learning and the Arts, 262; importance of political experience, 271

Baker, Augustine, 137
Baker, Sir Richard, 177, 179
Balance of Power, 4; principle of, 241
Bale, John, antiquary, 16, 23
Bancroft, Richard, bishop, letter of, 39
Barkham, John, 139, 143
Baronage, Sir William Dugdale, 43, 183
Baronius, Cesare, cardinal, 19
Bayle, Pierre, 314
Bedford (Francis Russell), earl of, 130
Behemoth, Thomas Hobbes, 171
Bennet, Sir John, 138
Bentley, Richard, 62
Berosus, forgeries of, 216
Bias; Selden accused of, xix; Coke's, 30; Soc. of Antiquaries, 100; *see also* Relevance; and names of historians
Bible (or Scriptures): and history, xix; Protestant view of, 18; contains God's words, 22; authority of, 23, 193, 201, 295, 313; historical parts of, 24; chronology in, 201; meaning of words in, 281
Bibliography, 162; *see also* Bibliographical Preface, xi-xii
Biography, 183–4
Blackstone, William, 319
Blundeville, Thomas, 57, 165
Bodin, Jean, use of term 'method', xvii; as humanist, 27, 28; *Methodus*, 165–6
Bodleian library, 63–5
Bodley, Sir Thomas, 35; *see also* Library
Bohun, Edmund, tr. *De Ratione . . . Legendi Historias*, 169
Bolde, William, 139
Bolingbroke (Henry Saint-John), viscount, 317; quoted, 319–20, 320–1;
Bolton, Edmund, 106, 143, 168, 171

Book and manuscript collections, 60–9
Book of Martyrs, John Foxe, 22
'Book of Seals', Sir Christopher Hatton, 66–7
Books, *see* individual titles
Borough, John, 142
Bossuet, Jacques-Bénigne, bishop, 313
Boswell, William, 142, 143
Bowyer, Robert: collections of, 36; ability, 75; member, Soc. Antiquaries, 76, 93; catalogue by, 83; pays for post, 86; helps Stow, 88; and Cotton, 132; record keeper, 142
Bowyer, William, 24, 76, 85, 142
Boyle, Robert, 111, 312
Bracton, Henry de, 31
Bradshaw, John, 91, 141
Brady Controversy, 112–13
Brady, Robert, 109, 114, 115
Brathwaite, Richard, 166–7; poem quoted, 168
Breviaries, defined, 160–1
Brewer, S. J., editor, 159
Brief Chronicle, Anthony Munday, 177, 179
Brief Description of Universal Mappes and Cardes, Thomas Blundeville, 57
Brisson, Barnabe, 277
Britannia, William Camden, 93, 99, 157, 166, 175, 179, 223, 233–6, 300
British Museum, 117
Brooke, Ralph, 43, 156
Browne, Sir Thomas, 48, 105, 117
Brute (Brutus), legend of, 16, 47, 178, 179, 216
Buck, Sir George, 57
Buckingham (George Villiers), duke of, 281
Buckle, Henry Thomas, 16
Budé, Guillaume, 277
Burckhardt, Jacob, 1
Bureaucracy, 73, 140–1; *see also* Civil Service

Burghley (William Cecil), Lord, 35, 63–4, 71, 128, 219, 230, 235
Busch, Wilhelm, criticism of Bacon's *Henry VII*, 265
Bush, Douglas, quoted, 9
Butler, Joseph, bishop, 315

Calendars, xviii, 60, 79
Calendars of State Papers, Domestic, xi
Calvin and Calvinism, 10, 19, 20, 23, 25, 302, 307
Cambria Triumphans, Percy Enderbie, 181
Cambridge, 36, 37
Camden Society, 251
Camden, William: 61, 63, 93, 99, 102, 121, 128, 144, 145, 154, 157, 166, 175, 177, 179, 181, 184, 189, 190, 215, 216, 223, 229, 230–52, 264, 270, 273, 300–1; library of, 36; as herald, 42–3; views on prerogative, 103, 131
BIOGRAPHY: birth and death, 230; patronage of, by Burghley, 230–1, 235; criticism of, 231–2; classical influences on, 232–3; conventions of thought, 232–3; submits *Annales* to King James, 231–2; knowledge of languages, 233; makes notebook collections, 233; continental writers influence, 234; patriotism, 234–5; Burghley gives access to papers, 235; humanist training, 242; religious views, 238–9; toleration, 243; establishes professorship, 252
HISTORICAL WRITING AND THOUGHT: *Annales*, significance of, 231; patriotism, 234; study of antiquities, 234; continuity and change, 235; progress, 235; conjecture, attitude toward, 236–7; interviews, 236; objectivity, 236, 237–8, 241, 250; use of records and sources, 236; content, 237, 239 ff.; ideas of explanation (causation), 237–8, 240–3, 245;

limits of freedom in history, 237–8; characters of Henry VIII, Elizabeth, and others, 238, 245–7, 250; 'mysteries of state', 238; emphasis on foreign affairs, 239, 242; footnotes, use of, 239; balance of power, 241; professional qualities, 241; bias, 243; relevance, 243–4; method, 244 ff.; historical inevitability, 246; unity of history, 246; evidence and proof, 247; imagination, 247; speeches, 247; critical judgment, 248; 'Laws of History', 248–9; rumours, 248; annalistic pattern, 249; decisive moments recognized, 249; significance of *Annales*, 251–2
Campion, Edward, 154
Canon law, 285–6, 289
Capitalism and Capitalists, 4, 8, 302
Carew, Richard, 34, 157, 180
Carr, Robert, earl of Somerset, 121–5
Cartography, 48, 57, 178
Casaubon, Isaac, 20
Catalogue of the Bishops of England, Francis Godwin, 156
Catalogue of English Kings, Princes and Peers, Ralph Brooke, 156
Catalogues, xviii, 60; library, 66; of treaties, 73; defined as history, 155–6
Catholicism, *see* Roman Catholics
Causation, xx; *see also* History, Method, esp. ideas of explanation; and names of historians
Cecil, William, *see* Burghley
Cecil, Sir Robert, 73; authorizes search in records, 89
Censorship and historical publication, 37–41; authority for, 38; premises of, 40
Chabod, Federico, quoted, 5, 14
Chance, in history, 11; *see also* History, theory
Change in history, 2, 178; *see also* Continuity

Characters: as form of history, xxi; defined, 157–8, 160; importance of, 159; and Lives, 159–60

Charles I, King of England, 130

Chelsea College, 39, 106

Christian humanism, *see* Humanism

Christian Virtuoso, Robert Boyle, 111

Christianity, 9, 18, 95; origins of, 95, 100; impact of science on, 111

Chronicle of the Kings of England, Sir Richard Baker, 179

Chronicles and Chroniclers: xxi; medieval, 9; 'chronicle' defined, 154; type of history, 154; use of, 177; examples of, 179; Tudor, 213

Chronology: *see* History, theory of; Periodization; and names of historians

Church, English: (*see also* Selden); and State, 19, 23, 24; role of, in scholarship, 20, 110–13, 301; study of, in 17th c., 100, 186; economic problems of, 279–81; infeodations, 285

Church History of Britain, Peter Heylyn, 187

Cicero, 194

Citation, of books in text, xi; of manuscripts, xii

Citizen, defined, 53–5

City of God, St. Augustine, 10

Civil history, 150–2; Bacon's subdivisions of, 153

Civil law, 285–6; *see also* Selden

Civil Service, 69–91; 139–42; *see also* Cotton; Records; Record Keeping

Civil Wars, impact of, on antiquarian and historical studies, 106–10; 112

Clapham, John, 64

Clarendon (Edward Hyde), earl of, xxi, 64, 160, 184–5, 301

Classical models, xxi, 9

Clientage (*see also* Patronage), bureaucratic, 118, 140

Coherence theory of history, 222, 291

Coke, Sir Edward: and common law, 29–30, 134–5; on records, 32; on Hayward's case, 39–40; legal collections of, 61, 129; defends Anglicanism, 84; on fees, 87; disregard of contexts, 108, 272; and Cotton, 125; political activity of, 134; scholarship of, 318

Colet, John, 15

Collation of manuscripts, 152

College of Arms, 42, 93, 141; *see also* Heralds; Heraldry

Collingwood, R. G., 255

Commentaries on the Laws of England, William Blackstone, 319

Commercial revolution, 6

Common law and lawyers: compared with French legal humanists, 31; interpretation of legal history, 102; and canon law, 285–6; *see also* Law

Compendium, Arthur Agarde, 73, 82, 83

Compleat Gentleman, Henry Peacham, 51, 166

Complete History of England, Robert Brady, 115

Concilia, Sir Henry Spelman, 68, 100

Conjecture: as opposed to proof, xv; attitude toward, of Soc. of Antiquaries, 97; *see also* Ralegh; Bacon; Camden; Stow; Selden

Conjectures, about historical revolution, 300, 304, 305–21

Constitution, Ancient, 28–9, 122

Contarini, 18

Content, definition of, xx–xxi; *see also* History, content; and names of historians

Contextualism in history, 104, 108; *see also* Historical contexts

Continuity and change in history, 2, 13, 111–12; *see also* names of historians

Cordell, Sir William, 72
Correspondence theory of history, 98, 99, 222–3
Cosmography, defined, 161; example of 'mixed history', 153
Cotton, Sir Robert Bruce: 24, 35, 36, 62, 63, 66, 88, 93, 96, 102, 114, 117–49, 178, 236, 277, 301
BIOGRAPHY: (*see also* political activities and career): significance of career, 117–18, 149; contemporary roles, 119; birth and education, 120–1; Bruce, importance of name, 120; knowledge of precedents and history, 121, 126, 131, 133; religion, and views on toleration, 124, 137; letters to, from various scholars, 136 ff.; treatises by, 132, 133, 137
LIBRARY: collections in British Museum, 117; administration and arrangement, 126 ff.; significance, 129–30, 147, 302; contents, 145–7; fire of 1731, 148
POLITICAL ACTIVITIES AND CAREER: 119–27, 131–4; service on Royal Commissions, 121; support of Somerset, 121–5; arrested 1615, 122; promotes Spanish match, 123–4; examined by Privy Council, 125; moves to opposition, 125–7; drafts speech of Eliot, 126; pattern of activities, 126; scheme to create Baronets, 128; prosecuted, 1629, 130–1; Stevenson conspiracy, 148
INFLUENCE: general, 127; on Court, officers of State, Parliament Men, 127–34; illustrative letter from Queen's secretary, quoted, 128; on legal profession, 134–6; on Church and Universities, 136–9; on Royal Officials, 139–42; on Record Keepers, 141–3; on scholars, historians and others, 142–9; helps gain access to records, 142–3
County history, *see* History, county

Courts of law, records of, 33, 70–1, 75, 186
Courts of record, defined, 32–3
Coventry, Thomas, Baron Coventry, 135
Crane, Sir Francis, 141
Cranfield, Lionel, 54, 55
Critical History of the Old Testament, Father Richard Simon, 313, 318
Cromwell, Oliver, 53, 209
Cronicon Preciosum, William Fleetwood, 316
Cujas, Jacques, 277; quoted, 28
'Custom and the Immemorial', 28, 30, 84, 97, 99, 107, 111, 289, 304

Dale, Robert, 183
Daniel, Samuel, 177
Davies, Sir John, 187, 244
De Augmentis, Sir Francis Bacon, 256
Dee, Dr. John, 48, 90, 104–5
De Laude Scriptorum, Johann von Trittenheim, abbot of Sponheim, 8
De Non Temerandis Ecclesias, Sir Henry Spelman, 296
De Ratione . . . Legendi Historias, Degory Wheare, 165, 169
Dering, Sir Edward, 66; warrant issued to, 89–90
Descartes, René, 315
Descriptio Globis Intellectualis, Sir Francis Bacon, 255–6
Description of England, William Harrison, 49, 54
Destiny, 198
De Thou, Jacques-Auguste (Thuanus), 234
Devil, role of in history, 205
D'Ewes, Sir Simonds, 63, 186; library of, 63; letter of, 85; *Journals of Elizabeth's Reign*, 90; indebtedness to Cotton, 144–5
Diatribae Upon the First Part of the Late History of Tithes, Richard Mountague, 293–5

Dictionaire Historique et Critique, Pierre Bayle, 314
Dictionary of National Biography, xi
Digests, historical, xxi
Digges, Sir Dudley, 133
'Dignity of History', 181, 238
Diodorus of Sicily, 202
Dionysius of Halicarnassus, 12, 40
Diplomatics, 115
Direction For Search of Records, Thomas Powell, 73, 79, 80
Discourses On Titus Livius, Machiavelli, 12
Discoverie of Errors, Augustine Vincent, 43, 156
Discoverie of the True Causes Why Ireland was never Entirely Subdued, Sir John Davies, 244
Divine right, *see* Selden
Divinity, implication of history for, 307
Doderidge, Sir John, 136, 183
Dodsworth, Roger, 63, 90, 147, 162, 181, 183
'Donation of Constantine', Lorenzo Valla, 18
Donne, John, epigram, 92
Douglas, David, quoted, 147–8, 188
Drayton, Michael, 46–7
Dryden, John, 305, 318
Ductor Dubitantium, Jeremy Taylor, 309
Dudley, Sir Robert, 130
Duello, John Selden, 279
Dugdale, Sir William, 43, 66, 67, 110, 143, 147, 162, 181, 182, 183, 229
Dupuy, Pierre, 144
Dykes, Oswald, 144

Earle, John, 92
Easy and Compendious Introduction For Reading All Sorts of Histories, Mathias Prideaux, 190
Ecclesiastical history, *see* History, ecclesiastical
Economic development, 2, 3, 305–6
Education, definition of, 44–5

Education and history, 44–8
Egerton, Sir Thomas (Baron Ellesmere), *see* Ellesmere
Eight Bookes Of The Peloponnesian Warre, Written by Thucydides, ed. and tr. by Thomas Hobbes, 171–2
Eirenarcha, William Lambarde, 76
Eliot, Sir John, 123; and Cotton, 125; spee~ 1625, 126; political activity, 134
Elizabeth I, Queen; history of, by Fletcher, 41; *see also* Annals; Camden; Church
Elizabethan Society of Antiquaries, *see* Society of Antiquaries
Ellesmere, Baron (Sir Thomas Egerton), 131, 143–4
Elsynge, Henry, 72, 132, 142, 186
Empiricism, xxiii; rise of, 53; and historians, 69; British, 254, 308, 314
Enderbie, Percy, 181
England, *see* titles of histories and names of historians
English Historical Library, William Nicolson, 113, 182
English Lawyer, Sir John Doderidge, 136
English, Old, study of, 42
Epicureans, 9
Episodic History, *see* History, episodic
Epitomes, 58, 189; defined, 160–1
Erasmus, Desiderius, 15, 18, 19
Erastianism, Hobbes, 314; *see also* names of major historians
Erdeswicke, Sampson, 181
Ethics, of individuals and states, 5
Europe, expansion overseas, 7
Eusebius, bishop of Caesarea, 201
Exact Catalogue of the Nobility of England and Lords Spiritual, Robert Dale, 183
Execution of Justice, William Cecil, 64
Exeter, city of, records, 34
Experience, appeal to, 306, 307–8

Explanation in history, xvii, xx; *see also* names of historians
Extension of Quantitative method, 306, 310–11

Fabyan, Robert, 215, 230
Fact, and theory, xvii
Faerie Queene, Edmund Spenser, 99, 207
Faith, and history, *see* Augustine; Ralegh; Secularism; Relevance
Family history, 183–4
Fanshawe, Sir Henry, 142
Fate, in history, 10, 198
Fauconberge, Thomas, 141
Felton, Henry, 193
Ferguson, Wallace K., quoted, 12
Feudalism, 3; history of, 32; definition of, by Spelman, 101; problem of, in history, 108–10, 285; English, context of, 115
Fideistic controversy, 313–14
Filmer, Sir Robert, 107–8
First Part of the Historie of England, Samuel Daniel, 177
First Part of Life and Reign of Henry IV, John Hayward, 39
Fitzstephens, William, 218, 220
Fleetwood, William, 316–17
Fletcher, Dr. Giles, letter of, 41
Florentine History, Machiavelli, 12
Foedera, Thomas Rymer, 162
Footnote form: books and manuscripts, xi–xii; purpose of, xi
Forgeries, 43, 291–2
Formulare Anglicanum, Thomas Madox, 115
Fortescue, Sir John, 28, 31
Fortuna, 10, 197
Fortune, in history, 11, 269
Foxe, John, 22, 40
Fragmentia Regalia, Sir Robert Naunton, 157
France, 6; *see also* French legal humanists
Freedom, in history, 10; *see also* Camden; Ralegh; Selden; History, theory

Free will, 198; *see also* Augustine; History, Theory; Ralegh
French legal humanists, 27, 28, 31, 99, 273, 277, 286, 303
French, Old, study of, 42
Froude, James Anthony, quoted, 251
Fuller, Thomas, 146, 155, 157, 187
Fundamental law, 30

Galbraith, V. H., on medieval historiography, xv
Gale, Roger, 105
Gale, Thomas, 110
Gardiner, S. R., quoted, 123, 130, 185
Genealogies: of the gentry, 17; interest in, 34; help to history, 45, 51, 162, 303; Speed's, 178, books on, 183
General Historie of the Turks, Richard Knolles, 176
Gentleman, defined, 50
Gentry, English: rise of, 17; defined, 49–51; and middle classes, 54
Geoffrey of Monmouth, 216
Geography, 48
Germany, 6
Gibbon, Edward, 319
Gibson, Edmund, 111, 113
Glossaries, xviii
God's judgments, 19, 195; *see also* names of historians; History, Theory
God's Law, and Selden's *Historie*, xix, 294–5
Godwin, Francis, 156, 177
Gondomar, *see* Sarmiento
Goodman, Godfrey, bishop, 173–4
Goodwin's case, 32
Governing class, English, defined, 50; and advancement of learning, 53
Government, offices of, 49, 127–34; *see also* Civil Service
Grafton, Richard, 175, 230
Greek, study of, 8, 45, 64, 103

Gresham College, 55, 105
Grindal, Edmund, bishop, 219
Guicciardini, 10, 163, 269
Guildhall, *see* London

Hakewill, George, 173–4
Hakluyt, Richard, 7, 57, 105
Hall, Arthur, 30
Hall, Edward, historian, 175, 215, 230
Hall, Joseph, bishop of Norwich, 209
Hallam, Henry, 67
Hampden, John, 209
Hardynge, John, 215
Harley, Robert, 63, 147–8
Harrington, James, 110
Harrington, Sir John, epigram quoted, 264
Harriot, Thomas, 105
Harrison, William, quoted, 49, 54
Hartwell, Abraham, 93
Hatfield House, State Papers at, 63
Hatton, Sir Christopher, 66, 105, 182
Hayward, Sir John, 39–40, 184
Hazard, Paul, 47
Hearne, Thomas, 158
Hebrew, study of, 8, 45, 64
Heckscher, Eli, quoted, 2–3, 6, 269–70
Help to English History, Peter Heylyn, 183
Heneage, Michael, 36, 88
Henry VII, Bacon's character of, 273
Heraldry, interest in, 34; knowledge of, 43, 112; decline of, 43; help to history, 45, 162, 303; books on, 183
Heralds, concern w. history, xv; forgeries of, 42; contribute to 'Book of Seals', 67
Herbert, Edward, Baron of Cherbury, 158–60
Heritage of antiquarianism, 113–16
Herodotus, 202, 224

Heylyn, Peter, 161, 170, 183, 186, 209
Heywood, Thomas, quoted, 184
Hickes, George, 113
Hill, Christopher, quoted, 281
Histoire Critique du Vieux Testament, Father Richard Simon, 313, 318
Historians: defined, xiv; skills required of, xiii; humanist, 8; classical, 9, 59; popular, 59; as opposed to antiquary, 114–15; *see also* names of historians
Historical contexts, 29, 98, 99, 104, 108–10, 303
Historical controversy: tradition of, 18; Brady, 112–13; Tithes, 275–98
Historical evidence, xiii, xiv; *see also* History, *Method*
Historical imagination, 101
Historical inquiry, modern problems of, xv
Historical jurisprudence, 102
Historical Manuscripts Commission, xi
Historical method, defined, xvii–xx; techniques and special skills, xviii; evidence and proof, xviii; explanation and relevance, xviii; paradox of, xx; *see also* History, *Method*; and names of antiquaries and historians
Historical politics, 95, 107, 112, 117
Historical relativism, *see* Relativism
Historical research: medieval problems and methods, xv; intensification of, 18; backwardness of English, 23; *see also* Records, Public; Records, use of; and names of historians
Historical revolt, xxiv
Historical Revolution: defined, 300–5; conjectural nature of effects, xv; dates of, xxii, 165; context of, 2, 68; based on scholarship, 48, 303; extent of,

102; and Spelman's theorem, 116; significance of, 188, 297; of 19th c., 251; compared w. scientific, 305; patterns of development, 306–21

Historical scepticism; rise of, 16, 307; defined, 314; and proof, 315

Historical studies, spread of in 17th c., xxii; *see also* History, popularity of

Historical writing, *see* Historiography

Historicism, paradox of, xvi; beginnings of, 5; modern, 220, 252, 320

Historie Conteyning the Warres . . . and other Occurents betweene England and Scotland, Edward Ayscue, 179

Historie of England, John Clapham, 64

Historie of Great Britaine, John Speed, 178, 268

Historie of Ireland, Collected By Three Learned Authors, James Ware, 155

Historie of Ireland, Edmund Campion, 154

Historie and Lives of Twentie Kings of England, William Martyn, 183

Historie of Tithes, John Selden, xi, xix, xxi, 100, 134, 277 ff.; *see also* Selden

Historiographer Royal, 112

Historiography: xiii–xiv; and climate of opinion, xxiv; popular, nature of, xxii; Renaissance beginnings of modern, 8; Greek and Roman, 46; humanist, 46; literary vs. scholarly tradition in, 47–8; middle–class formula in, 53; scope of, 59; changes in, 68; medieval, 299; continuity and change in, 305; *see also* History, Varieties; and names of historians

History of the Ancient and Modern Principality of Wales, Sir John Doderidge, 136

History and Antiquities of the Exchequer, Thomas Madox, 115

History of Henry III, Sir Robert Cotton, 132

History of the Rebellion, Edward Hyde, Earl of Clarendon, 64, 160, 184, 301

History of the Reign of King Henry VII, Sir Francis Bacon, 157, 158, 256, 258, 264–7, 269–70, 273

History of the Reigns of K. Henry VIII, K. Edward, Q. Mary and part of Elizabeth, Sir Francis Bacon, 266

History of Richard III, Sir Thomas More, 230

History of the Sabbath, Peter Heylyn, 187

History of St. Paul's Cathedral, Sir William Dugdale, 67, 182

History of Warwickshire, Sir William Dugdale, 67, 143

History of The World, Sir Walter Ralegh, xvi, 12, 59, 164, 167, 191–210

History, analogy in, 39–40, 167, 174, 299; *see also* names of historians

History, and ancillary disciplines, xviii, 152, 162

History, as drama, 167, 206

History, bias in, *see* Bias

History, biographical, 183–4; *see also* Bacon; Camden

History, Christian interpretation of, *see* History, Theory

History, civil, 150–1, 254

History, classification of, 150–90; *see also* History, Varieties; Bacon

History, and Conjecture, *see* Conjecture

History, comparative, 288; *see also* Soc. of Antiquaries; Camden; Ralegh; Selden; Spelman

History, constitutional, 302; *see also* History, legal; Soc. of Antiquaries; and names of constitutional historians

History, *Content*, defined, xx–xxi; and varieties of history, 150–1; 163–90; 300; significant changes in, 304

History, county, 180–2; *see also* names of county historians

History, cycles theory, 12; *see also* History, Theory

History: defined, xiii–xiv, *see also* 150–63; use of word in 17th c., 153; Selden's definition of, 163; Wheare's definition of, 169; a profession, 190

History, dictionary of, 103

History, divisions of, by Bacon, 150–3; Universal, Territorial, Problematic, 163–5; *see also* History, Varieties

History, ecclesiastical, 19; or sacred, 151; examples, 181–2, 186–8

History, economic, 316–17; *see also* Bacon; Camden; Ralegh; Selden; Stow

History, episodic, 184–5

History, family, 183–4

History of historiography, 17th c., xv, 182

History, Idea of (modern), xiii

History, of Learning and the Arts, 151, 262, 302

History, legal, 101–2, 108–10, 188, 302, 318–20; *see also* names of legal historians

History, lessons of, 13, 215; *see also* History, Varieties; and names of historians

History, linguistic, 102; *see also* Anglo-Saxon; Arabic; English; Latin; French; Greek; Hebrew

History, literary idea of, 46–8

History and literature, 317–18; *see also* History, *Style*; Soc. of Antiquaries

History, local, 179, 211–229, 303; *see also* Stow; and names of other local historians

History, *Method*: defined, xvii–xx; techniques and special skills, xviii–xix; evidence and proof, xix–xx; ideas of explanation and relevance, xx; difference between historical and antiquarian, 115; and varieties of history, 150 ff., 300, 303; importance of, 304, 311, 316; distinction bet. first and second causes, *see* Ralegh; *also* Soc. of Antiquaries; and names of historians

History and middle-class culture, 53–9

History, 'mixed', 153

History, natural, 48, 254; *see also* Bacon

History, parish, 179–80, 181–2

History, perfect, 151; *see also* Bacon

History, periodization, 9, 189, 304; *see also* names of historians

History, philosophy of, *see* History, Theory

History, popular, 7–8, 184

History, popularity of various types, xxii, 17, 58, 150–90

History, Problematic, defined, 163–4, 185–6; examples of, 185–90, 279; *see also* Selden

History, progress in writing of, xviii

History, *Purpose*, xiii; defined, xvi–xvii; and varieties of history, 150, 163–90, 300; significant changes in, 304

History, sacred, 151, 204; *see also* History, ecclesiastical

History, secular, 188, 200, 204, 307; *see also* Secularism

History, *Significance*, defined, xxii–xxiii, 300–21

History, special skills required, xviii

History, speeches in, 159; *see also* Camden; Bacon

History, *Style*, defined, xxi-xxii; and varieties of history, 150 ff.; inadequacy of English, 163, 300; changes in, 304–5; *see also* names of historians

History, Territorial, defined, 163–4; divisions of, 175; examples of, 175–85; importance of, 302; *see also* Camden; Stow

History and theology, 9, 10–12; *see also* 306–21, *passim*

History, Theory or Philosophy of, xvii; 10–12, 13, 164, 296, 301; *see also* History, Universal, Territorial, Problematic

History, Titles, problems of classification, 150–63; *see also* History, Varieties

History and tradition, 17

History, types of, *see* History, Varieties

History, Universal, 18, 152, 191–210; defined, 163–4; examples of, 165–75

History, utility of, 58, 59, 83, 95, 213, 262, 302; *see also* names of historians

History, Varieties of, xiv, xv; defined, 150 ff., 302; *see also* separate headings, e.g., Chronicles; Annals; History, civil; etc.

History, Whig interpretation of, 30, 109, 271–2

Hobbes, Thomas, 108–9, 162, 314; quoted, 170–1, 172

Holinshed, Raphael, 175, 234

Holles, Gervase, 183

Holme, Randle, herald, 89

Hooker, John (alias Vowel), 34

Hooker, Richard, 22, 309

Horseman, Nicholas, 169

Hoskins, W. G., quoted, 182, 225, 228

Howes, Edmund, 211

Humanism and Humanists: 7, 11, 15, 17, 27–8, 56; defined, 9; and historiography, 8; Christian, 7,

9; secular, 19; mottoes of, 15; French legal, 27, 28, 31, 99, 273, 277, 286, 303; ideals of, 45, 51, 153; *see also* names of historians

Hume, David, xx, 254, 315, 319

Hutchinson, Lucy, 56

Hyde, Edward, Earl of Clarendon, *see* Clarendon

Hydriotaphia, Sir Thomas Browne, 105

Hypercritica, Edmund Bolton, 168

Hypotheses of explanation, use of in this book, xv

Illyricus, Flacius, 20, 22

Impact of the Civil Wars (on antiquarian and historical studies), 106–110

Inns of Court: education in, 31, 46; libraries, 62; role of, 110, 301; decline of, 111

Industrialization, 'first', 17

Italy, 3, 4, 5–6, 9

James I, King of England, 32, 130

James, Richard, Cotton's librarian, 137–8

James, Thomas, Bodley's librarian, 65

Jesuits, historical propagandists, 20; church historians, 21

Johnson, Dr. Samuel, quoted, 176

Jordan, W. K., quoted, 137

Joscelyn, John, collections of, 36

Josephus, Flavius, 59

Journals of All the Parliaments during the Reign of Queen Elizabeth, Sir Simonds D'Ewes, 186

Jure divino theory of tithes, 282, 296

Jurisprudence, French historical, 27; comparative, 102; *see also* French legal humanists

Kendrick, Sir Thomas, quoted, 16

Kennett, White, 113, 180, 317
Knolles, Richard, 144, 176, 177

Lake, Thomas, 141
Lambarde, William: *Archaionomia*, 31; record keeper, 75, 79; catalogue by, 82-3; Anglo-Saxon studies, 100; 'Abreviate of Tower Records', 135; *Perambulation of Kent*, 180, 212, 224; *Archeion*, 188
Language studies, 102; *see also* Anglo-Saxon, Latin, etc.
Latin, study of, 8, 42, 45, 103
Laud, William, archbishop, 280
Law (*see also* names of historians): ancient, *see* Ancient Constitution; common, 26, 29, 30-3; courts of, *see* Courts; English, 26; fundamental, 30; history of, 32, 101-2; 108-10; 188, 302, 318-20; natural, 5, 30; Reception, 29; Roman, 27, 28; statute, 3
Laws of Ecclesiastical Polity, Richard Hooker, 22
'Laws of History', 248-9
Learned Societies, 60, 106, 168; *see also* Soc. of Antiquaries
Learning, territorialization of, 52; community of, 68
Legal history, *see* History, legal
Legal influences on history, 26-32
Legal record, and 'correspondence theory', 99; *see also* Records, public
Legate, John, the younger, 139
Legh, Gerard, 43
Leland, John, antiquary, 16, 23, 36, 233, 300; *Itinerary*, 63
Le Squyer, Scipio, 83
Letters and Papers of Henry VIII, S. J. Brewer, ed., 159
Leviathan, Thomas Hobbes, 171, 314
Lewis, C. S., quoted, 20
Libraries: catalogues of, 66; cathedral, 65; consolidation of, 36, 301; continental, access to, 64; growth of, 35; importance of, for history, 35-7, 60, 301; Inns of Court, 62, 65; scientific, 105; survey of, 61-6; town, 65-6
Library of: Thomas Allen, 105; Earl of Arundel, 64; Thomas Bodley (Oxford University), 37, 63-5; British Museum, 63; Duke of Buckingham, 64; Cambridge, colleges, 36, 37; the Cecils, 63-4; Sir Edward Coke, 129; Sir Robert Cotton, 63, 67, 118 ff.; 146-8; *see also* Cotton; Sir Simonds D'Ewes, 63; Dr. John Dee, 105; Duke Humphrey, 37; Robert Harley, 63-4; Lord Lumley, 65; Oxford, colleges, 36, 37; Royal, 65; Sion College, 66; *see also* names of antiquaries and historians
Licensing authorities, 38; *see also* Censorship
Life of Alfred the Great, Sir John Spelman, 157
Life of Edward VI, Sir John Hayward, 184
Life and Reign of Henry VIII, Edward Herbert, Baron of Cherbury, 158-60
Lilburne, John, 24, 188
Literacy, spread of, 55
Lives, defined, 157-8; and Characters, 159-60
Lives of Three Norman Kings, Sir John Hayward, 184
Livy, 12, 154, 162
Local history, *see* History, local
Local History in England, W. G. Hoskins, 225
Local Records, *see* Records, local
Locke, John, 254, 312-3
London, *see* Libraries; Stow; *Survey of London*; Records
Loyola, Ignatius, 18
Lucian, 172
Luther and Lutheranism, 10, 18, 19, 20
Lysle, William, 139

Machiavelli, Niccolo, and Machi-
avellism, 5, 10–15, 110, 163, 194,
197, 208, 209, 269, 271
Madox, Thomas, 83, 112, 115
Magazine of Honour, Sir John
Doderidge, 183
Magdeburg 'Centuries', 19, 20
Magna Carta, 30, 134
Maitland, Frederick William, 29,
31, 101, 189
Manuscripts, dispersal of, 23; *see
also* Records; names of anti-
quaries and historians
Maps and map-making, *see* Carto-
graphy
Maps, use of, by historians, 171
Marmora Arundeliana, John Selden,
130
Martyn, William, 183
Marx, Karl, 3
Master of the Rolls, *see* Record
Keepers
Mathew, David, quoted, 51
Medievalists, 1, 15, 16; stylistic
habits of, 115
Meinecke, Friedrich, quoted, 5
Melancthon, Philipp, 18
Memoirs, defined, 157–8
Memorials, defined, 151–2
Memorials of the Holles Family,
Gervase Holles, 183
Mercantilism, 3, 6, 51, 239, 304
Mercator, Gerard, 7
Method, historical, *see* Historical
method
*Methodus ad Facilem Historiarum
Cognitionem*, Jean Bodin, 165,
166
Microcosmography, John Earle,
92
Microcosmus, Peter Heylyn, 161,
170
Middle Ages, 9, 10, 19, 20 *see also*
Selden
Middle class, culture, 17, 54–5, 61,
213; definition of, 53–5; role of,
in history, 3, 6–7, 214–15;
utilitarianism of, 55, 58, 302

Milton, John, 25, 41, 45, 209
Moderns, vs. Ancients, 100, 210,
318
Monasticon, Roger Dodsworth, 63,
162, 183
Monuments, defined, 156–7
More, Sir Thomas, 15, 230
Morison, Richard, 14
Mountague, Sir Edward, 133
Mountague, Richard, impeached,
134; praises Cotton's library,
136; clerical objections to
Selden's *Historie*, 293–5
Munck, Levinus, 141
Munday, Anthony, 63, 177, 179
Mutability, doctrine of, 207–8
'Mysteries of state', 33

Narrations, defined, 151; example,
160
Nationalism, 3, 6, 214
Natural law, 5, 30
Naunton, Sir Robert, 157
Nef, John U., quoted, 309
'New Year's Gift', John Leland, 23
Nicolson, William, 111, 113, 182
*Nine Bookes of Various History
Concerning Women*, Thomas
Heywood, 184
Norden, John, 180
Novum Organum, Sir Francis
Bacon, 261
Nowell, Laurence, 36, 93, 102

Oaths of Office, 77
Oratorians, order of, 21
Original of Bishops, James Ussher,
100
Ortelius, Abraham, 234
Overbury, Sir Thomas, 121, 124
Owen, Sir Roger, 135
Oxford, 20, 36, 37
Oxford Reformers, 15

Paleography, 189
Palgrave, Sir Francis, quoted, 87
Papacy, 18, 20
Papist, *see* Roman Catholics

Parasceve, Sir Francis Bacon, 258–9
Parish history, *see* History, parish
Parker, Matthew, 23, 35, 93, 100, 102
Parkins (or Perkins), Dr., 89
Parliament, antiquity of, 95; history of, 98, 101, 186; debates in, 131
Parochial Antiquities, White Kennett, 180, 317
Pascal, Blaise, 148, 200, 307
Past, how related to present, xiii; remains of, xiii, xiv; *see also* Records; History; Custom and the Immemorial; Tradition
Patriarcha, Sir Robert Filmer, 107
Patrons and Patronage: rewards of, 49; importance of, 66; Renaissance, of letters, 112, 118; bureaucratic, 118, 140; lay patronage (Church), 279; *see also* Cotton; Camden; Soc. of Antiquaries
Patterns of intellectual development, 306
Peacham, Henry, 51, 166
Perambulation of Kent, etc., William Lambarde, 180, 212, 224
Perfect history, defined, 151–2; stylistic forms of, 151
Periodization, historical, 9, 189, 304
Peters, Hugh, modest proposal to burn records, 75
Petty, William, 316
Philology, study of, 48, 102, 103, 162, 189; importance of, xviii; *see also* Selden; Spelman, Sir Henry
Philosophy, importance of, xx; of history, xxii; *see also* History, Theory
Pickthorne, Kenneth, quoted, 272
Pirenne, Henri, quoted, 4
Plagiarism, 179
Plato, 201
Plutarch's Lives, 165, 166
Pocock, J. G. A., quoted, 27, 29, 47, 109

Pococke, Edward, Orientalist, 56–7
Pole, Reginal, cardinal, 14
Political theory, and history, 317; *see also* Soc. of Antiquaries; names of historians and antiquaries
Polybius, 154, 202, 233, 237
Polyolbion, Michael Drayton, 46
Popham, Sir John, 39–40
Popular histories, 7–8, 184
Postan, M. M., quoted, 53
Powell, Thomas, 73, 79, 80, 82
Powicke, F. M., quoted, 68
Precedents, English concern with legal, xiv, 32, 100, 108, 132, 319
Predestination, 197, 198
Presbyterians, 24; *see also* Calvin
Prideaux, Mathias, quoted, 190
Prince, The, Niccolo Machiavelli, 208
Principall Navigations, Richard Hakluyt, 57, 105
Printing, importance for scholarship, 7–8
Privy Council, letters of, 23; and records, 72
Probability, in history, 203, 268–9; *see also* names of historians, and History, *Method*, for related concepts
Problematic history, *see* History, Problematic
Proby, Peter, 72, 79
Process, awareness of, in history, 104, 299, 303; *see also* names of historians
Profession, history as, 190
Progress, in history, xviii, xix; in related fields, 311; idea of, xiv, 174–5, 235, 299, 302
'Proposal for Building a Royal Library', Richard Bentley, 62
Protestants and Protestantism, 18, 20, 21, 307
Providence, 10, 11, 25, 177, 205, 209, 256, 269, 296, 301; *see also* names of historians; and History, Theory

Prynne, William, 24, 75, 76, 107, 108
Public Record Office, 81, 82
Public Records and Record Keeping, 69–91; *see also* Records
Pulton, Ferdinando, 142
Purchas His Pilgrimage, Samuel Purchas, 57
Purchas, Samuel, 57
Purgatory, doctrine of, 10
Puritans and Puritanism: Tudor, 20; interest in history, 24–5, 56, 193; attack on hierarchy, 279; on Reason and Faith, 309; *see also* Calvin; Predestination; Providence
Purpose in history, defined, xvi–xvii
Putney, and Whitehall debates, 24
Pym, John, 134
Pyrrhonism, 47, 314

Quaestion of Tithes Revised, William Sclater, 296
Quantitative Method, 306, 310–11

Raison d'état, 5, 7, 12, 14
Ralegh, Sir Walter: xv, 59, 97, 164, 167, 191–210, 213, 304
  BIOGRAPHY: prisoner in Tower, 191; help received in writing history, 192; manuscript notebook of, 192; library in Tower, 192; religious beliefs, 192; scepticism, 192–3; as stylist, xxi, 210
  COMMENTARY ON *History of World*: popularity of, 193, 209; transitional, 193; typical of much 17th c. historiography, 194; traditional character of, 194, 196; frontispiece, 194; Augustinian, 196; Acton's praise of Ralegh, 207; baroque style, 210
  HISTORICAL THOUGHT: *History of World*, xvi, 12, 59, 164, 167, 191–210; idea of providence, xx; praise of history, 194–5; purpose of history, 195; symmetry bet. past and present, 195; moral judgments, 195–6; causation, 196–7; providence, 197–8; predestination, 197–8; fate and destiny, 198; use of conjecture, 199–204; criticism of Aristotle, 199–200; revelation, truths of, 200; Bible, authority of, 201; method, 201–5; evidence and proof, 202–5; authority, respect for, 203; secularism, 204; second causes, 204–6; Satan, 205; classical history, approach to, 205–10; role of individual, 205, 206; continuity and change, 205, 207; political lessons, 205, 208–9; history as drama, 206–7; mutability, 207; digressions, 208; on Machiavelli, 208–9; method, assumptions of, 210
Randolph, Ambrose, 142
Ranke, Leopold von, 283
Rationalism, xxiii; *see also* Reason; Secularism
Rationalization of Utility, 306, 309–10
Reason: and scriptural authority, 202; as form of history, 308; and Faith, 309, 312–3; image of, in 18th c., 320; role of (Bolingbroke), 320
Reasonableness of Christianity, John Locke, 313
Record Keepers: and Antiquaries, 85; at Four Treasuries, 73, 89; at Tower, 71, 72, 82, 85, 88, 89; disputes between, 72, 76; Exchequer Chamberlains, 71–2, 89, 91; Master of Rolls, 71, 72, 86; oaths of office, 77; problems faced by, 77–8; quality of, 75–6, 83; research of, 103
Record Offices, *see* Record Repositories; *also* Record Keepers; names of antiquaries and historians

Record Repositories: 33, 60, 69; importance of, 82, 83; Four Treasuries, 35, 70, 73, 74; Rolls House and Rolls Chapel, 71, 72, 73, 74, 80, 222; State Paper Office, 63, 71, 74, 77, 89, 141; Tower of London, 33, 35, 70, 71, 73, 74, 76, 80, 81, 85, 115, 222; other, 70–1

Records, books on searching, 33, 73, 79, 80, 82,

Records, family, 44

Records, local, 88; City of London, 88, 145–6

Records, monastic, 24; dispersal of, 18, 23

Records, Public: access to, 33, 40, 69, 86, 87–91; authority of, 223; Calendars of, 79, 80, 82, 83; citation of, 84; defined, 32–3; divisions of, 69; fees for search in, 33, 78, 80, 81, 86, 87; government policy toward, 74–5, 86; importance of, 83, 302; Irish and Scottish, 75; jurisdiction, 70, 72; locations of, 70–1, 73, 79–81; loss of, by borrowing, etc., 78, 81–2, 143; state of, 79, 81–2; transcripts of, 62, 115; use of, *see* Records, use of

Records, use of by historians and others, xiii, 32, 100, 141, 220, 222, 230; *see also* names of antiquaries and historians; Soc. of Antiquaries; Historical revolution

Reformation, English, xxiii–iv, 17, 23, 45, 99, 100, 215, 281, 300–1

Reformation, European: subject of controversy, xix; general, 1, 2, 15, 26, 29, 51; effects on historiography, 18–20, 114

Reformation politics and religion, 17–25, 100

Register, defined, 155; parish, 155–6

Relations, defined, 151; example, 160

Relativism, xvii, 14, 252, 294, 307, 318

Relevance: criterion of, xvii, 28, 303, 311; judgments of, xix; controversy about, xix, 279, 296; and bias, xx; problems of, 28, 319; *see also* names of historians and antiquaries

Religion: importance of, xx; controversy, 52; *see also* Church; Calvin; Secularism, Reformation; names of historians and antiquaries

Remains of a Greater Work, William Camden, 234

Renaissance: climate of opinion, 1–17; English, xxiii, 17, 99, 194; Elizabethan, 304; European, main trends of, 2–3; European movement, 26; and historical revolt, xiv; Italian, 1, 3; meaning of, 1–2, 15, 29; Northern, 1

Repertorie of Records, Thomas Powell, 79

Repertory books, City of London, 145–6

Restoration, English, 165, 185, 188, 304–5; importance of, 110; as turning point, 114

Revelation: relevant to history (Augustine), 11; truths of, 200, 297, 308, 313; appeals to, 308; *see also* Ralegh

Revolution: commercial, 6; economic, 306; industrial, 310; intellectual, 300, 310; in world of learning, 8; scientific, 274, 306–7, 310; *see also* Historical revolution

Robertson, William, 319

Roman Catholics and Catholicism, 18, 19, 20, 21, 24, 39, 84, 187

Round, J. H., quoted, 42

Rous, John, 15

Rowlands, Richard (alias Verstegan), 144

Royal College of Physicians and Surgeons, 105–6

Royal officials, *see* Civil Service

Royal Society, 105–6, 110–11, 263, 316

Russell, Francis, earl of Bedford, 130

Rymer, Thomas, 83, 112, 147, 162

Saint-John, Henry, *see* Bolingbroke

Samothes (eponymous King), 16

Sarmiento de Acuna, count of Gondomar, 123

Sarpi, Paolo, quoted, 20

Satan, 205

Savile, Sir Henry, 105, 162

Scaliger, Joseph, 20, 202

Scholarship, measure of significance of, xxii, 109; *see also* names of scholars and particular fields of scholarship

Scholasticism and Scholastic, xxiii, 9, 199, 253

Scholler's Medley, Richard Brathwaite, 166–7

Science and The Modern World, Alfred North Whitehead, quoted, xxiii–iv

Science and scientific movement: xiv; and history, 48, 200, 310, 315–16; methods of, 111–12, 316; intellectual ideal, 316; *see also* Bacon, Selden; Soc. of Antiquaries

Scientific revolution, 274, 306–7, 310

Scientific temper, xxiii–xxiv

Sclater, William, 296

Scriptures, *see* Bible

Second causes, 200, 204–5; *see also* History, *Method*; names of historians

Secularism: xxi, 3, 6, 13–14, 52, 187, 203, 205, 245, 261, 283, 301–2

Segregation, principle of, 25, 307, 309

Selden, John: BIOGRAPHY: comments on Cotton, 119, 135; political career, 123, 125, 134, 276; in

fluence of, 184, 189, 190, 303; common law training, 284, 286, 318; learning and languages, 275, 277–8, 286; influenced by French legal humanists, 277, 286; reply to Buckingham, 281–2; Erastian, 284; comments on clergy, 293; comments on religious disputes, 297; comments on scholarship, 298

COMMENTARY ON: prose style, 276; utility of history, 276–7; varieties of history written, 278–279; Tillesley's *Animad versions*, 276; *Historie of Tithes* suppressed, 279; *Tithes* example of problematic history, 279; *Selden Society*, 278; Mountague's *Diatribae*, 293–5

HISTORICAL WRITING AND THOUGHT: *Titles of Honour*, 156, 161–2, 163; *Anelecton Anglo-Britannicon*, 166; *Historie of Tithes*: purpose in writing, xi; divine right theory of tithes, 276, 281–2; implications for divinity, 281, 292, 294–5; and tithes controversy, 281; outline of thesis of, 282–8; continuity vs. change in, 283; fact vs. right in, 283; periodization in, 283; secular explanation in, 283; economic interpretation in, 284; jurisdiction of tithes, 285–6

METHOD, GENERAL: 286–93, 297–8; relevance and proof, 279, 286, 289–90, 296–8; contextualism and comparison, 288–9; coherence and synchronism, 291–3; philological tests, 291; problem of bias, 293; problem of inference, 293; limitations of, 297

Selden Society, founding of, 278

Sempil, Sir James, 296

'Seraglio of Antiquity', 138

Seventeenth century, as transition, xxiii

Shakespeare, William, 43, 193, 305

Shirley, Sir Thomas, 66
Short Title Catalogue, xi
Significance, definition of, xxii-xxiii; *see also* names of historians and antiquaries
Simon, Father Richard, 313, 318
Six Clerks Office, fire of 1621, 81
Smith, Thomas, librarian, 95
Society of Antiquaries, Elizabethan: 'Academy' proposed, 96; composition, 92-3, 120, 211; 'Discourses' of, 95 ff.; dissolution, 101; founding, 92; further research, 60, 88, 90; group research of, 94, 96; interests of, 100; methods of, 94-8; proposed sequels, 106
Society of Antiquaries (modern), founded, 105, 301; and study of history, 114
Somerset, Earl of, 121-5
Somner, William, 182
Sources, historical, collections of, 161-2; *see also* History, Varieties; Records; Soc. of Antiquaries
Sovereignty, doctrine of, 107-10; parliamentary, 108, 272; medieval, 214
Speeches, invented, 159; *see also* Camden; Bacon
Speed, John, 57, 145, 157, 177, 178, 266, 268
Spelman, Sir Henry: importance of, xv, 101-2, 115-16; scholarship, 68, 85, 189; and Soc. of Antiquaries, 95, 100-1; awareness of historical contexts, 99, 104; language studies by, 102-4; feudal interpretation, originality, 109, 240, 258; on tithes, 136, 296; mentioned, 147, 178, 190, 301, 303
Spelman, Sir John, 157; quoted, 158; *Life of Alfred*, 157-8
Spencer, John, 174
Spenser, Edmund, 207, 208
Spinoza, Benedict, 314
Sprat, Thomas, 105

Squirearchy, conception of, 51
Stafford, Edward, record keeper, 72
Star Chamber, Court of, 72
Starkey, Ralph, 63, 143
State Paper Office, *see* Record Repositories
State Papers, 60, 71, 88; *see also* Records, Public; and Record Repositories
Stationer's Company, agreement to deposit books at Oxford, 37
Statutes at Large, Ferdinando Pulton, 142
Stevenson conspiracy, 148
Stow, John: xv, 61, 62, 63, 74, 88, 90, 145, 211-29, 234, 301; historian, xiv, 175, 178; collections of, 36; *Survey of London*, xvi, 34, 63, 157, 211-29, 301; *Summarie of Englishe Chronicles*, 161; plagiarized, 179
BIOGRAPHY: member, Soc. of Antiquaries, 93, 211; education, 211-12; knowledge, of languages, 212, of London, 212; middle-class background, 213-14; psychological insecurity, 214-15; as propagandist, 215; belief in natural omens, 217; secular interests, 218; religion, 219-20
COMMENTARY ON: created new form of History, 212-13; *Annales* not a history, 216; *Survey*, value of to historians, 217, secular, 218-19, significance of, 229
HISTORICAL WRITING AND THOUGHT: utility, 213-15; importance of tradition, 214, attitude toward, 220; use of sources, 215-16, 218, 220, 222; sceptical of legendary history, 216, 223; awareness of historical change, 217; method, limitations of, 217-18; virtues of, 221-3; origins of London, 217-18; evidence and proof, 218, 221, 223; churches, attitude toward,

219; originality, 221, 223–4; authority, 222–3; relevance, 224–5, 226, 228–9; organization of *Survey*, 225–6; economic interpretation in, 226–8; significance of site, 225, 227; significance of street names, 226–7; population, 228; social mobility, 228; fieldwork, 228

Strafford (Thomas Wentworth), earl of, 130

Style, definition of, xxi–xxii; *see also* History, *Style*

Style, and development of characters, xxi

Summarie Abridged, John Stow, 222

Summarie of Englishe Chronicles, John Stow, 161, 213, 215

Survey: defined, 156–7; ignored by Bacon, 153; examples, 180–1

Survey of Cornwall, Richard Carew, 34, 157, 180

Survey of History, Richard Brathwaite, 166

Survey of London, John Stow, xvi, 34, 63, 157, 211–29, 301

Survey of Staffordshire, Sampson Erdeswicke, 181

Symbolic tools, 8

Symmetry, between past and present, 195; *see also* History, analogy

Table Talk, John Selden, 275; quoted, 293, 298

Tacitus, 40, 154, 162, 163, 233, 249

Talbot, Thomas, collections of, 36, 85, 88

Tate, Francis, 84, 145

Tawney, R. H., quoted, 141

Taylor, Jeremy, 308, 309

Techniques of research, early modern, xv

Territorial history, *see* History, Territorial

Testimony, historical, and Bible 22

Theatre of the Empire of Great Britaine, John Speed, 57, 157, 178

Theatre, and history, analogy, 167, 206–7

'Theorem', Spelman's, 101–2, 116, 258

Theory of confirmations, 30; *see also* Coke; Custom and the Immemorial; Law; Precedents

Theory, of history, *see* History, Theory

Thesaurus, George Hickes, 113

Third University of England, George Buck, 57

Thucydides, 60, 154, 162, 163, 170, 171, 172, 247, 273

Thynne, Francis, collections of, 36, 144; quoted 97

Tillesley, Dr. Richard, 277

Tithes: payment of, according to Selden, xix; controversy, 112–13; *jure divino* theory of, 282, 296; *see also Historie of Tithes*; Mountague, Richard; Selden; Spelman, Sir Henry

Titles of Honour, John Selden, 156, 163, 183, 288, 297

Topographical studies, 57

Tower of London, *see* Record Repositories

Tradition: authority of, xix; sanctions of, 213; historical, 214; *see also* names of historians

Translations and Translators, 162; 170–2

Treatise of Commerce, John Wheeler, 316

Trevor-Roper, H. R., quoted, 86

Trittenheim, Johann von, abbot of Sponheim, 8

Trojan: antiquity and genealogy, 16, 97, 104; causes of Trojan war, 204; *see also* Antiquities

Trojan Brute, *see* Brute, legend

True Order and Method of Wryting and Reading Histories, Thomas Blundeville, 165

Tudor revolution in government, 17, 140, 214

Twysden, Roger, 85

Ulpian's maxim, quoted, 309
Universal history, *see* History, universal
Universalism, 51
Universities, role of, in history, 52, 110–13, 301; *see also* Libraries
Use of history, *see* Utility; and History, utility of
Ussher, James, 102, 136, 186, 189, 190, 201, 275, 303
Utility and Utilitarianism: 13, 55–6, 58, 261–2, 302; rationalization of utility, 306, 309–10

Valerius Terminus, Sir Francis Bacon, 261
Valla, Lorenzo, 18
Van Eyck, portrait by, 4
Vergil, Polydore, 267
Verifiability, ideal of, 309, 310; *see also* History, *Method*; and names of historians
Verstegan, alias of Richard Rowlands, 144
Views, defined, 156–7
Vincent, Augustine, 43, 144, 156
Virtu, 1, 197
Vulgate, authority of, 19

Walsingham, Sir Francis, 35, 71, 231

Wanley, Humphrey, 105, 147
Ware, James, 155
Weever, John, 156
Wentworth, Sir Thomas, earl of Strafford, 130
Wernham, R. B., quoted, 69, 72
Wheare, Degory, 165, 169, 170
Wheeler, John, 316
Whelock, Abraham, librarian, 36
Whig interpretation of history, 30, 109, 271–2
Whitehead, Alfred North, quoted, xxiii–xxiv
Willey, Basil, quoted, xxiii
William of Malmesbury, 216
William of Worcester, 15
Williams, Roger, 310
Wilson, Dr. Thomas, 76
Wilson, Sir Thomas: 63; ability, 75; heads State Paper Office, 76–7, 141; problems faced by, 77; influence of, 78; attitude toward Cotton, 79; care of records, 89
Wolsey, Thomas, cardinal, 238
Wormald, B. W. G., quoted, 185
Worthies of England, Thomas Fuller, 146, 155, 157
Wotton, Sir Henry, 78
Wright, Dr. Louis B., quoted, 58

Yeomen, English, 50
Young, Patrick, Royal librarian, 65